Essentials of busi-
ness ethics

DATE DUE		
NOV 02 1993		
APR 3 0 1996		
OCT 1 1 1996		
MAR 1 2 1997		
DEC 1 9 1997		
DEC 2 2 1998		

ESSENTIALS OF BUSINESS ETHICS

Milton Friedman argues that the social responsibility of business is to increase its profits.

Inc. profiles a corporate "do-gooder" who also has done very well for his company.

Patricia H. Werhane presents a pair of "Bills of Rights"—one for employers, one for employees.

Myron Magnet traces the decline and fall of business ethics in America.

Exxon's John Rawl discounts any lasting damage from the Alaska oil spill.

Ralph Nader probes the anatomy of whistle-blowing.

These are just a few indications of the breadth of concern and diversity of viewpoints that make *Essentials of Business Ethics* truly the essential guide to the subject today.

PETER MADSEN, Ph.D., is Executive Director of the Center for the Advancement of Applied Ethics, Carnegie Mellon University. His articles on business ethics have been widely published in leading business journals.

JAY M. SHAFRITZ, Ph.D., is a Professor of Public and International Affairs, University of Pittsburgh, and is author of over two dozen reference and textbooks, including six anthologies.

ESSENTIALS OF
BUSINESS ETHICS

EDITED BY

Peter Madsen
and
Jay M. Shafritz

DISCARDED

A MERIDIAN BOOK

MERIDIAN
Published by the Penguin Group
Penguin Books USA Inc., 375 Hudson Street, New York,
New York, 10014, U.S.A.
Penguin Books Ltd, 27 Wrights Lane, London W8 5TZ, England
Penguin Books Australia Ltd, Ringwood, Victoria, Australia
Penguin Books Canada Ltd, 2801 John Street, Markham,
Ontario, Canada L3R 1B4
Penguin Books (N.Z.) Ltd, 182–190 Wairau Road, Auckland 10,
New Zealand
Penguin Books Ltd, Registered Offices: Harmondsworth,
Middlesex, England

First published by Meridian, an imprint of Penguin Books USA Inc.
Published simultaneously in Canada.

First Printing, May, 1990
10 9 8 7 6 5 4 3 2

 REGISTERED TRADEMARK—MARCA REGISTRADA

LIBRARY OF CONGRESS CATALOGING-IN-PUBLICATION DATA
Essentials of business ethics / edited by Peter Madsen and Jay M.
Shafritz.
    p.   cm.
  ISBN 0-452-01044-6
  1. Business ethics. I. Madsen, Peter, 1946–   . II. Shafritz,
Jay M.
HF5387.E75   1990
174'.4—dc20   89-13573
                                                    CIP

Printed in the United States of America
Set in Times Roman
Designed by Julian Hamer

CONTENTS

CONTENTS

INTRODUCTION

The task of defining business ethics is often described as "trying to nail Jell-O to a wall." There is simply no agreement on what the term means. Remember the story of the boy who went to the religious leader of his community and said, "I'll give you an apple if you tell me where God is!"? The religious leader replied, "But I'll give you two apples if you tell me where he or she isn't!" It is much the same with business ethics. One can hardly say where it isn't. Consequently, definitions of the field that tend to be narrow also tend to exclude significant elements. Conversely, definitions that are very broad and all-encompassing tend to be so broad as to be virtually meaningless. What to do? Since a book can hardly run from the challenge of defining its subject, we herewith offer ours to a skeptical world.

Business ethics is an example of applied ethics; it involves taking the pure theories, principles, and concepts of formal ethics and applying them to the world of work, which presents business professionals with any number of ethically charged but real-life situations. Pure ethics offers guideposts to answering the questions: "How does a business professional come to *know* what is right as opposed to what is wrong behavior in carrying out business tasks?" and "How can they then *do* what is right once they have recognized it?" Business ethics, in essence, is applied philosophy.

Business ethics can be divided into two separate areas, which, in turn, have two separate sets of issues, problems, and dilemmas. The first, called *managerial mischief*, concerns the illegal, unethical, or questionable practices of individual managers or organizations, as well as the causes of such behaviors and remedies available to eradicate them. The second, called *moral mazes in management*, is concerned with the numerous ethical quandaries managers must wrestle with, which are part of daily business decision making. Questions dealing with plant closings, AIDS policies, promotion decisions, and whistle-blowing are representative concerns of the moral mazes managers must resolve. Taken together—managerial mischief and moral mazes in management—these two sets of concerns comprise the field of business ethics.

Managerial Mischief

Many see an ethical crisis in American business today. Activities such as fraud and consumer deception, kickbacks and bribery, insider trading, government contracting improprieties, conflicts of interest, questionable advertising claims, illegal disposal of hazardous materials, intentional violations of workplace safety regulations, and the laundering of drug-trafficking money by financial institutions are becoming all too commonplace. When such illegal activity is coupled with legal but unethical or questionable activities—such as the "dumping" of pesticides banned in the U.S. in Third World countries; maintaining South African investments that directly support the practice of apartheid; engaging in less than honorable sales negotiations; using bluffing and deception to reach labor agreements; providing gratuities or sexual favors to prospective private buyers—it is no wonder that the public image of business and corporate life suffers.

Proof of this seeming ethical crisis is easy to find. A 1987 survey taken jointly by *Business Week* and Lou Harris asked the American public the following question: "How would you rate the ethical standards of business executives: excellent, pretty good, only fair, or poor?" Only 2% rated the standards of today's business executives as excellent, while 58% found them to be only fair or poor. These conclusions are made by business professionals themselves, who are on the inside and have firsthand knowledge of actual practices. In another 1987 survey of 722 businessmen and -women, the Chicago-based consulting firm of McFeely, Wackerly and Jett found that 84% of business professionals polled believed that people in business are at least occasionally unethical in their business dealings. The image of American business seems justly tarnished when the subject is ethics.

The literature of business ethics is certainly not unaware of the problems of managerial mischief. On the contrary, it is chock full of diverse explanations and diagnoses of this important issue. Textbooks, articles in academic journals, and research treatises have highlighted the illegal, unethical, or questionable practices of managerial mischief makers, trying to identify causes as well as recommending remedies for the problem. The most common explanation of what causes misconduct in business is that such behavior is due to someone's flawed character. People in business who tend to go over the line and commit illegalities or improprieties have a psychological disposition that makes them unable to control their desire to accumulate personal wealth. Many proponents of this view hold that if adequate deterrents, such as convicting more white-collar criminals or imposing stiffer fines and longer prison sentences, were instituted, then much illegal and improper behavior would be reduced in the workplace.

Another view holds that misconduct in business is a function of organizational pressures that push individuals into committing acts in which they normally would not engage. Thus stiff competition in the marketplace, the desire to succeed, corporate cultures that foster improprieties, emphasis on short-term profits, downturns in the business cycle, and indifference to misconduct from upper management have all been fingered as possible causes of managerial mischief.

The organizational view claims that corporate values and the peer pressures that attend them have a great influence on an individual's business conduct. If a corporate employee sees his or her culture as one that promotes success at any cost, then he or she is far more likely to engage in managerial mischief than someone who views his or her corporate culture as one that values high ethical standards. The oft-suggested remedy to managerial mischief caused by a wayward corporate culture is for American firms to insure that more positive values are operational. But an organization's top leadership may not want to change a culture that fosters such mischief. It might not be profitable to do so.

Moral Mazes in Management

While managerial mischief deals with issues that lend themselves to an evaluation of right and wrong, what we have called "moral mazes in management" offers a set of problems that are far more subtle. Today it is not enough that those who manage a firm be adept at technical business skills, such as corporate planning and strategizing, analyzing business data, buying and selling, etc. It is becoming increasingly clear that in addition to being competent in the technical arena, managers must also be moral philosophers.

The reasons for this seemingly rash pronouncement are many. The business environment is now so structured that there are any number of sectors that make imposing demands upon managerial decision making. Contemporary managers have obligations to their superiors; to the firm's shareholders, customers, suppliers, and employees; and to the community in which their company operates, as well as to society at large. Each of these sectors has a stake in the corporate decision-making process in that each may be affected for better or worse by management decisions. Sorting out the various obligations and responsibilities is a task requiring skills that are not taught in the typical business-school curriculum. And, as is usually the case, when demands upon managers are conflicting—as in the case where a plant closing is in the interests of the shareholders of a company but not its employees and its community—then the analysis of managerial responsibility and obligations passes from mere business decision making over into moral decision making. Thus, on this score, moral philosophy and moral reasoning would be a plus for any manager who must sort out the moral maze of the demands placed upon him or her.

The potential list of moral mazes in management is so long that it is useful to divide them into two levels: *macro mazes* and *micro mazes*. Micro moral mazes in management are concerned with those issues, problems, and dilemmas that have an ethical component and which make their appearance within the limited confines of an individual manager's organization. These are the commonplace quandaries of the workplace that every manager can expect to face. They include conflict of interest on the job, employee rights, fair performance appraisals, sexual harassment, proprietary information, confidentiality, discrimination, the accepting or offering of gifts, the treatment of "problem employees," and so on.

Micro moral mazes tend to be those that confront managers who are carrying out front-line responsibilities, while macro moral mazes are usually limited to upper-level managers because they involve the broadest dimension of corporate policy decision making. Put another way, macro moral mazes in management are organizational and ethical issues that have sweeping implications for companies and society; as opposed to micro issues, which are limited to individuals within a company. Macro moral mazes also tend to become public-policy issues. Their resolution is debated by many sectors of society. Often the only final resolution available is one imposed upon the corporate sector by the government.

Examples of macro ethical issues include corporate social responsibility, product liability, environmental ethics, multinational and transnational ethics, comparable worth, layoffs and downsizings, employee screening tests, the right of employees to privacy in the workplace, and corporate accountability.

Institutionalizing Business Ethics

The last major dimension of the field of business ethics concerns the various ways traveled and the steps that have been taken to institutionalize ethics in American business

INTRODUCTION

enterprise. It should come as no surprise to learn that the government at all levels (local, state, and federal) has had a good deal of input into business ethics. By means of various regulatory acts, governmental bodies have had a great impact upon the conduct of corporate and business activities in many of the thematic areas of concern mentioned above. In fact, many see government intrusion into private business matters as overregulation of the corporate sector. Be that as it may, there is no denying that such input has had great impact upon management decision making. Given the sheer number of local, state, and federal laws, regulatory agency findings, as well the decisions of the judiciary, managers are well advised to become quite clear about what is required of them in the legal area before they embark upon any corporate decision or action. But at the same time managers are also wise to realize that the law is but a "moral minimum" and that compliance with it only the beginning of ethical business conduct. What may be legal may not at the same time "automatically" be regarded as ethical.

The thematic concerns of business ethics have also received a good deal of interest from the academic community. College and universities have recognized the need for clear and rational thinking about the issues of managerial mischief and moral mazes and have taken various initiatives. There has been a significant rise in the number of courses now available to business students at both the graduate and undergraduate level. In addition, business-ethics research centers are now sponsored by quite a number of institutions of higher education. Still another example are the many workshops, symposia, and academic conferences that have been conducted on campuses throughout the nation on topics in business ethics. All this academic activity can be pointed to as another contribution toward the institutionalization of business ethics.

But just as the steps taken by governmental bodies have had their detractors, so, too, have there been those who are highly critical of the attempts by academia to engage in the discipline of business ethics. Here, the most prevalent criticism takes the form of a skepticism that argues one cannot learn to be ethical in college or university classrooms. An

Ivan Boesky, the most notorious of a recent series of inside traders, would still be Ivan Boesky, this line of reasoning goes, even if he had gotten an *A* in an ethics course. The debate over whether business ethics can be taught, let alone learned, is one that has grown quite vocal and has, in fact, spilled over from a purely academic question into a public debate as to whether or not courses in ethics and moral reasoning should be required courses in American schools of business and public administration.

But this skeptical outlook over whether ethics can be taught and learned in school misses the point of ethics education. Just as it would be a mistake to expect that a successful *A* student in Business Management 101 will be a successful executive in the real world of corporate life, so, too, is it unrealistic to expect the student of Business Ethics 101 to be the most ethical executive. Courses in ethics should not be construed as morally edifying in their content. The goal of ethics education is not character building; but rather, like all college course work, they attempt to share knowledge, build skills, and develop minds. A course in business ethics is a useful tool to assist students when as managers they face a decision with a major ethical component attached to it.

Many American corporations also have been seeking ways to institutionalize business ethics. Increasingly corporations are: implementing codes of ethics, formally articulating statements of corporate values, sponsoring training and educational programs in ethics, installing internal judiciary bodies that hear cases of improprieties, and creating telephone hot lines for reporting illegal, unethical, or questionable corporate practices.

All this—government regulation, academic interest and extensive corporate involvement—suggests that the field of business ethics is emerging not only as a major intellectual and legal concern but as a full-fledged social movement. Perhaps business ethics can be best described as a not so simple method by which people can come to *know* what is right from what is wrong and go on and *do* what is right in the business arena. It simply suggests what Mark Twain once said: "Always do right. This will gratify some people, and astonish the rest."

INTRODUCTION

The Purpose of This Book

The purpose of this book is twofold. The first is to serve business professionals who have an interest in the issues that comprise the field of business ethics. Given the complexities of ethical business decision making in today's corporate environment, a book that pinpoints and analyzes everyday ethical problems, dilemmas, and issues that successful managers must resolve in business should be welcomed. Furthermore, given the recent publicity of business misconduct, this work will also be valuable for its suggestions on ways for corporate managers to institutionalize ethics in the workplace and thereby take a step in reducing the possibility of wrongdoing and questionable practices.

Secondly, this book is designed to serve the requirements of students who are enrolled in college courses that in whole or in part are dedicated to business ethics. As the study of business ethics grows, and as more and more for-credit courses are being offered, the need for a text that examines the ethical dimensions of business practices in a straightforward manner and is free of the technical jargon of the academic specialist has become obvious. Thus both managers and managers-to-be should find this collection of readings and introductory analysis to be a helpful tool in gaining clarity and insight into the often murky field of business ethics.

This collection is designed to treat those topics that have emerged over the past few years as the most significant and pressing issues of business ethics. We have chosen selected pieces from both academic publications and popular periodicals primarily for the clarity of their presentation and their straightforward style. Classics in the field by academic stars such as Milton Friedman and Peter Drucker are included, along with original works by authors who have more recently gained notoriety as experts in business ethics.

After an opening chapter on definitions, the book progresses from a consideration of ethics as they have an impact on individuals, to ways in which ethics has become problematic for business organizations. Thus, Chapter 2, "The Ethical Treatment of Employees," examines the moral claims of individuals that have come to be known as employee rights, while Chapter 3, "Management Ethics," raises a host of problems and issues that relate to the ethical conduct and moral obligations of individuals who shoulder the responsibility of managing businesses.

Chapters 4 through 7, however, look to those ethical dilemmas and quandaries that confront the most pervasive and influential social institution of the day—the corporation. Here, we turn to analyze the complexities of corporate decision making with an eye toward the ethical ramifications of such decisions. Topics so covered include plant closings and downsizings, hostile takeovers and merger mania, product liability, advertising ethics, the social responsibilities of the corporation, the role of business in environmental matters, and the obligations of corporations that conduct multinational business. Hence, by means of this collection of essential readings, prefaced by a short introductory analysis, we hope to provide a clear channel through the often murky waters of business ethics for both the practicing manager and the student of management.

CHAPTER 1

DEFINING
BUSINESS ETHICS

Introduction

Business ethics is a multidimensional field that evades a one-dimensional definition. (It is a discipline that addresses numerous issues, problems, and dilemmas, and it does so from a variety of perspectives and methodologies.) Consequently, the objective of this first chapter is to survey these various dimensions of the field in the hope that an overview might be gained.

One way to present the complexities of business ethics is to explore the many kinds of issues having an ethical dimension that confront business professionals in the actual practice and conduct of business. The first selection in this chapter is just such an exploration. In 1988, the Conference Board, a nonprofit business-research organization, published a document titled "Corporate Ethics," which reported the findings of a survey of three hundred executives on the topic of ethics in business. The first section of the report, excerpted here, was designed to outline those ethical issues which the executives felt were the most pressing ones confronting their organizations and the individuals who worked in them. This research serves as an excellent point of departure to answer the questions of what issues fall under the purview of business ethics.

It is interesting to note that what the executives identified in 1988 as the most pressing issues confronting their organizations departs little from the sorts of issues business ethicists have been addressing for years in their studies. Issues such as corporate social responsibility, employee rights, whistle-blowing, ethical business conduct, business and the environment, the obligations of multinational corporations, and so on are constantly recurring themes. In short, they *are* the essentials of business ethics, and as such, they are examined in depth by the articles that follow.

(Business ethics can also be defined as an attempt to ascertain the responsibilities and ethical obligations of business professionals.) Here the focus is on people rather than issues, and the primary question deals with how individuals should conduct themselves in fulfilling the ethical requirements of their business lives. In today's complex corporate culture this question is increasingly important as managers and employees face numerous moral mazes and ethical dilemmas on the job that require hard choices.

Peter Drucker, in a chapter from his ground-breaking book, *Management: Tasks, Responsibilities, Practices,* sees business ethics in a somewhat critical light but, nonetheless, he, too, is concerned with the notion of responsibility as a main issue. In his commentary a strong argument is made that business professionals are no different than other professionals in that they should abide by what technically in the academic discipline of ethics is referred to as the "principle of nonmaleficence." Simply put, this principle holds that a chief obligation of professionals is to "do no harm." Drucker claims that such a principle needs to be followed more closely and cites instances where he feels it has not been embraced, leading to the conclusion that some executives are less than professional in their business dealings.

Laura Nash addresses this question of responsibility as well in her *Harvard Business Review* article, "Ethics Without the Sermon." Nash's main thesis is that there are strategies available to assist business professionals in reaching ethical decisions and carrying out their responsibilities. She presents one such strategy in the form of twelve practical guidelines that can serve as benchmarks of responsible business decision making. The reasoning in this approach is that if there are workable ethical guidelines, and if they are scrupulously followed in the process of business decision making, then such decisions ultimately will be the best for the individual and for the organization in which they work.

In addition to defining the field of business ethics as an identification of issues and an assigning of responsibilities as these three selections do, there are further ways in which to view the activities of business ethics. One can also find critical appraisals of business that attempt to establish the proposition that business is in great need of either self-policing or governmental regulation, or both. The business-ethics critics take up such issues as product liability, worker rights, environmental problems, white-collar crime, executive salaries, and the like. These critics of business usually point to instances of ethical misdeeds or mistakes in business conduct and conclude that business is an area of activity that requires watching through governmental regulation, which is, of course, anathema to business.

Others who write and publish under the banner of business ethics direct their concerns to individuals in the corporate workplace. Questions about the rights, responsibilities, and ethical decision making of managers and employees occupy the thoughts of these business ethicists. Here, theories about the relationship that exists between the individual and the organization are offered as explanations of why people in business do not always do what is legally or morally right. Such theoretical work usually ends in recommendations for organizational development and changes in the structures of the corporation and its culture. Management theories are offered and often debated as well, with an eye toward understanding what conduct is most ethical among those who manage others on the job. The last selection in this chapter, Albert Carr's now classic *Harvard Business Review* article "Is Business Bluffing Ethical?" is a fine example of this approach, which emphasizes the individual as it analyzes the differences between personal morality and business morality when business is understood as a kind of game like poker.

(A final way to define business ethics is through the philosophical approach. Here more fundamental and somewhat esoteric questions about business people and organizations are raised and debated.) For example, a number of academic business ethicists have contributed to the ongoing discussion over the issue of the essential nature of the corporation. What kind of an entity is the corporation? Can moral and ethical concepts be ascribed to corporations at all? Can we genuinely say that a corporation is good or bad in the same exact sense that we say an individual person is good or bad? Is there such a thing as a "corporate decision," or are all decisions made solely by individuals such that it would be wrong to condemn an organization for the acts of its members? Here the "ontological status" of the corporation—its manner of being—is investigated with an eye toward demarcating its moral status. Essentially the philosophical argument is that if corporations are not like people, in that they cannot count as moral or rational agents, then ascribing ethical concepts to them and making moral judgments of them may be an error.

Another example of this kind of philosophical questioning in business ethics concerns some fundamental problems that surface within the relationship between those who are employed by an organization and the organization itself. What is the best way to characterize the relationship between a corporation and those who choose to join it? Do top executives, managers, and workers merely "represent" the corporation, or are they in actuality the corporation itself? Put another way, are individuals only agents employed solely to further the interests of the corporation as in an agent/principal relationship, or are workers more than just agents having a vested interest themselves in the life of the organization? The answer to this fundamental question is important, since one's liability for unethical conduct may increase or decrease depending upon the type of relationship one holds to the organization. We would hold individuals accountable for their actions differently, for example, if they were acting on their own as opposed to acting on behalf of an organization. But in any case, these kinds of questions that present philosophical quandaries of a fundamental nature are an inherent part of the activities of business ethicists and as such must be counted within the purview of the discipline.

We are now in a better position to identify at least three separate tactics that can be employed in the analysis of

DEFINING BUSINESS ETHICS

ethical questions about business organizations and business executives. These three are:

- identifying practical issues and assigning responsibilities;
- critiquing the ethics of various business practices;
- raising fundamental philosophical problems and offering suggested resolutions to them.

As we shall see in the following chapters, these three approaches are among the most prevalent in the field of business ethics, and the reflective work done by business ethicists and others in this discipline manifest one or more of these three forms of analysis.

What, then, is business ethics? It is many things to many people. It is an application of ethics to the corporate community. It is the identification of important business and social issues. It is a way to determine responsibility in business dealings. It is a critique of business. And it is an attempt to unravel fundamental questions about the enterprise of business and those who engage in that enterprise. And although one single definition cannot encompass all the varied activities of business ethics, the discipline can still be viewed as a significant movement both in and outside of academia.

Defining Corporate Ethics
The Conference Board

In 1987 The Conference Board published its report of an international survey of three hundred executives, two thirds of whom were chief executive officers, on ethical issues within corporations. These executives had the opportunity to identify and prioritize twenty-seven separate issues. They identified those which they felt were the most pressing now and those which would be pressing five years from now. These issues were then categorized into four major areas: equity, rights, honesty, and exercise of corporate power.

SOURCE: *Corporate Ethics: Research Report No. 900*, Chapter One, The Conference Board, Inc., 1987. Reprinted with permission.

The issue of equity dealt with the CEOs' perceptions of how fair corporations are. The rights category referred to just claims individuals in corporations might make with respect to due process, privacy, sexual harassment, and so on. The third category of honesty included items such as conflicts of interest, gifts, questionable payments and the like. The final category of corporate power let the CEOs reflect on topics such as political-action committees, safety, and the environment.

———————

U.S. and European CEOs and senior managers view corporate ethics as a subject to be dealt with at three levels, each more specific than the last: (1) *the corporate mission*, (2) *constituency relations*, and (3) *policies and practices*.

The most easily recognized and universally applicable category is the *corporate mission*. Executives interviewed say that the enterprise in which they are engaged, and the products or services that they market, ought to serve an inherently ethical purpose. They believe that a company's primary ethical responsibilities are defined by the nature of its corporate objectives. Thus, a pharmaceutical concern will see its objectives as serving ethical purposes—promoting better health and saving lives. Food companies see their ethical mission as improving nutritional standards, while maintaining price levels that their poorest customers can afford.

Corporate managers speak of *constituency relations* in formulating their company's ethical standards. This effort usually entails statements of corporate responsibility to any or all of the following: employees, local communities, customers, suppliers, shareholders, home-country and foreign governments, and in some cases, the general public. The majority of the corporate codes of conduct examined describe the company's commitment to these groups, rather than prescribe ethical conduct for specific situations.

The former Chairman of a large Japanese company summarizes this view of constituency relations: "Our responsibility is not only to our stockholders, but to our clients, our employees and their families, our local community resi-

DEFINING BUSINESS ETHICS

dents, and indeed all of society at large. Our profit comes about through our effort to promote the prosperity of the community as a whole."

There are significant differences of opinion in the role that ethics ought to play at the third level—in evaluating *policies and practices*. Ethics, as the Vice President of Public Affairs of a Swiss multinational notes, can be "a key that opens all doors," the guiding principle behind every decision. But there is no widespread agreement among business leaders that this should always be the case. Some executives argue that ethical considerations are inappropriate for many management decisions and policies because, under certain circumstances, public commitments to ethical principles can give way to business and administrative priorities; or the potential connection between ethical commitments and broad social policies can make the company a target for pressure groups.

For example, while assigning ethics a place in business deliberations, an aerospace executive voices reservations: "The broad definition of ethics may permit the media, special interest groups, and the government to increase pressure on business to address areas that they are currently not equipped to handle. Companies should be concerned with business ethics in dealing with employees, suppliers, and customers. They should not be involved in social, political, or moral issues such as abortion, South Africa, sexual preference, and other personal moral issues."

Other executives are uneasy about the potential conflict between corporate ethics programs and management roles. The Director of a corporate ethics program commented that, among high level executives, "Discussion of the subject generates discomfort. The word suggests a mass confessional. It raises issues that are thought to be more relevant to philosophical discussions. People wonder what sort of new demands an ethics program will make on them. Will they be expected to act as judge, detective, guru, teacher, grand inquisitor, or guiding light to the employees that they supervise?" These roles and the tasks that go with them all imply new, difficult, and uncomfortable supervisory requirements for executives.

Current Issues in Corporate Ethics: The View from the Top

A corporation develops its ethical standards in response to the issues it confronts in pursuit of its business objectives. Viewed in this light, a profile of a company's ethical concerns sheds light on how it reconciles management and business priorities with public policy questions. The Conference Board asked CEOs of major companies which of 27 highly visible issues—in their personal opinion—also involve *ethical considerations* for business, how important each issue will be for business over the next five years, and which problems require further attention in their own companies.

These 27 problems generally fall into four basic (and somewhat overlapping) categories (Chart 1):

Equity is generally used to mean basic fairness, apart from any established legal or human right. For example, executive salary scales are sometimes the subject of controversy when critics say that it is inequitable for certain employees to annually receive thirty or forty times more than the lowest paid worker in the firm.[1] Some arguments for comparable worth are also rooted in an ethical appeal to greater fairness in determining the material rewards for work.

Equity issues are not limited to salary and pay considerations, however. They can also arise in the pricing discretion companies are permitted under applicable law. As is the case with compensation practices, ethical questions can be raised with regard to either results or the means used to attain them.

Rights are treatments to which a person has a just claim. The origin of the claim may be legislation, legal precedent, or community notions of dignity. Modern views of rights are generally protective in nature. They seek to defend individual autonomy from encroachment by powerful institutions or the community at large.

Societies accept the concept of rights to varying degrees. The Japanese, for example, rely heavily on their traditional concept of reciprocal obligation, which mandates discussion,

CHART 1: Ethical Categories of Current Corporate Issues

The issues CEOs were asked to comment on fall into these general categories:

Equity	Rights	Honesty	Exercise of Corporate Power
Executive Salaries	Corporate Due Process	Employee Conflicts of Interest	Political Action Committees
Comparable Worth	Employee Health Screening	Security of Company Records	Workplace Safety
Product Pricing	Employee Privacy Sexual Harassment	Inappropriate Gifts Unauthorized Payment to Foreign Officials	Product Safety Environmental Issues
	Affirmative Action Equal Employment Opportunity Shareholder Interests	Advertising Content	Disinvestment
	Employment at Will	Government Contract Issues Financial and Cash Management Procedures	Corporate Contributions
	Whistle-blowing	Conflicts between the Corporation's Ethical System and Accepted Business Practices in Foreign Countries	Social Issues Raised by Religious Organizations
			Plant/Facility Closures and Downsizing

conciliation, and adjustment of differences instead of an appeal to abstract concepts of justification. Rather than filing lawsuits, Japanese who allege discrimination usually form a "victims group" that negotiates with company representatives. The resulting accommodation does not set a precedent, but it establishes a basis for an ongoing dialogue.[2]

Corporate due process, protection for "whistle-blowers" and shareholders, and erosion of the employment-at-will doctrine are examples of "rights" issues that arise in the corporate context. Equal employment opportunity began as an equity problem, but has achieved the status of a "right" to some degree in the United States.

Dignity is a subcategory of rights, where protection is rooted in the community's sense of elemental decency rather than regulated by specific constitutional, judicial, or legislative mandates. For example, employee privacy and sexual harassment are issues subject to increasing legislative and judicial activity, but the legislative and judicial systems have yet to find an absolute formula for extending these rights to employees.

One of the more difficult dignity issues is employee health screening, because it can involve a conflict of ethical principles. Some see it as invading employee privacy in the interest of social responsibility. The CEO of a U.S. manufacturing company raised this issue when he said: "The right to screen, particularly for drug abuse, is essential to maintaining a safe, competitive work place. To the extent that there is inherent conflict between screening and employee privacy rights, the issue should be resolved in favor of safety and competitiveness."

Honesty in corporate ethics relates to the integrity and truthfulness of a company's actions or policies. Issues of honesty arise both in connection with corporate behavior and with employees acting under the company's nominal supervision. Misleading advertising, questionable financial and cash management procedures, "gifts" for foreign officials, and waste or fraud in the performance of government contracts are examples of corporate behavior that may be labeled dishonest.

Other honesty issues arise in connection with the compa-

DEFINING BUSINESS ETHICS

ny's responsibility to supervise those who act in its name, and the reciprocal obligation of employees to observe company and community standards in their business dealings. The misappropriation of proprietary information for personal enrichment, or to help a competitor, is an abuse of trust. Acceptance of inappropriate gifts can corrupt the purchasing process. Conflicts of interest between employee activities outside the workplace and company interests can create situations of divided loyalty. In all of these circumstances it is the employee who has an ethical responsibility, but a company cannot escape the consequences of lack of proper supervision.

Exercise of corporate power. Corporations recognize a responsibility to contribute to community enterprises that are consistent with their mission and with their commitments to the various constituencies they serve. Corporate financial and executive assistance and efforts to generate public support for programs are believed to be an important element of the company's ethical profile. Decisions of U.S. companies to support policy positions through political action committees are recognized as a responsible exercise of corporate power; but depending on the individual or policy supported, these activities may raise ethical questions.

Business organizations also acknowledge the ethical component of adhering to standards for workplace, product, and environmental safety. Workplace concerns appear to have given rise to a second generation of issues. For example, the CEO of a Canadian bank noted that there was some concern (which he believed to be unfounded) regarding "the longer term effects of CRT screens on physical or psychological health." A group of Swiss executives anticipate pressures in their company to restrict smoking to certain areas.

Beyond generally accepted responsibilities, more controversial positions advocated by religious or political groups may raise ethical questions that have an impact on corporate policy and practices. In recent years, companies have faced external pressures to disinvest from South Africa. The business community has been divided on this issue. Some companies have withdrawn from South Africa; but in interviews, one CEO and several top managers argued that the ethical position is to remain in South Africa, because they believe foreign investment is a critical lever for social change in that country.

Is This an Ethical Issue for Business?

Each of the 27 survey issues (Chart 1) was identified by a substantial number of respondents as posing ethical issues for business, but some topics were cited more often than others. The range among individual problems assessed as "ethical" varies from 37 to 91 percent (see Table 1). At the top of the list, with over 90 percent agreeing that the subject raised ethical questions for business, are *employee conflicts of interest, inappropriate gifts to corporate personnel,* and *sexual harassment.* At the other end of the spectrum are the three equity issues—*comparable worth* (43 percent), *product pricing* (42 percent), and *executive salaries* (37 percent).

U.S. and non-U.S. companies were in substantial accord as to the ethical content of all but four issues—affirmative action, sexual harassment, and whistle-blowing were regarded as more important by U.S. corporations; plant closures were of greater concern to the non-U.S. participants. Although 76 percent of the companies studied have a code of ethics, there was little difference between the responses of companies with and without codes.

Table 1: Is this an Ethical Issue for Business?
(300 Companies Worldwide)

Issue	Percent
Widespread Agreement (80 percent or more say "yes")	
Employee conflicts of interest	91%
Inappropriate gifts to corporate personnel	91
Sexual harassment	91
Unauthorized payments	85
Affirmative action	84
Employee privacy	84
Environmental issues	82

Issue	Percent

Moderate Level of Agreement (50–79 percent say "yes")

Employee health screening	79
Conflicts between company's ethics and foreign business practices	77
Security of company records	76
Workplace safety	76
Advertising content	74
Product safety standards	74
Corporate contributions	68
Shareholder interests	68
Corporate due process	65
Whistle-blowing	63
Employment at will	62
Disinvestment	59
Government contract issues	59
Financial and cash management procedures	55
Plant/facility closures and downsizing	55
Political action committees	55

No Consensus (less than half say "yes")

Social issues raised by religious organizations	47
Comparable worth	43
Product pricing	42
Executive salaries	37

Which Issues Will Be Most Important Over the Next Five Years?

CEOs who identified an issue as ethical in nature were also asked how serious they thought the problem would be for business in the next five years. *Environmental issues, product and workplace safety, employee health screening, security of company records*, and *shareholder interests* were cited by more than two-thirds of these participants as critical or serious concerns for business in the next five years (see Table 2). Companies with official codes of ethics regarded employee conflicts of interest and unauthorized payments to foreign governmental or business officials with greater concern.

U.S. and non-U.S. companies agreed substantially about the potential impact on business of 21 of the 27 issues. U.S. concern was considerably higher with regard to five of the six remaining subjects: sexual harassment, political action committees, social issues raised by religious organizations, employment at will, and employee health screening. Non-U.S. companies viewed only one problem with greater seriousness than did their U.S. counterparts—comparable worth.

Table 2: How Important Will This Issue Be for Business in the Next Five Years?

Issue	Number of Respondents Who Said Issue Gives Rise to Ethical Considerations for Business	Percent of This Group Who Think Issue will be "Critical" or "Serious"
Very Important (70 percent or more checked "critical" or "serious")		
Environmental issues	221	86%
Product safety	192	78
Employee health screening	230	77
Security of company records	216	73
Shareholder interests	194	70
Workplace safety	214	70
Moderately Important (40–69 percent checked "critical" or "serious")		
Affirmative Action/EEOC .	250	66
Disinvestment	137	64
Plant/facility closures and downsizing	149	64
Sexual harassment	266	64
Employment at will	179	59

DEFINING BUSINESS ETHICS

Issue	Number of Respondents Who Said Issue Gives Rise to Ethical Considerations for Business	Percent of This Group Who Think Issue will be "Critical" or "Serious"
Financial and cash management procedures	157	56
Corporate due process	188	51
Employee privacy	244	50
Governmental contract issues	132	49
Unauthorized payments	218	47
Conflicts between company's ethics and foreign business practices	193	46
Employee conflicts of interest	267	44
Product pricing	115	44
Political action committees	152	43
Comparable worth	121	41

Low Level of Concern (less than 40 percent checked "critical" or "serious")

Advertising content	200	37
Inappropriate gifts to corporate personnel	260	36
Executive salaries	107	32
Corporate contributions	202	31
Whistle-blowing	174	29
Social issues raised by religious organizations	119	21

Chart 2:

Ethical Issues that Require Additional Attention

(Responses among those companies that said issue gave rise to ethical considerations for business.)

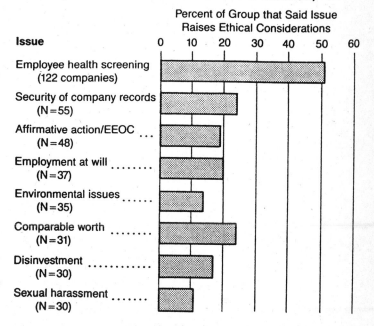

Percent of Group that Said Issue
Raises Ethical Considerations

(Issues checked by fewer than 30 companies are not listed.)

Which Issues Require Further Attention?

Only eight issues were regarded by at least 10 percent of the participants as requiring additional attention (Chart 2). *Employee health screening* was mentioned most often: Nearly half of the participants (122) said that their companies need to develop policies in this area, more than twice the number of respondents for the next most urgent issue, security of company records.

U.S. and non-U.S. companies have significant differences in outlook on health screening. Nearly 60 percent of the U.S. respondents thought their companies ought to pay

DEFINING BUSINESS ETHICS

more attention to it, while slightly less than one-third of the non-U.S. companies held that view. The issue is also regarded more seriously by U.S. companies—over 80 percent of them think it is a critical or serious problem, while only 37 percent of the non-U.S. firms see it in this light. Other differences between U.S. and non-U.S. companies include the great concern of U.S. respondents with employment-at-will issues and the emphasis of non-U.S. participants on product safety.

NOTES

1. For a good sample of opinion for and against high executive salaries and bonuses, see Robert C. Solomon and Kristine Hanson, *It's Good Business.* Harper and Row, 1985, p. 205.
2. Allen R. Janger and Ronald E. Berenbeim, *External Challenges to Management Decisions: A Growing International Business Problem.* The Conference Board, 1981, Report No. 808, pp. 46–48.

The Ethics of Responsibility
Peter Drucker

Peter Drucker has long enjoyed a reputation as the premier guru of American management. In his best-selling *Management: Tasks, Responsibilities, Practices,* Drucker argues that there is no such thing as a separate set of ethics for business; that "fastidiousness" is not necessarily a quality among leaders whether in or out of business. Drucker distinguishes between the manager as a group leader within an organization and the manager as an individual. This distinction allows Drucker to state that the ethics of "community responsibility"—being active on behalf of one's community and participating in furthering its causes—should not be forced on individual managers, since this would be an abuse of their leadership role. As members of a leadership group, managers are professionals. Like all professionals, they have

SOURCE: *Management: Tasks, Responsibilities, Practices,* by Peter F. Drucker. Copyright © 1973, 1974 by Peter F. Drucker. Reprinted by permission of Harper & Row, Publishers, Inc.

one fundamental ethical principle that should guide them: "Above all, do no harm." Drucker views this principle as the primary responsibility of managers.

Countless sermons have been preached and printed on the ethics of business or the ethics of the businessman. Most have nothing to do with business and little to do with ethics.

One main topic is plain, everyday honesty. Businessmen, we are told solemnly, should not cheat, steal, lie, bribe, or take bribes. But nor should anyone else. Men and women do not acquire exemption from ordinary rules of personal behavior because of their work or job. Nor, however, do they cease to be human beings when appointed vice-president, city manager, or college dean. And there has always been a number of people who cheat, steal, lie, bribe, or take bribes. The problem is one of moral values and moral education, of the individual, of the family, of the school. But there neither is a separate ethics of business, nor is one needed.

All that is needed is to mete out stiff punishments to those—whether business executives or others—who yield to temptation. In England a magistrate still tends to hand down a harsher punishment in a drunken-driving case if the accused has gone to one of the well-known public schools or to Oxford or Cambridge. And the conviction still rates a headline in the evening paper: "Eton graduate convicted of drunken driving." No one expects an Eton education to produce temperance leaders. But it is still a badge of distinction, if not of privilege. And not to treat a wearer of such a badge more harshly than an ordinary workingman who has had one too many would offend the community's sense of justice. But no one considers this a problem of the "ethics of the Eton graduate."

The other common theme in the discussion of ethics in business has nothing to do with ethics.

Such things as the employment of call girls to entertain customers are not matters of ethics but matters of esthetics. "Do I want to see a pimp when I look at myself in the mirror while shaving?" is the real question.

DEFINING BUSINESS ETHICS

It would indeed be nice to have fastidious leaders. Alas, fastidiousness has never been prevalent among leadership groups, whether kings and counts, priests or generals, or even "intellectuals" such as the painters and humanists of the Renaissance, or the "literati" of the Chinese tradition. All a fastidious man can do is withdraw personally from activities that violate his self-respect and his sense of taste.

Lately these old sermon topics have been joined, especially in the U.S., by a third one: managers, we are being told, have an "ethical responsibility" to take an active and constructive role in their community, to serve community causes, give of their time to community activities, and so on.

There are many countries where such community activity does not fit the traditional mores; Japan and France would be examples. But where the community has a tradition of "voluntarism"—that is, especially in the U.S.—managers should indeed be encouraged to participate and to take responsible leadership in community affairs and community organizations. Such activities should, however, never be forced on them, nor should they be appraised, rewarded, or promoted according to their participation in voluntary activities. Ordering or pressuring managers into such work is abuse of organizational power and illegitimate.

An exception might be made for managers in businesses where the community activities are really part of their obligation to the business. The local manager of the telephone company, for instance, who takes part in community activities, does so as part of his managerial duties and as the local public-relations representative of his company. The same is true of the manager of a local Sears, Roebuck store. And the local real estate man who belongs to a dozen different community activities and eats lunch every day with a different "service club" knows perfectly well that he is not serving the community but promoting his business and hunting for prospective customers.

But, while desirable, community participation of managers has nothing to do with ethics, and not much to do with responsibility. It is the contribution of an individual in his capacity as a neighbor and citizen. And it is something that lies outside his job and outside his managerial responsibility.

Leadership Groups but not Leaders

A problem of ethics that is peculiar to the manager arises from the fact that the managers of institutions are *collectively* the leadership groups of the society of organizations. But *individually* a manager is just another fellow employee.

This is clearly recognized by the public. Even the most powerful head of the largest corporation is unknown to the public. Indeed most of the company's employees barely know his name and would not recognize his face. He may owe his position entirely to personal merit and proven performance. But he owes his authority and standing entirely to his institution. Everybody knows GE, the Telephone Company, Mitsubishi, Siemens, and Unilever. But who heads these great corporations—or for that matter, the University of California, the Ecole Polytechnique or Guy's Hospital in London—is of direct interest and concern primarily to the management group within these institutions.

It is therefore inappropriate to speak of managers as leaders. They are "members of the leadership group." The group, however, does occupy a position of visibility, of prominence, and of authority. It therefore has responsibility. . . .

But what are the responsibilities, what are the ethics of the individual manager, as a member of the leadership group?

Essentially being a member of a leadership group is what traditionally has been meant by the term "professional." Membership in such a group confers status, position, prominence, and authority. It also confers duties. To expect every manager to be a leader is futile. There are, in a developed society, thousands, if not millions, of managers—and leadership is always the rare exception and confined to a very few individuals. But as a member of a leadership group a manager stands under the demands of professional ethics—the demands of an ethic of responsibility.

Primum Non Nocere

The first responsibility of a professional was spelled out clearly, 2,500 years ago, in the Hippocratic oath of the Greek physician: *primum non nocere*—"Above all, not knowingly to do harm."

No professional, be he doctor, lawyer, or manager, can promise that he will indeed do good for his client. All he can do is try. But he can promise that he will not knowingly do harm. And the client, in turn, must be able to trust the professional not knowingly to do him harm. Otherwise he cannot trust him at all. The professional has to have autonomy. He cannot be controlled, supervised, or directed by the client. He has to be private in that his knowledge and his judgment have to be entrusted with the decision. But it is the foundation of his autonomy, and indeed its rationale, that he see himself as "affected with the public interest." A professional, in other words, is private in the sense that he is autonomous and not subject to political or ideological control. But he is public in the sense that the welfare of his client sets limits to his deeds and words. And *primum non nocere*, "not knowingly to do harm," is the basic rule of professional ethics, the basic rule of an ethics of public responsibility.

There are important areas where managers, and especially business managers, still do not realize that in order to be permitted to remain autonomous and private they have to impose on themselves the responsibility of the professional ethic. They still have to learn that it is their job to scrutinize their deeds, words, and behavior to make sure that they do not knowingly do harm.

The manager who fails to think through and work for the appropriate solution to an impact of his business because it makes him "unpopular in the club" knowingly does harm. He knowingly abets a cancerous growth. That this is stupid has been said. That this always in the end hurts the business or the industry more than a little temporary "unpleasantness" would have hurt has been said too. But it is also a gross violation of professional ethics.

But there are other areas as well. American managers, in particular, tend to violate the rule not knowingly to do harm with respect to:

- executive compensation;
- the use of benefit plans to impose "golden fetters" on people in the company's employ; and
- in their profit rhetoric.

Their actions and their words in these areas tend to cause social disruption. They tend to conceal healthy reality and to create disease, or at least social hypochondria. They tend to misdirect and to prevent understanding. And this is grievous social harm.

Executive Compensation and Economic Inequality

Contrary to widespread belief, incomes have become far more equal in all developed countries than in any society of which we have a record. And they have tended to become steadily more equal as national and personal incomes increase. And, equally contrary to popular rhetoric, income equality is greatest in the United States.

The most reliable measure of income equality is the so-called Gini coefficient, in which an index of zero stands for complete equality of income and an index of 1 for total inequality in which one person in the population receives all the income. The lower the Gini coefficient, the closer a society is to income equality. In the U.S. the Gini in the early 1970s stood around 0.35—with about the same figure in Canada, Australia, and Great Britain, and probably also in Japan. West Germany and the Netherlands are about 0.40. France and Sweden are around 0.50.[1]

Specifically, in the typical American business the inequality of income between the lowest-paid people and the people in charge—that is, between the machine operator and the manager of a large plant—is at most 1 to 4, if taxes are taken into account. The take-home pay of the machine operator after taxes in 1970 was around $7,500 a year; the after-tax income of very few plant managers was larger than $25,000, all bonuses included. If fringes are taken into account, the ratio is even lower, i.e., one to three (or $12,000 to $35,000 maximum). And similar ratios prevail in other developed countries, e.g., in Japan. This, it should be said, is far greater income equality than in any communist country for the simple reason that the economic level of a communist country is lower.

In Soviet Russia, where there are practically no income taxes, the income differential between industrial worker and plant manager runs around 1 to 7, without taking into account the noncash benefits of the Russian manager. And Russian managers operate at an extreme of profit maximization; their profit-based bonus system of compensation so directs them. In China, the differential between workers and plant managers seems to run around 1 to 6 or so.

Whether the degree of inequality of incomes that actually prevails in the U.S. economy is "too high" or "too low" is a matter of opinion. But clearly it is much lower than the great majority of the American public accepts or even considers desirable. Every survey shows that an "income ratio of 1 to 10 or 12" between the blue-collar in the factory and the "big boss" would be considered "about right." That would make the "after-tax take-home pay" of the "big boss" somewhere around $75,000 to $100,000 a year, which would be equal to a pre-tax salary of at least $200,000. And only a mere handful of executives earn that much, bonuses included. If the comparison is made—as it should be—between total incomes, including fringes, deferred compensation, stock options, and all other forms of extra compensation, a 1 to 12 ratio would work out to an after-tax top figure of $150,000. And no more than a dozen or so top men in the very largest companies have pre-tax "total compensation package" of $300,000 and up, which is needed to produce an after-tax value of $150,000. The "extremely rich" are not employed executives—the tax system takes care of those (as it should); they are either a few heirs of the millionaires of pre-tax days or owners of small businesses.

And relative to the incomes of manual and clerical workers, after-tax executive compensation, and especially the income of the men at the very top, has been going down steadily for fifty years or more.

The facts of increasing income equality in U.S. society are quite clear. Yet the popular impression is one of rapidly increasing inequality. This is illusion; but it is a dangerous illusion. It corrodes. It destroys mutual trust between groups that have to live together and work together. It can only lead to political measures which, while doing no one any good, can seriously harm society, economy, and the manager as well.

In some considerable measure, the belief in growing income inequality in the U.S. reflects, of course, America's racial problem. The emergence into visibility, that is, into the big cities, of a disenfranchised nonworking population of Blacks has created a marginal but highly visible group suffering from extreme inequality of incomes. . . .

Another reason for the widespread belief in growing inequality is inflation. Inflation is a corrosive social poison precisely because it makes people look for a villain. The economists' explanation that no one benefits by inflation, that is, that no one gets the purchasing power that inflation takes away from the income recipients, simply makes no sense to ordinary experience. Somebody must have benefited, somebody "must have stolen what is rightfully mine." Every inflation in history has therefore created class hatred, mutual distrust, and beliefs that, somehow, "the other fellow" gains illicitly at "my" expense. It is always the middle class which becomes paranoid in an inflationary period and turns against the "system." The inflations of the sixties in the developed countries were no exceptions.

But the main cause of the dangerous delusion of increasing inequality of income is the widely publicized enormous *pre-tax* incomes of a few men at the top of a few giant corporations, and the—equally widely publicized—"extras" of executive compensation, e.g., stock options.

The $500,000 a year which the chief executive of one of the giant corporations is being paid is largely "make-believe money." Its function is status rather than income. Most of it, whatever tax loopholes the lawyers might find, is immediately taxed away. And the "extras" are simply attempts to

DEFINING BUSINESS ETHICS

put a part of the executive's income into a somewhat lower tax bracket. Economically, in other words, neither serves much purpose. But socially and psychologically they "knowingly do harm." They cannot be defended.

One way to eliminate the offense is for companies to commit themselves to a maximum range of *after-tax* compensation. The 1 to 10 ratio that the great majority of Americans would consider perfectly acceptable, would, in fact, be wider than the actual range of most companies. (There should, I would argue, be room, however, for an occasional exception: the rare, "once-in-a-lifetime," very big, "special bonus" to someone, a research scientist, a manager, or a salesman who has made an extraordinary contribution.)

But equally important is acceptance of social responsibility on the part of managers to work for a rational system of taxation,[2] which eliminates the temptation of "tax gimmicks" and the need for them.

There is a strong case for adequate incentives for performing executives. And compensation in money is far preferable to hidden compensation such as perquisites. If he gets money, the recipient can choose what to spend it on rather than, as in the case of "perks," taking whatever the company provides, be it a chauffeur-driven car, a big house, or (as in the case of some Swedish companies) a governess for the children. Indeed it may well be that real incomes in American business are not sufficiently unequal and that the compression of income differentials in the years since 1950 has been socially and economically detrimental.

What is pernicious, however, is the delusion of inequality. The basic cause is the tax laws. But the managers' willingness to accept, and indeed to play along with, an antisocial tax structure is a major contributory cause. And unless managers realize that this violates the rule "not knowingly to do damage," they will, in the end, be the main sufferers.

The Danger of "Golden Fetters"

A second area in which the manager of today does not live up to the commitment of *primum non nocere* is closely connected with compensation.

Since World War II compensation and benefits have been increasingly misused to create "golden fetters."

Retirement benefits, extra compensation, bonuses, and stock options are all forms of compensation. From the point of view of the enterprise—but also from the point of view of the economy—these are "labor costs" no matter how they are labeled. They are treated as such by managements when they sit down to negotiate with the labor union. But increasingly, if only because of the bias of the tax laws, these benefits are being used to tie an employee to his employer. They are being made dependent on staying with the same employer, often for many years. And they are structured in such a way that leaving a company's employ entails drastic penalties and actual loss of benefits that have already been earned and that, in effect, constitute wages relating to past employment.

This may be proper in a society which, like that of Japan, is built on lifetime employment and excludes mobility. Even in Japan, however, "golden fetters" are no longer acceptable to professional and technical employees who increasingly should have mobility in their own interest, in that of the Japanese economy, and even in that of the Japanese company. In the West, and especially in the United States, such golden fetters are clearly antisocial.

Golden fetters do not strengthen the company. They lead to "negative selection." People who know that they are not performing in their present employment—that is, people who are clearly in the wrong place—will often not move but stay where they know they do not properly belong. But if they stay because the penalty for leaving is too great, they resist and resent it. They know that they have been bribed and were too weak to say no. They are likely to be sullen, resentful, and bitter the rest of their working lives.

The fact that the employees themselves eagerly seek these

benefits is no excuse. After all, medieval serfdom also began as an eagerly sought "employee benefit."

It is incumbent, therefore, on the managers to think through
which of these benefits should properly—by their own
rationale—be tied to continued employment. Stock options
might, for instance, belong here. But pension rights, performance bonuses, participation in profits, and so on have
been "earned" and should be available to the employee
without restricting his rights as a citizen, an individual, and
a person. And, again, managers will have to work to get the
tax law changes that are needed.

The Rhetoric of the Profit Motive

Managers, finally, through their rhetoric, make it impossible for the public to understand economic reality. This violates the requirement that managers, being leaders, not
knowingly do harm. This is particularly true of the United
States but also of Western Europe. For in the West, managers still talk constantly of the profit motive. And they still
define the goal of their business as profit maximization.
They do not stress the objective function of profit. They do
not talk of risks—or very rarely. They do not stress the need
for capital. They almost never even mention the cost of
capital, let alone that a business has to produce enough
profit to obtain the capital it needs at minimum cost.

Managers constantly complain about the hostility to profit.
They rarely realize that their own rhetoric is one of the main
reasons for this hostility. For indeed in the terms management uses when it talks to the public, there is no possible
justification for profit, no explanation for its existence, no
function it performs. There is only the profit motive, that is,
the desire of some anonymous capitalists—and why that
desire should be indulged in by society any more than big-
amy, for instance, is never explained. But profitability is a
crucial *need* of economy and society.

Managerial practice in most large American companies is
perfectly rational. It is the rhetoric which obscures, and

thereby threatens to damage both business and society. To be sure, few American companies work out profitability as a *minimum* requirement. As a result, most probably underestimate the profitability the company truly requires (let alone the inflationary erosion of capital). But they, consciously or not, base their profit planning on the twin objectives of ensuring access to capital needed and minimizing the cost of capital. In the American context, if only because of the structure of the U.S. capital market, a high "price/earnings ratio" is indeed a key to the minimization of the cost of capital; and "optimization of profits" is therefore a perfectly rational strategy which tends to lower, in the long run, the actual cost of capital.

But this makes it even less justifiable to keep on using the rhetoric of the profit motive. It serves no purpose except to confuse and to embitter.

These examples of areas in which managers do not hold themselves to the rule "not knowingly to do harm" are primarily American examples. They apply to some extent to Western Europe. But they hardly apply to Japan. The principle, however, applies in all countries, and in the developing countries as much as in developed ones. These cases are taken from business management. The principle, however, applies to managers of all institutions in the society of organizations.

In any pluralist society responsibility for the public good has been the central problem and issue. The pluralist society of organizations will be no exception. Its leaders represent "special interests," that is, institutions designed to fulfill a specific and partial need of society. Indeed the leaders of this pluralist society of organizations are the servants of such institutions. At the same time, they are the major leadership group such a society knows or is likely to produce. They have to serve both their own institution and the common good. If the society is to function, let alone if it is to remain a free society, the men we call managers will remain "private" in their institutions. No matter who owns them and how, they will maintain autonomy. But they will also have to be "public" in their ethics.

In this tension between the private functioning of the

manager, the necessary autonomy of his institution and its accountability to its own mission and purpose, and the public character of the manager, lies the specific ethical problem of the society of organizations. *Primum non nocere* may seem tame compared to the rousing calls for "statesmanship" that abound in today's manifestos on social responsibility. But, as the physicians found out long ago, it is not an easy rule to live up to. Its very modesty and self-constraint make it the right rule for the ethics managers need, the ethics of responsibility.

NOTES

1. On this see the article by Sanford Rose, "The Truth about Income and Equality in the U.S." in *Fortune*, December 1972.

2. We know the specifications of such a system—and they are simple: *no* preferential tax rates for *any* personal income, whether from salaries or from capital gains, and a limit on the maximum tax—say 50 percent of total income received.

Ethics Without the Sermon
Laura L. Nash

When academic philosophers begin to discuss ethics with those who have more practical concerns (such as corporate executives), radically different styles, approaches, and biases become quite apparent. Taking these differences as her cue, Laura L. Nash offers a set of twelve questions that, while free of philosophical abstraction, nonetheless embody the central concerns of ethical reasoning as it is applied to business. Her twelve-point program of pertinent questions is a kind of checklist for help in answering the more general question: "Is my business decision also an ethical

SOURCE: Reprinted by permission of *Harvard Business Review*. "Ethics Without the Sermon," by Laura L. Nash, Vol. 59 (November/December 1981). Copyright © 1981 by the President and Fellows of Harvard College; all rights reserved.

decision?" Nash provides a framework that demonstrates the importance of critical thinking in business ethics. Throughout her analysis Nash refers to Lex Service Group, Ltd., a firm with operations in the United Kingdom and the United States, to demonstrate that her program works in a concrete setting; that it is not just a utopian, philosophical abstraction. Nash espouses the "good-puppy" theory of the corporation. This holds that the good toward which a firm should aim is an avoidance of "irretrievable social injury." (This is much like Peter Drucker's "do-no-harm" ethic.) For Nash, business ethics, then, is a practical exercise of critical thinking where the goal is a corporate practice that does not foster unnecessary social harm.

As if via a network TV program on the telecommunications satellite, declarations such as these are being broadcast throughout the land:

Scene 1. Annual meeting, Anyproducts Inc.; John Q. Moneypockets, chairman and CEO, speaking: "Our responsibility to the public has always come first at our company, and we continue to strive toward serving our public in the best way possible in the belief that good ethics is good business. . . . Despite our forecast of a continued recession in the industry through 1982, we are pleased to announce that 1981's earnings per share were up for the twenty-sixth year in a row."

Scene 2. Corporate headquarters, Anyproducts Inc.; Linda Diesinker, group vice president, speaking: "Of course we're concerned about minority development and the plight of the inner cities. But the best place for our new plant would be Horsepasture, Minnesota. We need a lot of space for our operations and a skilled labor force, and the demographics and tax incentives in Horsepasture are perfect."

Scene 3. Interview with a financial writer; Rafe Shortstop, president, Anyproducts Inc., speaking: "We're very concerned about the state of American business and our ability to compete with foreign companies. . . . No, I don't think we have any real ethical problems. We don't bribe people or anything like that."

Scene 4. Jud McFisticuff, taxi driver, speaking: "Anyproducts? You've got to be kidding! I wouldn't buy their stuff for anything. The last thing of theirs I bought fell apart in six months. And did you see how they were dumping wastes in the Roxburg water system?"

Scene 5. Leslie Matriculant, MBA '82, speaking: "Join Anyproducts? I don't want to risk my reputation working for a company like that. They recently acquired a business that turned out to have ten class-action discrimination suits against it. And when Anyproducts tried to settle the whole thing out of court, the president had his picture in *Business Week* with the caption, 'His secretary still serves him coffee.' "

Whether you regard it as an unchecked epidemic or as the first blast of Gabriel's horn, the trend toward focusing on the social impact of the corporation is an inescapable reality that must be factored into today's managerial decision making. But for the executive who asks, "How do we as a corporation examine our ethical concerns?" the theoretical insights currently available may be more frustrating than helpful.

As the first scene in this article implies, many executives firmly believe that corporate operations and corporate values are dynamically intertwined. For the purposes of analysis, however, the executive needs to uncoil the business-ethics helix and examine both strands closely.

Unfortunately, the ethics strand has remained largely inaccessible, for business has not yet developed a workable process by which corporate values can be articulated. If ethics and business are part of the same double helix, perhaps we can develop a microscope capable of enlarging our perception of both aspects of business administration—what we do and who we are.

Sidestepping
Triassic Reptiles

Philosophy has been sorting out issues of fairness, injury, empathy, self-sacrifice, and so on for more than 2,000 years. In seeking to examine the ethics of business, therefore, business logically assumes it will be best served by a "consultant" in philosophy who is already familiar with the formal discipline of ethics.

As the philosopher begins to speak, however, a difficulty immediately arises; corporate executives and philosophers approach problems in radically different ways. The academician ponders the intangible, savors the paradoxical, and embraces the peculiar; he or she speaks in a special language of categorical imperatives and deontological viewpoints that must be taken into consideration before a statement about honesty is agreed to have any meaning.

Like some Triassic reptile, the theoretical view of ethics lumbers along in the far past of Sunday School and Philosophy 1, while the reality of practical business concerns is constantly measuring a wide range of competing claims on time and resources against the unrelenting and objective marketplace.

Not surprisingly, the two groups are somewhat hostile. The jokes of the liberal intelligentsia are rampant and weary: *"Ethics and Business*—the shortest book in the world." "Business and ethics—a subject confined to the preface of business books." Accusations from the corporate cadre are delivered with an assurance that rests more on an intuition of social climate than on a certainty of fact: "You do-gooders are ruining America's ability to compete in the world." "Of course, the cancer reports on ——— [choose from a long list] were terribly exaggerated."

What is needed is a process of ethical inquiry that is immediately comprehensible to a group of executives and not predisposed to the utopian, and sometimes anticapitalistic, bias marking much of the work in applied business philosophy today. So I suggest, as a preliminary solution, a set of twelve questions that draw on traditional philosophical frame-

DEFINING BUSINESS ETHICS

works but that avoid the level of abstraction normally associated with formal moral reasoning.

I offer the questions as a first step in a very new discipline. As such, they form a tentative model that will certainly undergo modifications after its parts are given some exercise. The *Exhibit* on pages 43–44 poses the twelve questions.

To illustrate the application of the questions, I will draw especially on a program at Lex Service Group, Ltd., whose top management prepared a statement of financial objectives and moral values as a part of its strategic planning process.[1] Lex is a British company with operations in the United Kingdom and the United States. Its sales total about $1.2 billion. In 1978 its structure was partially decentralized, and in 1979 the chairman's policy group began a strategic planning process. The intent, according to its statement of values and objectives, was "to make explicit the sort of company Lex was, or wished to be."

Neither a paralegal code nor a generalized philosophy, the statement consisted of a series of general policies regarding financial strategy as well as such aspects of the company's character as customer service, employee-shareholder responsibility, and quality of management. Its content largely reflected the personal values of Lex's chairman and CEO, Trevor Chinn, whose private philanthropy is well known and whose concern for social welfare has long been echoed in the company's personnel policies.

In the past, pressure on senior managers for high profit performance had obscured some of these ideals in practice, and the statement of strategy was a way of radically realigning various competing moral claims with the financial objectives of the company. As one senior manager remarked to me, "The values seem obvious, and if we hadn't been so gross in the past we wouldn't have needed the statement." Despite a predictable variance among Lex's top executives as to the desirability of the values outlined in the statement, it was adopted with general agreement to comply and was scheduled for reassessment at a senior managers' meeting one year after implementation.

The Twelve Questions

1. Have you defined the problem accurately?

How one assembles the facts weights an issue before the moral examination ever begins, and a definition is rarely accurate if it articulates one's loyalties rather than the facts. The importance of factual neutrality is readily seen, for example, in assessing the moral implications of producing a chemical agent for use in warfare. Depending on one's loyalties, the decision to make the substance can be described as serving one's country, developing products, or killing babies. All of the above may be factual statements, but none is neutral or accurate if viewed in isolation.

Similarly, the recent controversy over marketing U.S.-made cigarettes in Third World countries rarely noted that the incidence of lung cancer in underdeveloped nations is quite low (from one-tenth to one-twentieth the rate for U.S. males) due primarily to the lower life expectancies and earlier predominance of other diseases in these nations. Such a fact does not decide the ethical complexities of this marketing problem, but it does add a crucial perspective in the assignment of moral priorities by defining precisely the injury that tobacco exports may cause.

Exhibit: Twelve Questions for Examining the Ethics of a Business Decision

1	Have you defined the problem accurately?
2	How would you define the problem if you stood on the other side of the fence?
3	How did this situation occur in the first place?
4	To whom and to what do you give your loyalty as a person and as a member of the corporation?
5	What is your intention in making this decision?
6	How does this intention compare with the probable results?
7	Whom could your decision or action injure?

DEFINING BUSINESS ETHICS

8	Can you discuss the problem with the affected parties before you make your decision?
9	Are you confident that your position will be as valid over a long period of time as it seems now?
10	Could you disclose without qualm your decision or action to your boss, your CEO, the board of directors, your family, society as a whole?
11	What is the symbolic potential of your action if understood? if misunderstood?
12	Under what conditions would you allow exceptions to your stand?

Extensive fact gathering may also help defuse the emotionalism of an issue. For instance, local statistics on lung cancer incidence reveal that the U.S. tobacco industry is not now "exporting death," as has been charged. Moreover, the substantial and immediate economic benefits attached to tobacco may be providing food and health care in these countries. Nevertheless, as life expectancy and the standards of living rise, a higher incidence of cigarette-related diseases appears likely to develop in these nations. Therefore, cultivation of the nicotine habit may be deemed detrimental to the long-term welfare of these nations.

According to one supposedly infallible truth of modernism, technology is so complex that its results will never be fully comprehensible or predictable. Part of the executive's frustration in responding to Question 1 is the real possibility that the "experts" will find no grounds for agreement about the facts.

As a first step, however, defining fully the factual implications of a decision determines to a large degree the quality of one's subsequent moral position. Pericles' definition of true courage rejected the Spartans' blind obedience in war in preference to the courage of the Athenian citizen who, he said, was able to make a decision to proceed in full knowledge of the probable danger. A truly moral decision is an informed decision. A decision that is based on blind or convenient ignorance is hardly defensible.

One simple test of the initial definition is the question:

2. How would you define the problem if you stood on the other side of the fence?

The contemplated construction of a plant for Division X is touted at the finance committee meeting as an absolute necessity for expansion at a cost saving of at least 25%. With plans drawn up for an energy-efficient building and an option already secured on a 99-year lease in a new industrial park in Chippewa County, the committee is likely to feel comfortable in approving the request for funds in a matter of minutes.

The facts of the matter are that the company will expand in an appropriate market, allocate its resources sensibly, create new jobs, increase Chippewa County's tax base, and most likely increase its returns to the shareholders. To the residents of Chippewa County, however, the plant may mean the destruction of a customary recreation spot, the onset of severe traffic jams, and the erection of an architectural eyesore. These are also facts of the situation, and certainly more immediate to the county than utilitarian justifications of profit performance and rights of ownership from an impersonal corporation whose headquarters are 1,000 miles from Chippewa County and whose executives have plenty of acreage for their own recreation.

The purpose of articulating the other side, whose needs are understandably less proximate than operational considerations, is to allow some mechanism whereby calculations of self-interest (or even of a project's ultimate general beneficence) can be interrupted by a compelling empathy for those who might suffer immediate injury or mere annoyance as a result of a corporation's decisions. Such empathy is a necessary prerequisite for shouldering voluntarily some responsibility for the social consequences of corporate operations, and it may be the only solution to today's overly litigious and anarchic world.

There is a power in self-examination: with an exploration of the likely consequences of a proposal, taken from the viewpoint of those who do not immediately benefit, comes a discomfort or an embarrassment that rises in proportion to the degree of the likely injury and its articulation. Like Socrates as gadfly, who stung his fellow citizens into a critical examination of their conduct when they became complacent, the discomfort of the alternative definition is meant to prompt a disinclination to choose the expedient over the most responsible course of action.

Abstract generalities about the benefits of the profit motive and the free market system are, for some, legitimate and ultimate justifications, but when unadorned with alternative viewpoints, such arguments also tend to promote the complacency, carelessness, and impersonality that have characterized some of the more injurious actions of corporations. The advocates of these arguments are like the reformers in Nathaniel Hawthorne's short story "Hall of Fantasy" who "had got possession of some crystal fragment of truth, the brightness of which so dazzled them that they could see nothing else in the whole universe."

In the example of Division X's new plant, it was a simple matter to define the alternate facts; the process rested largely on an assumption that certain values were commonly shared (no one likes a traffic jam, landscaping pleases more than an unadorned building, and so forth). But the alternative definition often underscores an inherent disparity in values or language. To some, the employment of illegal aliens is a criminal act (fact #1); to others, it is a solution to the 60% unemployment rate of a neighboring country (fact #2). One country's bribe is another country's redistribution of sales commissions.

When there are cultural or linguistic disparities, it is easy to get the facts wrong or to invoke a pluralistic tolerance as an excuse to act in one's own self-interest: "That's the way they do things over there. Who are we to question their beliefs?" This kind of reasoning can be both factually inaccurate (many generalizations about bribery rest on hearsay and do not represent the complexities of a culture) and philosophically inconsistent (there are plenty of beliefs, such as those of the environmentalist, which the same generalizers do not hesitate to question).

3. How did this situation occur in the first place?

Lex Motor Company, a subsidiary of Lex Service Group, Ltd., had been losing share at a 20% rate in a declining market; and Depot B's performance was the worst of all. Two nearby Lex depots could easily absorb B's business, and closing it down seemed the only sound financial decision. Lex's chairman, Trevor Chinn, hesitated to approve the closure, however, on the grounds that putting 100 people out of work was not right when the corporation itself was not really jeopardized by B's existence. Moreover, seven department managers, who were all within five years of retirement and had had 25 or more years of service at Lex, were scheduled to be made redundant.

The values statement provided no automatic solution, for it placed value on both employees' security and shareholders' interest. Should they close Depot B? At first Chinn thought not: Why should the little guys suffer disproportionately when the company was not performing well? Why not close a more recently acquired business where employee service was not so large a factor? Or why not wait out the short term and reduce head count through natural attrition?

As important as deciding the ethics of the situation was the inquiry into its history. Indeed, the history gave a clue to solving the dilemma: Lex's traditional emphasis on employee security *and* high financial performance had led to a precipitate series of acquisitions and subsequent divestitures when the company had failed to meet its overall objectives. After each rationalization, the people serving the longest had been retained and placed at Depot B, so that by 1980 the facility had more managers than it needed and a very high proportion of long-service employees.

So the very factors that had created the performance problems were making the closure decision difficult, and the very solution that Lex was inclined to favor again would exacerbate the situation further!

In deciding the ethics of a situation it is important to distinguish the symptoms from the disease. Great profit pressures with no sensitivity to the cycles in a particular industry, for example, may force division managers to be ruthless with employees, to short-weight customers, or even to fiddle with cash flow reports in order to meet headquarters' performance criteria.

Dealing with the immediate case of lying, quality discrep-

DEFINING BUSINESS ETHICS

ancy, or strained labor relations—when the problem is finally discovered—is only a temporary solution. A full examination of how the situation occurred and what the traditional solutions have been may reveal a more serious discrepancy of values and pressures, and this will illuminate the real significance and ethics of the problem. It will also reveal recurring patterns of events that in isolation appear trivial but that as a whole point up a serious situation.

Such a mechanism is particularly important because very few executives are outright scoundrels. Rather, violations of corporate and social values usually occur inadvertently because no one recognizes that a problem exists until it becomes a crisis. This tendency toward initial trivialization seems to be the biggest ethical problem in business today. Articulating answers to my first three questions is a way of reversing that process.

4. To whom and what do you give your loyalties as a person and as a member of the corporation?

Every executive faces conflicts of loyalty. The most familiar occasions pit private conscience and sense of duty against corporate policy, but equally frequent are the situations in which one's close colleagues demand participation (tacit or explicit) in an operation or a decision that runs counter to company policy. To whom or what is the greater loyalty—to one's corporation? superior? family? society? self? race? sex?

The good news about conflicts of loyalty is that their identification is a workable way of smoking out the ethics of a situation and of discovering the absolute values inherent in it. As one executive in a discussion of a Harvard case study put it, "My corporate brain says this action is O.K., but my noncorporate brain keeps flashing these warning lights."

The bad news about conflicts of loyalty is that there are few automatic answers for placing priorities on them. "To thine own self be true" is a murky quagmire when the self takes on a variety of roles, as it does so often in this complex modern world.

Supposedly, today's young managers are giving more weight to individual than to corporate identity, and some older executives see this tendency as being ultimately subversive. At the same time, most of them believe individual integrity is essential to a company's reputation.

The U.S. securities industry, for example, is one of the most rigorous industries in America in its requirements of honesty and disclosure. Yet in the end, all its systematic precautions prove inadequate unless the people involved also have a strong sense of integrity that puts loyalty to these principles above personal gain.

A system, however, must permit the time and foster the motivation to allow personal integrity to surface in a particular situation. An examination of loyalties is one way to bring this about. Such an examination may strengthen reputations but also may result in blowing the whistle (freedom of thought carries with it the risk of revolution). But a sorting out of loyalties can also bridge the gulf between policy and implementation or among various interest groups whose affiliations may mask a common devotion to an aspect of a problem—a devotion on which consensus can be built.

How does one probe into one's own loyalties and their implications? A useful method is simply to play various roles out loud, to call on one's loyalty to family and community (for example) by asking, "What will I say when my child asks me why I did that?" If the answer is "That's the way the world works," then your loyalties are clear and moral passivity inevitable. But if the question presents real problems, you have begun a demodulation of signals from your conscience that can only enhance corporate responsibility.

5. What is your intention in making this decision?

6. How does this intention compare with the likely results?

These two questions are asked together because their content often bears close resemblance and, by most calculations, both color the ethics of a situation.

Corporation Buglebloom decides to build a new plant in an underdeveloped minority-populated district where the city has been trying with little success to encourage industrial development. The media approve and Buglebloom adds

DEFINING BUSINESS ETHICS

another star to its good reputation. Is Buglebloom a civic leader and a supporter of minorities or a canny investor about to take advantage of the disadvantaged? The possibilities of Buglebloom's intentions are endless and probably unfathomable to the public; Buglebloom may be both canny investor and friend of minority groups.

I argue that despite their complexity and elusiveness, a company's intentions *do* matter. The "purity" of Buglebloom's motives (purely profit-seeking or purely altruistic) will have wide-reaching effects inside and outside the corporation—on attitudes toward minority employees in other parts of the company, on the wages paid at the new plant, and on the number of other investors in the same area—that will legitimize a certain ethos in the corporation and the community.

Sociologist Max Weber called this an "ethics of attitude" and contrasted it with an "ethics of absolute ends." An ethics of attitude sets a standard to ensure a certain action. A firm policy at headquarters of not cheating customers, for example, may also deter salespeople from succumbing to a tendency to lie by omission or purchasers from continuing to patronize a high-priced supplier when the costs are automatically passed on in the selling price.

What about the ethics of result? Two years later, Buglebloom wishes it had never begun Project Minority Plant. Every good intention has been lost in the realities of doing business in an unfamiliar area, and Buglebloom now has dirty hands: some of those payoffs were absolutely unavoidable if the plant was to open, operations have been plagued with vandalism and language problems, and local resentment at the industrialization of the neighborhood has risen as charges of discrimination have surfaced. No one seems to be benefiting from the project.

The goodness of intent pales somewhat before results that perpetrate great injury or simply do little good. Common sense demands that the "responsible" corporation try to align the two more closely, to identify the probable consequences and also the limitations of knowledge that might lead to more harm than good. Two things to remember in comparing intention and results are that knowledge of the future is always inadequate and that overconfidence often precedes a disastrous mistake.

These two precepts, cribbed from ancient Greece, may help the corporation keep the disparities between intent and result a fearsome reality to consider continuously. The next two questions explore two ways of reducing the moral risks of being wrong.

7. Whom could your decision or action injure?

The question presses whether injury is intentional or not. Given the limits of knowledge about a new product or policy, who and how many will come into contact with it? Could its inadequate disposal affect an entire community? two employees? yourself? How might your product be used if it happened to be acquired by a terrorist radical group or a terrorist military police force? Has your distribution system or disposal plan ensured against such injury? Could it ever?

If not, there may be a compelling moral justification for stopping production. In an integrated society where business and government share certain values, possible injury is an even more important consideration than potential benefit. In policymaking, a much likelier ground for agreement than benefit is avoidance of injury through those "universal nos" —such as no mass death, no totalitarianism, no hunger or malnutrition, no harm to children.

To exclude *at the outset* any policy or decision that might have such results is to reshape the way modern business examines its own morality. So often business formulates questions of injury only after the fact in the form of liability suits.

8. Can you engage the affected parties in a discussion of the problem before you make your decision?

If the calculus of injury is one way of responding to limitations of knowledge about the probable results of a particular business decision, the participation of affected parties is one of the best ways of informing that consideration. Civil rights groups often complain that corporations fail to invite participation from local leaders during the planning stages of community development projects and charitable programs. The corporate foundation that builds a tennis complex for disadvantaged youth is throwing away precious resources if most children in the neighborhood suffer from chronic malnutrition.

In the Lex depot closure case I have mentioned, senior executives agonized over whether the employees would choose redundancy over job transfer and which course would ultimately be more beneficial to them. The managers, however, did not consult the employees. There were more than 200 projected job transfers to another town. But all the affected employees, held by local ties and uneasy about possibly lower housing subsidies, refused relocation offers. Had the employees been allowed to participate in the redundancy discussions, the company might have wasted less time on relocation plans or might have uncovered and resolved the fears about relocating.

The issue of participation affects everyone. (How many executives feel that someone else should decide what is in *their* best interest?) And yet it is a principle often forgotten because of the pressure of time or the inconvenience of calling people together and facing predictably hostile questions.

9. Are you confident that your position will be as valid over a long period of time as it seems now?

As anyone knows who has had to consider long-range plans and short-term budgets simultaneously, a difference in time frame can change the meaning of a problem as much as spring and autumn change the colors of a tree. The ethical coloring of a business decision is no exception to this generational aspect of decision making. Time alters circumstances, and few corporate value systems are immune to shifts in financial status, external political pressure, and personnel. (One survey now places the average U.S. CEO's tenure in office at five years.)

At Lex, for example, the humanitarianism of the statement of objectives and values depended on financial prosperity. The values did not fully anticipate the extent to which the U.K. economy would undergo a recession, and the resulting changes had to be examined, reconciled, and fought if the company's values were to have any meaning. At the Lex annual review, the managers asked themselves repeatedly whether hard times were the ultimate test of the statement or a clear indication that a corporation had to be able to "afford" ethical positions.

Ideally, a company's articulation of its values should anticipate changes of fortune. As the hearings for the passage of the Foreign Corrupt Practices Act of 1977 demonstrated, doing what you can get away with today may not be a secure moral standard, but short-term discomfort for long-term sainthood may require irrational courage or a rational reasoning system or, more likely, both. These twelve questions attempt to elicit a rational system. Courage, of course, depends on personal integrity.

Another aspect of the ethical time frame stretches beyond the boundaries of Question 9 but deserves special attention, and that is the timing of the ethical inquiry. When and where will it be made?

We do not normally invoke moral principles in our everyday conduct. Some time ago the participants in a national business ethics conference had worked late into the night preparing the final case for the meeting, and they were very anxious the next morning to get the class under way. Just before the session began, however, someone suggested that they all donate a dollar apiece as a gratuity for the dining hall help at the institute.

Then just as everyone automatically reached into his or her pocket, another person questioned the direction of the gift. Why tip the person behind the counter but not the cook in the kitchen? Should the money be given to each person in proportion to salary or divided equally among all? The participants laughed uneasily—or groaned—as they thought of the diversion of precious time from the case. A decision had to be made.

With the sure instincts of efficient managers, the group chose to forgo further discussion of distributive justice and, yes, appoint a committee. The committee doled out the money without further group consideration, and no formal feedback on the donation was asked for or given.

The questions offered here do not solve the problem of

DEFINING BUSINESS ETHICS

making time for the inquiry. For suggestions about creating favorable conditions for examining corporate values, drawn from my field research, see the chart on pages 57–59.

10. Could you disclose without qualm your decision or action to your boss, your CEO, the board of directors, your family, or society as a whole?

The old question, "Would you want your decision to appear on the front page of *The New York Times*?" still holds. A corporation may maintain that there's really no problem, but a survey of how many "trivial" actions it is reluctant to disclose might be interesting. Disclosure is a way of sounding those submarine depths of conscience and of searching out loyalties.

It is also a way of keeping a corporate character cohesive. The Lex Group, for example, was once faced with a very sticky problem concerning a small but profitable site with unpleasant (though in no way illegal) working conditions, where two men with 30 years' service worked. I wrote up the case for a Lex senior managers' meeting on the promise to disguise it heavily because the executive who supervised the plant was convinced that, if the chairman and the personnel director knew the plant's true location, they would close it down immediately.

At the meeting, however, as everyone became involved in the discussion and the chairman himself showed sensitivity to the dilemma, the executive disclosed the location and spoke of his own feelings about the situation. The level of mutual confidence was apparent to all, and by other reports it was the most open discussion the group had ever had.

The meeting also fostered understanding of the company's values and their implementation. When the discussion finally flagged, the chairman spoke up. Basing his views on a full knowledge of the group's understanding of the problem, he set the company's priorities. "Jobs over fancy conditions, health over jobs," Chinn said, "but we always *must disclose.*" The group decided to keep the plant open, at least for the time being.

Disclosure does not, however, automatically bring universal sympathy. In the early 1970s, a large food store chain that repeatedly found itself embroiled in the United Farm Workers (UFW) disputes with the Teamsters over California grape and lettuce contracts took very seriously the moral implications of a decision whether to stop selling these products. The company endlessly researched the issues, talked to all sides, and made itself available to public representatives of various interest groups to explain its position and to hear out everyone else.

When the controversy started, the company decided to support the UFW boycott, but three years later top management reversed its position. Most of the people who wrote to the company or asked it to send representatives to their local UFW support meetings, however, continued to condemn the chain even after hearing its views, and the general public apparently never became aware of the company's side of the story.

11. What is the symbolic potential of your action if understood? if misunderstood?

Jones Inc., a diversified multinational corporation with assets of $5 billion, has a paper manufacturing operation that happens to be the only major industry in Stirville, and the factory has been polluting the river on which it is located. Local and national conservation groups have filed suit against Jones Inc. for past damages, and the company is defending itself. Meanwhile, the corporation has adopted plans for a new waste-efficient plant. The legal battle is extended and local resentment against Jones Inc. gets bitter.

As a settlement is being reached, Jones Inc. announces that, as a civic-minded gesture, it will make 400 acres of Stirville woodland it owns available to the residents for conservation and recreation purposes. Jones's intention is to offer a peace pipe to the people of Stirville, and the company sees the gift as a symbol of its own belief in conservation and a way of signaling that value to Stirville residents and national conservation groups. Should Jones Inc. give the land away? Is the symbolism significant?

If the symbolic value of the land is understood as Jones Inc. intends, the gift may patch up the company's relations with Stirville and stave off further disaffection with potential

DEFINING BUSINESS ETHICS

employees as the new plant is being built. It may also signal to employees throughout the corporation that Jones Inc. places a premium on conservation efforts and community relations.

If the symbolic value is misunderstood, however, or if completion of the plant is delayed and the old one has to be put back in use—or if another Jones operation is discovered to be polluting another community and becomes a target of the press—the gift could be interpreted as nothing more than a cheap effort to pay off the people of Stirville and hasten settlement of the lawsuit.

The Greek root of our word *symbol* means both signal and contract. A business decision—whether it is the use of an expense account or a corporate donation—has a symbolic value in signaling what is acceptable behavior within the corporate culture and in making a tacit contract with employees and the community about the rules of the game. How the symbol is actually perceived (or misperceived) is as important as how you intend it to be perceived.

12. Under what conditions would you allow exceptions to your stand?

If we accept the idea that every business decision has an important symbolic value and a contractual nature, then the need for consistency is obvious. At the same time, it is also important to ask under what conditions the rules of the game may be changed. What conflicting principles, circumstances, or time constraints would provide a morally acceptable basis for making an exception to one's normal institutional ethos? For instance, how does the cost of the strategy to develop managers from minority groups over the long term fit in with short-term hurdle rates? Also to be considered is what would mitigate a clear case of employee dishonesty.

Questions of consistency—if you would do X, would you also do Y?—are yet another way of eliciting the ethics of the company and of oneself, and can be a final test of the strength, idealism, or practicality of those values. A last example from the experience of Lex illustrates this point and gives temporary credence to the platitude that good ethics is good business. An article in the Sunday paper about a company that had run a series of racy ads, with pictures of half-dressed women and promises of free merchandise to promote the sale of a very mundane product, sparked an extended examination at Lex of its policies on corporate inducements.

One area of concern was holiday giving. What was the acceptable limit for a gift—a bottle of whiskey? a case? Did it matter only that the company did not *intend* the gift to be an inducement, or did the mere possibility of inducement taint the gift? Was the cut-off point absolute? The group could agree on no halfway point for allowing some gifts and not others, so a new value was added to the formal statement that prohibited the offering or receiving of inducements.

The next holiday season Chinn sent a letter to friends and colleagues who had received gifts of appreciation in the past. In it he explained that, as a result of Lex's concern with "the very complex area of business ethics," management had decided that the company would no longer send any gifts, nor would it be appropriate for its employees to receive any. Although the letter did not explain Lex's reasoning behind the decision, apparently there was a large untapped consensus about such gift giving: by return mail Chinn received at least twenty letters from directors, general managers, and chairmen of companies with which Lex had done business congratulating him for his decision, agreeing with the new policy, and thanking him for his holiday wishes.

Shared Conditions of Some Successful Ethical Inquiries

Fixed time frame	Understanding and identifying moral issues takes time and causes ferment, and the executive needs an uninterrupted block of time to ponder the problems.
Unconventional location	Religious groups, boards of directors, and professional associations have long recognized the value of the retreat as a way of stimulating fresh approaches to regular activities. If the group is going to transcend normal corporate hierarchies, it should hold

DEFINING BUSINESS ETHICS

the discussion on neutral territory so that all may participate with the same degree of freedom.

Resource person The advantage of bringing in an outsider is not that he or she will impose some preconceived notion of right and wrong on management but that he will serve as a midwife for bringing the values already present in the institution out into the open. He can generate closer examination of the discrepancies between values and practice and draw on a wider knowledge of instances and intellectual frameworks than the group can. The resource person may also take the important role of arbitrator—to ensure that one person does not dominate the session with his or her own values and that the dialogue does not become impossibly emotional.

Participation of CEO In most corporations the chief executive still commands an extra degree of authority for the intangible we call corporate culture, and the discussion needs the perspective of and legitimization by the authority if it is to have any seriousness of purpose and consequence. One of the most interesting experiments in examining corporate policy I have observed lacked the CEO's support, and within a year it died on the vine.

Credo Articulating the corporation's values and objectives provides a reference point for group inquiry and implementation. Ethical codes, however, when drawn up by the legal department, do not always offer a realistic and full representation of management's beliefs. The most important ethical inquiry for management may be the very formulation of such a statement, for the *process* of articulation is as useful as the values agreed on.

Homegrown topics	In isolating an ethical issue, drawing on your own experience is important. Philosophical business ethics has tended to reflect national social controversies, which though relevant to the corporation may not always be as relevant—not to mention as easily resolved—as some internal issues that are shaping the character of the company to a much greater degree. Executives are also more likely to be informed on these issues.
Resolution	In all the programs I observed except one, there was a point at which the inquiry was slated to have some resolution: either a vote on the issue, the adoption of a new policy, a timetable for implementation, or the formulation of a specific statement of values. The one program observed that had no such decision-making structure was organized simply to gather information about the company's activities through extrahierarchical channels. Because the program had no tangible goals or clearly articulated results, its benefits were impossible to measure.

The "Good Puppy" Theory

The twelve questions are a way to articulate an idea of the responsibilities involved and to lay them open for examination. Whether a decisive policy is also generated or not, there are compelling reasons for holding such discussions:

- The process facilitates talk as a group about a subject that has traditionally been reserved for the privacy of one's conscience. Moreover, for those whose consciences twitch but don't speak in full sentences, the questions
- help sort out their own perceptions of the problem and various ways of thinking about it.

DEFINING BUSINESS ETHICS

- The process builds a cohesiveness of managerial character as points of consensus emerge and people from vastly different operations discover that they share common problems. It is one way of determining the values and goals of the company, and that is a key element in determining corporate strategy.
- It acts as an information resource. Senior managers learn about other parts of the company with which they may have little contact.
- It helps uncover ethical inconsistencies in the articulated values of the corporation or between these values and the financial strategy.
- It helps uncover sometimes dramatic differences between the values and the practicality of their implementation.
- It helps the CEO understand how the senior managers think, how they handle a problem, and how willing and able they are to deal with complexity. It reveals how they may be drawing on the private self to the enhancement of corporate activity.
- In drawing out the private self in connection with business and in exploring the significance of the corporation's activities, the process derives meaning from an environment that is often characterized as meaningless.
- It helps improve the nature and range of alternatives.
- It is cathartic.

The process is also reductive in that it limits the level of inquiry. For example, the twelve questions ask what injury might result from a decision and what good is intended, but they do not ask the meaning of *good* or whether the result is "just."

Socrates asked how a person could talk of pursuing the good before knowing what the good is; and the analysis he visualized entailed a lifelong process of learning and examination. Do the twelve short questions, with their explicit goal of simplifying the ethical examination, bastardize the Socratic ideal? To answer this, we must distinguish between personal philosophy and participation as a corporate member in the examination of a *corporate* ethos, for the twelve questions assume some difference between private and corporate "goodness."

This distinction is crucial to any evaluation of my suggested process for conducting an ethical inquiry and needs to be explained. What exactly do we expect of the "ethical," or "good," corporation? Three examples of goodness represent prevailing social opinions, from that of the moral philosopher to the strict Friedmaniac.

- The most rigorous moral analogy to the good corporation would be the "good man." An abstract, philosophical ideal having highly moral connotations, the good man encompasses an intricate relation of abstractions such as Plato's four virtues (courage, godliness or philosophical wisdom, righteousness, and prudence). The activities of this kind of good corporation imply a heavy responsibility to collectively know the good and to resolve to achieve it.
- Next, there is the purely amoral definition of good, as in a "good martini"—an amoral fulfillment of a largely inanimate and functional purpose. Under this definition, corporate goodness would be best achieved by the unadorned accrual of profits with no regard for the social implications of the means whereby profits are made.
- Halfway between these two views lies the good as in "good puppy"—here goodness consists primarily of the fulfillment of a social contract that centers on avoiding social injury. Moral capacity is perceived as present, but its potential is limited. A moral evaluation of the good puppy is possible but exists largely in concrete terms; we do not need to identify the puppy's intentions as utilitarian to understand and agree that its "ethical" fulfillment of the social contract consists of not soiling the carpet or biting the baby.

It seems to me that business ethics operates most appropriately for corporate man when it seeks to define and explore corporate morality at the level of the good puppy. The good corporation is expected to avoid perpetrating irretrievable social injury (and to assume the costs when it unintentionally does injury) while focusing on its purpose as a profit-making organization. Its moral capacity does not extend, however, to determining by itself what will improve the general social welfare.

The good puppy inquiry operates largely in concrete experience; just as the twelve questions impose a limit on our moral expectations, so too they impose a limit (welcome, to some) on our use of abstraction to get at the problem.

The situations for testing business morality remain complex. But by avoiding theoretical inquiry and limiting the expectations of corporate goodness to a few rules for social behavior that are based on common sense, we can develop an ethic that is appropriate to the language, ideology, and institutional dynamics of business decision making and consensus. This ethic can also offer managers a practical way of exploring those occasions when their corporate brains are getting warning flashes from their noncorporate brains.

NOTES

1. The process is modeled after ideas in Kenneth R. Andrew's book *The Concept of Corporate Strategy* (Homewood, Ill.: Richard D. Irwin, 1980, revised edition) and in Richard F. Vancil's article "Strategy Formulation in Complex Organizations," *Sloan Management Review*, Winter 1976, p. 4.

Is Business Bluffing Ethical?

Albert Z. Carr

Business is often called a "game." Business people are fond of using sports metaphors and language, which suggests that they are involved in a kind of gamelike activity. Business people are "players" out to "win" in a "competitive situation." But don't these metaphorical references suggest that

SOURCE: Reprinted by permission of *Harvard Business Review*. "Is Business Bluffing Ethical?" by Albert Z. Carr, Vol. 46, (January/February 1968). Copyright ® 1968 by the President and Fellows of Harvard College. All rights reserved.

business is a unique and separate kind of activity that has rules of its own? But if people in business consider business to be more of a game than anything else, won't gamelike behaviors become increasingly acceptable? Albert Carr raises these and other questions about business as a game in his classic 1968 *Harvard Business Review* article "Is Business Bluffing Ethical?" He examines the common analogy that business is nothing more than a kind of poker game. If all the "players" fully know the "rules of the game" and if bluffing is part of the game, then isn't bluffing ethical in this context? Or, conversely, is bluffing nothing more than deception, a form of lying to be avoided? Carr holds that business is indeed a game; the rules of legality and the goal of profit are its sole ethical guideline. Thus, if one is to win at the "game of business," one must have a "game player's attitude," which means being able to divorce one's private morality from one's sense of right and wrong on the "playing field" of business.

A respected businessman with whom I discussed the theme of this article remarked with some heat, "You mean to say you're going to encourage men to bluff? Why, bluffing is nothing more than a form of lying! You're advising them to lie!"

I agreed that the basis of private morality is a respect for truth and that the closer a businessman comes to the truth, the more he deserves respect. At the same time, I suggested that most bluffing in business might be regarded simply as game strategy—much like bluffing in poker, which does not reflect on the morality of the bluffer.

I quoted Henry Taylor, the British statesman who pointed out that "falsehood ceases to be falsehood when it is understood on all sides that the truth is not expected to be spoken"—an exact description of bluffing in poker, diplomacy, and business. I cited the analogy of the criminal court, where the criminal is not expected to tell the truth when he pleads "not guilty." Everyone from the judge down takes it for granted that the job of the defendant's attorney is to get his client off, not to reveal the truth; and this is considered ethical practice. I mentioned Representative Omar Burleson, the Democrat from Texas, who was

DEFINING BUSINESS ETHICS

quoted as saying, in regard to the ethics of Congress, "Ethics is a barrel of worms"[1]—a pungent summing up of the problem of deciding who is ethical in politics.

I reminded my friend that millions of businessmen feel constrained every day to say *yes* to their bosses when they secretly believe *no* and that this is generally accepted as permissible strategy when the alternative might be the loss of a job. The essential point, I said, is that the ethics of business are game ethics, different from the ethics of religion.

He remained unconvinced. Referring to the company of which he is president, he declared: "Maybe that's good enough for some businessmen, but I can tell you that we pride ourselves on our ethics. In thirty years not one customer has ever questioned my word or asked to check our figures. We're loyal to our customers and fair to our suppliers. I regard my handshake on a deal as a contract. I've never entered into price-fixing schemes with my competitors. I've never allowed my salesmen to spread injurious rumors about other companies. Our union contract is the best in our industry. And, if I do say so myself, our ethical standards are of the highest!"

He really was saying, without realizing it, that he was living up to the ethical standards of the business game—which are a far cry from those of private life. Like a gentlemanly poker player, he did not play in cahoots with others at the table, try to smear their reputations, or hold back chips he owed them.

But this same fine man, at that very time, was allowing one of his products to be advertised in a way that made it sound a great deal better than it actually was. Another item in his product line was notorious among dealers for its "built-in obsolescence." He was holding back from the market a much-improved product because he did not want it to interfere with sales of the inferior item it would have replaced. He had joined with certain of his competitors in hiring a lobbyist to push a state legislature, by methods that he preferred not to know too much about, into amending a bill then being enacted.

In his view these things had nothing to do with ethics; they were merely normal business practice. He himself undoubtedly avoided outright falsehoods—never lied in so many words. But the entire organization that he ruled was deeply involved in numerous strategies of deception.

Pressure to Deceive

Most executives from time to time are almost compelled, in the interest of their companies or themselves, to practice some form of deception when negotiating with customers, dealers, labor unions, government officials, or even other departments of their companies. By conscious misstatements, concealment of pertinent facts, or exaggeration—in short, by bluffing—they seek to persuade others to agree with them. I think it is fair to say that if the individual executive refuses to bluff from time to time—if he feels obligated to tell the truth, the whole truth, and nothing but the truth—he is ignoring opportunities permitted under the rules and is at a heavy disadvantage in his business dealings.

But here and there a businessman is unable to reconcile himself to the bluff in which he plays a part. His conscience, perhaps spurred by religious idealism, troubles him. He feels guilty; he may develop an ulcer or a nervous tic. Before any executive can make profitable use of the strategy of the bluff, he needs to make sure that in bluffing he will not lose self-respect or become emotionally disturbed. If he is to reconcile personal integrity and high standards of honesty with the practical requirements of business, he must feel that his bluffs are ethically justified. The justification rests on the fact that business, as practiced by individuals as well as by corporations, has the impersonal character of a game—a game that demands both special strategy and an understanding of its special ethics.

The game is played at all levels of corporate life, from the highest to the lowest. At the very instant that a man decides to enter business, he may be forced into a game situation, as is shown by the recent experience of a Cornell honor graduate who applied for a job with a large company:

This applicant was given a psychological test which in-

DEFINING BUSINESS ETHICS

cluded the statement, "Of the following magazines, check any that you have read either regularly or from time to time, and double-check those which interest you most. *Reader's Digest, Time, Fortune, Saturday Evening Post, The New Republic, Life, Look, Ramparts, Newsweek, Business Week, U.S. News & World Report, The Nation, Playboy, Esquire, Harper's, Sports Illustrated.*"

His tastes in reading were broad, and at one time or another he had read almost all of these magazines. He was a subscriber to *The New Republic*, an enthusiast for *Ramparts*, and an avid student of the pictures in *Playboy*. He was not sure whether his interest in *Playboy* would be held against him, but he had a shrewd suspicion that if he confessed to an interest in *Ramparts* and *The New Republic*, he would be thought a liberal, a radical, or at least an intellectual, and his chances of getting the job, which he needed, would greatly diminish. He therefore checked five of the more conservative magazines. Apparently it was a sound decision, for he got the job.

He had made a game player's decision, consistent with business ethics.

A similar case is that of a magazine space salesman who, owing to a merger, suddenly found himself out of a job:

This man was 58, and, in spite of a good record, his chance of getting a job elsewhere in a business where youth is favored in hiring practice was not good. He was a vigorous, healthy man, and only a considerable amount of gray in his hair suggested his age. Before beginning his job search he touched up his hair with a black dye to confine the gray to his temples. He knew that the truth about his age might well come out in time, but he calculated that he could deal with that situation when it arose. He and his wife decided that he could easily pass for 45, and he so stated his age on his résumé.

This was a lie; yet within the accepted rules of the business game, no moral culpability attaches to it.

The Poker Analogy

We can learn a good deal about the nature of business by comparing it with poker. While both have a large element of chance, in the long run the winner is the man who plays with steady skill. In both games ultimate victory requires intimate knowledge of the rules, insight into the psychology of the other players, a bold front, a considerable amount of self-discipline, and the ability to respond swiftly and effectively to opportunities provided by chance.

No one expects poker to be played on the ethical principles preached in churches. In poker it is right and proper to bluff a friend out of the rewards of being dealt a good hand. A player feels no more than a slight twinge of sympathy, if that, when—with nothing better than a single ace in his hand—he strips a heavy loser, who holds a pair, of the rest of his chips. It was up to the other fellow to protect himself. In the words of an excellent poker player, former President Harry Truman, "If you can't stand the heat, stay out of the kitchen." If one shows mercy to a loser in poker, it is a personal gesture, divorced from the rules of the game.

Poker has its special ethics, and here I am not referring to rules against cheating. The man who keeps an ace up his sleeve or who marks the cards is more than unethical; he is a crook, and can be punished as such—kicked out of the game or, in the Old West, shot.

In contrast to the cheat, the unethical poker player is one who, while abiding by the letter of the rules, finds ways to put the other players at an unfair disadvantage. Perhaps he unnerves them with loud talk. Or he tries to get them drunk. Or he plays in cahoots with someone else at the table. Ethical poker players frown on such tactics.

Poker's own brand of ethics is different from the ethical ideals of civilized human relationships. The game calls for distrust of the other fellow. It ignores the claim of friendship. Cunning deception and concealment of one's strength and intentions, not kindness and openheartedness, are vital in poker. No one thinks any the worse of poker on that account. And no one should think any the worse of

DEFINING BUSINESS ETHICS

the game of business because its standards of right and wrong differ from the prevailing traditions of morality in our society.

Discard the Golden Rule

This view of business is especially worrisome to people without much business experience. A minister of my acquaintance once protested that business cannot possibly function in our society unless it is based on the Judeo-Christian system of ethics. He told me:

"I know some businessmen have supplied call girls to customers, but there are always a few rotten apples in every barrel. That doesn't mean the rest of the fruit isn't sound. Surely the vast majority of businessmen are ethical. I myself am acquainted with many who adhere to strict codes of ethics based fundamentally on religious teachings. They contribute to good causes. They participate in community activities. They cooperate with other companies to improve working conditions in their industries. Certainly they are not indifferent to ethics."

That most businessmen are not indifferent to ethics in their private lives, everyone will agree. My point is that in their office lives they cease to be private citizens; they become game players who must be guided by a somewhat different set of ethical standards.

The point was forcefully made to me by a Midwestern executive who has given a good deal of thought to the question:

"So long as a businessman complies with the laws of the land and avoids telling malicious lies, he's ethical. If the law as written gives a man a wide-open chance to make a killing, he'd be a fool not to take advantage of it. If he doesn't, somebody else will. There's no obligation on him to stop and consider who is going to get hurt. If the law says he can do it, that's all the justification he needs. There's nothing unethical about that. It's just plain business sense."

This executive (call him Robbins) took the stand that even industrial espionage, which is frowned on by some businessmen, ought not to be considered unethical. He recalled a recent meeting of the National Industrial Conference Board where an authority on marketing made a speech in which he deplored the employment of spies by business organizations. More and more companies, he pointed out, find it cheaper to penetrate the secrets of competitors with concealed cameras and microphones or by bribing employees than to set up costly research and design departments of their own. A whole branch of the electronics industry has grown up with this trend, he continued, providing equipment to make industrial espionage easier.

Disturbing? The marketing expert found it so. But when it came to a remedy, he could only appeal to "respect for the golden rule." Robbins thought this a confession of defeat, believing that the golden rule, for all its value as an ideal for society, is simply not feasible as a guide for business. A good part of the time the businessman is trying to do unto others as he hopes others will *not* do unto him.[2] Robbins continued:

"Espionage of one kind or another has become so common in business that it's like taking a drink during Prohibition—it's not considered sinful. And we don't even have Prohibition where espionage is concerned; the law is very tolerant in this area. There's no more shame for a business that uses secret agents than there is for a nation. Bear in mind that there already is at least one large corporation—you can buy its stock over the counter—that makes millions by providing counterespionage service to industrial firms. Espionage in business is not an ethical problem; it's an established technique of business competition."

"We Don't Make the Laws."

Wherever we turn in business, we can perceive the sharp distinction between its ethical standards and those of the churches. Newspapers abound with sensational stories growing out of this distinction:

DEFINING BUSINESS ETHICS

- We read one day that Senator Philip A. Hart of Michigan has attacked food processors for deceptive packaging of numerous products.[3]
- The next day there is a Congressional to-do over Ralph Nader's book, *Unsafe At Any Speed*, which demonstrates that automobile companies for years have neglected the safety of car-owning families.[4]
- Then another Senator, Lee Metcalf of Montana, and journalist Vic Reinemer show in their book, *Overcharge*, the methods by which utility companies elude regulating government bodies to extract unduly large payments from users of electricity.[5]

These are merely dramatic instances of a prevailing condition; there is hardly a major industry at which a similar attack could not be aimed. Critics of business regard such behavior as unethical, but the companies concerned know that they are merely playing the business game.

Among the most respected of our business institutions are the insurance companies. A group of insurance executives meeting recently in New England was startled when their guest speaker, social critic Daniel Patrick Moynihan, roundly berated them for "unethical" practices. They had been guilty, Moynihan alleged, of using outdated actuarial tables to obtain unfairly high premiums. They habitually delayed the hearings of lawsuits against them in order to tire out the plaintiffs and win cheap settlements. In their employment policies they used ingenious devices to discriminate against certain minority groups.[6]

It was difficult for the audience to deny the validity of these charges. But these men were business game players. Their reaction to Moynihan's attack was much the same as that of the automobile manufacturers to Nader, of the utilities to Senator Metcalf, and of the food processors to Senator Hart. If the laws governing their businesses change, or if public opinion becomes clamorous, they will make the necessary adjustments. But morally they have, in their view, done nothing wrong. As long as they comply with the letter of the law, they are within their rights to operate their businesses as they see fit.

The small business is in the same position as the great corporation in this respect. For example:

In 1967 a key manufacturer was accused of providing master keys for automobiles to mail-order customers, although it was obvious that some of the purchasers might be automobile thieves. His defense was plain and straightforward. If there was nothing in the law to prevent him from selling his keys to anyone who ordered them, it was not up to him to inquire as to his customers' motives. Why was it any worse, he insisted, for him to sell car keys by mail, than for mail-order houses to sell guns that might be used for murder? Until the law was changed, the key manufacturer could regard himself as being just as ethical as any other businessman by the rules of the business game.[7]

Violations of the ethical ideals of society are common in business, but they are not necessarily violations of business principles. Each year the Federal Trade Commission orders hundreds of companies, many of them of the first magnitude, to "cease and desist" from practices which, judged by ordinary standards, are of questionable morality but which are stoutly defended by the companies concerned.

In one case, a firm manufacturing a well-known mouthwash was accused of using a cheap form of alcohol possibly deleterious to health. The company's chief executive, after testifying in Washington, made this comment privately:

"We broke no law. We're in a highly competitive industry. If we're going to stay in business, we have to look for profit wherever the law permits. We don't make the laws. We obey them. Then why do we have to put up with this 'holier than thou' talk about ethics? It's sheer hypocrisy. We're not in business to promote ethics. Look at the cigarette companies, for God's sake! If the ethics aren't embodied in the laws by the men who made them, you can't expect businessmen to fill the lack. Why, a sudden submission to Christian ethics by businessmen would bring about the greatest economic upheaval in history!"

It may be noted that the government failed to prove its case against him.

DEFINING BUSINESS ETHICS

Cast Illusions Aside

Talk about ethics by businessmen is often a thin decorative coating over the hard realities of the game:

Once I listened to a speech by a young executive who pointed to a new industry code as proof that his company and its competitors were deeply aware of their responsibilities to society. It was a code of ethics, he said. The industry was going to police itself, to dissuade constituent companies from wrongdoing. His eyes shone with conviction and enthusiasm.

The same day there was a meeting in a hotel room where the industry's top executives met with the "czar" who was to administer the new code, a man of high repute. No one who was present could doubt their common attitude. In their eyes the code was designed primarily to forestall a move by the federal government to impose stern restrictions on the industry. They felt that the code would hamper them a good deal less than new federal laws would. It was, in other words, conceived as a protection for the industry, not for the public.

The young executive accepted the surface explanation of the code; these leaders, all experienced game players, did not deceive themselves for a moment about its purpose.

The illusion that business can afford to be guided by ethics as conceived in private life is often fostered by speeches and articles containing such phrases as, "It pays to be ethical," or, "Sound ethics is good business." Actually this is not an ethical position at all; it is a self-serving calculation in disguise. The speaker is really saying that in the long run a company can make more money if it does not antagonize competitors, suppliers, employees, and customers by squeezing them too hard. He is saying that oversharp policies reduce ultimate gains. That is true, but it has nothing to do with ethics. The underlying attitude is much like that in the familiar story of the shopkeeper who finds an extra twenty-dollar bill in the cash register, debates with himself the ethical problem—should he tell his partner?—and finally decides to share the money because the gesture will give him an edge over the s.o.b. the next time they quarrel.

I think it is fair to sum up the prevailing attitude of businessmen on ethics as follows.

We live in what is probably the most competitive of the world's civilized societies. Our customs encourage a high degree of aggression in the individual's striving for success. Business is our main area of competition, and it has been ritualized into a game of strategy. The basic rules of the game have been set by the government, which attempts to detect and punish business frauds. But as long as a company does not transgress the rules of the game set by law, it has the legal right to shape its strategy without reference to anything but its profits. If it takes a long-term view of its profits, it will preserve amicable relations, so far as possible, with those with whom it deals. A wise businessman will not seek advantage to the point where he generates dangerous hostility among employees, competitors, customers, government, or the public at large. But decisions in this area are, in the final test, decisions of strategy, not of ethics.

The Individual and the Game

An individual within a company often finds it difficult to adjust to the requirements of the business game. He tries to preserve his private ethical standards in situations that call for game strategy. When he is obliged to carry out company policies that challenge his conception of himself as an ethical man, he suffers.

It disturbs him when he is ordered, for instance, to deny a raise to a man who deserves it, to fire an employee of long standing, to prepare advertising that he believes to be misleading, to conceal facts that he feels customers are entitled to know, to cheapen the quality of materials used in the manufacture of an established product, to sell as new a product that he knows to be rebuilt, to exaggerate the curative powers of a medicinal preparation, or to coerce dealers.

There are some fortunate executives who, by the nature of their work and circumstances, never have to face problems of this kind. But in one form or another the ethical dilemma is felt sooner or later by most businessmen. Possibly the dilemma is most painful not when the company forces the action on the executive but when he originates it himself—that is, when he has taken or is contemplating a step which is in his own interest but which runs counter to his early moral conditioning. To illustrate:

- The manager of an export department, eager to show rising sales, is pressed by a big customer to provide invoices which, while containing no overt falsehood that would violate a U.S. law, are so worded that the customer may be able to evade certain taxes in his homeland.
- A company president finds that an aging executive, within a few years of retirement and his pension, is not as productive as formerly. Should he be kept on?
- The produce manager of a supermarket debates with himself whether to get rid of a lot of half-rotten tomatoes by including one, with its good side exposed, in every tomato six-pack.
- An accountant discovers that he has taken an improper deduction on his company's tax return and fears the consequences if he calls the matter to the president's attention, though he himself has done nothing illegal. Perhaps if he says nothing, no one will notice the error.
- A chief executive officer is asked by his directors to comment on a rumor that he owns stock in another company with which he has placed large orders. He could deny it, for the stock is in the name of his son-in-law and he has earlier formally instructed his son-in-law to sell the holding.

Temptations of this kind constantly arise in business. If an executive allows himself to be torn between a decision based on business considerations and one based on his private ethical code, he exposes himself to a grave psychological strain.

This is not to say that sound business strategy necessarily runs counter to ethical ideals. They may frequently coincide; and when they do, everyone is gratified. But the major tests of every move in business, as in all games of strategy, are legality and profit. A man who intends to be a winner in the business game must have a game player's attitude.

The business strategist's decisions must be as impersonal as those of a surgeon performing an operation—concentrating on objective and technique, and subordinating personal feelings. If the chief executive admits that his son-in-law owns the stock, it is because he stands to lose more if the fact comes out later than if he states it boldly and at once. If the supermarket manager orders the rotten tomatoes to be discarded, he does so to avoid an increase in consumer complaints and a loss of goodwill. The company president decides not to fire the elderly executive in the belief that the negative reaction of other employees would in the long run cost the company more than it would lose in keeping him and paying his pension.

All sensible businessmen prefer to be truthful, but they seldom feel inclined to tell the *whole* truth. In the business game truth-telling usually has to be kept within narrow limits if trouble is to be avoided. The point was neatly made a long time ago (in 1888) by one of John D. Rockefeller's associates, Paul Babcock, to Standard Oil Company executives who were about to testify before a government investigating committee: "Parry every question with answers which, while perfectly truthful, are evasive of *bottom* facts."[8] This was, is, and probably always will be regarded as wise and permissible business strategy.

For Office Use Only

An executive's family life can easily be dislocated if he fails to make a sharp distinction between the ethical systems of the home and the office—or if his wife does not grasp that distinction. Many a businessman who has remarked to his wife, "I had to let Jones go today" or "I had to admit to the boss that Jim has been goofing off lately," has been met with an indignant protest. "How could you do a thing like that? You know Jones is over 50 and will have a lot of trouble getting another job." Or, "You did that to Jim? With his wife ill and all the worry she's been having with the kids?"

If the executive insists that he had no choice because the

profits of the company and his own security were involved, he may see a certain cool and ominous reappraisal in his wife's eyes. Many wives are not prepared to accept the fact that business operates with a special code of ethics. An illuminating illustration of this comes from a Southern sales executive who related a conversation he had had with his wife at a time when a hotly contested political campaign was being waged in their state:

"I made the mistake of telling her that I had had lunch with Colby, who gives me about half my business. Colby mentioned that his company had a stake in the election. Then he said, 'By the way, I'm treasurer of the citizens' committee for Lang. I'm collecting contributions. Can I count on you for a hundred dollars?'

"Well, there I was. I was opposed to Lang, but I knew Colby. If he withdrew his business, I could be in a bad spot. So I just smiled and wrote out a check then and there. He thanked me, and we started to talk about his next order. Maybe he thought I shared his political views. If so, I wasn't going to lose any sleep over it.

"I should have had sense enough not to tell Mary about it. She hit the ceiling. She said she was disappointed in me. She said I hadn't acted like a man, that I should have stood up to Colby.

"I said, 'Look, it was an either-or situation. I had to do it or risk losing the business.'

"She came back at me with, 'I don't believe it. You could have been honest with him. You could have said that you didn't feel you ought to contribute to a campaign for a man you weren't going to vote for. I'm sure he would have understood.'

"I said, 'Mary, you're a wonderful woman, but you're way off the track. Do you know what would have happened if I had said that? Colby would have smiled and said, "Oh, I didn't realize. Forget it." But in his eyes from that moment I would be an oddball, maybe a bit of a radical. He would have listened to me talk about his order and would have promised to give it consideration. After that I wouldn't hear from him for a week. Then I would telephone and learn from his secretary that he wasn't yet ready to place the order. And in about a month I would hear through the grapevine that he was giving his business to another company. A month after that I'd be out of a job.'

"She was silent for a while. Then she said, 'Tom, something is wrong with business when a man is forced to choose between his family's security and his moral obligation to himself. It's easy for me to say you should have stood up to him—but if you had, you might have felt you were betraying me and the kids. I'm sorry that you did it, Tom, but I can't blame you. Something is wrong with business!' "

This wife saw the problem in terms of moral obligation as conceived in private life; her husband saw it as a matter of game strategy. As a player in a weak position, he felt that he could not afford to indulge an ethical sentiment that might have cost him his seat at the table.

Playing to Win

Some men might challenge the Colbys of business—might accept serious setbacks to their business careers rather than risk a feeling of moral cowardice. They merit our respect— but as private individuals, not businessmen. When the skillful player of the business game is compelled to submit to unfair pressure, he does not castigate himself for moral weakness. Instead, he strives to put himself into a strong position where he can defend himself against such pressures in the future without loss.

If a man plans to take a seat in the business game, he owes it to himself to master the principles by which the game is played, including its special ethical outlook. He can then hardly fail to recognize that an occasional bluff may well be justified in terms of the game's ethics and warranted in terms of economic necessity. Once he clears his mind on this point, he is in a good position to match his strategy against that of the other players. He can then determine objectively whether a bluff in a given situation has a good chance of succeeding and can decide when and how to bluff, without a feeling of ethical transgression.

To be a winner, a man must play to win. This does not mean that he must be ruthless, cruel, harsh, or treacherous. On the contrary, the better his reputation for integrity, honesty, and decency, the better his chances of victory will be in the long run. But from time to time every business-man, like every poker player, is offered a choice between certain loss or bluffing within the legal rules of the game. If he is not resigned to losing, if he wants to rise in his company and industry, then in such a crisis he will bluff—and bluff hard.

Every now and then one meets a successful businessman who has conveniently forgotten the small or large decep-tions that he practiced on his way to fortune. "God gave me my money," old John D. Rockefeller once piously told a Sunday school class. It would be a rare tycoon in our time who would risk the horse laugh with which such a remark would be greeted.

In the last third of the twentieth century even children are aware that if a man has become prosperous in business, he has sometimes departed from the strict truth in order to overcome obstacles or has practiced the more subtle decep-tions of the half-truth or the misleading omission. Whatever the form of the bluff, it is an integral part of the game, and the executive who does not master its techniques is not likely to accumulate much money or power.

N O T E S

1. *The New York Times*, March 9, 1967.
2. See Bruce D. Henderson, "Brinkmanship in Business," HBR March-April 1967, p. 49.
3. *The New York Times*, November 21, 1966.
4. New York, Grossman Publishers, Inc., 1965.
5. New York, David McKay Company, Inc., 1967.
6. *The New York Times*, January 17, 1967.
7. Cited by Ralph Nader in "Business Crime," *The New Republic,* July 1, 1967, p. 7.
8. Babcock in a memorandum to Rockefeller (Rockefeller Archives).

CHAPTER 2

THE ETHICAL TREATMENT OF EMPLOYEES

Introduction

Employee rights in the workplace have long been on the agenda of business ethicists as a primary and essential issue. In the not so distant past, unfortunately, the list of abuses of employees and their basic human rights was long. The phenomenon of the sweatshop—factories and workplaces where men as well as women and children were terribly exploited by unscrupulous owners—was prevalent throughout America. Long hours of very hard physical labor, highly unsafe and unhealthy working conditions, and unfairly low pay for a day's labor were once common characteristics of the American workplace.

In response to these cruel but not unusual workplace conditions, a strong labor movement made its appearance as workers united to combat exploitation on the job. Much legislation over the years at the federal, state, and local levels has been passed to outlaw sweatshops and to protect individuals at work with respect to their personal safety, occupational health, and economic justice—much of it in response to the demands of organized labor. Although the political clout of labor has been on the wane in recent years, the average American worker has benefited greatly from the advancements achieved through the lobbying efforts of unions and by means of collective bargaining agreements.

While great strides have been made in employee rights, the critics of business argue that much more still needs to be done in order to fully implement fair employment practices.

THE ETHICAL TREATMENT OF EMPLOYEES

Contemporary expressions of the employee-rights movement include critiques of business on such topics and issues as workplace privacy, job security, employee screening tests, lie-detector tests, a worker's right to know of hazardous materials in the workplace, equal employment opportunity and affirmative action, comparable worth, and freedom of speech and dissent in the workplace. Several of these issues are addressed by the selections in this chapter, which have been chosen to allow the reader to gain an overall perspective on the problem of employee rights.

Typically, those who choose to address employee rights in the workplace do so with the goal of pointing out and highlighting the instances where, they believe, business organizations fail to treat their employees in an ethical manner. For example, a number of critics see all too many corporations abridging the basic rights of workers by infringing on their workplace privacy through job tests and drug screening. These issues are taken up in the first three selections in this chapter, from accounts in *Business Week, Newsweek,* and *Fortune.* In the first, workplace privacy in general is reported; in the second, the prevalence of job testing is the focus; finally, in the third selection, the question of drug testing is raised in detail.

Of course, those corporations who engage in the kinds of screening practices which the critics claim abridge fundamental employee rights will not agree that job tests that attempt to measure the level of one's honesty, or gauge the nature of one's personality, or the random use of drug testing of workers are failures in the ethical treatment of employees. Rather, they will argue that these controversial tactics are exercises in fulfilling corporate responsibilities. On the issue of drug testing, for example, organizations claim that they have an obligation to insure that the workplace is free from hazards and that customers of their products and services have a moral and legal right to believe that the goods they purchase and the services they buy are safe and reliable. In fact, since the safety and reliability of products and services is so important, since so many might be affected by poor-quality workmanship or by workers who are impaired on the job, it is argued that the rights of workers to privacy must yield to the rights and responsibilities of corporations and their customers. Hence, drug testing is justified as a means toward these desirable ends.

Furthermore, this question of employee drug testing is not only an essential issue about the ethics of privacy rights in the workplace and the ethical treatment of workers, but also it is a question of law surrounded by a good deal of legal argument brought to the courts in a number of suits over the past few years. In fact, those who favor drug testing were given a boost in March of 1989 by the U.S. Supreme Court when it ruled that in certain safety-sensitive jobs the federal government has the right to screen its employees for drug use. Although the ruling was specifically applicable only to U.S. Customs agents engaged in drug interdiction work, legal scholars are conjecturing that when the Supreme Court hears a drug-testing case from the private sector, it will use the same reasoning and conclude that private employers also have a right to test employees engaged in safety-sensitive jobs. And it will be even more interesting to see the Supreme Court's ruling on testing those whose positions are not defined as safety-sensitive.

If this particular ruling appeared as a setback for the cause of privacy in the workplace, proponents could take heart in the recently passed Employee Polygraph Protection Act. With this legislation Congress greatly reduced the legal use of polygraph testing in private business. With a few exceptions—for industries in defense contracting and for national security purposes—firms are generally prohibited from using the lie detector on job applicants and their employees. Also restricted is the use of other mechanical devices, such as voice-stress analyzers and psychological-stress evaluators, which had been used increasingly as personnel tools. Not prohibited by the act, though, are paper-and-pencil tests that attempt to measure job applicant and employee honesty and dishonesty. Yet employee-rights advocates looked upon the passage of this act as a major victory in the battle for employee privacy.

The critics of business, however, see other problems in the ethical treatment of employees over and above those which deal with employee screening tests. They point to the

THE ETHICAL TREATMENT OF EMPLOYEES

lack of freedom that workers have at their place of employment and the few rights that are granted them in the workplace. David Ewing, a past editor of the *Harvard Business Review*, has remarked that most employees in this country surrender their basic constitutional rights when they arrive at work in the morning and have them suspended until they leave in the evening. Freedom of speech, the right to due process, the right to equality of treatment, the freedom to dissent, etc.—all of these rights, which Americans have come to take for granted, are abridged daily in the workplace, according to the most vocal business critics.

In recognition of the workers' rights problem, Patricia Werhane, business ethicist at Loyola University in Chicago, has proposed a Bill of Rights for Employees and Employers, which is reproduced here in its entirety from Werhane's book *Person, Rights and Corporations*. In it, Werhane suggests the minimum rights of both employees and employers in the context of twelve essential workplace issues, such as discrimination, equal pay for equal work, firings, due process on the job, job security, etc. Her program of workplace rights is unique in that it recognizes that employers as well as employees may lay claim to fundamental rights in the workplace. The two sets of rights, then, form something of a dialectic that have as their goal a more ethical organizational environment for both labor and management.

Whether or not such programs of reform will substantially change the workplace can be debated. Business will argue, no doubt, that such changes giving workers special new rights will have an expensive price tag that might put many businesses, especially smaller ones, in jeopardy. Or it might be argued that the cost of such changes would have to be passed along to the consumer, thereby driving up the price of goods and services. In any case, there will be business resistance to any reforms in the area of workers' rights.

For critics, this resistance is not surprising, for it has its source in what they would say is a questionable attitude on the part of business; namely, the attitude of seeing human labor solely as another cost of doing business. When the skills, talents, and abilities of human beings are equated with raw materials, energy, machinery, etc., when human labor is seen as just another operating expense necessary to conduct business, then, critics charge, exploitation of "human resources" will be the norm, and humans will be reduced to an item on an accountant's ledger. Many argue that until this fundamental attitude is overcome, there will always be tension between management and labor.

But there is some cause for hope in the resolution of this problem. For example, the trends toward "participatory management" and employee-owned companies suggest a redefinition of the traditional adversarial relationship between labor and management. In the service industry the emphasis is now on employee involvement rather than employee alienation. And in a number of American factories one can observe experiments based upon the success of Japanese management with "quality circles," which give labor a chance to voice their suggestions directly to their managers and become more of a part of the productive process. This is a far cry from the past where the factory as sweatshop was the norm, and these trends represent something of a change from the negative, devaluing attitude of American management toward labor to a more ethical treatment of employees. But no doubt the critics of business will feel that they will still have the need and the occasion to speak out again and raise this essential issue of business ethics.

Privacy in the Workplace

Business Week

This article from *Business Week* highlights the growing problem of the infringement of employee privacy by many corporations. This is an issue that poses an ethical dilemma for employers. On the one hand, they have the responsibility to ensure that the workplace is drug-free or free from dishon-

SOURCE: Reprinted from the March 28, 1988, issue of *Business Week* by special permission, copyright © 1988 by McGraw-Hill, Inc.

THE ETHICAL TREATMENT OF EMPLOYEES

est workers who might steal. Yet some degree of worker privacy may be abridged (or even completely sacrificed) to achieve this. With few legal precedents to serve as guidelines, finding a middle ground between an employer's myriad responsibilities and an employee's right to privacy is no easy task. Many companies engage in activities that civil libertarians find questionable; for example, random urine tests to discover drug use, computer surveillance of employee activities, telephone monitoring, breaches of the confidentiality of persons with AIDS, and the use of advanced technology to test worker suitability by means of genetic screening. Some perceive these kinds of employer tactics to promote the common good in the workplace as unacceptable infringements on a worker's rights. Note that the legislation mentioned in the article that would regulate the use of lie detectors by private industry has been passed as part of the Polygraph Protection Act of 1988; most companies are now prohibited from using the device to screen prospective and current employees.

On October 29, 1987, Eastern Air Lines Inc. apparently received an anonymous tip that some of its baggage handlers at Miami International Airport used drugs. Security guards rounded up ten workers in the plane-loading area. Then, in full view of other employees and passengers, the workers were marched down a guard-lined path to waiting vans—"like terrorists," as a lawsuit filed by the workers describes it. After questioning the men, supervisors put them aboard a bus—once again in front of onlookers—and took them to a hospital. Then came an ultimatum: Either take a urine test or be fired on the spot.

All ten employees, members of the International Association of Machinists, tested negative. Later they filed suit in federal court, seeking at least $30,000 each on charges of invasion of privacy, defamation, and intentional infliction of emotional distress. Eastern refuses to discuss the incident. In its motion to dismiss the case, Eastern contends that the complaint should be resolved in a union grievance procedure.

Wherever this case winds up, it's a gripping example of

the quintessential—and growing—American concern about privacy. The right to privacy, U.S. Supreme Court Justice Louis D. Brandeis wrote in 1928, is "the right to be let alone—the most prehensive of rights and the right most valued by civilized men." Brandeis was referring to the Fourth Amendment's guarantee against "illegal searches and seizures" by government. Today, Americans are asserting the "right to be let alone" by a different adversary: their employers. A nationwide controversy is erupting as companies probe deeper into workers' habits and health.

Unlike past labor uprisings, workers aren't mounting strikes over the privacy issue. Today's combat involves lawsuits, huge jury awards, and demands for leave-me-alone legislation. Individual employees and unions are filling court dockets with challenges to random drug testing. AIDS patients are suing employers for breach of confidentiality when co-workers learn about their condition. Employee advocates are demanding limits on electronic and telephone eavesdropping. And concern is growing over the potential for employers to delve into electronic data bases that collect the tiniest pieces of an employee's lifestyle under one neat label: the Social Security number.

Snooping?

The protests are being heard. Both the House and the Senate just passed bills restricting lie detector tests by private companies. Declares Paul Saffo, an expert on information technologies at the Institute for the Future: "After health care, privacy in the workplace may be the most important social issue in the 1990s."

It's not that most companies are idly snooping into their employees' lives. Behind the erosion of privacy lie pressing corporate problems. Drug use costs American industry nearly $50 billion a year in absenteeism and turnover. When employer groups opposed the lie detector bills, they cited employee theft, which is estimated at up to $10 billion annually. Moreover, in the litigious 1980s, failing to ensure a safe and drug-free workplace can subject an employer to millions in liability claims when people are injured by an errant employee or faulty products.

The difficulty is maintaining a proper balance between the common good and personal freedom. It may be laudable for companies to hold down soaring medical costs by giving employees checkups and offering exercise programs. But what keeps helpful advice on high blood pressure from becoming an ominous decision on an employee's promotion potential? There are few standards to help answer such questions. "It is an era of legal uncertainty," says Robert B. Fitzpatrick, a Washington lawyer who represents both companies and employees. "In a lot of states the law is in flux, and it is unclear what the rules are any longer."

"Fear of Abuse"

What is clear is that employers face a complex challenge. For years, American workers seemed to lack the body-and-soul dedication of their Japanese counterparts. Now, U.S. companies are beginning to gain the commitment of workers, who often build their private lives around the job—and the pension and health plans linked to it. But as this happens, employees also bring their off-the-job values—and demands—to work. Increasingly, says Alan F. Westin, a Columbia University professor who has studied individual rights in the corporation since the 1950s, "Americans are coming to believe that the rights we attach to citizenship in the society—free expression, privacy, equality, and due process—ought to have their echo in the workplace."

Privacy today matters to employees at all levels, from shop-floor workers to presidents. "I don't think politicians and corporate executives realize how strongly Americans feel about it," says Cliff Palefsky, a San Francisco lawyer who handles employee lawsuits. "It's not a liberal or a conservative issue, and the fear of abuse doesn't emanate from personnel policies. It's coming out of the larger, impersonal notion that workers are fungible, expendable items."

Huge jury awards in recent privacy cases reflect these concerns:

- A supervisor for Georgia-Pacific Corporation in Oregon fired a man based on an anonymous letter stating that the worker had been drunk in public. Then the supervisor repeated the allegation at a meeting of 100 employees. Concluding that such wide dissemination damaged the worker's reputation, a state appeals court upheld a $350,000 defamation award.
- A drugstore employee refused to take a lie detector test during an investigation of stock shortages at Rite-Aid of Maryland Inc. Though the company violated a state law in ordering the test, it forced the woman to resign. A state appeals court affirmed a $1.3 million award for behavior that "amounted to a complete denial of [her] dignity as a person."

These aren't isolated stories. A survey by Ira Michael Shepard and Robert L. Duston, members of a management law firm in Washington, turned up 97 jury verdicts against employers in privacy cases from 1985 to mid-1987. Damage awards averaged $316,000. Before 1980 employee suits for invasion of privacy rarely reached a jury.

They do now—largely because a decade of litigation and legislation involving employee rights has laid the groundwork. This movement has led to laws that give employees the right to know about hazardous workplace chemicals, that protect whistle-blowers, and that give workers access to medical and personnel records. Complaints of discrimination by age, race, and sex are also increasing fast. Meanwhile, nonunion workers, aided by state courts, are successfully challenging the once-undisputed employment-at-will doctrine. This gave private companies the right to dismiss employees without cause.

The erosion of the at-will concept clears the way for workers to sue employers over privacy issues. Otherwise, such cases are often difficult to file. State laws that regulate polygraph testing, for example, provide for prosecution of corporate violators but give no redress to wronged employees. But using precedents from employment-at-will cases, workers can often prove unfair dismissal—and win big awards.

THE ETHICAL TREATMENT OF EMPLOYEES

Turning Point

All these trends are creating chaos in the rules that govern the workplace. And the changes this will bring in the employer-employee relationship could be as far-reaching as those that followed the breakthrough of industrial unionism in the 1930s. The difference is that today the courts and Congress may do much more quickly what unions would take decades to achieve. "The idea that the employment relationship cannot be regulated will never be with us again," says William B. Gould, a labor law professor at Stanford University. "In some form or another, we're going to have regulation."

The tension over privacy, in fact, marks a turning point in the cycle of management-labor relations. Starting in the early 19th century and for decades after, employers exercised wide dominion over employees' lives. Companies built and ran company towns. In 1914, Henry Ford's workers were promised a $5-a-day wage only after Ford's "sociologists" visited their homes and deemed them morally qualified. The growth of unions, the improved education of the work force, and the civil-rights and civil-liberties movements of the 1960s seemed to kill off these Big Brother policies. In the 1980s, however, the cycle is reversing—as the controversy over these major issues indicates.

AIDS Discrimination

Employees with AIDS are already protected by federal and state laws that guarantee job rights for the handicapped. Nonetheless, some people with AIDS have been fired and in several instances not reinstated before they died.

Most companies have neither a policy nor an educational program on AIDS. Emerson Electric Co. in St. Louis has had "a couple" of employees with AIDS, says John C. Rohrbaugh, vice-president for corporate communications. Those who have the disease became known "because other employees didn't want to share phones or work in the same offices," Rohrbaugh adds. Typically, "We didn't take any type of action, and eventually the employee became more and more debilitated until he was too sick to work, and frankly, he died."

For many companies, such ad hoc handling of the situation may be a costly mistake, says David Herold, director of the Center for Work Performance Problems at the Georgia Institute of Technology. In a survey conducted for the center last year, 35% of 2,000 workers said they didn't believe that AIDS can be transmitted only by sexual contact or blood contamination. The same percentage of workers said they'd be "concerned" about using the same bathroom as people with AIDS.

Herold believes the costs of caring for AIDS sufferers could pale by comparison with the productivity losses if healthy employees refuse to work alongside them. And he disparages the policy of many companies to treat AIDS "like any other illness." Adds Herold: "If that's what they mean by policy, that's nonsense, because other employees will not treat it like any other illness."

Some thirty of the nation's largest employers agree. IBM, AT&T, and Johnson & Johnson, among others, have endorsed a ten-point bill of rights on AIDS issues. It calls for education to dispel fears, urges that medical records be kept confidential, and pledges not to test for the AIDS virus in hiring.

Polygraph Testing

Do lie detectors tell the truth? According to recent surveys, a lot of companies think they do. Studies show that about 30% of the largest companies and more than 50% of retail businesses use lie detectors to test honesty in pre-employment screening and to help investigate workplace thefts. Proponents contend that patterns of blood pressure, perspiration, and breathing recorded as a subject responds to questions reveal a liar's "internal blushes."

But many scientific and medical groups, including the American Medical Association, disagree. A strong response to a question could indicate guilt, fright, anger, "or indeed whether you artificially induced the reaction by, say, biting your tongue," says one critic. As a result, twenty-one states prohibit the use of tests as a condition of employment in

THE ETHICAL TREATMENT OF EMPLOYEES

private industry, and ten more place restrictions on the types of questions that can be asked.

Now, after years of trying, it appears that polygraph opponents will push through a federal law. A Senate bill passed on March 3, 1988 would bar most private employers from using polygraph exams in the hiring process, though it permits the testing of current employees during investigations of a theft or other incident causing "economic loss or injury." It also exempts private security firms and nuclear power plants.

A stronger House bill, passed in November 1987, forbids private employers to use the polygraph for any purpose, but exempts security firms and drug companies. A House-Senate committee will reconcile the two bills. Although [former] President Reagan earlier threatened to veto a polygraph law, he may approve one if the Senate version prevails.

Defamation and Negligent Hiring

Employees often sue when a former employer gives damaging information to a prospective employer. Because companies sometimes need to compare notes on hiring, their communications are considered "privileged." But they can lose this protection if they give information to too many people or hand out false information maliciously.

The fear of defamation suits has caused many companies, probably the majority, to refuse to say anything about a former employee except "name, rank, and serial number." But this practice is having an adverse effect on screening job applicants, which sometimes causes companies to hire people with unsavory backgrounds. Their unlawful conduct can lead to a negligent hiring suit and enormous damages. For example, in 1985 a car rental agency had to pay $750,000 in damages to atone for an employee who repeatedly hit a customer with "judo chops." In that case, a court found, the employer had ignored evidence of the worker's irascibility.

Confidentiality of Employee Records

Considerable private information about workers exists in computer data bases kept by practically every business and government agency—and it's available to a surprisingly wide range of snoops. A crazy quilt of state and federal laws, as well as court rulings, regulates employer access to such information. Some areas, such as medical data, are highly protected. But others aren't.

Credit bureaus, for instance, sell information on employees' bank accounts, outstanding bills, and tax liens or bankruptcies, although all negative records must be purged after seven years. Only recently, TRW Inc., the largest supplier of consumer credit information, began selling such data to employers. "It didn't sound like the kind of thing we wanted to be involved in," says Edward F. Freeman, vice-president and general manager of TRW's information services division. But "it's what our customers wanted, and all our competitors were doing it."

Certain employers, such as banks and nuclear power plants, can get criminal histories of prospective employees from the Federal Bureau of Investigation's Identification Division data base on more than 20 million people. In some states, other employers can get FBI information, too. Now the Bureau is considering lifting a major restriction on its criminal history data base: It may delete a rule requiring that information on people who are arrested but not convicted can't be disseminated after one year. Critics say this would add to the volume of potentially false information that employers can collect.

Many large employers have guidelines requiring managers to prove a specific business purpose before gaining access to sensitive information. But many don't. And the American Civil Liberties Union fears that voluntary guidelines won't work if the political climate changes. "What happens if society's pendulum shifts to be less concerned about personal liberty?" asks Jerry Berman, director of the ACLU's project on information technology and civil liberties.

Monitoring

Over the past decade, practically every major employer has gained the ability to monitor workers' performance through the computers and phones they use. This practice is already prevalent in service-oriented businesses such as insurance and telecommunications. And unless it's done carefully, workers resent it. "I don't think people mind having their work checked," says Morton Bahr, president of the Communications Workers of America (CWA). "It's the secretiveness of it. It's like being wired to a machine." The CWA is pushing a bill in Congress that would prohibit secret monitoring in all industries and require regular beeps when a supervisor is listening.

Worker advocates in Massachusetts are carrying the fight further in a bill that has raised strong objections by industry groups. In addition to requiring beeps, the proposal would limit the amount of monitoring and require employers to explain in writing the purpose and results of monitoring.

Genetic Screening

The most pernicious use of technology to invade privacy may be yet to come. Scientists already can identify genetic traits that indicate a predisposition to such diseases as heart disease and cancer. In 1980, Du Pont Co. came under fire for testing black employees and applicants for sickle cell anemia. The tests were given as a "service to employees," and the results were not used in hiring or career decisions, says Dr. Bruce W. Karrh, a Du Pont vice-president. But because of the controversy, the company now does testing only at workers' request.

Genetic testing might be used legitimately to ensure that employees susceptible to certain occupational diseases aren't put in the wrong work environments. And as far as anyone knows, no companies now use the tests to deny employment. But Mark A. Rothstein, director of the University of Houston's Health Law Institute, believes employers eventually will try that, if only to help hold down health care costs. "Unless we have some clear indication that employers aren't going to be engaged in screening, legislation may be necessary," he says.

A preview of this issue may come as companies mount more aggressive "wellness" programs that try to push employees toward healthier lifestyles. So far these programs seem aimed at helping employees live longer—and improving their productivity. But the logical next step is mandating off-the-job behavior. "I think employers are going to get deeper and deeper into the wellness business," says Columbia's Westin. "This is going to throw up a series of profound ethical and legal dilemmas about how they should do it and what we don't want them to do."

Most workplace privacy issues pose these kinds of difficult questions. They pit the needs of the company against the worker's feelings of dignity and worth. To sacrifice much of the latter would make work life untenable. So the U.S. must decide which rights of a citizen in society should extend to an employee in the corporation—and in what form. If employers don't voluntarily start this process, the courts or legislatures will do it for them.

—By John Hoerr in New York, with Katherine M. Hafner in San Francisco, Gail DeGeorge in Miami, Anne R. Field and Laura Zinn in New York, and bureau reports.

Can You Pass the Job Test?

Newsweek

Continuing the theme of worker privacy but with special emphasis on the use of various screening tests of prospective and current employees, the following article from *Newsweek* suggests that the practice of screening employees and job applicants is more widespread than commonly thought. In addition to drug testing on a random basis, many companies require screening tests that are designed to measure a worker's honesty, personality, health, and potential for disease. Again the essential issue is whether such tests serve a greater good or commit a wrong against those tested. Included are samples of questions used in tests designed to measure honesty and personality that should give the reader good insight into the nature of

SOURCE: Susan Dentzer and others, "Can You Pass the Job Test?" *Newsweek*, May 5, 1986. Reprinted with permission.

THE ETHICAL TREATMENT OF EMPLOYEES

such measurements. Critics ask if these paper-and-pencil tests are reliable predictors or just descriptions of employee traits.

. . . Proceeded on down the hall, gettin' more injections, inspections, detections, neglections, and all kinds of stuff that they was doin' to me. . . . I was there for a long time goin' through all kinds of mean, nasty, ugly things . . . and they was inspectin', injectin' every single part of me, and they was leavin' no part untouched.

When Arlo Guthrie sang his Vietnam-era ballad "Alice's Restaurant," his tormentor was that era's answer to Big Brother—the military draft board. Today John Sexton might cast someone else in the role of snooping archvillain: his former employer. Last year Sexton, then a $30,000-a-year dispatcher at Federal Express Corporation in Atlanta, was one of a group of employees ordered to submit urine samples for a drug test. Sexton tested positive; he says he had smoked marijuana at a party two weeks earlier, but he didn't appear impaired at the time of the test. Next he was ordered to take a lie-detector test or face suspension—but when he denied using drugs on the job or knowing anyone who did, the polygrapher running the test concluded he was holding something back. Fired last May, the 29-year-old college graduate hasn't been able to land another job since. Federal Express declines to comment on the episode but suggests that Sexton's firing was appropriate. Sexton, meanwhile, is preparing to sue Federal for wrongful discharge—and the American Civil Liberties Union (ACLU) of Georgia says he has a strong case.

Sexton's situation isn't unusual: in corporations across the United States, a frenzy of inspecting, detecting, selecting and rejecting is under way. Plans to test baseball players for illegal drug use have created a stir, but nearly a third of the corporations in the Fortune 500 also screen employees for abuse or even casual intake of such substances as marijuana and cocaine. Countless other firms monitor workers' honesty with lie detectors or written exams or probe their psyches with an array of personality tests. Some corporations have begun monitoring employees for diseases such as AIDS. And in quest of the perfect employee, many firms may one day be able to screen out workers with hundreds of genetic traits that could predispose them to serious and costly illnesses.

The boom in testing is fueling the growth of what was once a cottage industry: an array of labs, consulting firms, security specialists and other testing companies that together take in hundreds of millions of dollars in revenue each year. At the same time, it pits employees against management in a debate over whose interests tip the scales of justice. Which set of rights is paramount: those of companies seeking a productive and safe work force—or those of employees trying to protect their privacy? Does testing really identify drug abusers, in-house thieves and other undesirables, or are the innocent and employable also caught in the net? Is testing of employees the key to U.S. industrial competitiveness, or is it worsening labor-management relations at a time when more cooperation is needed? Does testing protect the commonweal, or does it run against the grain of American society—smacking of the oppressive utopias of Aldous Huxley's *Brave New World* or George Orwell's *1984*?

The debate should grow more contentious in the coming months. Lawsuits and union grievances challenging the use of drug testing are on the rise; California has barred testing for the AIDS virus or antibody as a condition of employment, and Congress may soon approve legislation to outlaw the use of lie detectors by most private employers. But whether these developments will dampen the current enthusiasm for testing is unclear. Many companies, alarmed by growing drug use and fearful of everything from wrongful-discharge suits to liability for faulty products, are embracing the use of testing as a vital defense. And advances in technology have made testing almost irresistible, yielding procedures that are "good enough and cheap enough that they are now an [inexpensive] management tool," says Bill Maher, a San Francisco supervisor who helped draft a city ordinance that bars most blanket drug testing.

Testing employees and job applicants is hardly new; in fact, the 1950s may have marked an earlier zenith of testing,

THE ETHICAL TREATMENT OF EMPLOYEES

as companies gathered reams of information on their prospective workers through psychological profiles, employment histories, criminal records and personal data. The shifting values and mores of the 1960s and 1970s changed all that, says Columbia University professor of public law Alan Westin. Federal equal-employment-opportunity guidelines put the onus on employers to ensure that testing was a scientifically valid selection tool and that it didn't discriminate against specific racial or social groups. As privacy laws were passed to protect the public from intrusive or discriminatory data collection by government and institutions such as credit agencies, private employers also began weeding out their personnel files and testing less.

Now that companies are turning to testing again, the privacy issue is back with a vengeance. Through the Fourth Amendment, only government workers have constitutional protection against unreasonable searches and seizures by their employer—a byproduct of the Founding Fathers' fear that unchecked government posed the greatest threat to citizens' rights. Nonetheless, many legal scholars believe that there also exists in society "a certain essential right of individuals to be left alone, and not to be subjected to . . . invasive activities without justification," as Geoffrey Stone, a professor of constitutional law at the University of Chicago, puts it. "Can you imagine the Founding Fathers saying that the major source of authority in [your] life"—your employer—"can make you drop your pants and urinate as a condition of getting or keeping a job?" asks Gene Guerrero, director of the Georgia ACLU. "It's ludicrous." But while employers argue that it's necessary, that's in a sense what many are compelling employees to do.

Honesty Tests: Are They Valid?

The late Senator Sam Ervin called them "twentieth-century witchcraft," but that hasn't stopped many employers from administering lie detectors, or polygraph tests. Almost 2 million are given to employees and job applicants each year—and they can be "a very effective tool in stopping employee crime," says Mark A. de Bernardo, a labor lawyer at the U.S. Chamber of Commerce. Brokerage firms such as E.F. Hutton and banks like Citicorp routinely give polygraphs—Hutton to all employees and Citicorp to most workers who physically handle money. Days Inns of America, a national motel chain based in Atlanta, testified in Congress last year that use of lie detectors helped cut its losses from employee crime to $115,000 in 1984, down from $1 million in 1975.

But polygraphs are undoubtedly more of a deterrent to crime than an effective means of determining an employee's guilt or innocence. The federal Office of Technology Assessment determined in 1983 that the scientific validity of lie-detector results couldn't be established. The American Psychological Association charges that polygraphs turn up "an unacceptable number of false positives"—that is, the subjects had not been lying. Because of these and other factors, few American courts will admit polygraph data as evidence.

Following the pattern of similar legislation in about twenty states, the House of Representatives [in March 1986] passed the Polygraph Protection Act, which would prohibit private employers from giving lie-detector tests to most current or prospective employees. (Many utility workers, pharmaceutical workers handling controlled substances, day-care workers and employees of private security companies could still be polygraphed.) [In June 1986] hearings were held on a similar measure introduced in the Senate by Republican Orrin Hatch of Utah, a conservative, and liberal Democrat Ted Kennedy. Opposed by the likes of attorney F. Lee Bailey—as well as polygraphers and many employers, who would prefer tighter regulation of the polygraph industry— the measure seems likely to pass.

To avoid the cost (about $40 to $50 per test) and ambiguity of polygraph tests, many companies have turned instead to written honesty tests. John E. Reid & Associates of Chicago, a pioneer in the field, markets its $9 tests to about 2,000 clients nationwide; Stanton Corp., based in Charlotte, NC, sells about a million tests each year to hotel chains,

THE ETHICAL TREATMENT OF EMPLOYEES

clothing retailers, convenience stores and other companies whose workers regularly handle money or merchandise for sale. Jim Walls, vice president of Stanton, contends that such screening is a necessity in an age when people move or change jobs frequently. "There's no way that [companies] can ever get to know the people they're hiring before they're hired," he says.

The Personality Test: Are You The Right One for the Job?

Personality tests often require job applicants to respond to hundreds of self-descriptive items designed to help employers determine an individual's traits. No single answer, or group of answers, is considered significant without taking into account the total pattern of responses. An individual's test score is measured against the response patterns of normal persons as well as those clinically diagnosed as suffering from such psychiatric disorders as depression, hysteria, paranoia and schizophrenia. Some personality tests can also predict, according to W. Grant Dahlstrom, professor of psychology at the University of North Carolina. For example, some tests may suggest which applicants are at risk of drug abuse; those who are unsuitable for employment in stressful positions at flight-control centers or nuclear power plants, or even those who would function well in jobs that involve frequent rejection (sales) or physical threat (psychiatric nursing). Questions similar to those below—which focus on experiences, relations and attitudes—are often incorporated in personality tests. Whether they are answered "true" or "false" may help detect the following traits and others.

Many honesty-test questions are almost disarmingly ingenuous. Dr. Homer B. C. Reed, a neuropsychologist at Tufts University's New England Medical Center and a consultant to Stanton, singles out one sample question: "The amount I stole from my employer was (a) 0 (b) $5 (c) $25 (d) $100 (e) $500," accompanied by a space for an explanation. Reed says many job applicants actually circle one of the last four answers. "You would think you can't identify scoundrels by asking them if they're scoundrels, but you can," he says.

Prompted by concerns that employers would use written

Can You Pass the Job Test?

	TRUE	FALSE	CAN'T SAY	
I have trouble going to sleep at night. I feel unhappy most of the time. I rarely see the bright side of things.	☐ ☐ ☐	☐ ☐ ☐	☐ ☐ ☐	TRUE responses to a large number of items similar to these could reveal extreme despondency.
Sometimes there is a feeling like something is pressing in on my head. My fingers sometimes feel numb.	☐ ☐	☐ ☐	☐ ☐	Physical complaints that have no organic causes may be symptomatic of underlying emotional problems.
I used to like to do the dances in gym class. I do not like sports. I like visiting art museums.	☐ ☐ ☐	☐ ☐ ☐	☐ ☐ ☐	The answers to these questions are used to gauge traditionally masculine and feminine interests.
It distresses me that people have the wrong ideas about me. There are those out there who want to get me.	☐ ☐	☐ ☐	☐ ☐	TRUE responses, reflecting extreme suspiciousness and fears of persecution, may signal paranoid traits.
I am often very tense on the job. I wish I could do over some of the things I have done. I worry about sexual matters. I can't keep my mind on what I'm doing.	☐ ☐ ☐ ☐	☐ ☐ ☐ ☐	☐ ☐ ☐ ☐	TRUE responses to such questions may indicate anxiety, indecisiveness and obsessive-compulsive tendencies.
The things that run through my head sometimes are horrible. I sometimes smell strange odors.	☐ ☐	☐ ☐	☐ ☐	TRUE responses to many items such as these may contribute to a pattern of a schizophrenic personality.
I never told a lie. Everything tastes salty. I never had a bad night's sleep. I'm more satisfied with life than my friends are.	☐ ☐ ☐ ☐	☐ ☐ ☐ ☐	☐ ☐ ☐ ☐	These items may help to determine if a person comprehends the testing task, is lying or is trying to influence the outcome.

THE ETHICAL TREATMENT OF EMPLOYEES

tests to pry too much into employees' backgrounds, as some lie-detector tests have done, a new Massachusetts state law prohibits employers from giving honesty tests that amount to "paper and pencil" polygraphs. Many experts are troubled for different reasons, calling some tests a useless tool that could actually screen out capable, honest employees. Columbia Professor Westin derides the absolutism of some tests in requiring "a Fearless Fosdick, Dick Tracy response to every situation"; he thinks they may be used to screen out "people more likely to join a union or challenge something on a job as being morally or ethically improper." Michael Merbaum, a psychologist with St. Louis-based Psychological Associates Inc., a management-consulting and training firm, concurs. He believes that the "correct" answers to many tests are too often based on strict definitions of honesty that may not be shared by test takers; for example, an employee who admits he once took office supplies may not believe he did anything wrong. A far better approach, says Merbaum, is interviewing prospective employees carefully to determine their level of emotional maturity —and to discover whether they have "the capability to appraise situations . . . judiciously so they will make the proper decisions."

The Honesty Test: Everyone's Guilty Some of the Time

Honesty tests are specialized variations of personality tests. A large number of questions are usually included to increase reliability, but most questions simply represent different ways to probe for dishonest behavioral tendencies and attitudes about society's punitive responses. Interpretations may be made by comparing an individual's profile with those of persons independently judged honest (possibly with polygraphs) and dishonest (possibly by courts of law). Following are samples of experimental questions provided by Stanton Corp., a testing service.

What would you do if your young child came home with a shoplifted item?
☐ A. Take him back to the store.   ☐ C. Send him back to the store.
☐ B. Give him a good talking to.   ☐ D. None of the above.

	YES	NO
	☐	☐

If you saw another person stealing on the job, would you
turn that person in to the boss?
Have you ever been disgusted with yourself because you did
something dishonest?
Is it very important for you to be trusted?
Is stealing from one's job a common occurrence at this time?
Have you ever been told, by a fellow employee, how to cheat
the company?
Do you think people who steal do it because they always have?
Joe always worked late without getting paid for it. Do you think it
would be right for him to take his carfare from petty cash?

YES	NO
☐☐☐	☐☐☐
☐☐	☐☐
☐	☐

Items in this section are designed to measure a
person's willingness to steal.
In the first question, the answer D suggests you
may behave dishonestly since you condone such
behavior in your child. NO answers
to the next three items suggest
condoning dishonesty, plus little concern
about image. YES answers to the next two
questions reveal a bent toward dishonesty that
may be shared with others. YES to the
last two? You rationalize dishonest behavior.

When you are wrong, do you usually admit it?
Do you ever worry about what other people think of you?
Did you ever cheat in school?
Have you ever thought about cheating anyone out of anything?
Did you ever lie to a teacher or policeman?
Have you ever stolen anything from an employer?
Have you ever looked in a mirror and wished you could
change something about yourself?

YES	NO
☐☐☐☐☐☐	☐☐☐☐☐☐
☐	☐

A YES to the first item in
this section and NOs to the rest
suggest you are probably lying in an
attempt to distort the test results.
Most tests do not penalize confessions to minor
dishonest acts or occasional ideas about such;
everybody's guilty sometime.

Are you always completely truthful with yourself?
Have you ever just thought about trying to steal something from anyplace?
Have you ever made a mistake on any of your jobs?

YES	NO
☐☐☐	☐☐☐

How candid were you? A YES answer to the
first question in this section and NOs
to the others may reveal some lack of candor.

Do you believe cheating people is worse than stealing money?
Have you ever wanted to be famous?
Do you think you are sometimes too honest?
Do you believe everyone is dishonest to a certain degree?
Do you agree with this: once a thief . . . always a thief?

YES	NO
☐☐☐☐☐	☐☐☐☐☐

Most test makers include a few
throwaways—filler questions with no specific
meanings—like these items. Your answers
probably don't matter.

THE ETHICAL TREATMENT OF EMPLOYEES

Drug Tests:
Legal Challenges

When guards conducted an early morning drug sweep of the Albuquerque Publishing Co. [in January 1985], company officials said it was for good reason: an estimated 20 percent of the firm's employees have "an abuse problem," says company president Thompson Lang—and of all the job applicants who've taken drug tests in recent months, "no one has passed." Few companies face problems quite so dramatic, but drug use does take a serious toll: the U.S. Chamber of Commerce estimates that drug and alcohol abuse among workers costs employers $60 billion a year— the total tab for lost productivity, accidents, higher medical claims, increased absenteeism and theft of company property (the means by which many workers finance their drug habits). Relatively few companies seem to be tackling alcohol abuse with as much conviction, but concern about drugs is plainly growing, and it has spread well beyond the private workplace. Last week [in June 1986] Boston's police commissioner called for mandatory drug testing of all officers, and in a recommendation hotly disputed by some panel members, President Reagan's Commission on Organized Crime recently called for testing of all federal workers in an attempt to control the spread of drugs.

To root out drug abusers among applicants or employees, meanwhile, companies such as Michigan-based Consumers Power Co., Westinghouse Electric Corp., the Du Pont Co. and Albuquerque Publishing have turned to relatively inexpensive urine tests, such as the EMIT (Enzyme Multiplied Immunoassay Test), manufactured by Syva Co., a subsidiary of Syntex Corp. of Palo Alto, CA. But whether use of these tests does much to control drug abuse is a matter of fierce debate. A major flaw of the most widely used tests is that they don't measure an employee's degree of impairment or level of job performance at the time of the test but show only traces of drugs in the urine. Cocaine may show up as much as three days after consumption; marijuana may be present from five days to three weeks afterward. A drug test, then, may nab even drug users who don't use them at the workplace. "What someone does outside the job isn't a concern for the employer unless it affects what they do on the job," argues Erwin Chemerensky, professor of constitutional law at the University of Southern California (USC).

An even bigger problem is that the tests aren't always accurate. Results can vary widely with the skills of the individuals carrying out the tests or the laboratories analyzing the results. Over-the-counter drugs such as Advil and Nuprin have shown up as illegal drugs on some tests, notes Kerry Shannon, marketing director of Bio-Analytical Technologies, a Chicago lab that conducts urinalysis tests. The most widely used tests claim a 95 to 99 percent accuracy rate; in companies where blanket testing is carried out, this means that, on average, 1 to 5 out of every 100 tests will produce inaccurate results. A recent Northwestern University study suggests an even worse record: it found that 25 percent of all EMIT tests that came up positive were really "false positives." And James Woodford, a forensic chemist in Atlanta and a consultant to the U.S. Public Health Service, contends that urinalysis tests may be racially biased. The reason: test results may be skewed by blacks' higher concentrations of the pigment melanin, which has an ion identical to THC, the active ingredient in marijuana—and which may also soak up body substances similar to THC.

Manufacturers of urine tests acknowledge some of their deficiencies. Michelle Klaich, a spokeswoman for Syntex, stresses that a positive reading on one test shouldn't by itself be a ground for firing; she says Syntex recommends follow-up tests and other measures to verify the results. To improve accuracy, meanwhile, some companies are at work on the next generation of testing devices. National Patent Analytical Systems, Inc., of Roslyn Heights, NY, is awaiting results of clinical tests of its Veritas 100 Analyzer, which uses computer hardware and software to analyze the electrical stimuli given off by the brain in the presence of certain drugs. Company president Joseph Boccuzi says the device measures only the presence of drugs at the time of the test and cuts the false-positive rate to less than 5 percent.

But Ira Glasser, executive director of the ACLU, worries

THE ETHICAL TREATMENT OF EMPLOYEES

that the growing testing industry will become its own reason for being, propounding the use of testing to justify its existence. He recommends "an unused method for detecting [drug abuse]—it's called 'two eyes.'" Most employees who are drug abusers reveal telltale signs of their problem, such as erratic behavior or inability to concentrate. A watchful supervisor, says Glasser, should be able to spot drug use and help an employee into a drug-rehabilitation program—an approach that ultimately may be most helpful in eliminating drug abuse.

Despite a growing number of lawsuits, courts so far have generally upheld the legality of drug testing. But some state and local legislatures are moving to restrict and regulate it. California Assemblyman Johan Klehs has proposed a bill that would require a company's testing policy to be in writing; test results would be kept confidential, and all labs that analyze tests of employees and job applicants would be licensed. The Civil Liberties Union of Massachusetts is drafting a bill that would allow testing of only those employees whose performance had a bearing on public safety—nuclear-plant operators, school-bus drivers and the like—and who show some signs of impairment. Similarly, in San Francisco, a new ordinance prohibits drug testing by private employers unless there is a high degree of what's known as individualized suspicion—that the employees to be tested are not only impaired but also pose a "clear and present danger" to themselves or others. Only through such measures will companies be barred from "rummaging through another person's biology," says San Francisco supervisor Maher, unless testing is absolutely necessary.

Personality Tests:
Probing the Psyche

Wanted: people with "kinetic energy," "emotional maturity" and the ability to "deal with large numbers of people in a fairly chaotic situation." No, not to be cohost of *Wheel of Fortune*; American Multi Cinema, the third largest theater chain in America, wants to hire candidates with these qualities to manage its movie houses. To identify the right employees, AMC is one of an increasing number of companies that administer personality or psychological tests to job applicants. Meanwhile, dozens of others such as General Motors, American Cyanamid, J.C. Penney and Westinghouse now rely on personality-assessment programs to evaluate and promote many current employees.

The tests that companies administer run the gamut. Some are standard psychological tests such as the 46-year-old MMPI (Minnesota Multiphasic Personality Inventory). Long used by psychiatrists and psychologists to test individuals for an array of personality traits, the MMPI consists of up to 566 statements and requires the answers "true," "false" or "cannot say" to questions such as "I avoid getting together with people" or "I have a great deal of self-confidence." Simpler tests include AMC's timed personality-profile exam, known as the PEP test, which among other things examines an applicant's level of mechanical interest and aptitude; people who score well "will be more likely to cope if the butter machine or the projection equipment develops problems," says an AMC district manager, Mario Marques.

Praendix Inc. of Wellesley Hills, MA, produces a personality-assessment test that consists of a list of phrases and adjectives—including "life of the party," "sympathetic" and "aggressive"—and two questions: "Which of these adjectives describes how you think you are expected to act by others?" and "Which of these adjectives describes who you really are?" Arnold Daniels, founder of Praendix, explains that people who select "patient" as an apt description of themselves might be good "detail" workers, such as researchers, and comfortable reporting to a higher authority. But those who select "impatient"—and think others expect them to be less so—might be good managers, focused on the big picture and eager to see tasks completed.

Many companies swear by the tests. Bobbi Ciarfella, an administrator of Yankee Cos., Inc., an oil-and-gas firm based in Massachusetts, says the Praendix test has helped the firm cut its high turnover rate and hire employees who thrive in a fast-paced environment. "You can't afford to make a mistake when you're hiring somebody in the $45,000 range,"

THE ETHICAL TREATMENT OF EMPLOYEES

she says. Others insist the objectivity of many tests benefits applicants by being even fairer than the typically subjective job interview.

Yet some employees may not fare so well. "For a large number of people, [tests] can predict" roughly who will perform a given job well, says Alexandra Wigdor of the National Research Council, which is currently conducting a study to devise an advanced testing system for the U.S. military. But for any one person, especially one who doesn't test well, "they can be hopeless," she concedes. Moreover, the human personality is so complex that not even the MMPI—considered by many psychiatrists to be the most objective of psychological tests—can give anything like a full and accurate reflection of the individual, says New York psychologist Juliet Lesser. Finally, there's the danger that employers will substitute test results for background checks or even old-fashioned intuition. "Anyone relying too much on tests is abdicating his responsibility as a manager," says New York industrial psychologist Brian Schwartz.

Genetic Tests:
Screening for Diseases

At Enserch Corp., a diversified energy company based in Dallas, officials were horrified: last summer the *maître d'hôtel* of the executive dining room was discovered to have AIDS. When the company summarily ordered mandatory AIDS tests for its other food-service workers, another was discovered to have the AIDS antibody. Both employees were suspended with full pay and medical benefits and escorted from the premises.

The consternation that followed among gay-rights groups and civil libertarians pointed up the controversy around a growing area of testing: monitoring employees' health. Examining blood or tissue samples for signs of disease or certain genetic traits could protect employees and the public from health risks—while sparing employers higher medical-insurance costs and reduced productivity. But as tests get increasingly sophisticated, they could also provide a powerful tool for discrimination against homosexuals, women, those predisposed to diseases or other groups of employees.

Testing for AIDS is especially problematic. Most of the tests offered have high rates of both false positives and "false negatives" (incorrect negative results)—traumatic enough in drug testing but particularly so with AIDS. Nor is it clear just what AIDS testing accomplishes, given most experts' belief that the disease isn't spread through the casual contact typical of the workplace but through sexual relations or contact with AIDS-contaminated blood. Yet so far [in 1986], only California has acted to prohibit AIDS testing as a condition of employment.

Looming on the horizon is genetic testing. Each year 390,000 workers contract occupational illnesses including lung, bladder and other cancers; about 100,000 die. The belief that some workers possessed genetic "hypersusceptibility" to some of these conditions that could be triggered by exposure to toxins in the workplace led companies like Du Pont and Dow Chemical to conduct tests on workers beginning in the 1970s. But "after a number of years we were not seeing what we thought we might find," says Dr. John Venable, medical director of Dow. Negative publicity about the tests—particularly Du Pont's testing of workers for sickle-cell trait, which leads to a condition that affects many blacks—further dampened corporate enthusiasm for testing. By the time a 1983 report by the Office of Technology Assessment determined that existing genetic tests couldn't predict what might happen on the job, most companies had quit the field.

Recently, however, biologists have discovered genetic "markers" for a number of genetic diseases such as cystic fibrosis and are now searching for others for more commonplace conditions such as Alzheimer's disease and breast cancer. "We're still many years away" from the time when genetic tests for such conditions could come into widespread use, asserts Alexander Morgan Capron, professor of law and medicine at USC. But since so many people may be prone to these diseases, there is the distant prospect that companies could one day undertake genetic screening—

declining to hire employees who seem likely to become sick on the job, use up expensive medical benefits or die young.

As the technology of testing advances, say the experts, so must the public's attention to the range of economic, ethical and legal issues it raises. Columbia's Westin is confident that such awareness will increase; as a consequence, he predicts, within ten years a "latticework of legislation" will be in place to balance employers' aims with employees' rights. Society has much to gain from careful and sophisticated testing—a potentially more productive corps of workers whose skills more closely match the requirements of their jobs. But the preeminent challenge for on-the-job testing will be whether it can avoid unwarranted encroachment on the rights and freedoms Americans hold dear.

Susan Dentzer in New York with Bob Cohn
in Washington, George Raine in San Francisco,
Ginny Carroll in Atlanta and
Vicki Quade in Chicago

Is Drug Testing Good or Bad?

Andrew Kupfer

Drug testing is the most hotly debated issue in employee rights today. At issue is whether or not workers should be forced to turn over a urine specimen—often produced under the watchful eyes of a witness to insure an untainted sample—which upon analysis will serve as proof that the worker is drug-free. This is a debate that weighs the privacy rights of individuals as opposed to the responsibility of employers to have their businesses operated by drug-free employees. This *Fortune* article asks the pivotal question of whether to randomly test all employees or just those whose jobs might be considered "safety-sensitive" such as airline pilots and railroad workers. It examines the reliability of drug tests and the problem of their false positives—results that tend to make those who are innocent appear guilty. It asks what use the tests will be put to by corporations. Will they fire those employees who fail? Will they make employee assistance programs available to help rehabilitate drug abusers who are exposed by the testing? How will American corporations assume and carry out the role of workplace policeman?

As the age of Aquarius turns to the age of abstinence, more and more companies are requiring job applicants and employees to take urine tests to prove they do not use drugs. Managers believe that drug-abusing workers cost millions in lost productivity, absenteeism, and medical expenses. Companies responsible for public safety live in fear of tragedies like the 1987 train wreck near Baltimore involving a Conrail engineer and brakeman who smoked marijuana before a fatal collision with an Amtrak train. The Department of Transportation recently announced a plan to require random tests of four million railroad, trucking, and airline workers—and has already been challenged by the unions. The tests are becoming so common throughout industry that classified ads in the drug-culture magazine *High Times* offer products such as Uri-Clean that promise to beat the system.

For all this popularity, there is great confusion over what drug tests prove. Some companies report that absenteeism, medical costs, and productivity have improved since they started testing job applicants and workers suspected of drug use. But these same companies say the tests were accompanied by a raft of managerial initiatives that may be equally responsible. The Navy, which performs more drug tests than any other American institution, has found only a low correlation between smoking marijuana, by far the most popular drug, and performance. As yet there is no solid evidence that candidates who flunk preemployment tests are more likely to perform poorly than those who pass. Part of the problem is that the drug tests reject the casual weekend

THE ETHICAL TREATMENT OF EMPLOYEES

marijuana smoker as readily as the daily injector of heroin. Another part of the problem is less-than-perfect testing.

No wonder managers are confused. When do drug tests make sense and when don't they? One place they clearly make sense: corporations whose operations involve public safety. Airlines, railroads, bus companies, and electric utilities can't be too careful. They have good reason to test job applicants for the presence of drugs.

What about preemployment drug testing in less "safety-sensitive" industries? Nearly half of all major U.S. companies, including IBM, Kodak, AT&T, Lockheed, 3M, and Westinghouse, require some or all job applicants to provide urine specimens. These companies say they have a responsibility to provide a safe, healthy, and productive environment for their workers and use preemployment drug tests in the hope of avoiding potential problems later on. If they lose some excellent potential employees, they have many more eager, qualified applicants. Companies in low-paying service industries cannot be so selective. Drug tests could eliminate so many candidates that these employers cannot fill all their slots.

Once on the job, which employees should be tested for drugs? Again, the case is strongest for industries involving public safety. That may mean subjecting employees to drug tests, even by surprise and at random, to protect themselves, their coworkers, and the general welfare. The Nuclear Regulatory Commission is drawing up guidelines for the random testing of power plant operators. But random testing stirs employee resentment, is not likely to yield many offenders, and may be an invasion of privacy. Though the courts are leaning toward that interpretation, they have not ruled conclusively.

As for less safety-sensitive companies, managers should try to spot drug-related problems without testing the entire work force. However, if a worker's performance or absenteeism makes a manager suspect that he is using drugs, a test is an appropriate way to confirm those suspicions and lead him to treatment. After that, further tests can monitor an employee's progress as part of a broad program of counseling and rehabilitation—with firing the last resort for those who continue to fail.

American laboratories will process 15 million to 20 million drug tests [in 1988]. About half will be for companies, the rest for prisons, police, and public drug-treatment programs. Of the corporate tests, 85% will be for preemployment screening. Businesses will pay about $200 million in 1988 for drug testing, a figure some experts estimate will reach $500 million a year by 1991.

Besides trying to generally improve worker productivity, companies might begin preemployment testing for several reasons. Other employers in their area may have done so and they could fear being swamped by drug rejects. They may worry about being sued for negligent hiring if an employee using drugs causes an accident that harms the company, the public, or fellow employees. And they may simply be responding to a fundamental change in the zeitgeist. In the 1960s many people looked upon drugs as a way of enhancing the imagination without serious side effects; now people tend to see them as detracting from performance and downright dangerous.

While drug tests are reliable, they are far from foolproof. First, testers have to make sure that the urine sample belongs to the person who fills the bottle. The only way of knowing, as any baseball fan can attest, is to see the ball enter the glove. But because watching someone urinate is taboo, observers often avert their eyes and may not see a specimen being tampered with. The new guidelines for testing federal employees say that the donor may produce a urine sample "in the privacy of a stall." Besides the possibility of the old switcheroo, adding common table salt to a sample may sneak it past some initial screenings.

Urinalysis is better than blood tests at detecting the presence of drugs. Impurities are more highly concentrated in urine by a factor of 10. The telltale signs of drugs remain in urine much longer than they do in the bloodstream. (However, a blood test is more efficient in determining drug use within the past few hours.)

The urine test is a high-tech, two-part affair, increasingly

THE ETHICAL TREATMENT OF EMPLOYEES

performed by such companies as PharmChem Laboratories in Menlo Park, California, whose only business is drug testing. Samples arrive by overnight courier in sealed bottles with a label signed by both the donor and the person who collected the specimen. First the lab runs each sample through a screening test for an array of substances, including marijuana, cocaine, opiates, amphetamines, barbiturates, and hallucinogens. Screening exams are simple to run and relatively cheap, usually under $10 each. The most common screen is the enzyme multiplied immunoassay technique, or EMIT, which is made by Syva Co. EMIT uses ultraviolet light to tell if a target drug in the urine binds with a drug antibody in the test mixture.

Screening exams are extremely sensitive, but not very specific; that is, many legal substances—such as poppy seeds and cold medicines—can set off alarm bells. The International Olympic Committee in Seoul prematurely announced that British runner Linford Christie had failed a drug test only to recant and let him keep his silver medal when it found that the banned substance in his urine came from ginseng tea. Up to 10% of samples will register as false positives.

So all positive results should be presumed innocent until the lab runs a more accurate confirmatory exam. Still, according to Northwestern University's Lindquist-Endicott Report, one-third of companies do not retest if the initial test is positive.

Companies should ask applicants to list any medications that might cause a positive test result. But as Washington management consultant Theodore Rosen says, "If you don't remember that two weeks ago the doctor gave you Tylenol Plus 3—the 3 being codeine—you're on the hot seat." Employers do not usually tell applicants why they failed to get a job unless they ask, so they rarely have the chance to explain an innocent cross-reaction. For that reason such states as Connecticut, Minnesota, and Vermont require that test results be sent directly to the applicant.

The best confirmatory test is called gas chromotagraphy/mass spectrometry, or GC/MS, which uses $100,000 machines made by Hewlett-Packard or Perkin-Elmer. GC/MS makes a positive identification by breaking down drugs into their constituent molecules. The test is intricate and expensive, costing $40 to $70 each. But if the complex GC/MS test is not administered expertly, false negatives and false positives can still pop up. The National Institute on Drug Abuse is compiling a list of laboratories that conform to its standards; companies should use one that does.

Mistakes and misrepresentations aside, what can a urine sample tell potential employers? A test can show only past exposure to drugs. It cannot tell how much of the drug was consumed or when. It cannot prove drug addiction or the degree to which the drug impairs the faculties of the user, if at all. A true positive result does not mean that a person was under the influence of the drug at the time of the test, for the metabolic byproducts may remain in the urine for up to a month in the case of marijuana. At the same time, a person in the worst stages of cocaine withdrawal may show no trace of the drug because it leaves the system in about three days.

Some companies avoid preemployment drug testing because it could wipe out their worker pool. Drug use is highest among men 18 to 35 years old without college degrees, who include most applicants for low-paying jobs. Attorney Jerry Glassman, a partner in a New York City management-labor law firm, reports that a government agency in the Northeast, which he won't identify, recently gave drug tests to 1,000 applicants for security guards: 980 failed. As it is, a general shortage of unskilled labor will hamstring business in the 1990s. Companies that need to fill a lot of these jobs face tough choices.

For all the problems with preemployment testing, some companies do it right. IBM requires a urine test of all job applicants. Unlike many corporations, IBM tells applicants if they failed the test and gives them a chance to come up with a solid medical reason. If they cannot, they can reapply after six months.

Companies that test job applicants often mistakenly assume that most employees with drug problems started using

THE ETHICAL TREATMENT OF EMPLOYEES

the substances before they were hired. But Thomas E. Backer, president of the Human Interaction Research Institute in Los Angeles, surveyed 1,238 employee assistance programs— confidential services that help workers with personal problems —and found that on-the-job pressure led to a large number of drug-abuse referrals to the programs. Says Backer: "Self-medication for stress is the single most unrecognized and unexplored reason for abuse of drugs in the workplace, and one that companies can't screen out with preemployment tests."

Most controversial is random testing of all employees. While it is a strong deterrent to drug use, random testing is not necessarily good management practice. An official with a nuclear power company that tests employees only when suspicions warrant does not look forward to the random testing required by the proposed Nuclear Regulatory Commission regulations. He says: "Our supervisors have been brought along to be able to spot employees to test for cause. If random testing occurs, they might take a step backward and say, 'Well, they'll get caught by the random test.' "

IBM does not perform random tests and tells managers to give employees every benefit of the doubt before recommending a drug test. If workers test positive, Big Blue offers treatment and gives them periodic drug tests during a one-year probationary period. If they fail during the year, or anytime thereafter, they may be fired.

Many companies say testing has helped lower costs and improve working conditions. The injury rate at Southern Pacific Transportation Co. is down over 60% since 1984, when it began preemployment and post-accident testing. Commonwealth Edison reports 25% to 30% lower absenteeism after six years with a drug program and a reduced rate of increase in medical costs. At Georgia Power sick days have fallen 23%, and serious accidents decreased from 39 in 1981, the year before drug testing was adopted, to 9 in 1987.

Georgia Power's program is unusual. The company encourages workers to go to its employee assistance program if they have a drug problem; if they do not come forward and managers suspect them of drug use, the company will order a drug test and dismiss them with no second chance if they fail. "You might say it's a nonrehabilitative approach, but we say the opposite," says labor relations coordinator Howard Winkler. "Since the price of detection is so high, it encourages employees to seek assistance before they're caught." The company has fired 75 to 100 employees who resisted the encouragement; 527 came forward for help. Over union objections, Georgia Power is about to start random testing of all employees. When it does, it will offer a second chance to those who fail.

Southern Pacific gives its drug tests total credit for the impressive improvement in its injury rate. At Commonwealth Edison and Georgia Power the drug program was part of wide-ranging attempts to curtail injuries and health costs and increase productivity.

To determine the relationship between drug testing and productivity, the U.S. Postal Service is conducting a novel study. Last year the post office told 5,400 job applicants in 20 cities that they had to take a urine test, which would be used for research only. The personnel managers doing the hiring had no access to the tests; they judged the applicants on other criteria. Only the Washington headquarters staff saw the results. The post office hired 4,156 of the people who took the test; 340 of them, or 8.2%, tested positive for drug use. The breakdown: 236 for marijuana, 71 for cocaine, and 33 for other illegal substances.

The post office will monitor the careers of the drug-positive hirees for two years to gauge their performance against that of other new workers. Lou Eberhardt, a post office spokesman, says that preliminary results will be available early in 1989, about halfway through the surveillance period.

When news of the study broke recently, union leaders complained about using workers as guinea pigs, and drug enforcement proponents criticized the government for hiring people known to take drugs. Both groups should cool down and wait for the results. On the one hand, the tests cost no potential union member a job. On the other, without the research there would have been no drug test, so the post office would have hired the drug-using applicants anyway.

* * *

An executive of a utility that routinely tests potential and current employees worries that companies are rushing to adopt drug testing without giving it much thought. "It's almost a case of managerial macho," he says. "If all you do is drug testing, if you don't train your supervisors to spot problems, or promote your employee assistance program, or communicate clearly and sympathetically with your employees, then you don't have a drug program."

Before joining the burgeoning ranks of willy-nilly drug testers, managers might want to consider the two companies that make the fancy mass spectrometers—Perkin-Elmer and Hewlett-Packard. Neither uses drug tests. They say that they know their employees, so they don't need to.

Plant Closing Bill Will Give Many Employers Their Day in Court

Stephen J. Cabot

In the early 1980s the country experienced a business downturn that resulted in a number of plant closings, predominantly in the so-called "rust belt" of the Midwest and Northeast. More and more companies felt the business pressure to reduce their employment rolls and actually closed down plants for good. In the wake of so many plant closings, Congress enacted the Worker Adjustment and Retraining Act, which requires employers to give their workers sixty days' advance notice before they can shut a plant down. Attorney Stephen J. Cabot examines this new law from the perspective of law and ethics. His thesis is that the law's intentions—simply to be fair to workers who are about to lose their livelihoods and to instill a sense of responsibility in those companies that are contemplating a shutdown—

SOURCE: *The Human Resources Professional,* Vol. 1, No. 1, November/December 1988.

has backfired because the bill Congress enacted is much more complex than generally thought. Cabot expects that there will be many long court battles over this bill before fairness and responsibility are seen in the context of plant closings.

The Worker Adjustment and Retraining Notification Act, better known as the Plant Closing Bill, passed both Houses of Congress in July [1988] and became law August 4, without the signature of President Reagan.

Prior efforts to pass similar legislation had all failed. In June, Congress had included a plant closing provision in the Omnibus Trade Bill. You'll remember that President Reagan vetoed the entire measure because of the plant closing provision, and Congress failed to muster the necessary votes for an override.

Is the newly passed legislation a simple measure requiring employers to give their workers sixty days' notice in the event of a plant shutdown, or is it more? It would seem that the controversy that brought this bill to the headlines will be nothing compared to the court battles that could ensue because of the bill's vagueness.

Remarks during the House debate by Representative Silvio Conte (R.-Mass.) characterized the legislation in a way that, arguably, few could oppose. He said the issue was:

> . . . about workers, their families, and their communities. It is a vote about fairness, and about responsibility. It is about understanding the human and economic costs of a plant shutdown or layoff. And it is a vote about the hard reality of business in America where fewer than 19 percent of businesses give more than one month's advance notice of plant shutdowns or mass layoffs.[1]

Surely it is desirable to provide workers with as much notice as possible in the event that a business is forced to lay off a significant number of employees or to close a facility. In fact, many companies have meaningful notice provisions

THE ETHICAL TREATMENT OF EMPLOYEES

as part of collective bargaining agreements—a much more appropriate method for dealing with this issue than federal intervention.

No Simple Measure

The measure, however, is not a *simple* notification bill. Rather, it is complex in its application to both plant closings *and* layoffs. In addition, the new law contains many complicated definitions and exemptions that must be interpreted by the courts.

The following discussion is designed to inform human resources professionals about the new law's key elements and its applicability in various situations.

As this article makes clear, however, it will be months before many of the provisions are defined adequately by federal regulations and court interpretation. Affected employers and key personnel should familiarize themselves with each section of the new law.

The effective date of the bill [is] February 4, 1989. It applies to any business with 100 or more full-time employees. It requires 60 days' notice if 50 or more workers at one site lose their jobs. The mass layoff provision would take effect if 50 or more workers lose their jobs and if the affected workers make up 33 percent or more of the work force at the site.

If 500 or more employees are laid off, notice of a layoff would be required even if that number did not represent one-third of the work force.

The rationale for advance notice is that communities must plan for such dislocation because of the significant economic disruptions brought about in local communities as well as for laid-off workers.

Highlighting the need for an advance notice measure, proponents in Congress cited a General Accounting Office (GAO) finding that one-third of all businesses with 100 or more employees that laid off workers gave no notice. Where advance notice was given, 36 percent of businesses gave less than two weeks' notice, and 50 percent gave less than one month.

In addition, a 1985 survey by the Bureau of Labor Statistics found that in more than half of the situations involving 50 or more laid-off employees, workers received no more than one day's notice.

Begin Preparing Now

Employers affected by the plant closing bill should review its implications carefully, and begin planning for events that could subject them to provisions of the law.

Preparation should include an early warning system that will allow them to predict layoffs and plant shutdowns more than sixty days in advance. They also must devise procedures to provide appropriate written notice to affected employees. Exact requirements should be clarified when federal regulations are issued.

Most American businesses are small. Studies indicate that less than 5 percent of all businesses in the U.S. have more than 100 employees, yet 49 percent of all employees in the private sector work for firms of 100 or more. Roughly half of the American work force, therefore, will be affected by this legislation, but only a small number of employers.

A substantial amount of litigation almost certainly will result from implementation of this measure. Affected workers surely will challenge employer use of exceptions from advance-notice requirements. Complicating matters further is the fact that the law is full of subjective legal tests.

Litigation Will Be Costly

Litigation, especially as the courts are interpreting the law initially, will be expensive. Employees also should be aware that the law gives courts the discretion to award reasonable attorney's fees as part of costs to the prevailing party.

The new law lists certain situations in which notification periods of less than sixty days are allowed. For instance,

THE ETHICAL TREATMENT OF EMPLOYEES

showing political sensitivity to the [1988] Summer draught's impact on farmers, Congress included the following language:

> No notice under this Act shall be required if the plant closing or mass layoff is due to any form of natural disaster, such as a flood, earthquake, or draught currently ravaging the farmlands of the United States.

Although the exception for natural disaster is fairly straightforward, others are much less clear.

Large Grey Areas

For example, the sixty-day notice period is reduced for any employer if "as of the time that notice would have been required the employer was *actively seeking* capital or business which, if obtained, would have enabled the employer to avoid or postpone the shutdown and the employer *reasonably and in good faith* believed that giving the notice required would have precluded the employer from obtaining the needed capital or business." (Emphasis added.)

A further exception allows for reduced notice if "the closing or mass lay-off is caused by business circumstances that were *not reasonably foreseeable* as of the time that notice would have been required." (Emphasis added.)

Who could possibly know what standards will be applied to employers in defining "actively seeking," "reasonably and in good faith," or "reasonably foreseeable"? It is clear from the face of the statute, however, that the burden of proof will be on the employer.

Some guidance on interpreting these and other sections of the law can be drawn from its legislative history.

The House and Senate passed identical versions of the Worker Adjustment and Retraining Notification Act (S. 2527). It was considered in the House under a rule that prohibited amendments.

When the measure first passed Congress in June as part of the trade bill, the houses passed different versions, so the bill went to a joint Conference Committee. The measure reintroduced and passed in July is virtually identical to that agreed to in Conference Committee in June.

A colloquy on the floor of the Senate between Senators John Chafee (R.-R.I.) and Howard Metzenbaum (D.-Ohio) indicates that the Conference Report language should be looked to for help in interpreting the measure.

Senator Chafee specifically raised his concern that the two exceptions discussed above would "produce endless litigation."[2] Senator Chafee was assured by Senator Metzenbaum that the Conference report contained explanatory language addressing the two exceptions. Senator Metzenbaum concluded, though, by saying that he could not "guarantee that these changes eliminate the potential for any litigation . . ."

What's a "Faltering Company"?

Referring to the "Faltering Company" exception, the Conference report stated that the provision was:

> . . . intended as a narrow one applicable only where it was unclear 60 days before the closing whether the closing would occur; the employer was actually pursuing measures that would avoid or indefinitely postpone closing; and the employer reasonably believed both that it had a realistic opportunity of obtaining the necessary capital or business, and that giving notice would prevent the employer's action from succeeding. . . . Thus, to avail itself of this defense an employer must prove the specific steps it had taken, at or shortly before the time notice would have been required, to obtain a loan, to issue bonds or stock, or to secure new business . . . Moreover, the employer must show the reasonable basis for its good faith belief that giving the required notice would have prevented the employer from obtaining the capital or business that the employer had a realistic opportunity to obtain. Finally, the employer also must show that, upon learning that the workplace would be closed, it promptly notified the employees and explained why earlier notice had not been given.[3]

THE ETHICAL TREATMENT OF EMPLOYEES

Despite Senator Metzenbaum's contention that the Conference language would clarify exceptions to the bill, this sort of language seems only marginally more helpful than the text of the law itself. The Conference language, for example, indicates that the employer must "prove" what specific steps it has taken. It also uses phrases such as "reasonable basis" or "good faith belief" without defining them. Stating that the "Faltering Company" provision is to be given narrow application is a clear signal that employers should be very circumspect about invoking it.

Referring to the "unforeseeable business circumstances" exception, the Conference Committee provided the following guidance for cases in which "unforeseeable events" would make it impossible for the employer to give the required sixty days' notice:

> For example, a natural disaster may destroy part of a plant; a principal client of the employee may suddenly and unexpectedly terminate or repudiate a major contract; or an employer may experience a sudden, unexpected and dramatic change in business conditions such as price, cost, or declines in customer orders. In those situations, the employer is required to give notice as soon as the closing or mass lay off becomes reasonably foreseeable, but the employer is permitted to implement the proposed closing or lay off without waiting until the end of the full notice.[4]

Here again, although the Conference report language may be modestly helpful, it hardly provides conclusive guidance regarding interpretation.

The law contains the above exceptions and certain exclusions touted by Congressional floor leaders as a means of securing sufficient votes to make the bill "veto-proof."

Earlier versions contained no such exemptions. However, the exemptions will be of little value if their exercise is subject to legal challenge followed by many months of court hearings and appeals. Uncertainty and expensive litigation actually might dictate against using the exemptions and exclusions.

Other sections of the bill raise different, but equally perplexing, issues. For instance, it sets forth complicated procedures for the sale of all or part of a business or cases in which a plant closing or layoff "constitutes a strike," or lock out.

Problems for Purchasers

In the case of a sale, the seller's full-time employees at the time of the sale are "considered [employees] of the purchaser immediately after the effective date of the sale."

Employees, in effect, become a third party beneficiary of the sales agreement. Apparently, employees are given a written employment contract with the buyer which, presumably, can be enforced in the courts. Also, this provision effectively provides for an automatic work force.

Another critical issue raised for purchasers relates to collective bargaining agreements with prior employers. Will the purchaser now be considered a "successor" bound to recognize an existing labor organization and fulfill terms of collective bargaining agreements because a majority of the union members are now its employees? Will consequences differ if the transaction is an asset or a stock purchase? These questions will certainly be subjects for debate.

Confusion Will Reign

Confusion also will reign in the cases of strikes. It is unclear what benefits employees would be owed, if any, were a company to go out of business because of a prolonged strike or if the employer were to replace economic strikers. The new measure says the Act shall not require an employer to give sixty days' notice:

> When permanently replacing a person . . . deemed to be an economic striker under the National Labor Relations Act; Provided that nothing in this Act shall be deemed to validate or invalidate any judicial or admin-

istrative ruling relating to the hiring of permanent replacements for economic strikers under the National Labor Relations Act.

In debate on the Senate Floor, Senator Metzenbaum, the bill's chief proponent, flatly stated the proposed legislation did not address this issue. He "clarified" his position as follows:

> If any confusion exists—and I want to make it loud and clear—our intention is to leave this complex issue to the National Labor Relations Act and the interpretations of that Act by the courts.

In Senator Metzenbaum's view, strikers themselves need not receive sixty days' notice when their strike brings about the plant shutdown. If the company's going out of business results from a strike, however, to what compensation would the strikers be entitled? Senator Metzenbaum acknowledges that the courts have given varying interpretations to the National Labor Relations Act regarding the circumstances under which permanent replacements may or may not be hired during an economic strike.

Senator Orrin Hatch (R.-Utah) argued vigorously that the new law would tip the "balance of rights" under traditional labor law. In Senator Hatch's view, the language in the bill is very ambiguous in those cases in which layoffs are caused by nothing except strikes. For example, let's say a company decides to replace production and maintenance employees who've struck over economic issues for three months, with no foreseeable resolution. Does the employer have to give the strikers sixty days' notice or other pay and benefits when it clearly is an economic strike?

Requiring employers to do so would certainly go to the heart of existing employee/employer relationships based on principles of the NLRA. Will some judges look at the law and determine that employees who voluntarily struck a plant over economic issues are entitled to sixty days' notice including pay and severance benefits? Only time will tell.

Some issues of interpretation may be clarified by regulations issued by the Secretary of Labor. Hopefully, those regulations will be in place before the effective date of the law. It is impossible to know, however, what assistance in interpretation the regulations will provide.

No Offset

One final consideration for employers is that collectively bargained severance pay and other termination benefits *do not* offset any obligations contained in the law when less than sixty days' notice is given. The conference report is very clear on that subject. It says:

> . . . Payments owing because of written or oral agreement, made on account of the employment loss, would not offset the backpay remedy. Such payment may include severance pay, pension benefits or any other kind of benefit that an employee is entitled to receive.[5]

Proponents cite a Department of Labor finding that all successful re-employment and re-training programs include advance notice of layoffs. Those same studies also found almost no evidence of disruption, theft, loss of customers, or declining productivity after plant closing or layoff notification.

Long-term Effects

Long-term effects of the measure are impossible to predict. But one thing is clear: The emphasis of this bill is on jobs that have already been lost. It does not focus on preventing job loss or encouraging job creation. The bill will not save one single job.

Supporters of the legislation, citing an Office of Technology Assessment Report, argue that there will be a savings of $250–400 million in unemployment compensation costs; that joblessness following displacement will be reduced by ap-

THE ETHICAL TREATMENT OF EMPLOYEES

proximately 3.8 weeks; and that displaced workers will earn $1–2 billion more on an annual basis.

If recently passed legislation providing $980 million for training pursuant to Title III of the Job Training Partnership Act is to be spent effectively, supporters argue, displaced workers must be given advance notice.

In contrast, opponents argue that the measure will actually result in fewer jobs. They argue that small- and medium-sized businesses are the backbone of job creation in the U.S. economy. The new law may well make American businesses, particularly smaller businesses, less willing to expand and to take on extra workers. There will be an incentive, for example, to keep employment levels in small businesses below 100. Employers will also be reluctant to create new jobs in marginal situations because each new position represents the potential for financial liability and litigation at the next economic downturn.

All the implications of the Worker Adjustment and Retraining Notification Act cannot be discussed adequately in this article. Businesses covered by the Act should be aware, however, that this bill will be effective in early 1989 and human resources professionals should begin establishing procedures for providing notice where required, and to take carefully documented steps, if exceptions or exclusions are to be used.

Suffice it to say that Representative Conte's remark about fairness and responsibility to the American worker, though it may be descriptive of the motivation of some of the measure's sponsors, greatly oversimplifies and disguises the complexity of the final product.

NOTES

1. Congressional Record, H5507, July 13, 1988.
2. Congressional Record, S. 8377, June 22, 1988.
3. Congressional Record, S. 8693, June 28, 1988.
4. Congressional Record, S. 8692, June 28, 1988.
5. Congressional Record, S. 8699, June 28, 1988.

A Bill of Rights for Employees and Employers

Patricia H. Werhane

In her provocative work *Persons, Rights and Corporations,* (1985) business ethicist Patricia Werhane argues that one can modify the relationship between corporations and their employees in such a way that justice can be done to both; so that employees can exercise their rights as human beings and corporations can still reap the benefits of the free-enterprise system. Her program for reform entails a recognition of the importance of moral rights in the workplace, which serves as the basis for this mutual relationship. Reprinted here is the appendix to her book, where she lists the kinds of moral rights she believes are necessary for both employees and employers, if workplace injustice is to be eradicated.

Employee Rights

1. Every person has an equal right to a job and a right to equal consideration at the job. Employees may not be discriminated against on the basis of religion, sex, ethnic origin, race, color, or economic background.
2. Every person has the right to equal pay for work, where "equal work" is defined by the job description and title.
3. Every employee has rights to his or her job. After a probation period of three to ten years every employee has the right to his or her job. An employee can be dismissed only under the following conditions:

SOURCE: Patricia H. Werhane, *Persons, Rights and Corporations,* © 1985, pp. 168–170. Reprinted with permission of Prentice-Hall, Inc., Englewood Cliffs, NJ.

THE ETHICAL TREATMENT OF EMPLOYEES

  a. He or she is not performing satisfactorily the job
     for which he or she was hired.
  b. He or she is involved in criminal activity either
     within or outside the corporation.
  c. He or she is drunk or takes drugs on the job.
  d. He or she actively disrupts corporate business ac-
     tivity without a valid reason.
  e. He or she becomes physically or mentally incapac-
     itated or reaches mandatory retirement age.
  f. The employer has publicly verifiable economic rea-
     sons for dismissing the employee, e.g., transfer of
     the company, loss of sales, bankruptcy, etc.
  g. Under no circumstances can an employee be dis-
     missed or laid off without the institution of fair
     due process procedures.

4. Every employee has the right to due process in the
   workplace. He or she has the right to a peer review, to
   a hearing, and if necessary, to outside arbitration before
   being demoted or fired.
5. Every employee has the right to free expression in the
   workplace. This includes the right to object to corporate
   acts that he or she finds illegal or immoral without
   retaliation or penalty. The objection may take the form
   of free speech, whistle-blowing, or conscientious objection. However, any criticism must be documented or
   proven.
6. The Privacy Act, which protects the privacy and confidentiality of public employees, should be extended to
   all employees.
7. The polygraph should be outlawed.
8. Employees have the right to engage in outside activities
   of their choice.
9. Every employee has the right to a safe workplace, including the right to safety information and participation
   in improving work hazards. Every employee has the
   right to legal protection that guards against preventable
   job risks.
10. Every employee has the right to as much information as
    possible about the corporation, about his or her job,

work hazards, possibilities for future employment, and any other information necessary for job enrichment and development.

11. Every employee has the right to participate in the decision-making processes entailed in his or her job, department, or in the corporation as a whole, where appropriate.

12. Every public and private employee has the right to strike when the foregoing demands are not met in the workplace.

Employer Rights

1A. Any employee found discriminating against another employee or operating in a discriminatory manner against her employer is subject to employer reprimand, demotion, or firing.

2A. Any employee not deserving equal pay because of inefficiency should be shifted to another job.

3A. No employee who functions inefficiently, who drinks or takes drugs on the job, commits felonies or acts in ways that prevent carrying out work duties has a right to a job.

4A. Any employee found guilty under a due process procedure should be reprimanded (e.g., demoted or dismissed), and, if appropriate, brought before the law.

5A. No employer must retain employees who slander the corporation or other corporate constituents.

6A. The privacy of employers is as important as the privacy of employees. By written agreement employees may be required not to disclose confidential corporate information or trade secrets unless not doing so is clearly against the public interest.

7A. Employers may engage in surveillance of employees at work (but only at work) with their foreknowledge and consent.

8A. No employee may engage in activities that literally harm the employer, nor may an employee have a second job whose business competes with the business of the first employer.

THE ETHICAL TREATMENT OF EMPLOYEES

9A. Employees shall be expected to carry out job assignments for which they are hired unless these conflict with common moral standards or unless the employee was not fully informed about these assignments or their dangers before accepting employment. Employers themselves should become fully informed about work dangers.

10A. Employers have rights to personal information about employees or prospective employees adequate to make sound hiring and promotion judgments so long as the employer preserves the confidentiality of such information.

11A. Employers as well as employees have rights. Therefore the right to participation is a correlative obligation on the part of *both* parties to respect mutual rights. Employers, then, have the right to demand efficiency and productivity from their employees in return for the employee right to participation in the workplace.

12A. Employees who strike for no reason are subject to dismissal.

Any employee or employer who feels he or she has been unduly penalized under a bill of rights may appeal to an outside arbitrator.

CHAPTER 3

MANAGEMENT ETHICS

Introduction

In the minds of many, the term *business ethics* is an oxymoron—two juxtaposed concepts that result in self-contradiction, like *jumbo shrimp*. The underlying reason for this cynical attitude probably has a great deal to do with the fact that recently there has been a rash of highly publicized instances of business executives allegedly engaged in unethical, questionable, or illegal activities. "Managerial mischief" appears to be on the increase, so much so that people become jaded and tend to think of business as inherently corrupt and beyond ethics.

Unfortunately, the list of these instances continues to grow. It includes the almost fictional escapades of Ivan Boesky, whose insider trading shook Wall Street. Likewise, Wall Streeter Michael Milken's potential fines for illegal behavior as an executive at Drexel Burnham Lambert will surely make the *Guinness Book of World Records* if he is eventually found guilty of the many violations of trading law the government says he has broken. Also, anyone familiar with the unfolding crisis of the nation's savings-and-loan industry knows that one main cause is the questionable and often illegal wheeling and dealing—not to mention outright fraud—of many leading savings-and-loan executives. Here we have a case where such conduct may bring an entire industry to its knees.

Another highly publicized record of managerial mischief within a single industry that has given business a bad name

MANAGEMENT ETHICS

concerns defense contracting. It often seems that this particular group of technically specialized businesses has a unique set of business values that promote unethical and illegal activity. Time-card fraud, overbilling of the government, the billing of personal items, intentional overpricing of materials, and the use of "Pentagon consultants" to garner inside information from government purchasers have all been well documented over the years.

Cases of wrongdoing in business are not confined to particular industries such as finance or defense contracting. They occur almost across the board, as exemplified by Beechnut, where apple juice for infants and children was switched with a nutritionally questionable substitute; by A. H. Robins, whose executives knew that its Dalcon Shield intrauterine device could cause injury but marketed the product nonetheless, with the result that some 88,000 women made claims against the firm; by Johns-Manville, which knew for some time that asbestos was carcinogenic but withheld its research from public disclosure and continued to sell it; by Chrysler Corporation, whose executives drove brand-new cars, illegally readjusted their odometers, and then sold them as new rather than used; and by Ford Motor Company, which knew its Pinto gas-tank design was flawed but opted for production, based upon a cost-benefit analysis that showed it would be less costly in the long run to settle lawsuits from those injured and the estates of those killed than it would be to change the design.

These cases and the startling rate of white-collar crime presents business ethicists with occasion for reflection upon the nature of American managerial practices. What are the generic causes of such mischief and illegality? Is the root cause a matter of individual psychological makeup, where greed and personal aggrandizement are the main motivations? Or are there organizational pressures that can be identified as causative? What preventative measure can be taken to stem white-collar crime and managerial mischief? Do the increasing instances of misconduct by managers warrant a whole-scale condemnation of the free-enterprise system? Or should we only conclude that "in every barrel there are a few rotten apples"? These are among some of the essential issues debated and questions raised by business ethicists within the context of managerial mischief. The first two selections in this chapter examine this problem. First, a *Fortune* magazine article by Myron Magnet explores the recent problems in the investment banking industry. It is followed by a *Time* magazine piece that identifies several major cases of business executives caught in illegal activities.

There is yet another set of issues that occupies the attention of those interested in understanding business ethics—the problems, issues, and dilemmas that have been called "moral mazes in management." While the critics of business may find managerial mischief to be at the crux of the field of business ethics, others with a more philosophical bent see the numerous quandaries managers must face in their careers as likewise worthy of attention. Thus the essential issues of "managerial mischief" and "moral mazes in management" both fall under the rubric of "management ethics." Consequently this chapter not only highlights the questionable practices of managers and their white-collar crimes, but also emphasizes the fact that managers must confront and resolve a wide variety of ethical situations in the workplace.

One of the more pressing moral mazes managers must navigate is that of whistle-blowing. If an illegal or unethical act were to be witnessed on the job, what obligations does a manager have to report it? Whistle-blowers in our society are not well received. Children have long been taught not to be a "squealer." In blowing the whistle one runs the risk of being ostracized by one's coworkers, losing one's job, and being blacklisted in one's field. Should the fact that whistle-blowing entails considerable personal risk be a factor in reaching the decision of whether or not to report wrongdoing? Or, on the other hand, do managers have an overriding responsibility to make such reports, regardless of the personal consequences?

Whistle-blowing has become an essential issue in the area of management ethics because it brings together so many difficult questions on both the personal and organizational levels. Individual managers must often wrestle with their conscience over their responsibility to blow or not blow the whistle on a colleague or their organization. Even after the decision to make a voluntary report of wrongdoing is reached, then the individual must make further crucial decisions. How should the whistle be blown? Does one report what is known anonymously? Should the report be made internally, or does one go to the proper legal authorities or even to the press? What protections, if any, are afforded the whistle-blower?

In this chapter there are two selections analyzing this moral maze of whistle-blowing. The first, "The Anatomy of Whistle-blowing," by consumer advocate Ralph Nader, provides instructive advice to those caught in the quandary of whether or not they are obliged to make reports of wrongdoing. A second article, "Whistle-Blowing: Its Moral Justification," by Gene G. James, argues that people who witness illegalities and unethical practices in the workplace have a positive obligation to report them.

But unfortunately, the dilemma of whistle-blowing is not the only moral maze managers must be prepared to resolve as they progress through their careers. In their daily work-day, any number of ethical issues might present themselves. A short list of such moral mazes would include: recognizing the problem of conflicts of interest and how to avoid them; deciding if a business gift is just a gift or more like a bribe; attaining fairness in employee-performance appraisals; reaching a decision to fire an employee; executing the order to downsize a unit; managing a problem employee; taking reports of wrongdoing on the job; safeguarding proprietary information and recognizing and balancing the legitimate interests of those who hold a stake in corporate decision making, such as shareholders, customers, employees, suppliers, and the communities in which they all live.

The contemporary manager is confronted with so many ethical issues that being adept at moral philosophy and possessing the skills of moral reasoning become necessities, along with having the technical know-how demanded by one's position. Being aware of one's managerial responsibilities and fulfilling them may mean the difference between professional success and failure. All too many careers have come to a grinding halt because of a neglected responsibility. Hence this chapter concludes with a classic piece in business ethics from the *Harvard Business Review* by Bowen H. McCoy entitled "The Parable of the Sadhu," which can be taken as an extended reflection on managerial responsibility. McCoy probes the issue by recalling an experience in the Himalayas where his group came across an Indian holy man—a sadhu—who was suffering from hypothermia and near death. What were McCoy's and his fellow climbers' responsibilities in such a situation? In posing this question, McCoy draws important parallels to managerial ethics and management responsibility.

The Decline and Fall of Business Ethics

Myron Magnet

This article from *Fortune* discusses the seeming rise in white-collar crime, with particular emphasis on the investment-banking industry, which recently has had more than its fair share of negative publicity about unethical and illegal practices. Thanks to the well-publicized insider-trading scams of Ivan Boesky and the alleged wrongdoings by Michael Milken, the "junk-bond king" of Drexel Burnham Lambert, investment banking's image is at an all-time low. The author, Myron Magnet, finds a kind of "profit-at-any-price" mentality in current investment-banking circles. He pinpoints particular problems as causes of the decline in ethics; for example, the loss of client loyalty and the loyalties of employees to their firms; the prevalence of conflicts of interest for brokers; and the negative effects of merger mania on professionalism in investment banking. While there is little doubt that investment banking is in the throes of an ethics crisis, the question Magnet concludes with is: Will the ethics crisis on Wall Street have a ripple effect and influence the rest of the business world?

SOURCE: Myron Magnet, "The Decline and Fall of Business Ethics," *Fortune,* © 1988 Time Inc. All rights reserved.

What is this—the business news or the crime report? Turn over one stone and out crawls Boesky's tipster, investment banker Dennis Levine, dirt clinging to his $12.6-million insider-trading profits. Turn over another and there's a wriggling tangle of the same slimy creatures, from minute grubs like the Yuppie Gang to plump granddads like jailed former Deputy Defense Secretary Paul Thayer. A shovel plunged into the ground above General Electric recently disclosed a bustling colony industriously faking time sheets to overcharge the government on defense contracts. Almost everywhere you look in the business world today, from the E.F. Hutton check-kiting scheme to the Bank of Boston money-laundering scandal, you glimpse something loathsome scuttling away out of the corner of your eye.

It's not just illegality. As if trapped by a thermal inversion, the ethical atmosphere of business, some executives mutter, is growing acrid. Says private investor and Fordham business school dean Arthur Taylor: "I can't do transactions on the telephone any more because people do not keep their word." Adds leveraged-buyout panjandrum Jerome Kohlberg of Kohlberg Kravis Roberts: "Agreements have got to be in writing, and writing is itself subject to interpretation." Laments Merle J. Bushkin, president of an investment banking boutique bearing his name: "I used to think that I could tell good guys from bad guys, and wouldn't deal with people I thought dishonest or unethical. But I've learned that I can't tell the difference. They look alike."

Not that Boy Scouts have always run American business: the Robber Barons didn't earn that name through philanthropy. But some eras are faster and looser than others, and in this one—at least in matters concerning the vast restructuring of U.S. industry now under way—the business climate has become less ethical than it was in the relatively aboveboard period from the Depression's end until the mid-seventies.

No place have standards dropped more vertiginously than in the investment banking trade that is presiding over this restructuring. While other areas of business are in most respects no more unethical than ever, wrongdoing in this central arena makes a crisis of business ethics seem in full swing. And with investment banking now largely manned by the young, is the erosion of ethics here an early warning of imminent trouble elsewhere in business as this generation rises to power?

Insider trading is investment banking's most widely publicized sin, and since extrasensory perception alone doesn't explain why the stock price of takeover targets regularly rises in advance of official announcement, doubtless plenty of insider traders besides Boesky's confederate Levine remain uncaught. But much more pervasive, if less heralded, is the unscrupulousness that now infects relations with clients. Says Herbert A. Allen, Jr., president of the Allen & Co. Inc. investment banking firm: "A major disquieting factor is the loss of confidentiality, well short of illegality. Important clients can find out anything about other important clients."

Formerly circumspect investment bankers now routinely trade confidential information, hoping to glean tips leading to new business. Information seeps out to other clients, too. In one example, a company preparing to go public to raise capital suddenly found itself faced with an unwelcome tender offer from another client of the investment banker arranging the stock offering.

Company chiefs are becoming understandably skittish about entrusting themselves to such leaky vessels. One divisional chief executive, hoping to buy his company out from its corporate parent, almost froze with fear when the time came to hire investment bankers to help structure the deal. If his boss discovered his plans before he could present the proposal in detail, he feared he'd be thought a traitor and get fired. "Here I am being asked to put my life in the hands of these people," he confided to Emory University business school professor Joseph McCann, "and for all I know the guy on the other end of the line is Dennis Levine."

This was no idle worry: such leaks have proven catastrophic. When management was trying to take U.S. Industries private in 1984, one of the investment bankers in the deal let out word that the company was for sale before the management group had lined up financing. The stock began to rise, and ultimately Britain's Hanson Trust snatched the company from under its astonished managers, compounding the injury by firing most of them as an economy move. A knowledgeable insider believes that the leaky banker, fearing that management might yet back off from the deal and assured by contract that the board would pay his firm if the company was sold to *anybody*, deliberately put U.S. Industries in play to guarantee the fee.

Perhaps, or maybe it was just an accident. But in many instances investment bankers haven't scrupled to work against their clients by putting them in play when that looked more profitable than working for them. A veteran of one august firm says of his colleagues: "When they speak ethics, you'd think they've worn white gloves all their lives. But these days they'll sell their clients out for a couple of million bucks in fees." Typically, says this veteran, you look over your client list, picking out a company that appears vulnerable. Somebody's going to put him in play, you sigh philosophically, so we'd better do it first—and accordingly you shop his company around behind his back.

A senior member of a more demotic firm reports a common variation on this technique. You tell a client who has come to you for some simple bankerly service that a raider is about to put his company in play and he'd better be scared; you gallantly offer your services in his defense; and then you look for a buyer yourself. "They take a healthy patient that walks in and make a cadaver," says this investment banker. "It happens so quick that the victim doesn't even know it's going on."

Rather than snatching a client's company, an investment banker might merely snatch his deal. Former ITT chief Harold Geneen and ex-Norton Simon chairman David Mahoney, for instance, recently came to Drexel Burnham Lambert to get financing for their proposed purchase of a W. R. Grace retail unit. To Geneen's outrage, another group—with close ties to Drexel and financed by the firm— ended up with the unit instead, after seeing, Geneen believes, the voluminous analysis of the unit's value that he had prepared and given to Drexel. (*Fortune* was unable to reach Drexel for comment.)

Clients contribute to the appearance of conflict of interest that hangs over some routine investment banking practices. When they hire firms to give fairness opinions on the terms of a deal, they conventionally pay a small retainer, with the bulk payable when the fairness letter is put into the proxy statement—where only a favorable letter can appear if the deal is to succeed. Or they hire firms to advise on whether to do a particular deal and how to structure it, with the fee contingent on the successful completion of the very deal whose wisdom is at issue.

Troubling, too, in terms of the appearance of conflict of interest is the investment banker's increasing propensity to turn up on all sides of a deal. In the pending sale of an equity stake in Western Union to Pacific Asset Holdings, Drexel not only advised the seller but also raised the financing for the buyer, an outfit, moreover, that includes among its partners Drexel junk-bond star Michael Milken and other present and former Drexel employees. It's all perfectly legal, of course.

For potential buyers, the auction process by which companies often get sold has become what one leveraged-buyout specialist calls "a nightmare of back-room dealing." Lucky you, you're the high bidder for Transylvania Airlines, and the investment banker running the auction says, "You've won, but you just need to sweeten your bid a little to make it totally palatable to the seller." So you up your offer, and regardless of what he's told you, the banker invites another high bidder to top it, and so on, all with jet speed and steam-engine pressure. "You can't believe anything anyone tells you in the process," says the leveraged-buyout specialist, who, like some other former participants, refuses to play the auction game again. Sums up Lazard Frères partner Felix Rohatyn: "The big business community views all investment bankers now as a bunch of samurais who will do anything for money."

What happened to turn a once sedate, gentlemanly business into such a free-for-all? The takeover movement fueled the change by pouring great gouts of money into investment banking and attracting hordes of aspirants to hold their buckets under the golden shower. The huge and numerous deals in turn produced such lightning stock appreciation that some quiet trading on your insider knowledge could make you seriously rich.

Changes in the structure of the business also have eroded standards of behavior. When clients pushed investment banks to buy up whole issues of their securities for later resale, most of the major private firms of fifteen years ago gained access to the needed capital by going public or selling out to big public companies. With that, each lost a measure of its distinctive character, along with the proprietary willingness to identify self-interest with the firm's interest, a willingness that used to characterize partners and those who knew that behaving like a partner was a good way to become one. Now even bigger and more bureaucratic, firms inspire still less loyalty. "Conscience is a fragile thing," says Dr. Abraham Zaleznik, a psychoanalyst and Harvard Business School professor. "It needs support from institutions, and that support is weakening."

With hopping from firm to firm becoming common, employees often think of their mission as doing as well for themselves as they can in the three to five years they spend on average at any given place. "These people see themselves as baseball free agents, not as belonging to anything larger than themselves that they feel a responsibility to protect," says Samuel L. Hayes III, investment banking professor at the Harvard Business School. Most junior investment bankers don't care what their firm's relationship with Mega Inc. will be two years hence. Their goal is to get the Mega deal done now, without worrying how Mega, or their own firm's reputation, will fare thereafter.

Loyalty between firms and clients has weakened no less conspicuously. Fifteen years ago, corporations still had long-term relationships with one or perhaps two investment bankers. The chief executive—often a company founder—dealt directly with the investment bank's chief, himself often a founder of his firm and frequently a member of his client's board. But when the SEC's adoption of shelf registration in 1982 made it possible to issue securities almost in a rote manner, which in turn allowed clients to force investment banks to compete on price, all that began to change.

The clients' focus moved from the relationship to the individual transaction: who could do it cheapest, and, since investment banks have different areas of expertise, who could do more complicated deals best? As had already happened with their commercial bankers, companies pushed to have loose connections with five or six investment banks, from whom they would buy particular services, depending on the particular deal. "The ethical equation has changed, because neither the adviser nor the client sees himself committed and held to the same standards as he did when the relationship was different," says Lazard's Rohatyn. Of course, not just honor kept you from behaving unethically in the days of stable relationships. Says Jerome Kohlberg of the black sheep: "Nobody would do business with you. Misconduct would hit you right in the pocketbook."

Twenty years ago, when investment bankers started at $9,000 a year, firms also felt less goaded to keep their new hires in perpetual motion than these days, when their numbers are legion and they start at up to $100,000. "There weren't the same hungry mouths needing a worm stuffed down them every day," says Harvard's Samuel Hayes. What's more, the deal being done now is much likelier to be a hostile takeover than two decades ago, when aggression in takeovers was less respectable. "Taking the gloves off," says Hayes, "creates an environment in which corners can be cut."

Because investment banking has become so competitive, so dependent on innovation, it has had to open itself to talent more than in the past, when a genteel oligarchy manned it. "The bottom quarter of the Yale class wasn't so bright," says Fordham's Arthur Taylor, "but it did share a sense of family and a sense of obligation." One mustn't romanticize this class's gentlemanly code—this wasn't a bunch of Sir Galahads, and few expansively lived out the ideals Groton or Exeter tried to teach them. But for all the oligarchy's snobbish exclusivity, it did promote a measure of probity and honor. The recruits that investment banking has attracted to its new meritocracy truly are the talented: business is this generation's hot career, and investment banking

MANAGEMENT ETHICS

the hottest part of it. What they often lack is the ethic that belonged not to the business but to the class that once ran it.

They have their own ethic, and it centers on money, as is increasingly true for the ethic of the culture at large. "Where we saw in the sixties the notion of public service, in the eighties money is the thing," says Hayes. For the get-rich-quick mergers and acquisitions generation, it sometimes seems that money is the only value. "The people with the most money are admired regardless of how they achieved it," says James Schreiber, a New York lawyer who specializes in cases involving securities fraud. The investment-banking boom gives these people their chance to be rich, and they are taking it. "For them, it's money *now*," says one of their elders in the business. "It's Las Vegas."

It's hard to know where they would get what used to be thought of as mainstream values, given schools that strive to be so inoffensively value-neutral that they shrink from telling pupils that it was God the Pilgrims were giving thanks to, or colleges that teach—when they teach anything beyond their preprofessional curriculum—that everything is relative, or a television culture celebrating instant gratification. It's hard to know where the new people would acquire a strong sense of responsibility for their actions when two of the chief social ideas they have been raised with are that the cause of wrongdoing is the economic or psychological environment of the wrongdoer and that it is right to hire and promote people not because of their personal merit but because they come from a particular group.

The ethic they have, half articulate but deeply felt, takes the idea of the free market and turns an economic theory into a personal moral code, making nonsense of reasonable propositions by exaggeration and distortion. "Okay," the rising generation says, "the mechanism of the market insures that each individual, pursuing his own interest in his own way, will augment the wealth of the nation, thereby advancing the public interest by self-interest. That means that whatever I do in my own race for wealth—spill this company's secrets or put that one into play or lie to a third—is fine. It is only mistaken sentimentality to say that these things are wrong." Observes Getty Foundation chief and ex-Norton Simon CEO Harold Williams: "The concept of 'Let the market govern' relieves one of one's sense of responsibility."

Members of the post-1975 generation of investment bankers don't sense that what they do advances the common weal only in some abstract, distant way. In fact, in their view they directly confer a vital social benefit. American industry fell behind in the seventies, they reasonably argue, because overregulation and a national emphasis on redistribution rather than production of wealth shackled competitiveness. But then they expand this point—and pervert it. "Rejecting talk of small is beautiful and eras of limitations," they argue, "our generation, stuck with this mess, rolled up its sleeves. Now, directed by investment bankers like us, and often opposed by contemptible entrenched management whose barren stodginess and porcine presumption helped make the country uncompetitive, U.S. industry is restructuring to be lean and strong, as changed conditions require. Only the strong and realistic survive in this competitive world—and you have to be strong and realistic as a nation, a company, and an individual."

But here the ethic turns into social Darwinism, and an appropriate tough-mindedness becomes mere hardness. "Part of the ethic is that the strong were meant to prevail over the weak, and the strong just do not have responsibility," says Fordham's Taylor. They can do what they want, and their success proves they were right to do it.

And how can what they do be wrong when they work so hard, with such virtuous self-denial? For the ethic of this new generation of investment bankers retains a nub of the Protestant ethic in its emphasis on hard work and dedication, if not to a "calling," at least to a career. Paradoxically, that virtue can turn into a license to misbehave. The 100-hour weeks, the lack of time for social or family life, the continual pressure, all breed resentment. "It's an inhuman way of life. You're at the firm's beck and call," says Dr. Mary Ann Goodman, a New York psychoanalyst. "There comes to be a feeling that they owe you—there's no way that they can repay what you've given up." Adds Harvard's Zaleznik,

"This leads to a sense of entitlement that weakens the conscience."

This may well be part of what drives people beyond the unethical into the illegal. But psychoanalysts think that what pushes some insider traders over the line, beyond mere greed, is a more primitive wish to flirt with danger, like stunt drivers. "As long as they're winning, they don't feel there's anything to stop them," says Goodman. "Clinically speaking," adds Zaleznik, "these people are fighting off major depressions" stemming from the "fear of being unloved, unlovable, and worthless."

Even their greed isn't always simple, as in the recent case of Kidder Peabody superbroker Peter Brant, a Great Gatsby for the eighties. Like F. Scott Fitzgerald's character, né Gatz, who reinvented himself according to his own ideal, Buffalo-born Brant rejected the name Bornstein in favor of something he apparently thought evoked Cary Grant, and went on to transform himself into a millionaire Racquet Clubman and polo player of swank Locust Valley, Long Island. To protect all this when his talent for picking stocks faltered, he induced *Wall Street Journal* reporter R. Foster Winans to disclose, prior to publication, what that paper's stock-tip column would be saying about individual companies, at least according to Winans's book, *Trading Secrets*. Like Gatsby trying to reveal his innermost soul by throwing open his wardrobe and pouring out the profusion of his handmade shirts—the outer surface he longed to make his identity—Brant needed the money to preserve not just his possessions but the sense of self tied up in them.

Because the eighties ethic now seems so pervasive, top executives in many businesses increasingly fear that wrongdoing could break out in their companies too. Executives worry that the industrial restructuring process could lower the standards of employee behavior by its relentless pressure to squeeze budgets and raise profits, by its fanning of fright and resentment among the survivors whenever employees are fired, and by its shredding of the corporate culture in which standards are embedded.

One of the worried is American Can Chairman William

Woodside, a champion restructurer who over the last five years has sold off most of his original company and put together a new one. "Two or three years ago," he says, "I thought, 'We're disassembling the culture we grew up in and spinning it off, and we're acquiring a lot of different cultures, but we have not the vaguest idea of what the underpinnings of those cultures are. We don't know how our family was brought up.' "

He decided to administer an ounce of prevention. Mindful that you shouldn't buy entrepreneurial companies and force them to conform to your corporate culture, Woodside instead put every middle manager at the newly constituted enterprise through an ethics course and outfitted him with an ethics manual. Equally uneasy, scores of other chief executives have tried the same remedy, making a boomlet for ethics consultants.

But the ethics experts who write such tomes and teach MBA students often aren't really sure what is ethical. Listen to Vernon Henderson, a retired minister who is an ethics consultant to the Arthur D. Little consulting firm: "Ethical behavior is always a function of a context. It is relative to a culture, an era, to the pressures exerted in a given job." Standards, moreover, are in constant flux, he says. "In a society like ours," he asks, "who's going to decide what's right and wrong?" One looks in vain in this kind of talk for anything that would prevent a person from pulling the lever at Auschwitz.

The result of such moral relativism is that every situation becomes a problem that every manager is expected to solve as if no one had ever faced it before. And the solutions become fairly zany, as in an example reported to Barbara L. Toffler, a professor of ethics at the Harvard Business School. When an employee came back to work at AT&T after a dangerous illness, he was a man transformed: formerly by far the worst of his superior's subordinates, he was now much the best. AT&T, then undergoing its breakup, had devised a new performance evaluation, requiring each manager to list subordinates in order of excellence. Should the manager rank her born-again subordinate first, as he deserved? Wouldn't this be unfair to her three other subordinates, she agonized, since higher-ups were bound to think them awful if she ranked them beneath an employee known to be the bottom of the barrel?

Her long-meditated solution: gradually improve the best employee's ranking, waiting several more quarters before anointing him number one. Toffler presents this case to her students approvingly; it takes a while for a visitor to get her to see that what the manager did was *lie*.

In the end, the business school ethicists may be as much a part of the problem as of the solution. Their main message starts off with the reasonable exhortation that the future managers in their classes must prevent the creation of cultures of corruption at the outfits they'll help run. Corporate cultures powerfully affect employee behavior, students rightly are told, so you mustn't have reward systems that encourage misreporting of revenue and expenses or that promote cheating on government contracts. But in practice all this talk about how employees are creatures of their culture ends up by tacitly accepting the notion that the individual employee really can't be held personally responsible for his actions. The result is to genuflect piously to the idea of ethics without requiring any person to be ethical.

The corporate employees in most danger nowadays are chief executives, for they are most susceptible to the contagion bred of corporate restructuring. In them it produces symptoms like questionably ethical golden parachutes, dealmaking in which CEOs don't always keep their word to each other, leveraged buyouts in which the management team that arguably hasn't maximized returns so far acts as both seller and buyer of the shareholders' assets, not to mention the host of company-bruising contortions chief executives have used to evade raiders and save their jobs.

Critics of restructuring fear that the process may not prove quite the panacea its supporters foresee, which makes the unethical behavior of the participants seem not just sordid but sinister. These critics admit that mismanagement bloated many companies that then needed shaping up. But by now, certain investment bankers and business leaders believe, it is not just poorly run companies that are being put through the wringer.

Some critics worry that the restructuring is mere financial manipulation. "The advent of junk bonds," says Felix Rohatyn, "took mergers and acquisitions away from where the industrial or business logic guided the merger to where the availability of finance became the guiding force." Companies have been bought simply to be broken up, he argues, not for any larger, constructive purpose. "We're not going to look back on this period and think that Boone Pickens performed a great service to U.S. interests or to the energy industry."

The vaunted restructuring may be making companies more profitable to shareholders, but that isn't necessarily the same thing as making them stronger global competitors. Their cultures destroyed, they may be stripped down not for competitive action but to pay off their new, restructuring-imposed burden of debt, a burden that could prove unsustainable when business turns down.

Presiding over all this, increasingly as instigators rather than mere intermediaries, are the investment bankers, saying, "Trust us, it's all for the best—trust us." But the steady barrage of their ethical lapses makes trusting them hard to do.

Having It All, Then Throwing It All Away

Time

Continuing the theme of the prevalence of illegal, unethical and questionable practices in business today, the following article from *Time* magazine underscores the fact that the business world has not seen such scandalous behavior since the "reckless 1920s" and "desperate 1930s." Details of white-

SOURCE: Stephen Koepp and others, "Having It All, Then Throwing It All Away," *Time*, May 25, 1987. Copyright © 1987 Time Inc. Reprinted with permission.

collar crime which costs the U.S. at least $40 billion annually (while street crime costs are estimated at only $4 billion) are documented. The question of what has caused this rash of business embarrassments is also raised. There are diverse explanations offered for the rise of business crime; for example, the Reagan Administration's *lassez faire* attitude toward the business sector, a wave of materialism caused by the post-war "baby boomers" coming into their prime earning years, the temptations of the computer and electronic fraud, competitive pressures upon individuals in corporations to produce, and the unknowns of deregulation.

———————

J. Michael Cook is an enthusiastic collector of oxymora, among them such alleged contradictions as airline food, jumbo shrimp and postal service. But Cook, chairman of the Big Eight accounting firm of Deloitte Haskins & Sells, bristles when wags tell him about the latest one: business ethics. The unamused Cook maintains that most business people can still be trusted. Yet he admits, "We have all been embarrassed by the events that make the *Wall Street Journal* read more like the *Police Gazette*."

That is hardly an exaggeration. Not since the reckless 1920s and desperate 1930s have the financial columns carried such unrelenting tales of vivid scandals, rascally characters and creative new means for dirty dealing (insider trading, money laundering, greenmailing). Consider these episodes, all hard to believe, all matters of record:

- A widely admired investment banker with a yearly income said to exceed $1 million sneaks into Wall Street alleys to sell insider tips, for which he later collects a briefcase stuffed with $700,000.
- Savings and loan officers in Texas, all with six-figure salaries and bonuses, loot their institution to buy Rolls-Royces and trips to Paris.
- A defense contractor with $11 billion in annual sales charges the government $1,118.26 for the plastic cap on a stool leg.

While questionable business practices are nothing new, the vulnerability of today's economy to rampant white-collar crime is setting off alarms. Particularly in the service industry, stealing has become easier than ever to pull off and to rationalize. White-collar workers are harried by competition, given new power by computers, tempted by electronic flows of cash, and possessed of a strong appetite for status symbols. Result: what began as the decade of the entrepreneur is fast becoming the age of the pinstriped outlaw, his prodigal twin. The white-collar crime wave is already spurring an antibusiness backlash, which could lead to a fresh dose of the regulations from which many industries have only recently won freedom. Says Michigan Democrat John Dingell, chairman of the House Energy and Commerce Committee: "I think the pressures on honest men have grown manifold, and they're leading them to mistakes they wouldn't have made before."

Of course, many of today's ethical transgressions go far beyond any gray area. [In May 1987] federal and New York City authorities cracked a phony tax-shelter scheme that allegedly bilked more than $115 million from at least 2,500 investors, including Comedian Eddie Murphy. The accused ringleader was John Galanis, 44, a hefty ex-con who managed to build a reputation as a financial wizard by spending lavishly on parties, automobiles and homes.

A day after Galanis was rounded up at his posh beach house in Del Mar, CA, Wall Street's insider-trading drama again burst into the headlines when prosecutors suddenly sought to drop charges against three defendants—Robert Freeman, Richard Wigton and Timothy Tabor—who had been scheduled to face trial. U.S. Attorney Rudolph Giuliani claimed that his prosecutors have found a much wider conspiracy and intend to come back to court soon with new charges against the same men and others. But the defendants, who were handcuffed in February [1986] while Wall Streeters watched agape, said the move shows that the government has a weak case and should never have arrested them in the first place.

Giuliani's hesitancy marks the first setback, perhaps only a temporary one, in the historic insider-trading crackdown that began a year ago last week with the arrest of Investment Banker Dennis Levine, who [has served] a two-year sentence in the federal penitentiary in Lewisburg, PA. In most cases the threat of going to prison, even one with a tennis court, has inspired accused insiders to squeal on their colleagues. Levine got a relatively light term for his cooperation in bringing down arbitrager Ivan Boesky (sentencing: August 21, [1987]), who in turn fingered Investment Banker Martin Siegel (June 11, [1987]) and others. To some observers, the Wall Street criminals are worse than many industrial scoundrels of the past. At least the fabled robber barons of the nineteenth century left a legacy of railroads and successful industrial companies; today's financial crooks are only paper shufflers and money changers. Critics think they will be far more socially productive now that they are making license plates and furniture.

Yet Wall Street does not have a corner on the greed industry. White-collar crime is as diverse as the economy, ranging from income tax evasion to false advertising, from check kiting to boiler-room operations that sell nonexistent gold. While common street crime costs the U.S. an estimated $4 billion a year in losses, white-collar lawbreaking drains at least $40 billion—and probably much more—from corporations and governments, not to mention millions of consumers and taxpayers. Marvin Warner, a financier and former Ambassador to Switzerland, was sentenced in March 1987 to 3½ years in prison for his role in the collapse of Cincinnati's Home State Savings Bank, which forced the temporary closing of 70 other thrift institutions in Ohio and cost that state an estimated $226 million. Business crime is just as insidious on a small scale: two tow-truck operators in New Jersey were convicted last year for pouring oil on a freeway ramp to cause accidents and boost their business.

Why a sleaze wave now? To some extent, it represents the dark side of President Reagan's emphasis on the free market and individual enterprise. A few entrepreneurs simply go too far. Says James Gattuso, a policy analyst for the Heritage Foundation, a conservative think tank: "We have more capitalism now, and it isn't always pretty." But Reagan deserves only part of the blame for America's current swing toward materialism, which has no doubt driven many status-crazed professionals over the line to meet the bills on their platinum cards.

If greed is the main motivator in the surge of white-collar crime, pressure to perform also plays a part. Many individuals and companies feel much more competitive stress these days. The flood of baby boomers into the job market has created a crowding effect as they squeeze toward the top. Observes Thomas Mulligan, an adjunct professor at the Duke University business school: "Unethical behavior is more the result of being too focused on their task than an overt intent to do something evil." At the same time, deregulation of industries from banking to broadcasting has made companies feel compelled to cut corners to keep up with rivals. Several U.S. airlines, notably Continental, have been accused of endangering passengers by cutting back on maintenance, a charge the carriers deny.

In any event, some of the worst ethical violations often result from the absence of conscientious naysayers rather than the presence of individual culprits. Manville's huge asbestos output and A.H. Robin's production of the tiny Dalkon Shield intrauterine device, both health hazards, might have been stopped earlier if employees had been encouraged to voice their misgivings. But whistle-blowing is usually a high-risk business. Says Richard Boland, professor of accountancy at the University of Illinois: "People who try to ask the embarrassing question have a very, very dismal record in succeeding in their later careers."

Management experts think ethics should start at the top. That may have been what General Electric officials had in mind [in May 1987] when they shook up the management at GE's Kidder Peabody investment division in the wake of insider-trading charges against two former employees and a third employee who is now suspended. Ralph DeNunzio, Kidder's chief executive for the past ten years, was ousted in favor of Silas Cathcart, former chairman of Illinois Tool Works, in a move that may be designed to inject a dose of heartland ethics into the Wall Street firm.

Already a new tide of more positive peer pressure appears to be coming to bear on the wayward Wall Streeters. Overreaching investment bankers are now widely lampooned for their herdlike compulsions, even their telltale yellow ties and red suspenders. Wrote Journalist Ron Rosenbaum in a blistering essay in *Manhattan, inc.*, a business magazine: "Throw them out, fellas. Wearing red suspenders these days is like wearing a sartorial scarlet letter that says: I BELONG TO A SHAMEFUL PROFESSION. I AM PROBABLY A CROOK." Another possible sign of change: hardly anyone seems interested anymore in the Parker Bros. board game called "Go for It! The Game Where You Can Have It All." Last week one store in Manhattan slashed the price of that fantasy from $13.49 to $3. —*By Stephen Koepp. Reported by Harry Kelly/ Chicago and Raji Samghabadi/New York*

The Anatomy of Whistle-Blowing

Ralph Nader

Probably no other issue can cause so much consternation to a manager who wants to do the right thing in his or her career as that of deciding whether or not to blow the whistle on his or her organization or coworkers. In this selection, consumer advocate Ralph Nader takes up the essential issue of whistle-blowing and managerial responsibility. Nader's approach is to argue that managers and all corporate employees have an overriding duty to public safety that must supersede loyalties to their organizations. He then goes on to list eight important questions the potential whistle-blower must contemplate; and he calls for workplace protections for those who do find it necessary to report violations of law and ethics in their midst. There is thus a need for what Nader labels a "new whistle-blower ethic," because the

SOURCE: Ralph Nader, Peter J. Petkas, and Kate Blackwell, editors, *Whistle Blowing* (New York: Grossman Publishers, 1972). Reprinted with permission of the author.

whistle-blower is the "last line of defense" the public has in its confrontation with massive institutions that wield such great power over the lives of ordinary citizens.

Americans believe that they have set for themselves and for the rest of the world a high example of individual freedom. That example inevitably refers to the struggle by a minority of aggrieved citizens against the royal tyranny of King George III. Out of the struggle that established this nation some chains were struck off and royal fiats abolished. Americans became a nation with the conviction that arbitrary government action should not restrict the freedom of individuals to follow their own consciences.

Today arbitrary treatment of citizens by powerful institutions has assumed a new form, no less insidious than that which prevailed in an earlier time. The "organization" has emerged and spread its invisible chains. Within the structure of the organization there has taken place an erosion of both human values and the broader value of human beings as the possibility of dissent within the hierarchy has become so restricted that common candor requires uncommon courage. The large organization is lord and manor, and most of its employees have been desensitized much as were medieval peasants who never knew they were serfs. It is true that often the immediate physical deprivations are far fewer, but the price of this fragile shield has been the dulling of the senses and perceptions of new perils and pressures of a far more embracing consequence.

Some of these perils may be glimpsed when it is realized that our society now has the numbing capacity to destroy itself inadvertently by continuing the domestic chemical and biological warfare against its citizens and their environments. Our political economy has also developed an inverted genius that can combine an increase in the gross national product with an increase in the gross national misery. Increasingly, large organizations—public and private—possess a Medea-like intensity to paralyze conscience, initiative, and proper concern for people outside the organization.

Until recently, all hopes for change in corporate and

government behavior have been focused on external pressures on the organization, such as regulation, competition, litigation, and exposure to public opinion. There was little attention given to the simple truth that the adequacy of these external stimuli is very significantly dependent on the internal freedom of those within the organization.

Corporate employees are among the first to know about industrial dumping of mercury or fluoride sludge into waterways, defectively designed automobiles, or undisclosed adverse effects of prescription drugs and pesticides. They are the first to grasp the technical capabilities to prevent existing product or pollution hazards. But they are very often the last to speak out, much less to refuse to be recruited for acts of corporate or governmental negligence or predation. Staying silent in the face of a professional duty has direct impact on the level of consumer and environmental hazards. But this awareness has done little to upset the slavish adherence to "following company orders."

Silence in the face of abuses may also be evaluated in terms of the toll it takes on the individuals who in doing so subvert their own consciences. For example, the twenty-year collusion by the domestic automobile companies against development and marketing of exhaust control systems is a tragedy, among other things, for engineers who, minionlike, programmed the technical artifices of the industry's defiance. Settling the antitrust case brought by the Justice Department against such collusion did nothing to confront the question of subverted engineering integrity.

The key question is, at what point should an employee resolve that allegiance to society (e.g., the public safety) must supersede allegiance to the organization's policies (e.g., the corporate profit), and then act on that resolve by informing outsiders or legal authorities? It is a question that involves basic issues of individual freedom, concentration of power, and information flow to the public. These issues in turn involve daily choices such as the following.

To report or not to report:

1. defective vehicles in the process of being marketed to unsuspecting consumers;

2. vast waste of government funds by private contractors;
3. the industrial dumping of mercury in waterways;
4. the connection between companies and campaign contributions;
5. a pattern of discrimination by age, race, or sex in a labor union or company;
6. mishandling the operation of a workers' pension fund;
7. willful deception in advertising a worthless or harmful product;
8. the sale of putrid or adulterated meats, chemically camouflaged in supermarkets;
9. the use of government power for private, corporate, or industry gain;
10. the knowing nonenforcement of laws being seriously violated, such as pesticide laws;
11. rank corruption in an agency or company;
12. the suppression of serious occupational disease data.

It is clear that hundreds and often thousands of people are privy to such information but choose to remain silent within their organizations. Some are conscience-stricken in so doing and want guidance. Actually, the general responsibility is made clear for the professional by codes of ethics. These codes invariably etch the primary allegiance to the public interest, while the Code of Ethics for United States Government Service does the same: "Put loyalty to the highest moral principles and to country above loyalty to persons, party, or Government department." The difficulty rests in the judgment to be exercised by the individual and its implementation. Any potential whistle-blower has to ask and try to answer a number of questions:

1. Is my knowledge of the matter complete and accurate?
2. What are the objectionable practices and what public interests do they harm?
3. How far should I and can I go inside the organization with my concern or objection?
4. Will I be violating any rules by contacting outside parties and, if so, is whistle-blowing nevertheless justified?

MANAGEMENT ETHICS

5. Will I be violating any laws or ethical duties by *not* contacting external parties?
6. Once I have decided to act, what is the best way to blow the whistle—anonymously, overtly, by resignation prior to speaking out, or in some other way?
7. What will be likely responses from various sources— inside and outside the organization—to the whistle-blowing action?
8. What is expected to be achieved by whistle-blowing in the particular situation?

. . . The decision to act and the answers to all of these questions are unique for every situation and for every individual. Presently, certitudes are the exception.

There is a great need to develop an ethic of whistle-blowing which can be practically applied in many contexts, especially within corporate and governmental bureaucracies. For this to occur, people must be permitted to cultivate their own form of allegiance to their fellow citizens and exercise it without having their professional careers or employment opportunities destroyed. This new ethic will develop if employees have the right to due process within their organizations and if they have at least some of the rights— such as the right to speak freely—that now protect them from state power. In the past . . . whistle-blowing has illuminated dark corners of our society, saved lives, prevented injuries and disease, and stopped corruption, economic waste, and material exploitation. Conversely, the absence of such professional and individual responsibility has perpetuated these conditions. In this context whistle-blowing, if carefully defined and protected by law, can become another of those adaptive, self-implementing mechanisms which mark the relative difference between a free society that relies on free institutions and a closed society that depends on authoritarian institutions.

Indeed, the basic status of a citizen in a democracy underscores the themes implicit in a form of professional and individual responsibility that places responsibility to society over that to an illegal or negligent or unjust organizational policy or activity. These themes touch the right of free

speech, the right to information, the citizen's right to participate in important public decisions, and the individual's
obligation to avoid complicity in harmful, fraudulent, or
corrupt activities. Obviously, as in the exercise of constitutional rights, abuses may occur. But this has long been
considered an acceptable risk of free speech within very
broad limits. . . .

    . . . The willingness and ability of insiders to blow the
whistle is the last line of defense ordinary citizens have
against the denial of their rights and the destruction of their
interests by secretive and powerful institutions. As organizations penetrate deeper and deeper into the lives of people—
from pollution to poverty to income erosion to privacy
invasion—more of their rights and interests are adversely
affected. This fact of contemporary life has generated an
ever greater moral imperative for employees to be reasonably protected in upholding such rights regardless of their
employers' policies. The corporation, the labor unions and
professional societies to which its employees belong, the
government in its capacity as employer, and the law must all
change or be changed to make protection of the responsible
whistle-blower possible.

    Each corporation should have a bill of rights for its em-
ployees and a system of internal appeals to guarantee these
rights. As a condition of employment, workers at every
level in the corporate hierarchy should have the right to
express their reservations about the company's activities and
policies, and their views should be accorded a fair hearing.
They should have the right to "go public," and the corporation should expect them to do so when internal channels of
communication are exhausted and the problem remains
uncorrected.

    Unions and professional societies should strengthen their
ethical codes—and adopt such codes if they do not already
have them. They should put teeth into mechanisms for
implementing their codes and require that they be observed
not only by members but also by organizations that employ
their members. Unions should move beyond the traditional
"bread and butter" issues, the societies should escape their
preoccupation with abstract professionalism, and both should

MANAGEMENT ETHICS

apply their significant potential power to protecting members who refuse to be automatons. Whistle-blowers who belong to labor unions have fared only slightly better than their unorganized counterparts, except when public opinion and the whistle-blower's fellow workers are sufficiently aroused. This is partly a result of the bureaucratized cooptation of many labor leaders by management and the suppression of rank and file dissent within the union or local. . . .

All areas of the law touching upon the employee-employer relationship should be reexamined with an eye to modifying substantially the old rule that an employer can discharge an employee for acts of conscience without regard to the damage done to the employee. Existing laws that regulate industry should be amended to include provisions protecting employees who cooperate with authorities. The concept of trade secrecy is now used by business and government alike to suppress information that the public has a substantial need to know. A sharp distinction must be drawn between individual privacy and corporate secrecy, and the law of trade secrecy is a good place to begin. The Freedom of Information Act, which purports to establish public access to all but the most sensitive information in the hands of the federal government, can become a toothless perversion because civil servants who release information in the spirit of the act are punished while those who suppress it are rewarded.

Whistle-blowing is encouraged actively by some laws and government administrators to assist in law enforcement. Under the recently rediscovered Refuse Act of 1899, for example, anyone who reports a polluter is entitled to one-half of any fine collected—even if the person making the report is an employee of the polluting company. And corporations constantly probe government agencies to locate whistle-blowers on their behalf. Consumers need routine mechanisms to encourage the increased flow of information that deals with health, safety, environmental hazards, corruption, and waste inside corporate and governmental institutions. Whistle-blowing can show the need for such systemic affirmations of the public's right to know. . . .

The rise in public consciousness among the young and

among minority groups has generated a sharper concept of duty among many citizens, recalling Alfred North Whitehead's dictum, "Duty arises from our potential control over the course of events." But loyalties do not end at the boundaries of an organization. "Just following orders," was an attitude that the United States military tribunals rejected in judging others after World War II at Nuremberg. And for those who set their behavior by the ethics of the great religions, with their universal golden rule, the right to appeal to a higher authority is the holiest of rights.

The whistle-blowing ethic is not new; it simply has to begin flowering responsibly in new fields where its harvests will benefit people as citizens and consumers. . . . The realistic tendency of such an internal check within General Motors or the Department of the Interior will be to assist traditional external checks to work more effectively in their statutory or market-defined missions in the public interest. . . .

However, the exercise of ethical whistle-blowing requires a broader, enabling environment for it to be effective. There must be those who listen and those whose potential or realized power can utilize the information for advancing justice. Thus, as with any democratic institutions, other links are necessary to secure the objective changes beyond the mere exposure of the abuses. The courts, professional and citizen groups, the media, the Congress, and honorable segments throughout our society are part of this enabling environment. They must comprehend that the tyranny of organizations, with their excessive security against accountability, must be prevented from trammeling a fortified conscience within their midst. Organizational power must be insecure to some degree if it is to be more responsible. A greater freedom of individual conviction within the organization can provide the needed deterrent—the creative insecurity which generates a more suitable climate of responsiveness to the public interest and public rights.

Whistle-Blowing: Its Moral Justification*

Gene G. James

To blow or not to blow the whistle on one's organization or coworkers. That is the question Gene James examines. He finds that a moral argument for whistle-blowing to protect the public safety can be logically made. This is in contrast to the contentions of Richard DeGeorge, that James cites in this article, and who claims that while whistle-blowing may be "morally permissible" in many cases, it is not always "morally obligatory." In other words, for DeGeorge, individuals in organizations need not feel absolutely obliged in every case to blow the whistle and become what he calls a "moral hero." James takes issue with such a position, especially in cases where harm or injury can be prevented. He itemizes the factors that a potential whistle-blower should contemplate and ends with a discussion of what organizations can do to change their cultures in ways that will prevent the need for whistle-blowing.

Introduction

Whistle-blowing may be defined as the attempt of an employee or former employee of an organization to disclose what he or she believes to be wrongdoing in or by the organization. Like blowing a whistle to call attention to a thief, whistle-blowing is an effort to make others aware of practices one considers illegal or immoral. If the wrongdoing is reported to someone higher in the organization, the

SOURCE: Reprinted with permission of the author

* This article is a substantial revision and expansion of an earlier article "In Defense of Whistle-Blowing" initially published in the first edition of *Business Ethics: Readings and Cases in Corporate Morality,* eds., Michael Hoffman and Jennifer Moore, and reprinted in a number of places. A much shorter edited version of the current article will appear in the second edition of the above work.

whistle-blowing may be said to be *internal*. If the wrongdoing is reported to outside individuals or groups, such as reporters, public interest groups, or regulatory agencies, the whistle-blowing is *external*. If the harm being reported is primarily harm to the whistle-blower alone, such as sexual harassment, the whistle-blowing may be said to be *personal*. If it is primarily harm to other people that is being reported, the whistle-blowing is *impersonal*. Most whistle-blowing is done by people currently employed by the organization on which they are blowing the whistle. However, people who have left an organization may also blow the whistle. The former may be referred to as *current* whistle-blowing, the latter as *alumni* whistle-blowing. If the whistle-blower discloses his or her identity, the whistle-blowing may be said to be *open*; if the whistle-blower's identity is not disclosed, the whistle-blowing is *anonymous*.

Whistle-blowers differ from muckrakers because the latter do not have any ties to the organizations whose wrongdoing they seek to disclose. Whistle-blowers also differ from informers and stool pigeons because the latter usually have self-interested reasons for their disclosures, such as obtaining prosecutorial immunity. The term *whistle-blower*, on the other hand, is usually used to refer to people who disclose wrongdoing for moral reasons. However, unless whistle-blowing is arbitrarily defined as disclosure of wrongdoing for moral reasons, the distinction cannot be a sharp one. Thus, although most whistle-blowers act for moral reasons, one cannot take for granted that their motives are praiseworthy.

The organization involved may be either private or public. It may also be either an organization for profit such as a commercial corporation or a nonprofit organization such as a philanthropic foundation. The public organizations that are the most frequent targets of whistle-blowing are, of course, government agencies, from the county or city level to the federal. Whistle-blowing at the federal level may concern either activities that involve national security or more ordinary activities such as waste, fraud, or permitting activities that are harmful to the public. Whistle-blowing that concerns national security usually involves agencies such as the National Security Council and the CIA, but it may

MANAGEMENT ETHICS

also involve private commercial firms such as defense contractors. This type of whistle-blowing raises a number of issues not raised by more ordinary whistle-blowing, in particular the issue of balancing the public's right to know against the need for secrecy. One major problem here is that appeal to secrecy and classification of information have frequently been used to hide illegal and immoral activities. Although some of the comments in this article apply to whistle-blowing involving national security, because it raises issues that are more complicated than whistle-blowing involving most commercial firms, or government agencies dealing with domestic matters, the present discussion is limited to whistle-blowing of the latter type.

Whistle-blowers almost always experience retaliation. If they work for private firms and are not protected by unions or professional organizations, they are likely to be fired. They are also likely to receive damaging letters of recommendation, and may even be blacklisted so that they cannot find work in their profession. If they are not fired, they are still likely to be transferred, given less interesting work, denied salary increases and promotions, or demoted. Their professional competence is usually attacked. They are said to be unqualified to judge, misinformed, etc. Since their actions may threaten both the organization and their fellow employees, attacks on their personal lives are also frequent. They are called traitors, rat finks, disgruntled, known troublemakers, people who make an issue out of nothing, self-serving, and publicity seekers. Their life-styles, sex lives, and mental stability may be questioned. Physical assaults, abuse of their families, and even murder are not unknown as retaliation to whistle-blowing.

Whistle-Blowing and The Law[1]

The law does not at present offer whistle-blowers very much protection. Agency law, the area of common law which governs relations between employees and employers, imposes a duty on employees to keep confidential any information learned through their employment that might be detrimental to their employers. However, this duty does not hold if the employee has knowledge that the employer either has committed or is about to commit a felony. In this case the employee has a positive obligation to report the offence. Failure to do so is known as misprision and makes one subject to criminal penalties.

One problem with agency law is that it is based on the assumption that unless there are statutes or agreements to the contrary, contracts between employees and employers can be terminated at will by either party. It therefore grants employers the right to discharge employees at any time for any reason or even for no reason at all. The result is that most employees who blow the whistle, even those who report felonies, are fired or suffer other retaliation. One employee of thirty years was even fired the day before his pension became effective for testifying under oath against his employer, without the courts doing anything to aid him.

This situation has begun to change somewhat in recent years. In *Pickering* v. *Board of Education* in 1968, the Supreme Court ruled that government employees have the right to speak out on policy issues affecting their agencies provided doing so does not seriously disrupt the agency. A number of similar decisions have followed and the right of government employees to speak out on policy issues now seems firmly established. But employees in private industry cannot criticize company policies without risking being fired. In one case involving both a union and a company doing a substantial portion of its business with the federal government, federal courts did award back pay to an employee fired for criticizing the union and the company, but did not reinstate or award him punitive damages.

A few state courts have begun to modify the right of employers to dismiss employees at will. Courts in Oregon and Pennsylvania have awarded damages to employees fired for serving on juries. A New Hampshire court granted damages to a woman fired for refusing to date her foreman. A West Virginia court reinstated a bank employee who reported illegal interest rates. The Illinois Supreme Court upheld the right of an employee to sue when fired for reporting and testifying about criminal activities of a fellow employee. However, a majority of states still uphold the right of employers to fire employees at will unless there are statutes or agreements to the contrary. To my knowledge only one state, Michigan, has passed a law prohibiting employers from retaliating against employees who report violations of local, state, or federal laws.

A number of federal statutes contain provisions intended to protect whistle-blowers. The National Labor Relations Act, Fair Labor Standards Act, Title VII of the 1964 Civil Rights Act, Age Discrimination Act, and the Occupational Safety and Health Act all have sections prohibiting employers from taking retaliatory actions against employees who report or testify about violations of the acts. Although these laws seem to encourage and protect whistle-blowers, to be effective they must be enforced. A 1976 study[2] of the Occupational Safety and Health Act showed that only about 20 percent of the 2,300 complaints filed in fiscal years 1975 and 1976 were judged valid by OSHA investigators. About half of these were settled out of court. Of the sixty cases taken to court at the time of the study in November 1976, one had been won, eight lost, and the others were still pending. A more recent study[3] showed that of the 3,100 violations reported in 1979, only 270 were settled out of court and only sixteen litigated.

Since the National Labor Relations Act guarantees the right of workers to organize and bargain collectively, and most collective-bargaining agreements contain a clause requiring employers to have just cause for discharging employees, these agreements would seem to offer some protection for whistle-blowers. In fact, however, arbitrators have tended to agree with employers that whistle-blowing is an act of disloyalty which disrupts business and injures the employer's reputation. Their attitude seems to be summed up in a 1972 case in which the arbitrator stated that one should not "bite the hand that feeds you and insist on staying for future banquets."[4] One reason for this attitude, pointed out by David Ewing, is that unions are frequently as corrupt as the organizations on which the whistle is being blown. Such unions, he says, "are not likely to feed a hawk that comes to prey in their own barnyard."[5] The record of professional societies is not any better. They have generally failed to come to the aid or defense of members who have attempted to live up to their codes of professional ethics by blowing the whistle on corrupt practices.

The Moral Justification of Whistle-Blowing

Under what conditions, if any, is whistle-blowing morally justified? Some people have argued that whistle-blowing is never justified because employees have absolute obligations of confidentiality and loyalty to the organization for which they work. People who argue this way see no difference between employees who reveal trade secrets by selling information to competitors, and whistle-blowers who disclose activities harmful to others.[6] This position is similar to another held by some business people and economists that the sole obligation of corporate executives is to make a profit for stockholders. If this were true, corporate executives would have no obligations to the public. However, no matter what one's special obligations, one is never exempt from the general obligations we have to our fellow human beings. One of the most fundamental of these obligations is to not cause avoidable harm to others. Corporate executives are no more exempt from this obligation than other people. Corporations in democratic societies are chartered with the expectation that they will function in ways that are compatible with the public interest. If they cease to behave this way, they violate the understanding on which they are based and may legitimately be penalized or even have their charters revoked. Corporations in democratic societies are also chartered with the expectation that they will not only obey the laws governing their activities, but will not do anything that undermines basic democratic processes, such as bribing public officials. In addition to having the obligation to make money for stockholders, corporate executives have the obligation to see that these expectations are complied with. They also have obligations to the company's employees, e.g., to maintain a safe working place. It is the failure of corporate executives to fulfill obligations of the types mentioned that creates the need for whistle-blowing.

Just as the special obligations of corporate executives to stockholders cannot override their more fundamental obligations to others, the special obligations of employees to employers cannot override their more fundamental obligations. In particular, obligations of confidentiality and loyalty cannot take precedence over the fundamental duty to act in ways that prevent unnecessary harm to others. Agreements to keep something secret have no moral standing unless that which is to be kept secret is itself morally justifiable. For example, no one can have an obligation to keep secret a conspiracy to murder someone, because murder is an immoral act. It is for this reason also that employees have a legal obligation to report an employer who has committed or is about to commit a felony. Although there are obvious differences between the situations of employees who work for government agencies and those who work for private firms, if we leave aside the special case in which national security is involved, then the same principles apply to both. The Code of Ethics of Government Service to which all government employees are expected to conform requires that employees put loyalty to moral principles and the national interest above loyalty to political parties or the agency for which they work. Nor can one justify participation in an illegal or immoral activity by arguing that one was merely following orders. Democratic governments repudiated this type of defense at Nuremberg.

It has also been argued that whistle-blowing is always justified because it is an exercise of the right to free speech. However, the right to free speech is not absolute. An example often used to illustrate this is that one does not have the right to shout "Fire" in a crowded theater because that is likely to cause a panic in which people may be injured. Analogously, one may have a right to speak out on a particular subject, in the sense that there are no contractual agreements which prohibit one from doing so, but it nevertheless may be the case that it would be morally wrong for one to do so because it would harm innocent people, such as one's fellow workers and stockholders who are not responsible for the wrongdoing being disclosed. The mere fact that one has the right to speak out does not mean that one ought to do so in every case. But this kind of consideration cannot create an absolute prohibition against whistle-blowing because one must weigh the harm to fellow workers and stockholders caused by the disclosure against the harm to others caused by allowing the organizational wrong to continue. Furthermore, the moral principle that one must consider all people's interests equally prohibits giving priority to one's own group. There is, in fact, justification for not giving as much weight to the interests of the stockholders as to those of the public, because stockholders investing in corporate firms do so with the knowledge that they undergo financial risk if management acts in imprudent, illegal, or immoral ways. Similarly, if the employees of a company know that it is engaged in illegal or immoral activities and do not take action, including whistle-blowing, to terminate the activities, then they too must bear some of the guilt for the actions. To the extent that these conditions hold, they nullify the principle that one ought to refrain from whistle-blowing because speaking out would cause harm to the organization. Unless it can be shown that the harm to fellow workers and stockholders would be *significantly greater* than the harm caused by the organizational wrongdoing, the obligation to avoid unnecessary harm to the public must take precedence. Moreover, as argued above, this is true even when there are specific agreements which prohibit one from speaking out, because such agreements are morally void if the organization is engaged in illegal or immoral activities. In that case one's obligation to the public overrides one's obligation to maintain secrecy.

If the foregoing arguments are sound, then neither the position that whistle-blowing is never justified because it involves violations of loyalty and confidentiality, nor the position that whistle-blowing is always right because it is an exercise of the right to free speech, is a morally justifiable position. The right to free speech confers a presumption in favor of whistle-blowing, making it a morally permissible action, unless: (a) one is bound by specific agreements to maintain secrecy, and (b) the harm resulting from the wrongdoing isn't great. If these two conditions hold, then one's right to free speech is overridden by the special agreement into which one has entered. Furthermore, even if the harm resulting from the wrongdoing is great, there may be situations in which one ought not blow the whistle because the harm from blowing the whistle would be even greater. However, these are special situations. In general, the fundamental obligation to prevent avoidable harm to others overrides special obligations of confidentiality and loyalty, creating an obligation to blow the whistle on illegal or immoral activities.

Criteria For Justifiable Whistle-Blowing

The argument in the foregoing section is an attempt to show that unless special circumstances hold, one has an obligation to blow the whistle on illegal or immoral actions—an obligation that is grounded on the fundamental human duty to avoid preventable harm to others. In this section I shall attempt to spell out in greater detail the conditions under which blowing the whistle is morally obligatory. Since Richard DeGeorge has previously attempted to do this, I shall proceed by examining the criteria he has suggested.[7]

DeGeorge believes there are three conditions that must hold for whistle-blowing to be morally permissible, and two additional conditions that must hold for it to be morally obligatory. The three conditions that must hold for it to be morally permissible are:

1. The firm, through its product or policy, will do serious and considerable harm to the public, whether in the person of the user of its product, an innocent bystander, or the general public.
2. Once an employee identifies a serious threat to the user of a product or to the general public, he or she should report it to his or her immediate superior and make his or her moral concern known. Unless he or she does so, the act of whistle-blowing is not clearly justifiable.
3. If one's immediate superior does nothing effective about the concern or complaint, the employee should exhaust

the internal procedures and possibilities within the firm. This usually will involve taking the matter up the managerial ladder, and, if necessary—and possible—to the board of directors.

The two additional conditions which DeGeorge thinks must hold for whistle-blowing to be morally obligatory are:

4. The whistle-blower must have, or have accessible, documented evidence that would convince a reasonable, impartial observer that one's view of the situation is correct, and that the company's product or practice poses a serious and likely danger to the public or to the user of the product.
5. The employee must have good reason to believe that by going public the necessary changes will be brought about. The chance of being successful must be worth the risk one takes and the danger to which one is exposed.[8]

One problem with these criteria is that they are intended to apply only to situations involving commercial firms. However, as pointed out above, if national security is not involved, then there are many similarities between the issues facing whistle-blowers in corporate settings and those facing them in governmental settings. Consequently, I shall treat the proposed criteria as if they were intended to cover all acts of whistle-blowing not involving national security. Some of the comments that follow may also be applicable to whistle-blowing involving national security, but it is not my intention to address this topic here.

DeGeorge intends for the proposed criteria to apply to situations in which a firm's policies or products cause physical harm to people. Indeed, the first criterion he proposes is intended to restrict the idea of harm even more narrowly to threats of serious bodily harm or death. He offers the following reasons in support of restricting the concept of harm in this way: (1) Non-physical harm, such as financial harm to one's interests as a result of fraud, seems to be quite different from physical harm. (2) To suffer non-physical harm is not as serious an injury as suffering physical harm.

For example, "An immoral practice that increases the cost of a product by a slight margin may do serious harm to no individual, even if the total amount when summed adds up to a large amount."[9] (3) "If the harm threatened by a product is slight or not certain, it might not be greater than the harm done to the firm [by the whistle-blowing]."[10] (4) Even if the policy or product does cause minor harm to the public, there may be routine procedures by which the harm can be eliminated. "The slight harm that is done, say, by the use of a product, can be corrected after the product is marketed (e.g., as a result of customer complaint)."[11]

DeGeorge apparently believes that situations which involve threats of serious bodily harm or death are so different from those involving other types of harm that the kind of considerations which justify whistle-blowing in the former situations could not possibly justify it in the latter. Thus, he says, referring to the former type of whistle-blowing: "We shall restrict our analysis to this type of whistle-blowing because, in the first place, the conditions that justify whistle-blowing vary according to the type of case at issue."[12] A few sentences later he adds: "As a paradigm, we shall take a set of fairly clear-cut cases, namely, those in which serious bodily harm—including possible death—threatens either the users of a product or innocent bystanders."[13]

One problem in restricting discussion to clear-cut cases of this type, regarding which one can get almost universal agreement that whistle-blowing is justifiable, is that it leaves us with no guidance when we are confronted with more usual situations involving other types of harm. Although DeGeorge states that his "analysis provides a model for dealing with other kinds of whistle-blowing as well,"[14] his criteria in fact provide no help in deciding whether one should blow the whistle in situations involving such wrongs as sexual harassment, violations of privacy, industrial espionage, insider trading, and a variety of other harmful actions. A second problem is that even if we were to restrict our attention to the type of situations DeGeorge suggests, his criteria are formulated in such a way that they cover only possible harm to users of a firm's products and the general public. He totally ignores, for example, possible harm to workers because of unsafe work practices.

No doubt, one of the reasons DeGeorge restricts his treatment the way he does is to avoid having to define harm. This is indeed a problem. For if we fail to put any limitations on the idea of harm, it seems to shade into the merely offensive or distasteful and thus offer little help in resolving moral problems. But, on the other hand, if we restrict harm to physical injury, as DeGeorge does, it then applies to such a limited range of cases that it is of minimal help in most of the moral situations which confront us. The only defensible way of dealing with this problem, in my opinion, is to first recognize that the notion of harm, like most moral concepts, is not amenable to precise definition. No matter how carefully we define it, borderline cases are likely to arise. However, this is precisely what we should expect. As Aristotle pointed out, it is the mark of an educated person not to look for more precision than a subject matter allows. The most difficult moral problems are frequently those in which we are confronted with shades of gray rather than black-and-white situations. This is not to say that we should not strive for as much precision as possible without arbitrarily limiting the situations taken into consideration. This can be done in the case of harm by correlating it with violations of fundamental human rights such as the rights to due process, privacy, and property, in addition to the right to freedom from physical harm. Thus, not only situations which involve threats of physical harm, but also those involving actions such as sexual harassment which violates the right to privacy and causes psychological harm, compiling unnecessary records on people, and financial harm due to fraudulent actions, are situations which may justify whistle-blowing. Correlating harm with the violation of fundamental human rights does not, of course, relieve us of the necessity to deal with borderline cases, since there is no way to avoid these in making moral decisions. But it does provide a guideline for helping decide when whistle-blowing is justified. Fortunately, the law recognizes that people may be harmed in a number of ways and makes most infractions of fundamental human rights illegal.

MANAGEMENT ETHICS

The fact that a company or agency is engaged in illegal actions is, therefore, always a prima facie reason for blowing the whistle, whether or not the action causes physical injury.

A still greater problem with DeGeorge's analysis is that even in cases where there is a threat of serious physical harm or death, he believes that this only makes whistle-blowing morally permissible, rather than creating a strong prima facie obligation in favor of whistle-blowing. His primary reasons for believing this seem to be those stated in criterion 5. Unless one has reason to believe that the whistle-blowing will eliminate the harm, and the cost to oneself is not too great, he does not believe whistle-blowing is morally obligatory. He maintains that this is true even when the person involved is a professional whose code of ethics requires her or him to put the public good ahead of private good. He argued in an earlier article, for example:

> The myth that ethics has no place in engineering has . . . at least in some corners of the engineering profession . . . been put to rest. Another myth, however, is emerging to take its place—the myth of the engineer as moral hero. . . . The zeal . . . however, has gone too far, piling moral responsibility upon moral responsibility on the shoulders of the engineer. This emphasis . . . is misplaced. Though engineers are members of a profession that holds public safety paramount, we cannot reasonably expect engineers to be willing to sacrifice their jobs each day for principle and to have a whistle ever at their sides.[15]

He contends that engineers have only the obligation "to do their jobs the best they can."[16] This includes reporting their concerns about the safety of products to management, but does *not* include "the obligation to insist that their perceptions or . . . standards be accepted. They are not paid to do that, they are not expected to do that, and they have no moral or ethical obligation to do that."[17] He also states that even though engineers are better qualified than other people to determine cost versus safety features of products, decisions about acceptable risk should be left to management. Under ideal conditions he thinks the public itself should make this kind of decision. "A panel of informed people, not necessarily engineers, should decide . . . acceptable risk and minimum standards."[18] This information should then be provided to consumers so they can decide whether they wish to buy the product.

To take a specific case, DeGeorge maintains that even though some Ford engineers had grave misgivings about the safety of Pinto gas tanks, and several people had been killed when tanks exploded after rear-end crashes, the engineers did not have an obligation to make their misgivings public. DeGeorge's remarks are puzzling because the Pinto case would seem to be exactly the kind of clear-cut situation which he says provides the paradigm for justified whistle-blowing. Indeed, if the Ford engineers did not have an obligation to blow the whistle, it is difficult to see what cases could satisfy his criteria. They knew that if Pintos were struck from the rear by vehicles traveling thirty miles per hour or more, their gas tanks were likely to explode, seriously injuring or killing people. They also knew that if they did not speak out, Ford would continue to market the Pinto. Finally, they were members of a profession whose code of ethics requires them to put public safety above all other obligations.

DeGeorge's remarks suggest that the only obligation the Ford engineers had was to do what management expected of them by complying with their job descriptions, and that so long as they did that no one should find fault with them or hold them accountable for what the company did. It is true that when people act within the framework of an organization, it is often difficult to assess individual responsibility. One reason for this is that organizational decisions are frequently the product of groups or committees rather than of individuals. Another is that because committee members often serve temporary terms, none of the people who helped make a particular decision may be members when it is implemented. Implementation is also likely to be the responsibility of others. Finally, even when decisions are made by individuals, they may have little control over the outcome. The result is frequently that no one feels responsible for the consequences of an organizational decision. Top management does not because it only formulates policy rather than implementing it. Those at the bottom and middle of the chain of authority do not because they merely implement it. If challenged to assume moral responsibility for their actions, those at the top respond that they never intended those consequences, while those at the bottom reply they were simply carrying out orders. But as DeGeorge points out, absence of the feeling of obligation does not mean absence of obligation. The fact that one is acting as a member of an organization does not relieve one of moral obligations. The exact opposite is true. Because most of the actions we undertake in organizational settings have more far-reaching consequences than those we undertake in our personal lives, our moral obligation to make sure that we do not harm others is *increased* when we act as a member of an organization. The amount of moral responsibility one has for any particular organizational action depends on the extent to which: (a) the consequences of the action are foreseeable, and (b) one's own action or failure to act is a cause of those consequences. It is important to include failure to act here, because frequently it is easier to determine what will happen if we do not act than if we do, and because we are morally responsible for not preventing harm as well as for causing it.

DeGeorge thinks that the Ford engineers would have had an obligation to blow the whistle only if they believed doing so would have been likely to prevent the harm involved. But we have an obligation to warn others of danger even if we believe they will ignore our warnings. This is especially true if the danger will come about partly because we did not speak out. DeGeorge admits that the public has a right to know about dangerous products. If that is true, then those who have knowledge about such products have an obligation to inform the public. This is not usurping the public's right to decide acceptable risk; it is simply supplying people with the information necessary to exercise that right.

DeGeorge's comments also seem to imply that in general it is not justifiable to ask people to blow the whistle if it would threaten their jobs. It is true that we would not necessarily be justified in demanding this if it would place them or their families' lives in danger. But this is not true if only their jobs are at stake. It is especially not true if the people involved are executives and professionals who are accorded respect and high salaries not only because of their specialized knowledge and skills, but also because of the special responsibilities we entrust to them. Frequently, as in the case of engineers, they also subscribe to codes of ethics which require them to put the public good ahead of their own or the organization's good. Given all this, it is difficult to understand why DeGeorge does not think the Ford engineers had an obligation to blow the whistle in the Pinto case.

Although DeGeorge rejects the view that loyalty to an organization creates an absolute prohibition against whistle-blowing, he believes that it is one of three factors which collectively create a presumption that it is not justified, so that the burden of justification always falls on the whistle-blower. The reasons he gives for loyalty creating a presumption against whistle-blowing are: (1) "There is a strong tradition within American mores against 'ratting,' or telling on others. We find this to be true of children . . . and . . . folk wisdom."[19] (2) The view of the vast majority of workers is, therefore, that the whistle-blower is a kind of traitor. (3) Workers owe a debt of gratitude to their company or organization for their job, "no small consideration in a society in which 4 percent unemployment is considered normal."[20] The second factor which he believes creates a presumption that whistle-blowing is not justified is that it may be seen as an act of disobedience. "Disobedience typically requires justification if it is to be considered moral—whether . . . civil disobedience, disobedience to the corporation, or a child's disobedience to its parents. Under the appropriate conditions, obedience is the expected and required moral way to act."[21] The third factor is that whistle-blowing is likely to harm the organization's reputation, subjecting it to bad publicity and possible investigation.

The fact that whistle-blowing harms the organization is one of the reasons DeGeorge believes that for it to be

MANAGEMENT ETHICS

justified it must disclose threats of serious bodily harm or death. It was argued above that this is far too narrow a criterion. The belief that whistle-blowing is an act of disloyalty and disobedience, on the other hand, seems to underlie his second and third criteria that for whistle-blowing to be justified, the whistle-blower must have first reported the wrongdoing to his or her immediate superior and, if nothing was done, taken the complaint as far up the managerial ladder as possible.

Some of the problems with adopting these suggestions as general criteria for justified whistle-blowing are: (1) It may be one's immediate supervisor who is responsible for the wrongdoing. (2) Organizations differ considerably in both their procedures for reporting, and how they respond to, wrongdoing. (3) Not all wrongdoing is of the same type. If the wrongdoing is of a type that threatens people's health or safety, exhausting channels of protest within the organization may result in unjustified delay in correcting the problem. (4) Exhausting internal channels of protest may give people time to destroy evidence needed to substantiate one's allegations. (5) Finally, it may expose the employee to possible retaliation, against which she or he might have some protection if the wrongdoing were reported to an external agency.

His fourth criterion, that the whistle-blower have documented evidence which would convince an impartial observer, is intended to reduce incidences of whistle-blowing by curbing those who would blow the whistle on a mere suspicion of wrongdoing. It is true that one should not make claims against an organization based on mere guesses or hunches, because if they turn out to be false one will have illegitimately harmed the organization and innocent people affiliated with it. But DeGeorge also wishes to curb whistle-blowing because he thinks that if it were widespread, that would reduce its effectiveness. He argues that "any condition that makes whistle-blowing mandatory in large numbers of cases may possibly reduce [its] . . . effectiveness. . . . If this were the result, and the practice were to become widespread, then it is doubtful that we would all be better off."[22] Another argument against the claim that "many people very often have the obligation to blow the whistle," in his opinion, is that it "goes against the common view of the whistleblower as a moral hero, and against the commonly held feeling that whistle-blowing is only rarely morally mandatory."[23] DeGeorge's fourth and fifth criteria are, therefore, deliberately formulated in such a way that if they are satisfied, "people will only rarely have the moral obligation to blow the whistle."[24]

DeGeorge's fear, that unless strict criteria of justification are applied to whistle-blowing it might become widespread, is unjustified. If it is true, as he himself claims, that there is a strong tradition in America against "ratting," that most workers consider themselves to have an obligation of loyalty to their organization, and that whistle-blowers are commonly looked upon as traitors, then it is unlikely that whistle-blowing will ever be a widespread practice. (The last statement that whistle-blowers are usually seen as traitors, incidentally, contradicts the one quoted in the preceding paragraph that they are commonly thought of as moral heroes.) However, there is a more basic reason that whistle-blowing will never become widespread. Workers usually have a feeling of loyalty to their organization according to DeGeorge. What is the basis of this feeling? DeGeorge gives the following answer to this question:

> In one view, loyalty is based appropriately on gratitude. . . . But even if the worker feels no gratitude, both the worker and the employer profit from their mutual contract. . . . The worker . . . has a stake in the firm for which he or she works. The stake is appropriately translated into positive concern for the firm, if not full identification with it—a concern that is in part what people mean by *loyalty*.[25]

In other words what people call loyalty to the organization is frequently merely self-interest, the very same factor that accounts for organization wrongdoing. Furthermore, contrary to DeGeorge, if the organization is engaged in wrongdoing, it is *not* morally appropriate for self-interest to be translated into loyalty to the organization. Indeed, even if it is genuine loyalty based on gratitude that makes a worker feel an obligation to the organization, as argued above, this cannot override one's obligation to blow the whistle on activities harmful to the public.

DeGeorge argues both: (1) whistle-blowing is not likely to be effective unless it is done by a previous loyal employee who blows the whistle publicly for moral reasons, and (2) if whistle-blowing is not likely to be effective, then it is not morally justified. He states, e.g., that for whistle-blowing to be effective the whistle-blower "must usually be willing to be identified, to testify publicly, to produce verifiable evidence, and to put oneself at risk."[26] He attempts to support this claim by drawing a parallel between the whistle-blower and the civil disobedient. "As with civil disobedience, what captures the conscience of others is the willingness of the whistle-blower to suffer harm for the benefit of others, and for what he or she thinks is right."[27] And he maintains that if a whistle-blower is "disaffected" from the organization for which she or he works, then the whistle-blowing is not likely to be taken seriously. Thus he thinks that it is necessary to determine the whistle-blower's motives before one can determine whether whistle-blowing is justified. He concedes that this may be difficult, but argues that it is a practical rather than a theoretical problem. "To sift out the claims and concerns of the disaffected worker from the genuine claims and concerns of the morally motivated employee is a practical problem. It may be claimed that this problem has nothing to do with the moral permissibility of the act of whistle-blowing; but whistle-blowing is a practical matter. If viewed as a technique for changing policy or actions, it will be justified only if effective."[28]

One problem with these claims is that they contradict his stipulation in criterion 5 that one does not have an obligation to blow the whistle if the personal cost is great. However, they also raise several other questions. Is it true that anonymous whistle-blowing is likely to be ineffective? If whistle-blowing is likely to be ineffective, is it morally unjustified? Is it necessary for the whistle-blower to testify openly for whistle-blowing to be justified? Or is anonymous whistle-blowing sometimes justified? Is it necessary that in addition to testifying openly, the whistle-blower must show a "willingness to suffer" in order for whistle-blowing to be either effective or morally justified? Does one need to determine the whistle-blower's motives in order to decide whether whistle-blowing is justified?

In my opinion, whenever anonymous whistle-blowing is ineffective, it is more likely to be due to lack of documentation than to its anonymity. It should not be forgotten, e.g., that one of the most effective and dramatic whistle-blowing incidents in recent years, Deep Throat's disclosure of Richard Nixon's betrayal of the American people, was an instance of anonymous whistle-blowing. Moreover, anonymity is a matter of degree. For whistle-blowing to be anonymous, the whistle-blower's identity does not have to be unknown to everyone, only to those on whom the whistle is blown and the general public. A few key investigators may know her or his identity.

The statement that for whistle-blowing to be morally justified, it must be probable that it will end the wrongdoing has already been responded to above, where it was argued that we have an obligation to warn others about possible harm even if we think they will ignore our warnings. One reason people may disregard warnings of danger is that whistle-blowers are sometimes unable to adequately document threats of harm. DeGeorge believes that if one is unable to document wrongdoing without recourse to illegal or immoral means, this relieves one of the obligation to blow the whistle. He argues:

> One does not have an obligation to blow the whistle simply because of one's hunch, guess, or personal assessment of possible danger, if supporting evidence and documentation are not available. One may, of course, have the obligation to attempt to get evidence if the harm is serious. But if it is unavailable—or unavailable without using illegal or immoral means—then one does not have the obligation to blow the whistle.[29]

I have already indicated above that I do not think one has an obligation to blow the whistle on possible wrongdoing on the basis of a mere guess or hunch because this might harm innocent people. But if one has good reason to believe that wrongdoing is occurring, even though one cannot document it without oneself engaging in illegal or immoral actions, this does not relieve one of the obligation to blow the whistle. Indeed, if this were true, one would almost never have an obligation to blow the whistle, because employees are rarely in a position to satisfy DeGeorge's fourth criterion that the whistle-blower "must have, or have accessible, documented evidence that would convince a reasonable, impartial observer that one's view of the situation is correct." Indeed, it is precisely because employees are rarely ever in a position to supply this type of documentation without themselves resorting to illegal or immoral actions that they have an obligation to inform others who have the authority to investigate the possible wrongdoing. The attempt to secure such evidence on one's own may even thwart the gathering of evidence by the proper authorities. Thus, instead of DeGeorge's criterion being a necessary condition for justifiable whistle-blowing, the attempt to satisfy it would prevent its occurrence. One has an obligation to gather as much evidence as one can so that authorities will have probable cause for investigation. But, if one is convinced that wrongdoing is occurring, one has an obligation to report it even if one is unable to adequately document it. One will have then done one's duty even if the authorities ignore the report.

The claim that it is usually necessary for the whistle-blower to speak out openly for whistle-blowing to be morally justified implies that anonymous whistle-blowing is rarely, if ever, justified. Is this true? It has been argued that anonymous whistle-blowing is never justified because it violates the right of people to face their accusers. But, as Frederick Elliston has pointed out, although people should be protected from false accusations it is not necessary for the identity of whistle-blowers to be known to accomplish this. "It is only necessary that accusations be properly investigated, proven true or false, and the results widely disseminated."[30]

Some people believe that because the whistle-blower's motive is not known in anonymous whistle-blowing, this suggests that the motive is not praiseworthy and in turn raises questions about the moral justification of anonymous whistle-blowing. DeGeorge apparently believes this, because in addition to stating that only public whistle-blowing by previously loyal employees who display their sincerity by their willingness to suffer is likely to be effective and morally justified, he mentions at several places that he is restricting his attention to whistle-blowing for moral reasons. He says, e.g., that "the only motivation for whistle-blowing we shall consider . . . is moral motivation."[31] However, in my opinion, concern with the whistle-blower's motive is irrelevant to the moral justification of whistle-blowing. It is a red herring which takes attention away from the genuine moral issue involved: whether the whistle-blower's claim that the organization is doing something harmful to others is true. If the claim is true, then the whistle-blowing is justified regardless of the motive. If the whistle-blower's motives are not moral, that makes the act less praiseworthy, but this is a totally different issue. As DeGeorge states, whistle-blowing is a "practical matter." But precisely because this is true, the justification of whistle-blowing turns on the truth or falsity of the disclosure, not on the motives of the whistle-blower. Anonymous whistle-blowing is justified because it can both protect the whistle-blower from unjust attacks and prevent those who are accused of wrongdoing to shift the issue away from their wrongdoing by engaging in an irrelevant ad hominem attack on the whistle-blower. Preoccupation with the whistle-blower's motives facilitates this type of irrelevant diversion. It is only if the accusations prove false or inaccurate that the motives of the whistle-blower have any moral relevance. For it is only then, and not before, that the whistle-blower rather than the organization should be put on trial.

The view that whistle-blowing is prima facie wrong because it goes against the tradition that "ratting" is wrong is indefensible because it falsely assumes both that we have a general obligation to not inform others about wrongdoing and that this outweighs our fundamental obligation to prevent harm to others. The belief that whistle-blowers should suffer in order to show their moral sincerity, on the other

MANAGEMENT ETHICS

hand, is not only false and irrelevant to the issue of the moral justification of whistle-blowing, but is perverse. There are *no* morally justifiable reasons a person who discloses wrongdoing should be put at risk or made to suffer. The contradictory view stated by DeGeorge that "one does not have an obligation to put oneself at serious risk without some compensating advantage to be gained,"[32] is also false. Sometimes doing one's duty requires one to undertake certain risks. However, both individuals and society in general should attempt to reduce these risks to the minimum. In the next section I consider some of the actions whistle-blowers can take to both make whistle-blowing effective and avoid unnecessary risk. In the last section I briefly consider some of the ways society can reduce the need for whistle-blowing.

Factors to Consider in Whistle-blowing

Since whistle-blowing usually involves conflicting moral obligations and a wide range of variables, and has far-reaching consequences for everyone concerned, the following is not intended as a recipe or how-to-do list. Like all complicated moral actions, whistle-blowing cannot be reduced to such a list. Nevertheless, some factors can be stated which whistle-blowers should take into consideration in disclosing wrongdoing if they are to also act prudently and effectively.

Make sure the situation is one that warrants whistle-blowing.
Make sure the situation is one that involves illegal or immoral actions which harm others, rather than one in which you would be disclosing personal matters, trade secrets, customer lists, or similar material. If the disclosure would involve the latter as well, make sure that the harm to be avoided is great enough to offset the harm from the latter.

Examine your motives.
Although it is not necessary for the whistle-blower's motives to be praiseworthy for whistle-blowing to be morally

justified, examining your motives can help in deciding whether the situation is one that warrants whistle-blowing.

Verify and document your information.

Try to obtain information that will stand up in regulatory hearings or court. If this is not possible, gather as much information as you can and indicate where and how additional information might be obtained. If the only way you could obtain either of these types of information would be through illegal procedures, make sure the situation is one in which the wrongdoing is so great that it warrants this risk. Although morality requires that in general we obey the law, it sometimes requires that we break it. Daniel Ellsberg's release of the Pentagon papers was a situation of this type in my opinion. If you do have to use illegal methods to obtain information, try to find alternative sources for any evidence you uncover so that it will not be challenged in legal hearings. Keep in mind also that if you use illegal methods to obtain information you are opening yourself to ad hominem attacks and possible prosecution. In general, illegal methods should be avoided unless substantial harm to others is involved.

Determine the type of wrongdoing involved and to whom it should be reported.

Determining the exact nature of the wrongdoing can help you both decide what kind of evidence to obtain and to whom it should be reported. For example, if the wrongdoing consists of illegal actions such as the submission of false test reports to government agencies, bribery of public officials, racial or sexual discrimination, violation of safety, health, or pollution laws, then determining the nature of the law being violated will help indicate which agencies have authority to enforce the law. If, on the other hand, the wrongdoing is not illegal but is nevertheless harmful to the public, determining this will help you decide whether you have an obligation to publicize the actions and if so how to go about it. The best place to report this type of wrongdoing is usually to a public-interest group. Such an organization is more likely than the press to: (1) be concerned about and

MANAGEMENT ETHICS

advise the whistle-blower how to avoid retaliation, (2) maintain confidentiality if that is desirable, (3) investigate the allegations to try to substantiate them, rather than sensationalizing them by turning the issue into a "personality dispute." If releasing information to the press is the best way to remedy the wrongdoing, the public-interest group can help with or do this.

State your allegations in an appropriate way.

Be as specific as possible without being unintelligible. If you are reporting a violation of law to a government agency, and if possible to do so, include technical data necessary for experts to verify the wrongdoing. If you are disclosing wrongdoing that does not require technical data to substantiate it, still be as specific as possible in stating the type of illegal or harmful activity involved, who is being harmed and how.

Stick to the facts.

Avoid name-calling, slander, and being drawn into a mud-slinging contest. As Peter Raven-Hansen wisely points out: "One of the most important points . . . is to focus on the disclosure. . . . This rule applies even when the whistle-blower believes that certain individuals are responsible. . . . The disclosure itself usually leaves a trail for others to follow the miscreants."[33] Sticking to the facts also helps the whistle-blower minimize retaliation.

Decide whether the whistle-blowing should be internal or external.

Familiarize yourself with all available internal channels for reporting wrongdoing and obtain as much data as you can both on how people who have used these channels were treated by the organization and what was done about the problems they reported. If people who have reported wrongdoing in the past have been treated fairly and the problems corrected, use internal channels. If not, find out which external agencies would be the most appropriate to contact. Try to find out also how these agencies have treated whistle-blowers, how much aid and protection they have given them, etc.

Decide whether the whistle-blowing should be open or anonymous.

If you intend to blow the whistle anonymously, decide whether partial or total anonymity is required. Also document the wrongdoing as thoroughly as possible. Finally, since anonymity may be difficult to preserve, anticipate what you will do if your identity becomes known.

Decide whether current or alumni whistle-blowing is required.

Sometimes it is advisable to resign one's position and obtain another before blowing the whistle. This is because alumni whistle-blowing helps protect one from being fired, receiving damaging letters of recommendation, or even being blacklisted in one's profession. However, changing jobs should not be thought of as an alternative to whistle-blowing. If one is aware of harmful practices, one has a moral obligation to try to do something about them, which cannot be escaped by changing one's job or location. Many times people who think the wrongdoing involved is personal, harming only them, respond to a situation by simply trying to remove themselves from it. They believe that "personal whistle-blowing is, in general, morally permitted but not morally required."[34] For example, a female student subjected to sexual harassment, and fearful that she will receive low grades and poor letters of recommendation if she complains, may simply change departments or schools. However, tendencies toward wrongdoing are rarely limited to specific victims. By not blowing the whistle the student allows a situation to exist in which other students are likely to be harassed also.

Make sure you follow proper guidelines in reporting the wrongdoing.

If you are not careful to follow any guidelines that have been established by organizations or external agencies for a particular type of whistle-blowing, including using the proper forms, meeting deadlines, etc., wrongdoers may escape detection or punishment because of "technicalities."

MANAGEMENT ETHICS

Consult a lawyer.

Lawyers are advisable at almost every stage of whistle-blowing. They can help determine if the wrongdoing violates the law, aid in documenting it, inform you of any laws you might break in documenting it, assist in deciding to whom to report it, make sure reports are filed correctly and promptly, and help protect you from retaliation. If you cannot afford a lawyer, talk with an appropriate public-interest group that may be able to help. However, lawyers frequently view problems within a narrow legal framework, and decisions to blow the whistle are moral decisions, so in the final analysis you will have to rely on your own judgment.

Anticipate and document retaliation.

Although not as certain as Newton's law of motion that for every action there is an equal reaction, whistle-blowers whose identities are known can expect retaliation. Furthermore, it may be difficult to keep one's identity secret. Thus whether the whistle-blowing is open or anonymous, personal or impersonal, internal or external, current or alumni, one should anticipate retaliation. One should, therefore, protect oneself by documenting every step of the whistle-blowing with letters, tape recordings of meetings, etc. Unless one does this, she or he may find that regulatory agencies and the courts are of little help in preventing or redressing retaliation.

Beyond Whistle-blowing

What can be done to eliminate the wrongdoing which gives rise to whistle-blowing? One solution would be to give whistle-blowers greater legal protection. Another would be to change the nature of organizations so as to diminish the need for whistle-blowing. These solutions are of course not mutually exclusive.

Many people are opposed to legislation to protect whistle-blowers because they think that it is unwarranted interference with the right to freedom of contract. However, if the right to freedom of contract is to be consistent with the public interest, it cannot serve as a shield for wrongdoing. It does this when threat of dismissal prevents people from blowing the whistle. The right of employers to dismiss at will has been previously restricted by labor laws which prevent employers from dismissing employees for union activities. It is ironic that we have restricted the right of employers to fire employees who are pursuing their economic self-interest, but allowed them to fire employees acting in the public interest. The right of employers to dismiss employees in the interest of efficiency should be balanced against the right of the public to know about illegal, dangerous, and unjust practices of organizations. The most effective way to achieve this goal would be to pass a federal law protecting whistle-blowers.

Laws protecting whistle-blowers have also been opposed on the grounds that: (1) employees would use them to mask poor performance, (2) they would create an "informer ethos," and (3) they would take away the autonomy of business, strangling it in red tape.

The first objection is illegitimate because only those employees who could show that an act of whistle-blowing preceded their being penalized or dismissed, and that their employment records were adequate up to the time of the whistle-blowing, could seek relief under the law.

The second objection is more formidable, but nevertheless invalid. A society that encourages snooping, suspicion, and mistrust does not conform to most people's idea of the good society. Laws which encourage whistle-blowing for self-interested reasons, such as the federal tax law which pays informers part of any money that is collected, could help bring about such a society.[35] However, laws protecting whistle-blowers from being penalized or dismissed are quite different. They do not reward the whistle-blower; they merely protect him or her from unjust retaliation. It is unlikely that state or federal laws of this type would promote an informer society.

The third objection is also unfounded. Laws protecting whistle-blowers would not require any positive duties on the part of organizations—only the negative duty of not retaliating against employees who speak out in the public interest.

MANAGEMENT ETHICS

However, not every act of apparent whistle-blowing should be protected. If (1) the whistle-blower's accusations turn out to be false and, (2) it can be shown that she or he had no probable reasons for assuming wrongdoing, then the individual should not be shielded from being penalized or dismissed. Both of these conditions should be satisfied before this is allowed to occur. People who can show that they had probable reasons for believing that wrongdoing existed should be protected even if their accusations turn out to be false. If the accusation has not been disproved, the burden of proof should be on the organization to prove that it is false. If it has been investigated and proven false, then the burden of proof should be on the individual to show that she or he had probable reasons for believing wrongdoing existed. If it is shown that the individual did not have probable reasons for believing wrongdoing existed, and the damage to the organization from the false charge is great, it should be allowed to sue or seek other restitution. Since these provisions would impose some risks on potential whistle-blowers, they would reduce the possibility of frivolous action. If, on the other hand, it is found that the whistle-blower had probable cause for the whistle-blowing and the organization has penalized or fired him or her, then that person should be reinstated, awarded damages, or both. If there is further retaliation, additional sizable damages should be awarded.

What changes could be made in organizations to prevent the need for whistle-blowing? Some of the suggestions which have been made are that organizations develop effective internal channels for reporting wrongdoing, reward people with salary increases and promotions for using these channels, and appoint senior executives, board members, ombudspersons, etc., whose primary obligations would be to investigate and eliminate organizational wrongdoing. These changes could be undertaken by organizations on their own or mandated by law. Other changes which might be mandated are requiring that certain kinds of records be kept, assessing larger fines for illegal actions, and making executives and other professionals personally liable for filing false reports, knowingly marketing dangerous products, failing to monitor how policies are being implemented, and so forth.

Although these reforms could do much to reduce the need for whistle-blowing, given human nature it is highly unlikely that this need can ever be totally eliminated. Therefore, it is important to have laws which protect whistle-blowers and for us to state as clearly as we can both the practical problems and moral issues pertaining to whistle-blowing.

NOTES

1. For discussion of the legal aspects of whistle-blowing see Lawrence E. Blades, "Employment at Will vs. Individual Freedom: On Limiting the Abusive Exercise of Employer Power," *Columbia Law Review*, vol. 67 (1967); Philip Blumberg, "Corporate Responsibility and the Employee's Duty of Loyalty and Obedience: A Preliminary Inquiry," *Oklahoma Law Review*, vol. 24 (1967); Clyde W. Summers, "Individual Protection Against Unjust Dismissal: Time for a Statute," *Virginia Law Review*, vol. 62 (1976); Arthur S. Miller, "Whistle Blowing and the Law," in Ralph Nader, Peter J. Petkas, and Kate Blackwell, *Whistle Blowing*, New York: Grossman Publishers, 1972; Alan F. Westin, *Whistle Blowing!*, New York: McGraw-Hill, 1981. See also vol. 16, no. 2, Winter 1983, *University of Michigan Journal of Law Reform*, special issue, "Individual Rights in the Workplace: The Employment-At-Will Issue."

2. For a discussion of this study which was conducted by Morton Corn, see Frank von Hipple, "Professional Freedom and Responsibility: The Role of the Professional Society," *Newsletter on Science, Technology and Human Values*, vol. 22, January 1978.

3. See Westin, op. cit.

4. See Martin H. Marlin, "Protecting the Whistleblower From Retaliatory Discharge," in the special issue of the *University of Michigan Journal of Law Reform*, op. cit.

5. David W. Ewing, *Freedom Inside the Organization*, New York: E. P. Dutton, 1977, pp. 165-66.

6. For a more detailed discussion of this argument, see Gene G. James, "Whistle Blowing: Its Nature and Justification," *Philosophy in Context*, vol. 10 (1980).

7. See Richard T. DeGeorge, 2nd ed., *Business Ethics*, New York: Macmillan, 1986. Earlier versions of DeGeorge's criteria can be found in the first edition (1982), and in "Ethical Responsibilities of Engineers in Large Organizations," *Business and Professional Ethics Journal*, vol. 1, no. 1, Fall 1981.

8. DeGeorge, *Business Ethics*, 2nd ed., pp. 230-34.

9. *Ibid.*, p. 223.

10. *Ibid.*, p. 230.

11. *Ibid.*

12. *Ibid.*, p. 223.

13. *Ibid.*

14. *Ibid.*, p. 237.

15. DeGeorge, "Ethical Reponsibilities of Engineers in Large Organizations," p. 1.

16. *Ibid.*, p. 5.

17. *Ibid.*

18. *Ibid.*, p. 7.
19. DeGeorge, *Business Ethics*, 2nd ed., p. 226.
20. *Ibid.*, p. 227.
21. *Ibid.*, p. 229.
22. *Ibid.*, p. 235.
23. *Ibid.*
24. *Ibid.*
25. *Ibid.*, p. 227.
26. *Ibid.*, p. 236.
27. *Ibid.*
28. *Ibid.*, p.231.
29. *Ibid.*, p. 234.
30. Frederick A. Elliston, "Anonymous Whistleblowing," *Business and Professional Ethics Journal*, vol. 1. no. 2, Winter 1982.
31. DeGeorge, *Business Ethics*, 2nd ed., p. 223.
32. *Ibid.*, p. 234.
33. Peter Raven-Hansen, "Dos and Dont's for Whistleblowers: Planning for Trouble," *Technology Review*, May 1980, p. 30. My discussion in this section is heavily indebted to this article.
34. DeGeorge, *Business Ethics*, 2nd ed., p. 222.
35. People who blow the whistle on tax evaders in fact rarely receive any money because the law leaves payment to the discretion of the Internal Revenue Service.

The Parable of the Sadhu

Bowen H. McCoy

While on a mountain-climbing expedition in the Himalayas, Bowen McCoy, a managing director of Morgan Stanley & Co., Inc., at the time, experienced a life-and-death situation that has had a lasting impact on his understanding of the moral obligation of individuals in corporate organizations. "The Parable of the Sadhu" recounts that experience and raises a host of ethical issues about values, solving moral dilemmas, the pressures of organizational life on ethical conduct, and the tensions managers face between personal morality and the morality of their corporation. The life-changing experience McCoy relates is the decision on the mountainside he and his international cadre of fellow climb-

SOURCE: Reprinted by permission of *Harvard Business Review*. "The Parable of the Sadhu," by Bowen H. McCoy, Vol. 61 (September/October 1983). Copyright © 1983 by the President and Fellows of Harvard College. All rights reserved.

ers had to make between offering help to an Indian holy man—the sadhu—whom they encountered on a perilous trail in a semiconscious state or continuing up the mountain to achieve a "once-in-a-lifetime" feat. McCoy's Himalayan experience prompts a serious consideration of a whole range of factors that supplies the backdrop for ethical managerial decision making and managerial responsibility. Moreover, he suggests that management ethics needs to be considered right alongside many of the more typical business considerations that define the functional responsibilities of those who lead our corporate institutions.

[In 1982], as the first participant in the new six-month sabbatical program that Morgan Stanley has adopted, I enjoyed a rare opportunity to collect my thoughts as well as do some traveling. I spent the first three months in Nepal, walking 600 miles through 200 villages in the Himalayas and climbing some 120,000 vertical feet. On the trip my sole Western companion was an anthropologist who shed light on the cultural patterns of the villages we passed through.

During the Nepal hike, something occurred that has had a powerful impact on my thinking about corporate ethics. Although some might argue that the experience has no relevance to business, it was a situation in which a basic ethical dilemma suddenly intruded into the lives of a group of individuals. How the group responded I think holds a lesson for all organizations no matter how defined.

The Sadhu

The Nepal experience was more rugged and adventuresome than I had anticipated. Most commercial treks last two or three weeks and cover a quarter of the distance we traveled.

My friend Stephen, the anthropologist, and I were halfway through the 60-day Himalayan part of the trip when we reached the high point, an 18,000-foot pass over a crest that we'd have to traverse to reach to the village of Muklinath, an ancient holy place for pilgrims.

Six years earlier I had suffered pulmonary edema, an acute form of altitude sickness, at 16,500 feet in the vicinity of Everest base camp, so we were understandably concerned about what would happen at 18,000 feet. Moreover, the Himalayas were having their wettest spring in 20 years; hip-deep powder and ice had already driven us off one ridge. If we failed to cross the pass, I feared that the last half of our "once in a lifetime" trip would be ruined.

The night before we would try the pass, we camped at a hut at 14,500 feet. In the photos taken at that camp, my face appears wan. The last village we'd passed through was a sturdy two-day walk below us, and I was tired.

During the late afternoon, four backpackers from New Zealand joined us, and we spent most of the night awake, anticipating the climb. Below we could see the fires of two other parties, which turned out to be two Swiss couples and a Japanese hiking club.

To get over the steep part of the climb before the sun melted the steps cut in the ice, we departed at 3:30 A.M. The New Zealanders left first, followed by Stephen and myself, our porters and Sherpas, and then the Swiss. The Japanese lingered in their camp. The sky was clear, and we were confident that no spring storm would erupt that day to close the pass.

At 15,500 feet, it looked to me as if Stephen were shuffling and staggering a bit, which are symptoms of altitude sickness. (The initial stage of altitude sickness brings a headache and nausea. As the condition worsens, a climber may encounter difficult breathing, disorientation, aphasia, and paralysis.) I felt strong, my adrenaline was flowing, but I was very concerned about my ultimate ability to get across. A couple of our porters were also suffering from the height, and Pasang, our Sherpa sirdar (leader), was worried.

Just after daybreak, while we rested at 15,500 feet, one of the New Zealanders, who had gone ahead, came staggering down toward us with a body slung across his shoulders. He dumped the almost naked, barefoot body of an Indian holy man—a sadhu—at my feet. He had found the pilgrim lying on the ice, shivering and suffering from hypothermia. I cradled the sadhu's head and laid him out on the rocks. The New Zealander was angry. He wanted to get across the pass before the bright sun melted the snow. He said, "Look, I've done what I can. You have porters and Sherpa guides. You care for him. We're going on!" He turned and went back up the mountain to join his friends.

I took a carotid pulse and found that the sadhu was still alive. We figured he had probably visited the holy shrines at Muklinath and was on his way home. It was fruitless to question why he had chosen this desperately high route instead of the safe, heavily traveled caravan route through the Kali Gandaki gorge. Or why he was almost naked and with no shoes, or how long he had been lying in the pass. The answers weren't going to solve our problem.

Stephen and the four Swiss began stripping off outer clothing and opening their packs. The sadhu was soon clothed from head to foot. He was not able to walk, but he was very much alive. I looked down the mountain and spotted below the Japanese climbers marching up with a horse.

Without a great deal of thought, I told Stephen and Pasang that I was concerned about withstanding the heights to come and wanted to get over the pass. I took off after several of our porters who had gone ahead.

On the steep part of the ascent where, if the ice steps had given way, I would have slid down about 3,000 feet, I felt vertigo. I stopped for a breather, allowing the Swiss to catch up with me. I inquired about the sadhu and Stephen. They said that the sadhu was fine and that Stephen was just behind. I set off again for the summit.

Stephen arrived at the summit an hour after I did. Still exhilarated by victory, I ran down the snow slope to congratulate him. He was suffering from altitude sickness, walking fifteen steps, then stopping, walking fifteen steps, then stopping. Pasang accompanied him all the way up. When I reached them, Stephen glared at me and said: "How do you feel about contributing to the death of a fellow man?"

I did not fully comprehend what he meant.

"Is the sadhu dead?" I inquired.

"No," replied Stephen, "but he surely will be!"

MANAGEMENT ETHICS

After I had gone, and the Swiss had departed not long after, Stephen had remained with the sadhu. When the Japanese had arrived, Stephen had asked to use their horse to transport the sadhu down to the hut. They had refused. He had then asked Pasang to have a group of our porters carry the sadhu. Pasang had resisted the idea, saying that the porters would have to exert all their energy to get themselves over the pass. He had thought they could not carry a man down 1,000 feet to the hut, reclimb the slope, and get across safely before the snow melted. Pasang had pressed Stephen not to delay any longer.

The Sherpas had carried the sadhu down to a rock in the sun at about 15,000 feet and had pointed out the hut another 500 feet below. The Japanese had given him food and drink. When they had last seen him he was listlessly throwing rocks at the Japanese party's dog, which had frightened him.

We do not know if the sadhu lived or died.

For many of the following days and evenings Stephen and I discussed and debated our behavior toward the sadhu. Stephen is a committed Quaker with deep moral vision. He said, "I feel that what happened with the sadhu is a good example of the breakdown between the individual ethic and the corporate ethic. No one person was willing to assume ultimate responsibility for the sadhu. Each was willing to do his bit just so long as it was not too inconvenient. When it got to be a bother, everyone just passed the buck to someone else and took off. Jesus was relevant to a more individualistic stage of society, but how do we interpret his teaching today in a world filled with large, impersonal organizations and groups?"

I defended the larger group, saying, "Look, we all cared. We all stopped and gave aid and comfort. Everyone did his bit. The New Zealander carried him down below the snow line. I took his pulse and suggested we treat him for hypothermia. You and the Swiss gave him clothing and got him warmed up. The Japanese gave him food and water. The Sherpas carried him down to the sun and pointed out the easy trail toward the hut. He was well enough to throw rocks at a dog. What more could we do?"

"You have just described the typical affluent Westerner's response to a problem. Throwing money—in this case food and sweaters—at it, but not solving the fundamentals!" Stephen retorted.

"What would satisfy you?" I said. "Here we are, a group of New Zealanders, Swiss, Americans, and Japanese who have never met before and who are at the apex of one of the most powerful experiences of our lives. Some years the pass is so bad no one gets over it. What right does an almost naked pilgrim who chooses the wrong trail have to disrupt our lives? Even the Sherpas had no interest in risking the trip to help him beyond a certain point."

Stephen calmly rebutted, "I wonder what the Sherpas would have done if the sadhu had been a well-dressed Nepali, or what the Japanese would have done if the sadhu had been a well-dressed Asian, or what you would have done, Buzz, if the sadhu had been a well-dressed Western woman?"

"Where, in your opinion," I asked instead, "is the limit of our responsibility in a situation like this? We had our own well-being to worry about. Our Sherpa guides were unwilling to jeopardize us or the porters for the sadhu. No one else on the mountain was willing to commit himself beyond certain self-imposed limits."

Stephen said, "As individual Christians or people with a Western ethical tradition, we can fulfill our obligations in such a situation only if (1) the sadhu dies in our care, (2) the sadhu demonstrates to us that he could undertake the two-day walk down to the village, or (3) we carry the sadhu for two days down to the village and convince someone there to care for him."

"Leaving the sadhu in the sun with food and clothing, while he demonstrated hand-eye coordination by throwing a rock at a dog, comes close to fulfilling items one and two," I answered. "And it wouldn't have made sense to take him to the village where the people appeared to be far less caring than the Sherpas, so the third condition is impractical. Are you really saying that, no matter what the implications, we should, at the drop of a hat, have changed our entire plan?"

The Individual vs. the Group Ethic

Despite my arguments, I felt and continue to feel guilt about the sadhu. I had literally walked through a classic moral dilemma without fully thinking through the consequences. My excuses for my actions include a high adrenaline flow, a superordinate goal, and a once-in-a-lifetime opportunity—factors in the usual corporate situation, especially when one is under stress.

Real moral dilemmas are ambiguous, and many of us hike right through them, unaware that they exist. When, usually after the fact, someone makes an issue of them, we tend to resent his or her bringing it up. Often, when the full import of what we have done (or not done) falls on us, we dig into a defensive position from which it is very difficult to emerge. In rare circumstances we may contemplate what we have done from inside a prison.

Had we mountaineers been free of physical and mental stress caused by the effort and the high altitude, we might have treated the sadhu differently. Yet isn't stress the real test of personal and corporate values? The instant decisions executives make under pressure reveal the most about personal and corporate character.

Among the many questions that occur to me when pondering my experience are: What are the practical limits of moral imagination and vision? Is there a collective or institutional ethic beyond the ethics of the individual? At what level of effort or commitment can one discharge one's ethical responsibilities?

Not every ethical dilemma has a right solution. Reasonable people often disagree; otherwise there would be no dilemma. In a business context, however, it is essential that managers agree on a process for dealing with dilemmas.

The sadhu experience offers an interesting parallel to business situations. An immediate response was mandatory. Failure to act was a decision in itself. Up on the mountain we could not resign and submit our résumés to a headhunter. In contrast to philosophy, business involves action and implementation—getting things done. Managers must come up with answers to problems based on what they see and what they allow to influence their decision-making processes. On the mountain, none of us but Stephen realized the true dimensions of the situation we were facing.

One of our problems was that as a group we had no process for developing a consensus. We had no sense of purpose or plan. The difficulties of dealing with the sadhu were so complex that no one person could handle it. Because it did not have a set of preconditions that could guide its action to an acceptable resolution, the group reacted instinctively as individuals. The cross-cultural nature of the group added a further layer of complexity. We had no leader with whom we could all identify and in whose purpose we believed. Only Stephen was willing to take charge, but he could not gain adequate support to care for the sadhu.

Some organizations do have a value system that transcends the personal values of the managers. Such values, which go beyond profitability, are usually revealed when the organization is under stress. People throughout the organization generally accept its values, which, because they are not presented as a rigid list of commandments, may be somewhat ambiguous. The stories people tell, rather than printed materials, transmit these conceptions of what is proper behavior.

For twenty years I have been exposed at senior levels to a variety of corporations and organizations. It is amazing how quickly an outsider can sense the tone and style of an organization and the degree of tolerated openness and freedom to challenge management.

Organizations that do not have a heritage of mutually accepted, shared values tend to become unhinged during stress, with each individual bailing out for himself. In the great takeover battles we have witnessed during past years, companies that had strong cultures drew the wagons around them and fought it out, while other companies saw executives, supported by their golden parachutes, bail out of the struggles.

Because corporations and their members are interdependent, for the corporation to be strong the members need to share a preconceived notion of what is correct behavior, a "business ethic," and think of it as a positive force, not a constraint.

As an investment banker I am continually warned by well-meaning lawyers, clients, and associates to be wary of conflicts of interest. Yet if I were to run away from every difficult situation, I wouldn't be an effective investment banker. I have to feel my way through conflicts. An effective manager can't run from risk either; he or she has to confront and deal with risk. To feel "safe" in doing this, managers need the guidelines of an agreed-on process and set of values within the organization.

After my three months in Nepal, I spent three months as an executive-in-residence at both Stanford Business School and the Center for Ethics and Social Policy at the Graduate Theological Union at Berkeley. These six months away from my job gave me time to assimilate twenty years of business experience. My thoughts turned often to the meaning of the leadership role in any large organization. Students at the seminary thought of themselves as antibusiness. But when I questioned them they agreed that they distrusted all large organizations, including the church. They perceived all large organizations as impersonal and opposed to individual values and needs. Yet we all know of organizations where people's values and beliefs are respected and their expressions encouraged. What makes the difference? Can we identify the difference and, as a result, manage more effectively?

The word "ethics" turns off many and confuses more. Yet the notions of shared values and an agreed-on process for dealing with adversity and change—what many people mean when they talk about corporate culture—seem to be at the heart of the ethical issue. People who are in touch with their own core beliefs and the beliefs of others and are sustained by them can be more comfortable living on the cutting edge. At times, taking a tough line or a decisive stand in a muddle of ambiguity is the only ethical thing to do. If a manager is indecisive and spends time trying to figure out the "good" thing to do, the enterprise may be lost.

Business ethics, then, has to do with the authenticity and integrity of the enterprise. To be ethical is to follow the business as well as the cultural goals of the corporation, its owners, its employees, and its customers. Those who cannot serve the corporate vision are not authentic business people and, therefore, are not ethical in the business sense.

At this stage of my own business experience I have a strong interest in organizational behavior. Sociologists are keenly studying what they call corporate stories, legends, and heroes as a way organizations have of transmitting the value system. Corporations such as Arco have even hired consultants to perform an audit of their corporate culture. In a company, the leader is the person who understands, interprets, and manages the corporate value system. Effective managers are then action-oriented people who resolve conflict, are tolerant of ambiguity, stress, and change, and have a strong sense of purpose for themselves and their organizations.

If all this is true, I wonder about the role of the professional manager who moves from company to company. How can he or she quickly absorb the values and culture of different organizations? Or is there, indeed, an art of management that is totally transportable? Assuming such fungible managers do exist, is it proper for them to manipulate the values of others?

What would have happened had Stephen and I carried the sadhu for two days back to the village and become involved with the villagers in his care? In four trips to Nepal my most interesting experiences occurred in 1975 when I lived in a Sherpa home in the Khumbu for five days recovering from altitude sickness. The high point of Stephen's trip was an invitation to participate in a family funeral ceremony in Manang. Neither experience had to do with climbing the high passes of the Himalayas. Why were we so reluctant to try the lower path, the ambiguous trail? Perhaps because we did not have a leader who could reveal the greater purpose of the trip to us.

Why didn't Stephen with his moral vision opt to take the sadhu under his personal care? The answer is because, in part, Stephen was hard-stressed physically himself, and because, in part, without some support system that involved our involuntary and episodic community on the mountain, it was beyond his individual capacity to do so.

MANAGEMENT ETHICS

I see the current interest in corporate culture and corporate value systems as a positive response to Stephen's pessimism about the decline of the role of the individual in large organizations. Individuals who operate from a thoughtful set of personal values provide the foundation for a corporate culture. A corporate tradition that encourages freedom of inquiry, supports personal values, and reinforces a focused sense of direction can fulfill the need for individuality along with the prosperity and success of the group. Without such corporate support, the individual is lost.

That is the lesson of the sadhu. In a complex corporate situation, the individual requires and deserves the support of the group. If people cannot find such support from their organization, they don't know how to act. If such support is forthcoming, a person has a stake in the success of the group, and can add much to the process of establishing and maintaining a corporate culture. It is management's challenge to be sensitive to individual needs, to shape them, and to direct and focus them for the benefit of the group as a whole.

For each of us the sadhu lives. Should we stop what we are doing and comfort him; or should we keep trudging up toward the high pass? Should I pause to help the derelict I pass on the street each night as I walk by the Yale Club en route to Grand Central Station? Am I his brother? What is the nature of our responsibility if we consider ourselves to be ethical persons? Perhaps it is to change the values of the group so that it can, with all its resources, take the other road.

CHAPTER 4

CORPORATE ETHICS

Introduction

While the last chapter dealt with the individual conduct and responsibilities of managers, this one deals with the organizational ethics of the corporation. While management ethics focuses on the ethical quality of decison making and the resulting actions of managers, corporate ethics examines the propriety of decision making and actions made by corporate entities. The former is thus individual, while the latter is collective in scope.

The collective actions of corporate entities come in a variety of forms. First, they may take place within internal policies and directives that give the organization its particular structure and culture. They define the way things are done within the firm; as such, these policies and directives can be evaluated from an ethical perspective. Are these policies and directives fair and just? Could they create circumstances that might lead to unethical action on the part of the organization's members? And do they espouse desirable values and belief systems worthy of an excellent corporate culture? These are typical of the questions that are posed from this perspective.

Corporate actions may also take the form of business strategies where the future directions of the firm are enunciated. Strategic plans about markets, products, cost reduction, and the use of existing facilities are examples of the kind of corporate action where ethical evaluations and considerations can be brought to bear. Indeed, it is in this realm of strategic business decision making where many of the essential issues of business ethics have often made their appearance.

One barometer of a corporation's practice of ethics can be seen in the strategic responses that are made in times of corporate crises. Crisis management and the way a firm handles imminent threats to their operations say much about the culture of a company. Take, for example, the 1989 response of Exxon Corporation in the wake of the nation's worst oil spill in Valdez, Alaska. Exxon has been roundly criticized for its apparent inaction in Valdez and for what many have called a lack of genuine concern for the disastrous environmental effects of this tragedy upon the fishing industry and natural wildlife in Prince William Sound. The conclusion is that not only had there been negligence that caused the accident and irresponsible planning in the event of such a spill, but also that responsible corporate behavior was not part of Exxon's crisis management immediately after the event.

Contrast this with the 1982 Johnson & Johnson Tylenol crisis. After learning that tampering with Tylenol had occurred in the Chicago area, leading to the death of several Tylenol users, Johnson & Johnson took the highly extraordinary and highly expensive step of recalling every single unsold bottle of Tylenol on the market in America. Their reaction was swift and decisive. Business commentators lauded this crisis management as a fine example of corporate responsibility. And in the end, Johnson & Johnson not only won back its market share but also increased it, at least in part thanks to their ethical concern for the health of the American public.

Other corporate strategies such as downsizings, plant closings, diversification, takeovers, and mergers are among those which have been given a great deal of attention and scrutiny both in the literature of business ethics and in the headlines of the nation's daily newspapers. In addition, decisions about marketing and advertising tactics, product lines, and capital allocations can be taken as more examples of corporate strategies that have ethical ramifications. The articles in this section first examine the internal structures and cultures of corporations; then the ethical dimensions of two kinds of strategic business decisions: advertising and the hostile takeover.

Robert Jackall looks at the issue of corporate culture and ethics from a unique perspective. Jackall suggests that there are various "rules-in-use" in the American corporate workplace that guide the business decisions of managers. These corporate rules differ markedly from personal ethical rules (the objective standards of behavior set by society) and are driven by the values of survival and success in business. In his revealing book, *Moral Mazes*, to which he refers as an "interpretive sociological account" of the occupational ethics of modern corporate bureaucracies, Jackall presents data to prove his thesis that corporate cultures enforce an unspoken ethos that requires managers to "bracket" social and personal morality, if they are to survive and succeed. His empirical work demonstrates that questionable conduct within business organizations is an accepted fact of life. Its eradication will be no easy task, given the ingrained organizational ethos that appears to condone and promote questionable behavior.

One way that many business organizations have attempted to address ethics within their corporate structure is by means of a code of business conduct. These business ethics codes contain provisions that are designed to advise, guide, and regulate behavior on the job. They usually include reference to such activities as conflicts of interest, proper use of company assets and property, safeguarding proprietary information, insider information, compliance with the law, maintaining a high standard of business conduct, and the like. But while corporations will often point to the existence of a code of ethics within their organization, critics have claimed that they merely serve as window dressing and that employees pay them but lip service.

In "A Different Look at Codes of Ethics" by Donald Robin and others, these same criticisms are made after an extensive examination of their contents. But where most critics have ended their analysis of corporate codes of ethics with the judgment that they are not worth the paper they are written on, this article suggests a fresh perspective and makes some interesting recommendations to the corporate community on ways in which their codes may become vital and living documents.

The theme that unethical corporate activities may be due to the very way in which corporations are structured is further developed by Manuel Velasquez in his "Corporate Ethics: Losing It, Having It, Getting It." Velasquez answers the question of why unethical behavior seems so prevalent in business with a thesis that such behavior is systemic in the sense that corporations have created systems and encourage practices that pressure people to do things they might not ordinarily do. Thus, if corporate ethics is a problem at the systemic level within the organization, then one needs to identify remedies that will "cure" the corporation of its "systemic ills." Velasquez makes several recommendations for such a cure by creating a new system within the corporate system that would institutionalize ethics and in turn create a valuable new asset for the corporation.

The final two selections can be taken as individual studies of two separate issues in corporate ethics: namely, advertising and the corporate-merger phenomenon. In "Advertising and Corporate Ethics," Vincent Barry examines the extent to which corporations engage in questionable practices by means of the advertising they use to publicize their consumer goods or services. Barry demonstrates the ways in which ambiguity, concealed facts, exaggeration, and psychological appeals make their way into advertising and the impacts they can have on consumers. His main thrust is to suggest that morality and ethics are matters that many corporations seem willing to discard in their ads, as long as their persuasive functions are successful and the consumer buys the product or service. As Barry's article demonstrates, advertising can be an ethically problematic area for corporations whose values accent profitability over honesty and fairness in consumer communications.

For some business ethicists, advertising is one of the most crucial issues in corporate ethics because of its pervasiveness and because of its power to mold consumer thinking and behavior. For example, many have argued that advertising is a form of behavior control, given its subtle psychological persuasion and its repetitiveness. One such argument holds that advertising creates in the mind of the consumer a need— not just a want—for that which is advertised. By making the consumer feel dependent upon the product or service so advertised, their freedom of choice in the matter of consumption appears to be constrained, and as such, advertising becomes tantamount to propaganda. And when the consumer in question happens to be a child subjected to a barrage of TV ads about toys, sugared cereals, candy, and so on, then the ethics of advertising taken as a form of behavior control is even more crucial.

In their essay titled "The Ethical Side of Takeovers and Mergers," Robert Allan Cooke and Earl Young delve into many questions about the propriety of the current rage of merger mania and hostile takeover attempts. This is the well publicized arena where raiders meet white knights, executives don golden parachutes while offering the raiders greenmail (a kind of bribe to make a raider go away) and their shareholders poison pills, and where junk bonds are more likely to be found than hard-earned cash. This Alice in Wonderland realm of mergers and takeovers may have many profitable payoffs for the central actors in the transactions, but for many others, takeovers and mergers mean trouble and hardship. Cooke and Young recommend that the ethics of takeovers and mergers can be evaluated by means of a "stakeholder analysis." Who has a stake in the takeover and merger "game" and how will those who have such a stake be affected? Are there those who will be unnecessarily harmed in a business consolidation? How can business executives who are contemplating mergers and takeovers, whether friendly or not, incorporate ethics within their operational decision making throughout the various stages along the way to takeover or merger? These are among the important themes Cooke and Young develop.

Business as a Social and Moral Terrain

Robert Jackall

Robert Jackall's *Moral Mazes* is a sociological study of how corporate bureaucracy shapes the moral consciousness of managers. Through interviews with managers responsible for the day-to-day operations of a firm, Jackall was able to uncover what he calls the "rules for survival and success" within the contemporary corporation. "Business as a Social and Moral Terrain," reprinted here, is the introductory chapter to his book. Jackson sought to find those "evaluative rules" managers use to guide their work relationships with superiors, subordinates, and peers—as well as with those with whom they have contact who are not part of their organization. He seeks to measure the extent to which these rules are determined by the corporation, its culture, and its bureaucracy. His is thus a work in "descriptive ethics" in the sense that it does not offer rules that should be obeyed in business (as is the case in "prescriptive ethics"). Rather, Jackall provides his reader with an empirical description of how corporate morality is really established in an objective, noncritical light. What Jackall uncovers as the "rules-in-use" in corporate organizations are highly contextual and situational moral guidelines that managers divorce from their own personal set of moral beliefs. Consequently the world of work can be seen as a realm where everyday morality has no place except to serve the interests of public relations.

Corporate leaders often tell their charges that hard work will lead to success. Indeed, this theory of reward being commensurate with effort has been an enduring belief and a moral imperative in our society, one central to our self-

---

image as a people, where the main chance is available to anyone of ability who has the gumption and persistence to seize it. Hard work, it is also frequently asserted, builds character. This notion carries less conviction because business people, and our society as a whole, have little patience with those who, even though they work hard, make a habit of finishing out of the money. In the end, it is success that matters, that legitimates striving, and that makes work worthwhile. What if, however, men and women in the corporation no longer see success as necessarily connected to hard work? What becomes of the social morality of the corporation —the everyday rules-in-use that people play by—when there is thought to be no fixed or, one might say, objective standard of excellence to explain how and why winners are separated from also-rans, how and why some people succeed and others fail? What rules do people fashion to interact with one another when they feel that, instead of ability, talent, and dedicated service to an organization, politics, adroit talk, luck, connections, and self-promotion are the real sorters of people into sheep and goats?

This is one important puzzle that confronted me. I went into . . . organizations to study how bureaucracy—the prevailing organizational form of our society—shapes moral consciousness. I stayed to study managers' rules for survival and success in the corporation because these goals proved to be uppermost in their minds. I suggest . . . that managers' rules for survival and success are at the heart of what might be called the bureaucratic ethic, a moral code that guides managers through all the dilemmas and vicissitudes that confront them in the big organization.

This book analyzes the occupational ethics of corporate managers. By occupational ethics, I mean the moral rules-in-use that managers construct to guide their behavior at work, whether these are shaped directly by authority relationships or by other kinds of experiences typical in big organizations. I refer here to experiences such as the deep anxiety created by organizational upheavals that jumble career plans, or the troubling animosity generated by intense rivalries that pit managers against one another in struggles for prestige and say-so, or the emotional aridity caused by continually honing one's self to make hard choices with ambiguous outcomes.

As they are popularly used, of course, the notions of morality and ethics have a decidedly prescriptive, indeed moralistic, flavor. They are often rooted in religious doctrines or vague cultural remnants of religious beliefs, like the admonition to follow the Golden Rule. However, this book treats ethics and morality sociologically, that is, as empirical, objective realities to be investigated. Therefore, in using the terms morality and ethics, I do not refer to any specific or given, much less absolute, system of norms and underlying beliefs. Moreover, I imply no judgment about the actions I describe from some fixed, absolute ethical or moral stance, as the terms are often used in popular discourse, sometimes even by corporate managers themselves.

I mean to explore rather the actual evaluative rules that managers fashion and follow in their work world, the rules that govern their stances toward and interaction with their superiors, subordinates, and peers; their friends, allies, and rivals; their business customers and competitors; regulators and legislators; the media; and the specific publics they address and the public at large. I examine, as well, the particular conceptions of right and wrong, of proper and improper, that underpin those rules. Even more specifically, I analyze how the work that managers do and, in particular, how the social and bureaucratic context of their work—the warp across which the threads of their careers are stretched—shape their occupational moralities. In this sense, the book is also a sociology of the peculiar form of bureaucracy dominant in American business.

As it happens, the field of business ethics is rapidly becoming big business. Among other developments, the last fifteen years have seen the proliferation of a great number of books and articles on ethical problems in business;[1] the emergence of several centers and institutes at least partly dedicated to the subject or to related problems like the role of values in scientific, technological, or public policy work;[2] the spread of business ethics courses in both college and business school curricula;[3] and even, in some corporations, the development of seminars in ethics for executives. This

groundswell of attention to ethical issues in business continues a historical tradition that in different forms dates at least
to the turn of this century, when the corporation became a
paramount institution in our society.[4] The current upsurge
in concern over ethics was prompted undoubtedly by the
Watergate crisis and its spillover into business. It has been
stimulated more recently by a series of corporate and governmental scandals headed by revelations about insider trading on the stock market and by glimpses of high federal
officials illegally diverting funds and systematically deceiving
Congress and the public during the Iran-contra affair. At
the same time, the accelerating pace of scientific and technological change that continually overturns taken for granted
notions about our universe has prompted widespread discussions of ethical issues. All of this has been a boon to moral
philosophers, normally a precariously positioned occupational group in a social order where the mantle of intellectual supremacy has long since passed from a discipline once
called the queen of the sciences. With the titles of "ethicist"
or even "ethician," moral philosophers have applied their
considerable mental acumen to unraveling the conundrums
of the fast-paced, hurly-burly worlds of commerce and industry or more sedate scientific milieux. In doing so, they
have extended in quite new directions the much longer
tradition of moral casuistry, that is, the process of applying
general principles to specific situations in order to resolve
moral quandaries, an art that may involve the invention of
wholly new rules and legitimations for action.[5] Unfortunately,
most of this analysis has been of hypothetical cases, of
real-life situations abstracted from their intricate organizational contexts, of public testimony before various commissions and hearings by officials who, as it happens, are
well-versed in fencing with their adversaries, or of the jour-
nalistic accounts of the many highly publicized corporate
scandals in recent years. In fact, certain vocabularies have
become so institutionalized in some philosophical circles that
whole sets of assumptions and taken-for-granted analyses,
often complete with settled moral judgments, are often in-
voked simply by cryptic references to, say, the "Pinto Case"
or the "Dalkon Shield Affair." Despite the emergence of a

new industry that one might call Ethics Inc., however, the philosophers at least have done little detailed investigation of the day-to-day operations, structure, and meaning of work in business and of how the conditions of that work shape moral consciousness.

But only an understanding of how men and women in business actually experience their work enables one to grasp its moral salience for them. Bureaucratic work shapes people's consciousness in decisive ways. Among other things, it regularizes people's experiences of time and indeed routinizes their lives by engaging them on a daily basis in rational, socially approved, purposive action; it brings them into daily proximity with and subordination to authority, creating in the process upward-looking stances that have decisive social and psychological consequences; it places a premium on a functionally rational, pragmatic habit of mind that seeks specific goals; and it creates subtle measures of prestige and an elaborate status hierarchy that, in addition to fostering an intense competition for status, also makes the rules, procedures, social contexts, and protocol of an organization paramount psychological and behavioral guides. In fact, bureaucratic contexts typically bring together men and women who initially have little in common with each other except the impersonal framework of their organizations. Indeed, the enduring genius of the organizational form is that it allows individuals to retain bewilderingly diverse private motives and meanings for action as long as they adhere publicly to agreed-upon rules. Even the personal relationships that men and women in bureaucracies do subsequently fashion together are, for the most part, governed by explicit or implicit organizational rules, procedures, and protocol. As a result, bureaucratic work causes people to bracket, while at work, the moralities that they might hold outside the workplace or that they might adhere to privately and to follow instead the prevailing morality of their particular organizational situation. As a former vice-president of a large firm says: "What is right in the corporation is not what is right in a man's home or in his church. *What is right in the corporation is what the guy above you wants from you. That's what morality is in the corporation.*" Of course, since public legitimacy and respectability depend, in part, on perceptions of one's moral probity, one cannot admit to such a bracketing of one's conventional moralities except, usually indirectly, within one's managerial circles where such verities are widely recognized to be inapplicable except as public relations stances. In fact, though managers usually think of it as separate from decision making, public relations is an extremely important facet of managerial work, one that often requires the employment of practitioners with special expertise.

Managers do not generally discuss ethics, morality, or moral rules-in-use in a direct way with each other, except perhaps in seminars organized by ethicists. Such seminars, however, are unusual and, when they do occur, are often strained, artificial, and often confusing even to managers since they frequently become occasions for the solemn public invocation, particularly by high-ranking managers, of conventional moralities and traditional shibboleths. What matters on a day-to-day basis are the moral rules-in-use fashioned within the personal and structural constraints of one's organization. As it happens, these rules may vary sharply depending on various factors, such as proximity to the market, line or staff responsibilities, or one's position in a hierarchy. Actual organizational moralities are thus contextual, situational, highly specific, and, most often, unarticulated.

NOTES

1. For a comprehensive listing of these works, see Donald G. Jones, *A Bibliography of Business Ethics, 1971–1975* (Charlottesville, Va.: University Press of Virginia, 1977); and Donald G. Jones and Helen Troy, eds., *A Bibliography of Business Ethics, 1976–1980* (Charlottesville, Va.: University Press of Virginia, 1982).

2. These include the Center for the Study of Applied Ethics at the Darden Graduate Business School, University of Virginia; the Center for the Study of Values at the University of Delaware; the Center for Business Ethics at Bentley College; the Center for the Study of Ethics in the Professions at the Illinois Institute of Technology; the Center for Applied Philosophy at the University of Florida; and the Center for Public Philosophy at the University of Maryland. A comprehensive list of such centers is available from the Ethics Resource Center, 1025 Connecticut Avenue, N.W., Suite 1003, Washington, D.C. 20036.

3. See, for instance, the *Report of the Committee for Education in Business Ethics* sponsored by the National Endowment for the Humanities (Skokie, Ill.: Fel-Pro Incorporated, 1980); Charles W. Powers and David Vogel, *Ethics in the Education of Business Managers* (Hastings-on-Hudson, N.Y.: The Hastings Center, 1980); and Opinion Research Corporation, *Codes of Ethics in Corporations and Trade Associations and the Teaching of Ethics in Graduate Business Schools,* a survey conducted for the Ethics Resource Center (Princeton, N.J.: Opinion Research Corporation, June 1979). Sixteen percent of graduate schools of business responding to this survey (57 out of 134 schools, or 43 percent) offered a separate course in ethics; almost all claimed that ethics was included in other courses. In early 1987, the Harvard Business School received a gift of $30 million to support a program on ethics in its curriculum. Most of the gift came from John S. R. Shad, the outgoing chairman of the Securities and Exchange Commission. See Alison Leigh Cowan, "Harvard to Get $30 Million Ethics Gift," *The New York Times,* Tuesday, March 31, 1987, D1, cols. 3–5 and D8, cols. 5, 6. According to the article, one purpose of the gift was to help the Harvard Business School ". . . forge a weapon to curb abuses on Wall Street."

4. For a useful listing of some of the main works in this tradition going back to 1900, see Portia Christian with Richard Hicks, *Ethics in Business Conduct: Selected References from the Record—Problems, Attempted Solutions, Ethics in Business Education* (Detroit, Mich.: Gale Research Company, 1970).

5. Wherever there are human moral quandaries, there is, of course, casuistry; it is as ancient as human thought itself. For two fine summaries of the main historical developments in moral casuistry, see R. M. Wenley, "Casuistry," *Encyclopedia of Religion and Ethics,* Vol. 3 (Edinburgh: T. T. Clark, 1910), pp. 239–247; and Benjamin Nelson, "Casuistry," *Encyclopedia Britannica,* Vol. 5 (1973 edition), pp. 51–52.

A Different Look at Codes of Ethics

Donald Robin, Michael Giallourakis, Fred R. David, and Thomas E. Moritz

Corporate codes of ethics have been praised as excellent mechanisms to enforce ethical behavior in business. They are lauded as highly useful guidelines to assist the members of the organization in determining the ethically right course of action, in conducting themselves aboveboard, and in furthering the shared values and beliefs of the corporate culture. Nevertheless, these codes also have been lambasted as

SOURCE: Reprinted from *Business Horizons* (January/February 1989). Copyright © 1989 by the Foundation for the School of Business at Indiana University. Used with permission.

being actually unrelated to ethics (broadly defined), useless in enforcing acceptable forms of corporate conduct, and serving only as window dressing for more serious problems that the corporation has been slow to address. The four authors of "A Different Look at Codes of Ethics" attempt to plot a middle ground between these two views of the efficacy of corporate codes. They test the relationship of the content of a corporation's code of ethics to the prevailing ethical theories of utilitarianism and deontology (both of these theoretical positions are defined in the article). After surveying the various expectations that managers have of codes of ethics, they recommend that such codes can be improved by including the core values of the corporation so that these documents—the codes—might become a living statement of the corporation's culture.

Organizational codes of ethics are: 1. very different; 2. often similar; 3. not connected with ethics; 4. perceived as an important tool for fostering ethical conduct; and 5. not very effective in a broad ethical sense. A welter of contradictions? Indeed, all of the above statements are true—and this fact makes an analysis of ethical codes extremely difficult. However, in order to understand why codes are not very effective (point five), we must be able to analyze them. And in order to perform any kind of analysis, we must deal with points one through four.

Point one frustrates the analysis of ethical codes because the differences seem to prevent us from classifying the items found in them. We are then faced with the problem of analyzing codes one at a time, which reduces our ability to offer any general means of improvement. Point two, however, offers some hope. If there are any important similarities, they can form a basis for our grouping activities. With clusters of code items to analyze, we can: make statements about their ethical content (point three); attempt to determine why they haven't been very effective (point five); and suggest what might be done to improve them. If codes were not used by organizations as important tools for fostering ethical conduct (point four), none of this discussion would be interesting or important. But businesses do seem to perceive them in that way.

One of the similarities among the codes is their tendency to be legalistic. The first title in Motorola's summary of their "Code of Conduct" is "Improper Use of Company Funds and Assets," with the following two entries:

> 1. The funds and assets of Motorola may not be used for influential gifts, illegal payments of any kind or political contributions whether legal or illegal.
> 2. The funds and assets of Motorola must be properly and accurately recorded on the books and records of Motorola.

Under "Dealings with Distributors or Agents," one finds, "Motorola shall not enter into any agreements with dealers, distributors, agents or consultants which are not in compliance with U.S. laws and the laws of any other country that may be involved; or which provide for the payment of a commission or fee that is not commensurate with the services to be rendered." The other two titles, "Customer/ Supplier/Government Relationships" and "Conflict of Interest," contain similar legalistic statements, all of the form "Thou shall . . ." or "Thou shall not . . ." Motorola's approach is far from unique. It appears in almost every code that we studied.

The headings in the code of the Coca-Cola Company are also narrow and legalistic, but they can be compared to Motorola's code as an example of the *differences* that occur between code items from various companies. The Coca-Cola "Code of Business Conduct" contains nine, rather than Motorola's four, major headings. These titles include, among others: "General," which begins: "The Company, its employees and agents shall comply with all applicable legal requirements . . ."; "Political Campaign Contributions"; "Payments, Gifts and Entertainment Involving Customers and Suppliers"; "Accuracy and Completeness of Company Books and Records"; and "Business Conduct Inquiries." While Coca-Cola's code is different from Motorola's in important ways, there are several similarities in the *content* of these two codes. For example, the use and recording of company funds and dealings with persons outside the firm appear in both codes. Thus, although substantive differences existed between codes, important similarities in their character and content also could be discerned.

In order to use the similarities in the codes as the basis for analysis, some form of classification was necessary. Classification involves the division of items into groups that are homogeneous with respect to some criteria. There are two approaches to classification, both of which are used in this study. With groups established, it becomes possible to suggest what characteristics of codes aren't working, why they aren't working, and what might be done to improve them.

Organization of Code by Category

In a survey of the organizations appearing in the *Business Week* 1000, firms were asked for a copy of their code of ethics, if one existed. They returned 84 codes, while 168 responses to a separate and additional questionnaire were also received. The difference in the two figures is due to either the nonexistence of a code or the company's unwillingness to send one to the authors. The 84 codes came from some of the largest service and manufacturing organizations in the United States.

A two-step process was developed to provide an initial grouping of the code items. The first step used the personal judgment of two reviewers to evaluate the items listed and group them under broader, more descriptive headings where appropriate. The second step involved a third reviewer to test the results of the first two. The lists generated by these reviewers were then compared and titles composed for the groupings. The final list contains 30 categories.

It was also desirable to statistically group the 30 categories based on their usage by the different companies. Three clusters of items from codes of ethics resulted from this analysis, accounting for 24 of the 30 categories. **Table 1** is a presentation of all 30 categories with suggested labels for the clusters.

Ethical Tools to Evaluate Clusters

To assess the clusters, we must first define the tools of evaluation. The most important of these tools is philosophical ethics. Philosophers have been struggling for centuries to provide us with approaches for defining right and wrong. Unfortunately, philosophical ethics is often viewed as non-specific in character by people who aren't familiar with it. However, the discipline actually offers very specific advice about how to behave ethically. The study of ethics existed long before the business disciplines were formally developed; over that time period it has generated several philosophies that can be used to direct our behavior. These philosophies are similar to those in economics in that they sometimes disagree over the approach that should be used to solve a problem. Nevertheless, like the economic philosophies, the ethical philosophies can provide us with considerable guidance.

Of the several ethical philosophies that have been developed, two major traditions currently dominate the literature—deontology and utilitarianism. Deontology is probably favored over utilitarianism by moral philosophers today, although both are popular. Many of the attacks on business come from a deontological tradition, but utilitarianism has historically been used to provide most of the ethical justification for the modern economic systems found in capitalistic democracies. Each philosophy is briefly described in the following sections.

Deontology

This branch of moral philosophy focuses on universal statements of right and wrong, concerning the duties and rights of individuals. The most telling criticism of deontology is that exceptions to universal statements can almost always be found. Some deontologists have dealt with the problem by suggesting that there are *prima facie* universals that allow exceptions in certain situations. Thus, while we may believe the universal statement, "It is wrong to lie," a little thought should produce instances where lying can prevent major harm for an individual or society. To deal adequately with these necessary exceptions, the burden of proof is shifted to the individual who breaks the universal, and anyone who does so must be prepared to justify his or her action.

Immanuel Kant provided much of the background for modern deontology. He formulated what he called the "categorical imperative," which states that "one ought never to act unless one is willing to have the maxim on which one acts become universal law." Thus, we would ask whether we would be willing to live in a world where everyone lied whenever it was in his or her best interest to do so. If we would not like to live in that way, then, according to the categorical imperative, we must consider lying unethical. Further, it becomes our duty not to lie. In fact, the term *deontology* is derived from the word *duty*.

Many of the ethical judgments attained by using a deontological approach are the same as those developed by utilitarianism. However, the two approaches differ in important ways.

Utilitarianism

There are many variations of utilitarianism, just as there are of deontology; however, the key concepts are not difficult. The utilitarian ideal can be summarized as "the greatest good for the greatest number." Reaching this ideal involves performing a social cost/benefit analysis of the action in question and acting on the results. The individual is required to identify and somehow measure all social and economic benefits deriving from the action. A similar approach is used for all of the social and economic costs, and these costs are subtracted from the benefits. If the net result is positive (favors the benefits), the action is considered ethical. If two actions are compared, then the one with the largest positive result is preferable. The problems of trying to quantify all social and economic benefits and costs should be apparent. However, utilitarians might respond that if a person does the best that he or she can, then that person is acting ethically.

The concepts of utilitarianism are easy for business to understand and accept because of their ties to the justification of capitalism. Adam Smith and others have argued that capitalism provides the greatest *economic* good for the greatest number. The concept of "utility," the core term in utilitarianism, is also familiar to modern economists. However, in ethical analysis, utility includes social as well as economic benefits and costs.

The most important criticism of utilitarianism, for the purposes of this presentation, is its proposed "unjust" distribution of utility. Severe harm to an individual or to small groups can be offset by small gains to a large number of other individuals. This result is viewed as unethical by the critics of utilitarianism. If utilitarianism is to be useful to business, this issue must be dealt with. For example, it is possible (but by no means assured) that in the case of Nestle's sale of infant formula to Third World mothers, a utilitarian analysis would have suggested that it was acceptable to continue the sale. However, the outcome of that case favored a deontological analysis, resulting in very severe restrictions on the sale of infant formula in Third World countries. The telling arguments revolved around the severe harm incurred by individuals, even though the sale also did considerable good. Although this case emphasized deontology, many ethical decisions lend themselves to a utilitarian analysis. Thus, both philosophical systems can be useful in evaluating corporate codes of ethics.

Evaluation of Clusters

In the current study of codes of ethics, one cluster was labeled, "Be a dependable organizational citizen" (Table 1). The categories included in this cluster all direct the employee to be a nice, dependable person. Such dictates may or may not describe desirable outcomes for the organization, but they have very little to do with ethical conduct. Deontology and utilitarianism have little or nothing to say about these dictates, and their appearance in a code of ethics suggests a lack of understanding or a mislabeling on the part of those organizations that use them. Furthermore, these rules are very specific, providing only limited

Table 1: Clusters of Categories Found in Corporate Codes of Ethics

Cluster 1
"Be a dependable organization citizen."

1. Demonstrate courtesy, respect, honesty, and fairness in relationships with customers, suppliers, competitors, and other employees.
2. Comply with safety, health, and security regulations.
3. Do not use abusive language or actions.
4. Dress in business-like attire.
5. Possession of firearms on company premises is prohibited.
6. Use of illegal drugs or alcohol on company premises is prohibited.
7. Follow directives from supervisors.
8. Be reliable in attendance and punctuality.
9. Manage personal finances in a manner consistent with employment by a fiduciary institution.

Cluster 2
"Don't do anything unlawful or improper that will harm the organization."

1. Maintain confidentiality of customer, employee, and corporate records and information.
2. Avoid outside activities which conflict with or impair the performance of duties.
3. Make decisions objectively without regard to friendship or personal gain.
4. The acceptance of any form of bribe is prohibited.
5. Payment to any person, business, political organization, or public official for unlawful or unauthorized purposes is prohibited.
6. Conduct personal and business dealings in compliance with all relevant laws, regulations, and policies.
7. Comply fully with antitrust laws and trade regulations.
8. Comply fully with accepted accounting rules and controls.
9. Do not provide false or misleading information to the corporation, its auditors, or a government agency.
10. Do not use company property or resources for personal benefit or any other improper purpose.

CORPORATE ETHICS

11. Each employee is personally accountable for company funds over which he or she has control.
12. Staff members should not have any interest in any competitor or supplier of the company unless such interest has been fully disclosed to the company.

Cluster 3
"Be good to our customers."

1. Strive to provide products and services of the highest quality.
2. Perform assigned duties to the best of your ability and in the best interest of the corporation, its shareholders, and its customers.
3. Convey true claims for products.

Unclustered Items

1. Exhibit standards of personal integrity and professional conduct.
2. Racial, ethnic, religious, or sexual harassment is prohibited.
3. Report questionable, unethical, or illegal activities to your manager.
4. Seek opportunities to participate in community services and political activities.
5. Conserve resources and protect the quality of the environment in areas where the company operates.
6. Members of the corporation are not to recommend attorneys, accountants, insurance agents, stockbrokers, real estate agents, or similar individuals to customers.

direction for employees. Service organizations such as banks and utilities were heavy users of categories in this cluster. . . .

Another cluster is entitled, "Don't do anything unlawful or improper that will harm the organization." This cluster contained the largest number of categories and was by far the group most subscribed to. Over fifty companies included some of these categories in their codes of ethics. The legalistic character of the items in this cluster make it a set of rules designed to protect the organization, rather than a set of values to guide behavior. . . .

The ethics literature does deal with some of the issues raised in the second cluster, but in the context of ethics, these issues lead to reasoned and rational decisions based on certain central values. For example, two of the categories in this cluster deal with bribery. Within the context of this cluster, the issue seems to be one of prohibiting bribery because it is against the law, and the organization could get into trouble if bribes are given or taken. The message is actually "Don't break the law." This message, while certainly desirable, is substantially different from a deontological value that might, for example, state: "Always act in such a manner that you would be willing to live and work in a world where everyone acted as you do." This latter statement effectively prohibits bribery just as well as the rules that are part of this cluster, but it does many other things as well. The organizational value suggested above is a restatement of Kant's categorical imperative and obviously goes far beyond merely obeying the law. Thus, this cluster also seems to lack ethical thought or content.

The final cluster was entitled "Be good to our customers." It contained only three categories, which roughly dealt with ways in which the behavior of employees could satisfy customers. While these three categories lack the breadth of, say, Peters and Waterman's "Close to the Customer" from *In Search of Excellence*,[1] the intent is somewhat broader than in the other clusters. The first item from this cluster in Table 1 was adopted by only 10 companies, item two by 15, and item three by 24 out of the 84 companies represented in the study. There was no obvious tendency toward one or more particular industries. The cluster is somewhat more suggestive of ethical thought, since both deontological and utilitarian reasoning could be used to justify the statements. For example, the marketing concept suggests that following cluster three suggestions is efficient and will produce utility for all. The approach also satisfies deontological requirements. However, all of the clusters need a more thoughtful and organized use of ethical study for the final result to be called a true code of "ethics."

The six unclustered items also appear in Table 1. Item one of this group was adopted by 31 companies. It is not an ethical dictate and could be confusing to individuals attempting to apply it, since personal integrity and professional conduct can mean different things to different people. The second item, dealing with harassment, could be the result of an ethical analysis, or it could simply be a reaction to societal concerns. Of the 84 codes that were analyzed, this item appeared in 19.

Item three also appeared in 19 codes, but it simply supplies directions on how to deal with perceived unethical occurrences. Directions about reporting such occurrences ought to be in every code, but they probably should not be part of the ethical statements in the code itself. The most popular of these six unclustered items was number four, dealing with community and political service, which was adopted by 46 companies. It would be difficult to fit this item into any of the most popular moral philosophies, but it does have social responsibility connotations.

Item five, conservation of the environment, again reflects social responsibility issues rather than ethics, but it could be the result of an ethical analysis. Only 12 companies used this category in their codes. Finally, item six lacks both ethical and social responsibility ties. It was adopted by three financial institutions and was the only one of the six that suggested any specific usage.

Before moving to the second grouping effort, we need to examine the expectations for, and effectiveness of, codes of ethics. The following discussion sets the stage for selection of appropriate categories in the second grouping and for evaluation of the results.

Management Expectations for Codes of Ethics

It was argued in the preceding sections that current codes were for the most part not ethical statements, but dictates or rules that either prohibited or demanded specific behaviors. It is suggested in this section that despite the fact that codes are currently not very effective, business has high expectations for them.

A considerable amount of work has been spent in analyzing codes of ethics. However, two relatively recent articles summarize the general feeling by many (not all) researchers that codes lack much impact. Cressey and Moore, in an elaborate analysis of corporate codes of ethics, are convinced "that any improvements in business ethics taking place in the last decade are not a consequence of business leaders' calls for ethics or of the codes themselves. We believe that, instead, any changes have stemmed from conditions imposed by outsiders."[2] Further, an empirical study by Chonko and Hunt involving marketing managers found that "the existence of corporate or industry codes of ethics seems to be unrelated to the extent of ethical problems in marketing management."[3]

Both results suggest that codes of ethics are not a major factor in important decisions involving ethical questions. Codes may communicate the specific rules suggested by the three clusters in the last section, but they have little impact on what might be considered the *important* problems of business. Unfortunately, corporate management seems to expect more from them. The Center of Business Ethics at Bentley College published the results of a study in which they inquired whether the respondent's company had been "taking steps to incorporate ethical values and concerns into the daily operations of [its] organization" and, if they had, what they hoped to achieve by doing so. About 80 percent of the 279 respondents said that they had taken such steps, with five major objectives. In order of perceived importance they were: "to be a socially responsible corporation"; "to provide guidelines for employees' behavior"; "to improve management"; "to comply with local, state, or federal guidelines"; and "to establish a better corporate culture." The first two were substantially more important, while the last three were seen as about equal in importance. Codes of conduct were used by 93 percent of the respondents to achieve these objectives. The next most popular approach, employee training in ethics, was used by only 44 percent of the respondents.[4]

In a study published in January 1988 by Touche Ross, respondents again cited the adoption of business codes of ethics as "the most effective measure for encouraging ethical business behavior." In this study, 39 percent of the respondents selected codes of ethics as most effective, 30 percent selected a "more humanistic curriculum in business education," and 20 percent selected "legislation." Interestingly, 55 percent selected "legislation" as *least* effective.[5] Thus, codes are still seen by managers as the most viable approach for dealing with ethical problems.

However, there is a gap between what managers hope to accomplish with corporate codes and what is actually accomplished. Compliance with local, state, or federal guidelines might be achieved based on the categories in cluster one. Also, *very specific* guidelines for employees' behavior might be set based on the character of the categories, but broad guidelines and other objectives seem to be beyond what is currently attainable. To the degree the codes analyzed in this article are representative, their content and apparent intent lack the ability to truly aid in ethical decision making.

Cressey and Moore, in their analysis of corporate codes of ethics, believe that these documents "tend to imitate the criminal law and thus contain few innovative ideas about how the ethical standards of a firm, let alone of business in general, can be improved."[6] A quick review of the 30 categories listed in Table 1 and the examples presented throughout this article should verify that our findings confirm this belief. Rule-based statements dominate, while broad, shared values are almost absent.

Logical Partition of Codes by Dimension of Guidance

Since ethical guidance of employees is the desired outcome of adopting a code, two dimensions of guidance were used in another grouping effort. Figure 1 employs the second grouping approach, logical partition, to evaluate the degree of guidance provided by current codes of ethics. The horizontal categories identify the degree of specificity in the code items, while the vertical categories classify the code items according to type of guidance—rule-based or value-based. All of the code items seem to fit easily into two of

Figure 1
A Partition of Code Items

Degree of Guidance

	Low (Little Specific Guidance)		High (Very Specific Guidance)	
Rule-Based	Cell 1		Cell 2	
	(None of the rule-based statements were weak enough to be placed in this cell)		Cluster 1 (All Items) Cluster 2 (All Items) Cluster 3 (Items 2 and 3) Unclustered Items 2, 3, 4, and 6	
Value-Based	Cell 3		Cell 4	
	Cluster 3 (Item 1) Unclustered Items 1 and 5			

Type of Guidance

the four cells, with all of the items in clusters one and two falling into the same cell.

Many of the early attempts at developing codes of ethics were broad value-based statements of the "Be good!" type. They tended to be altruistic and unattainable, to confuse rather than aid understanding. Cell three in Figure 1 is designed to cover these statements. The problems that occur with cell three statements revolve around whose values are used in describing "personal integrity" or determining "quality" and what is meant by these broad, ill-defined value statements. Only three items were placed into cell three—item one of cluster three, and items one and five of the unclustered group.

Historically, the critic's reaction to the ineffective cell three statements is a call for more specificity. The reaction of business to this call is cell two—specific guidance state-

CORPORATE ETHICS

ments. All of the items in clusters one and two, two of the items in cluster three, and four of the unclustered items have been placed in cell two. In all, this cell accounts for 27 of the 30 items. Cell one has been left blank, but arguably some of the rule-based items in cell two could be classified as providing a relatively low level of guidance. However, since rules are supposed to provide very specific guidance, and since the item labels were composites created by the authors, the companies using them have been given the benefit of the doubt. It is the *intent* of the companies in creating the code items that is important in this article, and the intent seems to have been the creation of cell two statements.

Perhaps the most interesting part of the partition is cell four. If very specific guidance could be combined with a value-based approach to social responsibility and corporate ethics, it could have an important impact on performance. There is simply no way to create enough rules to cover even the most ethically important occurrences, even if they could be identified before they occurred. Perhaps this situation helps explain why most of the code items, including all of those in clusters one and two, are turned inward toward the firm itself. Creating rule-type statements to deal with all of the important issues from the organization's environment is simply too massive an undertaking to be handled effectively. However, if core values could be created to direct organizational behavior—values felt and understood by everyone in the organization—they could be the basis of a very effective code of ethics. This approach seems to call for the study and development of a specific corporate culture. The principal determinant of any culture is its values or guides to behavior. If such values were established as part of a corporate culture to guide the ethical behavior of an organization, many unforeseen events could be dealt with ethically. Unfortunately, cell four is void. It may be that some firms are using a cell four approach without recording it, but this study and recent literature on the subject does not find pervasive use of such an approach.

What would a cell four code look like? What role would it play in directing corporate behavior? A cell four code of ethics would be a statement of the company's ethical and socially responsible values. These values could be derived from an evaluation of potential threats and opportunities using both deontological and utilitarian reasoning. It would be a document that is open to all of the organization's publics and a constant reminder to employees about the expected approach for conducting all activities. Such a code would be a tool in the training program for new employees and part of the broad effort to enculturate all employees. Eventually, it would become an aid in spreading the folklore of the organization, providing the themes around which corporate myths and heros are created. However, only if the code is used in conjunction with strong enculturation efforts would it reach the high level of guidance that is part of cell four.

Some progress in this direction seems to be occurring. A February 1988 document by The Business Roundtable made the following observation:

> In the growing movement among major U.S. corporations to develop and refine mechanisms to make their ethics effective, there are two interrelated purposes:
> —First, there is the aim to ensure compliance with company standards of conduct. At work is the realization that human consciences are fragile and need the support of institutions.
> —Second, there is the growing conviction that strong corporate culture and ethics are a vital strategic key to survival and profitability in a highly competitive era.[7]

We believe that the most effective results will occur when these two purposes are combined. When standards of conduct become ethically determined values and are integrated into a strong corporate culture, then corporate behavior will become more ethical.

NOTES

1. Thomas J. Peters and Robert H. Waterman, Jr., *In Search of Excellence* (NY: Harper & Row, Publishers, 1982).

2. Donald R. Cressey and Charles A. Moore, "Managerial Values and Corporate Codes of Ethics," *California Management Review,* Summer 1983, p. 73–4.

3. Lawrence B. Chonko and Shelby D. Hunt, "Ethics and Marketing Management: An Empirical Analysis," *Journal of Business Research,* August 1985, p. 356.

4. Center for Business Ethics, "Are Corporations Institutionalizing Ethics?" *Journal of Business Ethics,* October 1986, p. 86.

5. Touche Ross, *Ethics in American Business* (Detroit: Touche Ross, January 1988).

6. Cressey and Moore (see note 2), p. 73.

7. The Business Roundtable, *Corporate Ethics: A Prime Business Asset* (NY: The Business Roundtable, February 1988), p. 6.

Corporate Ethics: Losing It, Having It, Getting It

Manuel G. Velasquez

If an exploration of a corporation's ethics is a matter of identifying what it does that can be judged as either good or bad, or right or wrong, then a discussion of how the corporation might acquire a character where ethics is actually important would seem to be in order. Manuel Velasquez surveys the conditions under which corporations often fail to be ethical, as well as ways in which they typically maintain and keep an ethical corporate culture intact. For Velasquez, corporate ethics is a systemic matter. Things go wrong in business organizations when the culture is so structured that people find rationalizations for unethical conduct or feel pressured into doing things in the name of the corporation that they would not do under other circumstances. Thus the acquisition of a corporate character where ethics dominates is a matter of paying close attention to the systemic factors of the corporate culture. Velasquez makes several good specific recommendations on how the corporation can improve their cultures and instill corporate ethics.

SOURCE: Previously unpublished article. Reprinted with permission of the author.

Losing It

Although only a minority of firms are involved in unethical activities, that minority is still surprisingly large. Between 1970 and 1980, 11 percent of the largest American firms were convicted of lawlessness, including bribery, criminal fraud, illegal campaign contributions, tax evasion, or price-fixing. Well-known companies with four or more convictions included Braniff International, Gulf Oil, and Ashland Oil. Firms with at least two convictions included Allied, American Airlines, Bethlehem Steel, Diamond International, Firestone, Goodyear, International Paper, National Distillers, Northrop, Occidental Petroleum, Pepsico, Phillips Petroleum, R. J. Reynolds, Schlitz, Seagram, Tenneco, and United Brands. The recent Union Carbide disaster in Bhopal is well known, as is the E. F. Hutton fiasco, the General Dynamics fraud, and of course, the Wall Street scandals involving Ivan Boesky, David Levine, and Michael Milken.

It is a mistake to think that such unethical behavior in business is just a matter of bad individuals: vicious characters whose wrongdoing is exposed and publicized by the media. There are ample instances of wrongdoing by individuals, of course—such as Ivan Boesky and David Levine—who know that they are doing wrong from the beginning and who deliberately go ahead and do it, anyway. But it is a mistake to think that unethical behavior is restricted to evil individuals who act alone or in small groups and who happen to get caught.

Unethical behavior in business more often than not is a *systemic* matter. To a large degree it is the behavior of generally decent people who normally would not think of doing anything illegal or immoral. But they get backed into doing something unethical by the systems and practices of their own firms or industries. Unethical behavior in business generally arises when business firms fail to pay explicit attention to the ethical risks that are created by their own systems and practices.

The example of Pacific Bell Telephone Company, which serves northern California, provides a good illustration of

CORPORATE ETHICS

the kinds of systemic problems that produce corporate misbehavior. Pacific Bell markets its services through sales representatives who answer the phone when a new customer calls to get a new telephone hookup. In 1984, in an attempt to get representatives to increase their sales, Pacific Bell's marketing managers began to impose increasingly stiff quotas on sales representatives and began to place them on probation if they failed to meet their quotas. Sales representatives gradually resorted to telling customers they had to pay a "standard price" for new telephone service, without telling customers that this "standard price" included several expensive options that the customer did not have to purchase. A representative describes the deceptive tactics that were soon being practiced on 65 percent of the company's new customers:

> I'm going to tell you [a new customer] that "You will get unlimited local calling, Touchtone service, our four custom-calling services and a 20 percent discount in the Pacific Bell service area; the central office fee to turn the services on is $37.50 and I have all of these things available and it's only $22.20 a month." Most customers will say, "That's fine." It isn't a bad deal, but how many people know they don't have to buy all those things, that they can get basic service for $9.95? The company says, "People should be intelligent enough to ask. Why should it be Pac Bell's job to tell them?" People who don't speak English, well, they end up with those services.[1]

Pacific Bell was subsequently ordered to refund $60 million to customers and to put $16.5 million into a consumer-education trust fund.

National Semiconductor, a manufacturer of computer semiconductors provides another example of a company whose systemic practices gradually led to unethical corporate behaviors. Government regulations require that all semiconductors intended for use in airplanes, nuclear warheads, guidance systems, satellites, and other sensitive security purposes must undergo a lengthy, costly, and rigorous period of testing to ensure that each one will function perfectly. Between 1979 and 1981, however, demand for semiconductors grew so fast that National's managers felt intense pressure to take shortcuts as the company fell farther and farther behind in its attempts to meet contract schedules. National Semiconductor subsequently admitted that during this period it had gradually begun to omit the required government tests and had been falsifying records to cover the omissions. An employee describes the situation that gradually developed:

> I'd say that over 100 employees had to know. To say that dozens participated would be a very conservative estimate. . . . Just about everybody in production control knew about it who had been there for six months. . . . I would borrow my gals' [identification] stamps [and] tell them, "You don't know I'm using your stamp." Yeah, we did make it up. There was a lot of documentation I personally dummied up. . . . When I realized how deeply things were being falsified, I just couldn't believe it. . . . I asked, "How did things get the way they were?" Nobody seemed to be able to give me a good answer.[2]

In 1984 National Semiconductor was fined $1.75 million in civil and criminal penalties for failing to adequately test some twenty-six million semiconductors, which by then were installed in ships and planes scattered throughout the world; they could no longer be tracked down.

What creates unethical behavior in business? Any of several factors including:

• Cutting corners to meet tight corporate objectives;
• Behaviors motivated by system incentives or disincentives;
• A corporate or industry culture that rationalizes or ignores unethical behavior;
• Factors that encourage obeying orders without considering their impact;
• Performance evaluations that encourage shortsighted decision making or set unrealistic goals.

Systemic factors like these gradually create pressures on business people until they edge over into unethical behavior. They deviate into unethical behavior when they are trying to meet goals, and have to cut corners to do it. Or they do something unethical because of the pressures of the budgeting system, or the promotion system, or the merit-pay system under which they work. Or they feel that management wants them to save money here and there, even at the price of unethical behavior. Or they follow the orders of someone without thinking that the manager who gave the order might not know what is really going on. Or they make a poor decision without allowing themselves to think fully about all the implications of that decision.

A well-documented illustration of how corporate systemic factors can gradually draw employees into unethical behavior is provided by the electrical price-fixing conspiracy of the early 1960s. In 1960, managers of General Electric, Westinghouse, Allis-Chalmers, and Federal Pacific were successfully prosecuted for getting together and fixing prices in their industry for several years. Clarence Burke, a G.E. manager, testified during the trials that his general manager had always insisted on a "reach budget," which required him each year to increase the percent of net profit to sales over what it had been the year before. In addition, he explained, he and his fellow managers at G.E. were told that to "get ahead" and have the "goodwill" of their superiors, they would have to attain these goals. The only way to attain these goals, the managers felt, was by fixing prices. Burke told how he was gradually introduced into the details of a practice that became accepted throughout the company and how he rationalized this widespread breaking of the law:

> I was taught [the techniques] by my superiors back as far as 1945, who took me to meetings with them and told me that, instead of showing Pittsburgh [the place of the meetings] in your expense account, let's all show so-and-so. . . . From then on it was just inbred in me. . . . I ascertained that it [was the usual way to act] because my superiors at Pittsfield were doing it and asking me to do it. So it was their practice. . . . [But] we were not meeting for the purpose of getting

the most that the traffic could bear. It was to get a value for our product. . . . I knew I violated the technicalities of the law. I salved my own conscience by saying I was not violating the spirit of the law. Because I was not establishing prices that would gouge the public, and I thought the spirit of the law was to prevent you from establishing abnormal prices, from making huge profits.[3]

Because unethical corporate behavior is a systemic matter, creating a corporate commitment to ethics is also a systemic matter. But beyond this, achieving a corporate commitment to ethics not only requires a systemic approach to ethical decision making: The achievement of a corporate commitment to ethics also will yield broad systemic benefits. A corporate commitment to ethics is, in fact, a firm's most valuable asset, one which impacts favorably on every function of a firm.

Having It

Before continuing, it should be remarked that although a commitment to ethics is the most valuable asset a firm can possess, it would be misleading to suggest that ethics always pays off. It does not. In fact, one of the primary functions of ethical norms is to carry people through those troubling times when doing what's right is not the easiest, nor the most profitable, course of action. Ethics sometimes requires self-sacrifice, foregoing personal gains or bearing significant costs and burdens. In such difficult times, people are sustained by the ethical norms that they have cultivated and that provide them with the personal incentives and inner motivations that enable them to do what is right in spite of the costs.

Nevertheless, although doing right does not always pay off, an ongoing commitment to ethics repeatedly proves to be a strategically valuable business asset. Corporations, such as IBM, that have cultivated a tradition of ethical treatment of employees have found that they have unusually low turnover rates, that their employees are extremely loyal to the company and willing to work harder and longer than those at other companies, and that their employees are unlikely to engage in company theft or fraud and do not have to be continually watched through expensive monitoring or auditing systems. On the other hand, companies that pay little attention to how they are treating their employees find not only that their turnover rates raise their training costs, but also that employee pilfering, theft, and other employee problems create noticeable expenses for the company. A tradition of high ethical standards toward employees can pay off on the bottom line.

Similarly, firms that maintain high ethical standards in their treatment of customers find that their customers are willing to pay a premium to the firm for good treatment, that customers will be more likely to become repeat buyers and more likely to recommend the firm's products to other customers. As a result, such firms have been able to increase their market share while raising their prices.

Thus a commitment to ethics can pay handsomely. In fact, one can cite companies, such as Hewlett-Packard, where good ethics have been the basis of a spectacularly profitable history. Hewlett-Packard early on developed an enviable reputation for ethical dealings with purchasers. Any machine purchased from H-P could be returned to H-P by the customer, in any condition for any reason, no questions asked. The company immediately responded to any and all consumer requests for service and help. Product quality was consistently outstanding, and product claims were always carefully understated. As a result, H-P quickly came to dominate several electronic markets, even though its products were always priced much higher than those of its competitors.

There are numerous other examples of companies that have found that a consciously sustained commitment to high ethical standards has paid off, including Borg-Warner Corporation, J.C. Penney, General Mills, Quaker Oats, Advanced Micro Devices, Chemical Bank of New York, Champion International, Levi-Strauss, Caterpillar, and many others.

The prime example of how a systemic commitment to ethics pays off, however, is Johnson & Johnson, the pharmaceutical manufacturer. When seven individuals died after consuming Tylenol capsules contaminated with poison, Johnson & Johnson managers in many different parts of the company, scattered over many different parts of the country, had to decide what to do. To a remarkable extent their decisions were uniformly and instinctively aimed at protecting the public: local managers independently pulled lots of Tylenol capsules off local shelves, marketing managers halted all advertising for Tylenol, all managers joined in support of a full public disclosure of the situation, and a massive recall of all Tylenol capsules was launched (a move that cost the company an estimated $50 million after taxes). A Johnson & Johnson manager described how this company-wide commitment to ethical values stabilized the company and ensured a coordinated response in a critical and potentially disastrous situation:

> It was astounding. Here you had all these people, outsiders and insiders, running into [CEO] Burke's office with information, opinions, and no pat answers. Sometimes people would be shouting at each other across the table. Meanwhile, out in the Company people were making hundreds of separate decisions which in retrospect I feel completely supported the Credo.[4]

This corporate commitment to the health and safety of consumers was rooted in Johnson & Johnson's systematic attention to inculcating in all managers the values embedded in the company Credo. The Credo states, and all employees are taught to believe, that "our first responsibility is to the doctors, nurses, hospitals, mothers, and all others who use our products." For several years the company had invested considerable time and resources into developing the Credo, communicating it to all employees and ensuring that it was genuinely integrated into every aspect of management thinking, including product choice, advertising, employee compensation, research, delivery times, costs, and financial reserves. James E. Burke, chairman and CEO of

Johnson & Johnson, describes how the investment paid off in their exemplary response to the Tylenol crisis:

> [The crisis] required literally dozens of people at Johnson & Johnson to make hundreds of decisions in a painfully short period of time. Most of the decisions were complicated, involving considerable risk. And we had no historical precedent to rely on. The guidance of the Credo played the single most important role in our decision making. . . . There was no way we could have instructed our people on how to make the decisions they did. Yet, somehow, they reached the same conclusions independently.[5]

Today, as a result of the trust and confidence that Johnson & Johnson's response created, the company has completely recovered its losses. Sales of Tylenol are once again at high levels, and the firm is prospering. A crisis that easily might have destroyed the company, became, instead, a catalyst that boosted its image in the eyes of millions of consumers.

Getting It

While a commitment to ethics is among the most valuable assets a firm can possess, it is also among the most difficult of assets to acquire and maintain, as well as among the easiest to lose. Even a company with a long tradition of being committed to ethics has no assurance that it will remain so committed.

For example, early in its history, Boeing Company acquired a reputation as a highly ethical and reputable company under the leadership of William Allen, who became CEO in 1945. Allen formed an Ethics Committee to report directly to the Board and had an ethics policy drafted and put in place. Older employees at Boeing today still recall the "Allen Era" as a period of uncompromisingly high standards and "squeaky-clean ethics."[6]

Allen was succeeded at Boeing by T. A. Wilson, who expanded the company until a disastrous collapse of the airplane market in 1969 forced him to reduce the company from 150,000 employees to about 55,000. For the next several years the firm was consumed with financial and operational problems, and ethics was gradually neglected as the company struggled to stay alive. Then, in 1974, several Boeing employees in one of the company's divisions were caught making foreign bribes. Ten years later, in 1984, the company was suspended from doing business with the federal government because employees in a different division were found to have used inside government information when submitting bids for a government contract. The two incidents taught the company a lesson: In 1974, Wilson immediately instituted an ethics program in the division that had been involved with foreign bribes, and his successor substantially strengthened and expanded this program to all divisions after the 1984 incident. The Boeing ethics program is now among the best and most extensive programs in the country.

Changes in management, the buffetings of a turbulent economy, or any of the many other shocks to which companies are inevitably subjected, can lead companies to neglect paying explicit attention to ethics. What can they do to regain the ethical culture they have lost?

Because unethical behavior is a systemic matter, building a commitment to ethics requires systemic methods. Several companies—including Boeing—have developed programs that introduce systemic changes into the corporation and are designed to institutionalize the company's commitment to ethics. Among some of the crucial elements of these programs are the following.

1. *The commitment of top management.* A recent study of ten companies with successful ethics programs conducted by the Business Roundtable revealed that top management plays a crucial role in securing a company's commitment to ethics.[7] The commitment of top management is essential to ensure that adequate resources are invested in the company's ethics program, that ethical behavior is truly supported throughout the company, to provide constant leadership through personal example, and to ensure that ethics is folded into every aspect of corporate life, including the strategic plan-

ning process. The recently instituted ethics program of McDonnell Douglas Corporation, for example, was spearheaded by CEO Sandy McDonnell, who personally oversaw the development of the program and its integration into the company's planning and management procedures. And the first employees to be exposed to the ethics training workshops the company conducted were the top nineteen senior members of McDonnell Douglas management.

Under the leadership of Sandy McDonnell, McDonnell Douglas folded ethics into its strategic planning process by formulating and implementing the "five keys" that formed the basis of the company's corporate reorganization: (1) strategic management; (2) human resource management; (3) participative management; (4) quality/productivity improvement; and (5) ethical decision making. Ethical considerations are integrated into each of these areas. The formulation of corporate goals and objectives, central to the company's new emphasis on the strategic management process, is explicitly conducted in light of the ethical values to which the company has committed itself and which the company views as crucial for its survival. Human resource management is now deliberately aimed at developing each employee's highest potential and attainment, so that the company serves employees rather than making employees into mere servants of the company. Participative management is emphasized because the company believes that respect for persons means that individuals should be allowed to participate in decisions that affect them. Quality/productivity improvements are achieved primarily through reorganization of the workplace in ways that increase participative decision making and heightened levels of trust and respect. To secure ethical decision making, all employees at all levels are given training in ethical reasoning. Thus, through the deliberate commitment of top management, ethics at McDonnell Douglas has come to permeate all levels of the company.

2. *Assignment of responsibility.* If an ethics program is to succeed, someone has to be made responsible for the development and implementation of the program. Because a large element of the program will involve the training of employees, responsibility for programs is often delegated to

a top-level manager in the human resources department. In McDonnell Douglas, for example, the corporate vice president of human resources was assigned responsibility for the company's ethics program, and a full-time manager was assigned to her to implement the program. Other companies, such as Boeing, developed a new high-level position, a corporate ethics officer, who assumed responsibility for administering the company's ethical program.

3. *Clarifying the company's ethical standards.* The foundation of every corporate ethics program is a clearly written statement of the company's core ethical values. Such statements are called "Codes of Ethics" or "Credos." Ideally, the statement will contain: (1) a description of the company's fundamental mission, purpose, or "beliefs"; (2) a description of the main constituencies (e.g., stockholders, employees, suppliers, consumers, community, etc.) or "stakeholders" to whom the company believes it is obligated in the pursuit of its mission; (3) the specific obligations the company believes it has toward these groups; (4) concrete examples of the behaviors required or permitted by these obligations; and (5) an indication of the kinds of sanctions the company will impose upon transgressions of these obligations.

Unfortunately, many companies still have codes of ethics that are too vague to help employees and which serve merely as a public relations document. If a company is going to take control of its ethics, it has to know what its own values are and has to communicate these clearly and in concrete and specific language to everyone in the organization. It is not enough, for example, to write that "integrity is expected of every employee of XYZ Corporation." The company has to spell out what integrity means when charging costs to a project, or when a conflict of interest arises, or when dealing with customers, or when accepting gifts from suppliers, and so on. The code, in short, must address the real ethical issues that employees will face in their particular positions as they deal with the various constituencies toward whom the company believes it is obligated.

Because codes must address the real issues employees face, the *process* by which the code is put together is critical:

Employees at all levels of the organization must take part in drawing up a code. This can be done by adopting a process that draws in representatives from various levels and sectors of a company. Security Pacific Bank, for example, began by having 70 senior managers participate in writing up the first draft of its corporate credo through lengthy discussions of the company's core values and of the kinds of specific dilemmas they and their staffs encountered. The draft was then reviewed by 250 employees in a series of 26 "focus-group" sessions, and subsequently revised to incorporate their concerns. The senior managers then reviewed the results of these sessions and made the final decisions about what the code would look like. Unless employees are drawn into the process of drafting the code in this or a similar fashion, the code will not address their real concerns and will not be "owned" by them.

Finally, if the code is to be more than a piece of paper that everyone dutifully reads and then files away and forgets, it must be enforced with realistic sanctions. Disciplinary actions have to be taken against employees who violate the ethics codes, or the efforts taken to draft the code will have been wasted.

4. *Building systems that support ethical behavior.* As the last point suggests, a company has to make sure it has systems to monitor and enforce the ethical behavior described in the code of ethics, and has to make sure that its systems provide incentives for ethical behavior rather than disincentives. Hewlett-Packard Company, for example, makes monitoring of compliance with its "Standards of Business Conduct" part of its annual internal audit function. During the annual audit, Hewlett-Packard's auditors check for any deviations from these standards, interview managers and employees to ascertain knowledge and observance of the standards, check to see that the standards have been reviewed by managers and that new employees are being informed of the standards, and report on the corrective actions that managers have taken to remedy any deviations from the standards that were reported in the last audit. In addition, the annual evaluations of managers include observance of the company's standards, and deviations from these

standards are noted in the manager's files. GTE Corporation explicitly states in its ethics guidelines that "personal integrity and moral fiber are as important to advancement within GTE as technical competence."

5. *Communicating the company's values.* Communication plays a key role in securing a company's commitment to ethics. Three kinds of communication systems have to be put into place if an ethics program is to succeed. First, the company has to communicate its standards to all employees, through orientation programs, training programs, in-house communications, pamphlets, management letters, word of mouth, and the personal example of management. This last is the most important. Nothing communicates a company's real ethics to an employee better than the example of his superiors.

Secondly, management has to have channels that let employees alert the company about any unethical behavior that is going on. "Internal whistle-blowing," as this is sometimes called, allows the upper management of a company to become aware of any ethical violations, and to deal with them before they become explosive situations. FMC corporation, for example, has an "ethics hot line"—a telephone number that any employee can call anonymously, and without fear of punishment, to report suspected legal or ethical violations to an "ethics officer," who then investigates the incident. The "ethics officer" can then take the results of her investigation to higher management, including, if necessary, the audit committee of the Board of Directors. Any supervisor who retaliates against an employee who reports a violation is subject to punishment.

Thirdly, a company should install some kind of advisory system. Because a written code cannot cover every contingency, employees sometimes have questions about whether or not something is ethical. Companies have therefore found it useful to set up a method of answering employee questions about ethics. Boeing, for example, has Ethics Advisers in every department, and at company headquarters. Employees can go to the Ethics Advisers to get clarification about company policies or about an issue not covered by these policies, and the Ethics Advisers themselves have ready access to company headquarters to which they can turn when they encounter questions that they feel unable to resolve.

6. *Employee training.* A particularly effective means for communicating the company's values to employees and for ensuring a uniformly high level of ethics throughout the organization is the use of workshops that provide explicit and annual training in ethics for employees. Implementation of an ethics program cannot succeed unless employees regularly are given adequate training in ethics, are made aware of the company's commitment to ethics and the means by which the company supports ethics, and are instructed as to the contents of the company's ethics code.

Ethics workshops in companies range from half a day (two to three hours) to three days. Depending on their length, they involve a number of elements, including: (1) an overview of the company's code of ethics; (2) discussion of several "cases" or incidents that illustrate the code; (3) discussion of some cases that involve "dilemmas" possibly not covered by the code; (4) description of some practical methods of making an ethical decision when faced with an issue not covered by the code; (5) explanation of any assistance the company provides when faced with a dilemma, including its "ethics hot line" and its Ethics Advisers; and (6) discussion of the factors that employees believe impede or discourage ethical behavior in their departments.

Different companies have devised different ways of implementing these workshops. A number of companies—including Boeing, FMC, McDonnell Douglas, General Electric, and Hughes Aircraft Company—have developed videotapes that provide much of the content of their workshops. Other companies deliver their training through more traditional training methods.

The most successful kinds of ethics workshops are those where the workshops are led *not* by trainers with staff functions (such as human resource trainers) but by line managers and supervisors. In Boeing, for example, top management was first to go through ethics training. These managers then led the workshops, in which they trained their own immediate subordinates with the help of the human resources staff; each subordinate then led workshops in which *their* immediate subordinates were trained, and so on. In this way, training cascaded downward from the top levels of the organization to the bottom. Having line managers present the workshops not only ensured that these managers had a good grasp on the substance of the ethics programs (the best way to learn a subject is by teaching it), it also communicated strongly to each employee that ethical behavior would be supported by management at all levels of the company.

Perhaps the greatest variation in ethics training programs is found in the "practical methods" that are suggested to aid ethical decision making when employees are faced with a difficult ethical dilemma. Some training programs suggest very simple tests, e.g., "Ask yourself whether you would want to explain what you did on television." Other fuller programs, such as those conducted by the author, teach more detailed methods of ethical analysis such as the following:

When faced with an ethical decision, ask yourself:

1. What are the facts; what are my alternatives?
2. What parties will be affected?
3. What do I owe each of these parties?
   a. What would produce the greatest benefits for all parties?
   b. What rights does each party have, and how can these rights best be respected?
   c. Are all parties treated fairly and justly?
4. On balance, what is the most ethical alternative?
5. How do I best implement this alternative?

All programs incorporate discussions of cases that call for an ethical decision. Some programs use off-the-shelf vignettes, many of which are available on videotape as dramatized incidents. But the better programs use cases that are specifically developed for their own employees and which address the specific ethical dilemmas their employees typically encounter. Through the use of employee focus groups or individual interviews with employees, cases and vignettes can be constructed that are based on the experiences of a company's own employees and which can be used as the basis for discussing what the company expects in the particular situations employees will face.

*   *   *

Every firm manages its ethics. Some do it by simply ignoring ethics. That is a kind of management by neglect. Like any other management technique, management by neglect has its consequences. But the consequences are unintended and undesirable: They are the gradual appearance and growth of areas in which the company lies exposed to those risks of unethical behavior that its systemic omissions have created. Only a concerted and systematic attention to ethics will reduce and eliminate such risks. The value of achieving a corporate commitment to ethics, however, makes the attainment well worth the effort.

NOTES

1. Quoted in Ed Pope, "Pac Bell's Sales Quotas," *San Jose Mercury News*, 24 April 1986, p. 1C.

2. David Willman and David Sylvester, "How Tests Were Faked at National," *San Jose Mercury News*, 3 June 1984, p. 12A.

3. U.S. Congress, Senate, *Administered Prices: Hearings Before the Subcommittee on Antitrust and Monopoly of the Committee on the Judiciary*, 87th Congress, 1st session, May-June, 1961, pp. 16772, 16790.

4. Laura Nash, ed., "Johnson & Johnson's Credo," in the Business Roundtable, *Corporate Ethics: A Prime Business Asset* (New York: The Business Roundtable, 1988), p. 97.

5. Quoted in Robert W. Goddard, "Are You An Ethical Manager?" *Personnel Journal*, March 1988, pp. 38–47.

6. Kirk Hanson and Manuel Velasquez, "The Boeing Company: Managing Ethics and Values," in *Corporate Ethics: A Prime Business Asset*, p. 13.

7. *Ibid.*

Advertising and Corporate Ethics

Vincent Barry

Most commercial advertising is regulated so that truth in advertising should be the norm. Yet there continue to be instances where corporations stretch the truth, engage in

SOURCE: From *Moral Issues in Business,* second edition, by Vincent Barry, © 1979, 1983 by Wadsworth, Inc. Reprinted with permission of the publisher.

subtle forms of deception, or make claims about their products or services that are exaggerations, or worse. Vincent Barry surveys such advertising tactics and highlights the most prevalent forms of questionable advertising ploys. In the course of demonstrating that ambiguity, the concealment of facts, exaggerated claims, and appeals to emotion are inherent to corporate marketing strategies and advertising campaigns, Barry contends that the goal of these tactics is to persuade—rather than to inform—the public. Since competitive pressures are so great, many corporations are all too willing to engage in deception and puffery in order to generate sales at the expense of bona fide consumer education about their products and services. There is thus a clear line between advertising as pure persuasion and advertising as a vehicle for consumer information. All it takes is one step in the wrong direction to put a corporation on the wrong ethical track when it comes to its commercial advertising.

Most moral issues related to advertising exist because of a conflict between its informative and persuasive functions. On the one hand, advertising functions to provide consumers information about the goods and services available to them. On the other hand, it serves to persuade them to purchase one product rather than another. These two functions are not always compatible. In an attempt to persuade, advertisers often obfuscate, misrepresent, or even lie. Moral issues arise when, in an attempt to persuade, advertisers are ambiguous, conceal facts, exaggerate, or employ psychological appeals. . . .

Ambiguity. When ads are ambiguous, they can be deceiving. Suppose, for example, a government study found that Grit filter cigarettes were lower in tar and nicotine than their filter-tip competitors. As part of its advertising, Grit claims, "Government Supported Grit Filters." *Supported* here is ambiguous. It can not only mean that government research supports Grit's claim that it's lower in tar and nicotine than its competitors but also that the government endorses the use of Grit. The Continental Baking Company was charged with such ambiguity by the Federal Trade Commission (FTC). In advertising its Profile Bread, Continental implied that eating the bread would lead to weight loss. The fact was that Profile had about the same number of calories per ounce as other breads but each slice contained seven fewer calories only because it was sliced thinner than most breads. Continental issued a corrective advertisement.

In all aspects of advertising, much potential moral danger lies in the interpretation. The Profile ad is a good example. A large number of people interpreted that ad to mean that eating Profile Bread would lead to a weight loss.[1] Likewise, for years consumers have inferred from its advertisements that Listerine mouthwash effectively fought bacteria and sore throats. Not so; in 1978 the FTC ordered Listerine to run a multimillion-dollar disclaimer. In such cases, advertisers and manufacturers invariably deny intending the inference that consumers draw. But sometimes the ad is so ambiguous that a reasonable person couldn't infer anything else. Thus, when a cold tablet advertises, "At the first sign of a cold or flu—Coricidin," what is the consumer likely to think? The fact is that neither Coricidin nor any other cold remedy can cure the common cold. At best it can only provide temporary symptomatic relief. But a consumer is left to draw his or her own conclusion, and it's likely to be the wrong one.

A striking example of this "open-to-interpretation" aspect of ambiguity can be seen in the battle over a seemingly harmless topic—buying a tire. Uniroyal advises consumers to buy the numbers: use the numbers and letter molded into the sidewalls under a federally mandated tire-grading system to select the best tire value. Goodyear counters that the numbers are misleading and that the only reliable way to buy a tire is by brand name and dealer recommendations. (It is hardly any coincidence, of course, that Uniroyal has the highest tread-wear number on its first-line radials, those supplied to auto dealers; and Goodyear has the best-known brand, the biggest advertising budget, and the most stores and dealers.)

The dispute is long-standing. In the mid-sixties the government responded to concern about quality and safety by proposing a quality grading system. Producers fought tire grading for over ten years, but a 1979 court decision forced them to start using grade labels. Under the law, each manufacturer can grade its own tires, and the government randomly checks to see that the tires measure up to the ratings. Although grading began with the bias-ply tires, in 1980 tire makers also had to begin putting separate A, B, or C grade ratings on radials for traction and ability to withstand heat buildup from high-speed driving. In response, tire makers simply put on a number to indicate expected wear and left it at that.

But early in 1981 Uniroyal, which had rated its "Steeler" at 220 (indicating 66,000 miles of useful life[2]), started advertising that its Steelers were better than Goodyear's Custom Polysteel, which had been rated at 170 (51,000 miles), and other competing brands. As a result, Goodyear, Firestone Tire and Rubber, B. F. Goodrich, and General Tire were put in the ludicrous position of having to convince tire dealers and motorists that their grade ratings were really meaningless, and that no one should take them seriously.

Each of these companies insisted that the test results on which the ratings were based are so variable that they are not reliable. Goodyear, for example, said tests on its Polysteel tires ranged from 160 to 420, with a 13-inch size ranking the lowest. Goodyear therefore assigned a grade of 160 for 13-inch tires and 170 for 14- and 15-inch sizes to assure that all tires met the grade. Fair or not, Goodyear began running ads declaring that, in comparative tests, its Custom Polysteel Tires averaged 229 and 329 ratings in 14- and 15-inch sizes, higher than the 250 and 277 averaged for Uniroyal's Steelers. For its part, Uniroyal insisted that the records of the tests they had run showed that the Goodyear tires didn't test as well as the Steelers.

What, then, does a tire grade mean? What kind of information does it provide the consumer? You be the judge.

Aiding and abetting ambiguity in ads is the use of "weasel" words, words used to evade or retreat from a direct or forthright statement or position. Consider the weasel *help*. *Help* means "aid" or "assist" and nothing else. Yet, as one author has observed, " 'help' is the one single word which, in all the annals of advertising, has done the most to say something that couldn't be said."[3] Because the word *help* is used to qualify, once it's used almost anything can be said after it. Thus, we're exposed to ads for products that "help us keep young," "help prevent cavities," "help keep our houses germ-free." Consider for a moment how many times a day you hear or read phrases like these: "helps stop," "helps prevent," "helps fight," "helps overcome," "helps you feel," "helps you look." And, of course, *help* is hardly the only weasel. "Like," "virtual" or "virtually," "can be," "up to" (as in "provides relief *up to* eight hours"), "as much as" (as in "saves *as much as* one gallon of gas"), and numerous other weasels function to say what can't be said.

That ads are open to interpretation doesn't exonerate advertisers from the obligation to provide clear information. Indeed, this fact intensifies the responsibility, because the danger of misleading through ambiguity increases as the ad is subject to interpretation. At stake is not only people's money but also their health, loyalties, and expectations. The potential harm a misleading ad can cause is great, not to mention its cavalier treatment of the truth. For these reasons ambiguity in ads is of serious moral concern.

A final word about this topic. As far back as 1944 the United States Supreme Court, speaking about the issue of truthful advertisement, proposed a standard whose spirit might still be used in evaluating ads. In insisting on the literal truthfulness of an ad, the Court recommended "a form of advertising clear enough so that, in the words of the prophet Isaiah, 'wayfaring men, though fools, shall not err therein.'"[4]

Concealed facts. When advertisers conceal facts, they suppress information which is unflattering to their products. Put another way, a fact is concealed when its availability would probably make the desire, purchase, or use of the product less likely than in its absence. The case of Pertussin is a case in point. Surely if consumers had known of the potentially fatal ingredients the vaporizer contained, they'd have been less likely to purchase the product than they apparently were. Concealed facts concern us in ethics not only because they can exploit by misleading as much as ambiguity can but also because they wantonly undermine truth telling.

Truth rarely seems foremost in the minds of advertisers. As Samm Sinclair Baker writes in *The Permissible Lie:* "Inside the agency the basic approach is hardly conducive to truth telling. The usual thinking in forming a campaign is first what can we say, true or not, that will sell the product best? The second consideration is, how can we say it effectively and get away with it so that (1) people who buy won't feel let down by too big a promise that doesn't come true, and (2) the ads will avoid quick and certain censure by the FTC."[5] In this observation we see the business person's tendency to equate what's legal with what's moral, an attitude we previously alluded to. It's precisely this outlook that leads to advertising behavior of dubious morality.

One needn't look far to find examples of concealed facts in ads. You may recall the old Colgate-Palmolive ad for its Rapid Shave Cream. It showed Rapid Shave being used to shave "sandpaper": "Apply, soak, and off in a stroke." This was an impressive ad for any man who's ever scraped his way awake. Unfortunately, what Colgate concealed was that the sandpaper in the ad was actually Plexiglas and that actual sandpaper had to be soaked in Rapid Shave for about eighty minutes before it came off in a stroke.[6]

More recently Campbell vegetable soup ads showed pictures of a thick, rich brew calculated to whet even a gourmet's appetite. Supporting the soup were clear glass marbles deposited into the bowl to give the appearance of solidity.

Then there's the whole area of feminine deodorant sprays (FDS), one rife with concealed facts. Currently an industry in excess of $55 million, FDS ads not only fail to mention that such products in most cases are unnecessary but that they frequently produce unwanted side effects: itching, burning, blistering, and urinary infections. A Food and Drug Administration (FDA) "caution" now appears on these products.

If business has obligations to provide clear, accurate, and adequate information, we must wonder if it meets this charge when it hides facts relevant to the consumer's need and desire for or purchase of a product. Hiding facts raises serious moral concerns relative to truth telling and consumer exploitation. This exploration takes the form of real injuries that can result to users of products and also of abridgements to consumers' personal freedom. When consumers are deprived of comprehensive knowledge about a product, their choices are constricted.

Exaggeration. Advertisers can mislead through exaggeration; that is, by making claims unsupported by evidence. For example, claims that a pain reliever provides "extra pain relief" or is "50% stronger than aspirin," that it "upsets the stomach less frequently," or that it's "superior to any other non-prescription pain killer on the market" contradict evidence which indicates that all analgesics are effective to the same degree.[7]

In recent years the FTC has been making numerous companies substantiate their claims, as in the Profile and Listerine cases. In the tire industry, the FTC has questioned Goodyear's claim that its Double-Eagle Polysteel Tires can be driven over ax blades without suffering damage. It has also asked Sears, Roebuck and Company to prove its claim that its steel-belted radial tires can give 60,000 to 101,000 miles of service. In the auto industry, the FTC has questioned Volkswagen's claim that its squareback sedan gets about 25 miles per gallon and that it gives drivers 200 gallons of gas more a year compared with the average domestic compact. In addition, the FTC has asked General Motors to verify its claim that its Vega's ground beams provide more side-impact collision protection than those of any other comparable compact. And it has questioned Chrysler's claim that its electronic system never needs tuning.[8]

Clearly the line between deliberate deception and what advertising mogul David Ogilvy has termed *puffery* is not always clear. By *puffery* Ogilvy means the use of "harmless" superlatives. Thus advertisers frequently boast of the merits of their products by using words such as *best, finest,* or *most.* In many instances the use of such puffery is indeed harmless, as in the claim that a soap is the "best loved in America." Other times, however, it's downright misleading, as in the Dial soap ad which claimed that Dial was "the most effective deodorant soap you can buy." When asked to substantiate that claim, Armour-Dial Company insisted that it was not claiming product superiority; all it meant was that Dial soap was *as effective as* any other soap.

Of moral importance in determining the line between puffery and deliberate deception would seem to be the advertiser's intention and the likely interpretation of the ad. Are the claims intended as no more than verbal posturing, or are they intended to sell through deceptive exaggeration? Are advertisers primarily interested in saying as much as they can without drawing legal sanction or in providing consumers with accurate information? But even when the intention is harmless, advertisers must consider how the ad is likely to be interpreted. What conclusion is the general consuming public likely to draw about the product? Is that conclusion contrary to likely performance? Without raising questions like these about their ads, advertisers and manufacturers run risks of warping truth and injuring consumers, two significant moral concerns.

Psychological appeals. A psychological appeal is one that aims to persuade exclusively by appealing to human emotions and emotional needs and not to reason. This is potentially the area of greatest moral concern in advertising. An automobile ad that presents the product in an elitist atmosphere peopled by members of the "in" set appeals to our need and desire for status. A life insurance ad that portrays a destitute family woefully struggling in the aftermath of a provider's death aims to persuade through pity and fear. Reliance on such devices, although not unethical per se, raises moral concerns because rarely do such ads fully deliver what they promise.

Ads that rely extensively on pitches to power, prestige, sex, masculinity, femininity, acceptance, approval, and the like aim to sell more than a product. They are peddling psychological satisfaction.

Psychological messages raise serious moral questions about inner privacy. Perhaps the best example is the increasingly explicit and pervasive use of sexual pitches in ads.

Scene: An artist's skylit studio. A young man lies nude, the bedsheets in disarray. He awakens to find a tender note on his pillow. The phone rings and he gets up to answer it.

CORPORATE ETHICS

Woman's Voice: "You snore."
Artist (smiling): "And you always steal the covers."

More cozy patter between the two. Then a husky-voiced announcer intones: "Paco Rabanne. A cologne for men. What is remembered is up to you."[9]

Although sex has always been used to sell products, it has never before been used as explicitly in advertising as it is today. And the sexual pitches are by no means confined to products like cologne. The California Avocado Commission supplements its "Love Food From California" recipe ads with a campaign featuring leggy actress Angie Dickinson, who is sprawled across two pages of some eighteen national magazines to promote the avocado's nutritional value. The copy line reads: "Would this body lie to you?" Similarly, Dannon Yogurt recently ran an ad featuring a bikini-clad beauty and the message: "More nonsense is written on dieting than any other subject—except possibly sex."

Some students of marketing claim that ads like these appeal to the subconscious mind of both marketer and consumer. Purdue University psychologist and marketing consultant Jacob Jacoby contends that marketers, like everyone else, carry around sexual symbols in their subconscious that, intentionally or not, they use in ads. A case in point: the widely circulated Newport cigarette "Alive with Pleasure" campaign. One campaign ad featured a woman riding the handlebars of a bicycle driven by a man. The main strut of the bike wheel stands vertically beneath her body. In Jacoby's view, such symbolism needs no interpretation.

Author Wilson Bryan Key, who has extensively researched the topic of subconscious marketing appeals, claims that many ads take a subliminal form. *Subliminal advertising is advertising that communicates at a level beneath our conscious awareness,* where some psychologists claim that the vast reservoir of human motivation primarily resides. Most marketing people would likely deny that such advertising occurs. Key disagrees. Indeed, he goes so far as to claim: "It is virtually impossible to pick up a newspaper or magazine, turn on a radio or television set, read a promotional pamphlet or the telephone book, or shop through a supermarket without having your subconscious purposely massaged by some monstrously clever artist, photographer, writer, or technician."[10]

Concern with the serious nature of psychological appeals is what the California Wine Institute seemed to have in mind when it adopted an advertising code of standards. The following restrictions are included:

- No wine ad shall present persons engaged in activities which appeal particularly to minors. Among those excluded: amateur or professional sports figures, celebrities, or cowboys; rock stars, race car drivers.
- No wine ad shall exploit the human form or "feature provocative or enticing poses or be demeaning to any individual."
- No wine ad shall portray wine in a setting where food is not presented.
- No wine ad shall present wine in "quantities inappropriate to the situation."
- No wine ad shall portray wine as similar to another type of beverage or product such as milk, soda, or candy.
- No wine ad shall associate wine with personal performance, social attainment, achievement, wealth, or the attainment of adulthood.
- No wine ad shall show automobiles in a way that one could construe their conjunction.

As suggested, the code seems particularly sensitive to the subtle implications that wine ads often carry. In a more general sense it alerts us to the psychological nuances of ads. In adopting such a rigorous code of advertising ethics, the California Wine Institute recognizes the inextricable connection between *what* is communicated and *how* it is communicated. In other words, as media expert Marshall McLuhan always insisted, content cannot be distinguished from form, nor form from content. Sensitivity to this proposition would go far toward raising the moral recognition level in advertising and toward alerting business people to the moral overtones of psychological appeals. . . .

NOTES

1. See "Mea Culpa, Sort Of," *Newsweek,* September 27, 1971, p. 98.
2. A rating of 100 supposedly equals 30,000 miles of useful life.
3. Paul Stevens, "Weasel Words: God's Little Helpers," in *Language Awareness,* ed. Paul A. Eschhol, Alfred A. Rosa, Virginia P. Clark (New York: St. Martin's Press, 1974), p. 156.
4. "Charles of the Ritz District Corporation v. FTC, 143,F.2d 276 (2d Cir. 1944)," in David A. Aaken and George S. Day, *Consumerism: Search for the Consumer Interest* (New York: The Free Press, 1974), p. 140.
5. Samm Sinclair Baker, *The Permissible Lie* (New York: World Publishing Co., 1968), p. 16.
6. Ibid.
7. The editors of *Consumers Reports, The Medicine Show* (Mt. Vernon, N.Y.: Consumers Union, 1972), p. 14.
8. Fred Luthans and Richard M. Hodgetts, *Social Issues in Business* (New York: Macmillan, 1976), p. 353.
9. Gail Bronson, "Sexual Pitches in Ads Become More Explicit and Pervasive," *The Wall Street Journal,* November 18, 1980, p. 1.
10. Wilson Bryan Key, *Subliminal Seduction* (New York: New American Library, 1972), p. 11.

The Ethical Side of Takeovers and Mergers

Robert Allan Cooke and Earl Young

Perhaps no other issue in corporate ethics has received as much attention from the press as that of takeovers and mergers. But the attention in the nation's newspapers and magazines has been primarily geared toward the wheeling and dealing of raiders and top management. Rarely is there a more considered approach to takeovers and mergers that looks at them globally, with an eye toward the consequences of this business movement. Robert Allan Cooke and Earl Young provide a balanced examination of these phenomena by providing a "stakeholder analysis" of them. Simply put, *stakeholder analysis* means paying attention to the conse-

---

SOURCE: This article is a modification of "Mergers From an Ethical Perspective," *Business and Professional Ethics Journal,* Vol. 6, 1987. Published with permission of the authors.

quences of a decision or a business activity. It asks who will be affected and to what extent will those who have a stake in the decision or activity be so affected. Cooke and Young review the large number of parties who might qualify as stakeholders in any given takeover or merger. After arguing that the stakeholder approach is a desirable form of analysis, they then employ the Golden Rule Model, the Ethical Egoist Model and the Utilitarian Model to the issue, each of which leads to a series of questions. These in turn function as a set of guidelines that should help determine the ethical or unethical character of a proposed takeover or merger.

Background

Over the last fifteen years there has been a dramatic increase in the number of mergers in the United States.[1] Terms like *mergers, acquisitions, takeovers, arbitrage,* and *leveraged buyouts* have become part of our common vocabulary. Yet this so-called "merger mania" has not been accompanied by many in-depth examinations of the ethical issues generated by these developments. This lack of analysis is not only surprising, but also it may have contributed to the apparent insensitivity to the negative consequences mergers and takeovers have for certain individuals or groups affected by these business changes.

In the absence of such a framework, certain key developments have occurred. On the one hand, government regulators have sent mixed signals to companies about such changes. During the first half of this period, though mergers were on the upswing, the use of judicial, regulatory, and legislative safeguards was also increasing. Mergers that sought to increase the dominance of a corporation within a given industry were usually opposed, e.g., Mobil's attempts to purchase Connoco and Marathon Oil. Yet mergers that tended to diversify a company's holdings normally went unchallenged[2] e.g., the diversification of Beatrice Foods to over two hundred companies is an extreme example of this laissez-faire attitude.[3]

What are the general characteristics of these mergers or takeovers? Several observations are appropriate.

First, though numerous mergers seem friendly, a growing number involve bitter conflicts. For the purposes of this paper we want to distinguish between these friendly and hostile situations in the following way: When we refer to a *merger,* we mean that two or more companies or firms have decided it is to their mutual interest to combine into one larger company or firm. When there is conflict and hostility because one company is taking over an unwilling partner, we refer to this as a *hostile takeover.*[4] Such hostile takeovers seem to have become the norm during the last decade. And this phenomenon has given rise to the emergence of so-called *white knights,* companies willing to rescue the besieged company through an acquisition. Of course, most of these besieged companies want to be left alone, but they find acquisition by a white-knight company preferable to acquisition by a hostile company.[5] For example, when Mobil Oil attempted to acquire Marathon Oil, it was met with stiff resistance. Marathon found a white knight in the form of U.S. Steel (now USX). One of the major points of contention was that Marathon wanted to keep its corporate headquarters in Findlay, Ohio. The acquisition by U.S. Steel guaranteed corporate headquarters would remain there.

Second, a growing number of hostile takeovers have been initiated by individual investors or groups of investors, not companies. These investors fall into two general categories. The first group, *reform-minded investors,*[6] are unhappy with the existing corporate policy and direction. Their goal is to replace top management with people who share their concerns and will implement the necessary changes. These concerns may involve earnings per share, return on investment, or issues not directly related to profit, such as corporate image or corporate history.[7]

The second group, *corporate raiders,* are also convinced that top management needs to be replaced, but their primary goal is profit for the shareholders—in particular, themselves. Corporate raiders like T. Boone Pickens and Carl Icahn are masterful in the art of making money through the threat of a takeover. Raiders simply buy a significant percentage of the outstanding stock of a given company. Then they threaten to buy enough additional stock to gain a controlling interest in the company. To prevent this second step, management is often forced to buy back the stock from the raider at a premium. This technique is called *greenmail,* an analogy to blackmail. If the strategy works, the corporate raider makes a handsome profit, and the value of stock increases for all shareholders.

Third, in light of the preceding developments, many companies have adopted complex defensive strategies to prevent hostile takeovers. These plans are usually described as *poison pills* or *doomsday strategies*. In other words, the vulnerable company constructs a series of complex steps that must be completed before anyone can gain a controlling interest in the company. For example, a company may issue a special class of stock in addition to their common and preferred stock, so that a potential raider will have to spend more capital to acquire control. Or the company may put a larger percentage of its stock into the employee stock option plan (ESOP).[8] These steps, in combination with changes in corporate bylaws and other maneuvers, are designed to wear down the potential raider or aggressor company by making it very costly to gain control. The hope is that the raider will not be able to raise the necessary capital or will become hesitant about tying up his liquid assets; the price of controlling interest is too much of a pill to swallow.

It should be noted that any given company is vulnerable to a hostile takeover. There was a time when takeovers or mergers usually involved a financially sound company merging with or acquiring a company that had financial weaknesses. Today, anyone with a significant percentage of outstanding stock is susceptible to a takeover. In fact, many companies have purchased much of their outstanding stock to repel potential takeovers. This strategy may work in the short run, but in the long term it may put such a strain on liquidity that the company is weakened financially and therefore vulnerable. The strategy may actually make the company more susceptible to the takeover it was designed to prevent. For that matter, it is unclear how effective any of the preventive strategies are.[9]

CORPORATE ETHICS

Fourth, today's mergers and acquisitions are often motivated by the need to diversify rather than to dominate a given industry. Such diversification may decrease overhead costs[10], or it may protect a given company from economic downturns in its basic industry, e.g., U.S. Steel's acquisition of Marathon Oil. This diversification enables the company to cover some of its losses through the existing assets and profits generated by the company that was acquired.[11]

Fifth, many takeovers are coming from within, through mechanisms such as *leveraged buyouts.* In other words, the corporate board of directors must not only be on guard against external threats for control, but also it must be sensitive to the possibility that the company's top management may engineer a buyout from within, with capital from external sources. This relatively new business phenomenon has created a new growth industry for firms that plan and engineer such buyouts.

Finally, as mergers and hostile takeovers have become more commonplace, an increasing number of upper-level managers have negotiated contracts with provisions that protect them in the event of a merger or hostile takeover. These safety nets, commonly known as *golden parachutes,* provide lucrative cash and stock settlements in the event that a merger or takeover occurs. Such parachutes are designed to protect executives from the displacement that ensues. Of course, this technique does little, if anything, for middle and lower management. And these safety nets may have a "*double effect*":[12] Although they may protect given executives, such strategies may lessen the incentive to resist takeovers, since top management's interest is protected in any case.

When all is said and done, the rise in merger and takeover activity during the last decade seems to indicate that such consolidations are popular because it is economically sound to consolidate in an ever-changing business climate—even though this trend may limit competition. Yet studies indicate that the overall economic strength of companies engaged in merger or takeover activity has actually declined.[13]

Obviously such financial data should concern everyone. Yet there are also public-policy and ethics issues to be considered.

The Stakeholder Concept

The primary focus of this paper is on a neglected area of business-decision analysis; namely, the ethical issues embedded in the operational evaluation of mergers. The best way to begin such an analysis is to introduce the concept of *stakeholder*. A stakeholder is any individual or group that has a stake in the outcome of a corporation's actions or policies. For example, stockholders, creditors, customers, competitors, managers, employees, suppliers, and the government are actual or potential stakeholders in any given situation. Just which stakeholders are involved is determined in part by whether or not we are looking at systemic issues facing our economic system and the global economy, issues related to the interrelations among a given corporation and other organizations, or micro issues within the company.[14]

In any case, though the frequency of mergers continues to expand, most stakeholders have little, if any, imput—either before or after the deal is consummated.[15] Even though the need for secrecy in a competitive environment is understandable, this does not eliminate the importance of assessing the impact of mergers on the appropriate stakeholders. It is important for at least two reasons:

1. Ignoring the effects of mergers on stakeholders may unfairly and arbitrarily hurt innocent stakeholders, or it may encourage unethical business conduct; and
2. Ignoring such impacts may undermine profit growth in the long run.

Since most stakeholders are usually without influence in the merger process, management has a responsibility to consider stakeholder interests during merger negotiations and implemention. In order to protect stakeholders' interests, management must:

• identify the critical problem areas that arise in a merger;
• identify the key operational considerations in the merger process;

- identify the key ethical considerations in the merger process;
- develop a set of decision criteria for the merger;
- integrate ethical considerations in the plan to merge;
- integrate ethical concerns in the implementation plan; and
- develop a set of design criteria for inclusion in the implementation plan.

Although each of these tasks could be the focus of a separate paper, one must intially understand the underlying process of integrating ethical analysis into the merger decision.

It is our contention that the very separation of ethical analysis from operational considerations in the decision process is a primary reason for the fact that the ethical consequences of mergers are usually ignored. In short, not knowing how to interject ethical import into the decision process is as much of a deterrent to ethical conduct as is any premeditated decision to take ethical shortcuts.

Most companies simply are not prepared to handle the full range of issues and problems that emerge in the merger process. They seldom have a comprehensive and systematic procedure for planning and implementation because they lack:

- *a merger strategy*. Too often the steps taken in the merger are reactions to internal and external pressures. Thus there is little deliberation about how the merger will or will not enhance the corporate mission;
- *policies to guide merger activities*. Since the average company has no experience with mergers, it is not surprising that it is difficult for many companies to identify what the salient concerns should be, and to formulate alternative solutions;
- *an understanding of the potential harm that may ensue.* In an effort to respond to immediate pressures, top management often ignores the long-term impact on the relevant stakeholders. The initial euphoria that often follows the merger masks the chain of events that continue to effect jobs, careers, and work assignments; and

• *an appreciation of the dynamics of postmerger activity.* Since mergers create a new organization with a new management structure, it is difficult to predict the policies and directions of top management.

This lack of a comprehensive merger strategy is serious because of the fact that there are legitimate reasons for considering this option. These include: a lack of funds to compete effectively with companies with better plant facilities, newer equipment, and a large work force; a growing number of competitors who have solidified their economic positions through mergers and acquisitions; an environment of deregulation that has economically weakened many companies not accustomed to a competitive marketplace; intense technological competition, which makes it more difficult to attain economies of scale and to retain key personnel; and the emergence of foreign competitors with substantial resources to challenge the market share in all industries.

Within such a business climate it is easy to understand why mergers have become commonplace. Few will dispute the operational necessities that make this option more attractive. Yet these operational considerations should not be evaluated in isolation from the ethical costs that ensue from any consolidation.

The Ethical Side: Some General Comments

When examining the ethical dimension of mergers, we must realize that mergers benefit some stakeholders and hurt others. And the degree of harm or benefit may vary quite dramatically. For instance, most stockholders benefit from mergers; but the average employee may face reassignment, relocation, or worse. Even if both stockholders and employees benefit, other stakeholders are bound to suffer some loss.

Moreover, the effects will vary on the basis of when the effects begin [*immediacy*], how long the effects last [*duration*], and whether or not the effects are direct or indirect [*proximity*].[16] This means that each stakeholder will have a

CORPORATE ETHICS

somewhat biased view of the harms and benefits of the merger.

Just how any one individual or group evaluates the relative harm or benefit of mergers depends, in part, on the ethical framework they use. For the purposes of this paper, we identify three common frameworks: the Golden Rule Model, the Enlightened Egoist Model, and the Utilitarian Model.[17]

One of the oldest models of moral conduct, the Golden Rule Model, is based upon the belief that an individual's actions toward another should be evaluated in light of how that individual would wish to be treated in the same situation.[18] This perspective requires the moral agent to examine the anticipated effects from the vantage point of those affected. For example, in a merger situation, those initiating the consolidation should assess the probable impacts on all stakeholders as if they were those stakeholders. Would they wish to be treated this way?

If the answer is negative, then a reexamination of the process is needed, for the dignity and importance of each stakeholder must be preserved in the merger process. If the dignity of any stakeholder is at risk, steps should be taken to alleviate or remove the harmful consequences that threaten the stakeholder(s). Any individual who uses this framework of ethical analysis should raise the following questions in the merger deliberations and implementation:

- Are there ways to initiate the anticipated merger that will not have negative consequences for any stakeholder?
- Will each stakeholder be treated with dignity and respect in the merger process?
- If certain harmful effects are unavoidable, what steps can be taken to alleviate the impact?
- Is it possible and feasible to spread these losses among all stakeholders, so that no individual or group bears the full brunt of these losses?
- If not, and certain stakeholders do suffer most of the harmful effects from the merger, what steps are needed to alleviate these losses?
- Will these measures ensure that all stakeholders are treated with dignity and respect?

By way of contrast, the Enlightened Egoist is motivated by prudential concerns. Whether or not the anticipated merger will benefit the parties who initiate it is the fundamental question. If the merger fails to provide the necessary benefits to these initiating parties, or to those stakeholders they represent, then the merger is unacceptable.[19] Any ethical considerations are focused primarily on the harms and benefits these initiating parties, or those stakeholders they represent, will face.

Yet there is also some concern for the effects on other stakeholders. If prudential benefits can be realized without causing unnecessary harm to other stakeholders or can be parlayed into some benefit for these stakeholders, so much the better. This concern is not altruistic. The Enlightened Egoist believes it may be in his or her self-interest to be sensitive to the harmful effects for other stakeholders. This is a long-term strategic consideration that increases the likelihood that the initiating parties will devise measures in the merger process to lessen the harmful effects on various stakeholders. The individual(s) who adopt this model should raise the following questions:

- Is it in my interest to pursue this anticipated merger?
- If it is, what actions will maximize the probable benefits from the merger?
- Will the stakeholders I (we) represent also benefit from this transaction?
- Will there be harmful consequences for other stakeholders? How severe will these losses be?
- Are these anticipated losses arbitrary or unfair?
- Will these stakeholder losses offset or diminish the prudential benefits in the short term or the long term?
- Are there ways to modify the merger process that will alleviate or diminish these losses?
- If such losses are unavoidable, what steps can be taken to minimize reciprocal actions that may lessen my benefits?

Like the Enlightened Egoist, the Utilitarian is interested in maximizing the positive consequences of mergers and in lessening the harm, if possible. Yet this concern is not motivated by self-interest. It is based upon the belief that ethics requires the maximization of benefits for all stakeholders. Thus the utilitarian would oppose any merger that resulted in an overall balance of loss for the majority of stakeholders—even if the initiating parties benefited.

Even if the majority of stakeholders did benefit, the Utilitarian would still be concerned with lessening the negative impact on other stakeholders. An agent utilizing this model of moral reasoning must raise certain questions.

- Will the anticipated merger benefit a majority of the stakeholders?
- Can we maximize these benefits for a majority of the stakeholders?
- If the merger will hurt certain stakeholders, will the overall benefits outweigh these losses?
- If the benefits do outweigh the harms for a majority of the stakeholders, what measures will lessen the harmful effects?
- If the harmful and beneficial effects of the anticipated merger are weighted according to duration, immediacy, and proximity, will this change our evaluation of the merger?[20]

It should be obvious that these three models may lead to conflicting courses of action. The initiating agent has a choice to make when integrating such ethical analysis into the decision procedures for determining whether or not to merge. In spite of these differences, it is important to note the following points.

- In a given situation, the same course of action may be taken, whichever model is chosen.
- Although the process of reasoning differs, each model requires some sensitivity to the potential harms and benefits for all stakeholders.
- Each model provides a systematic method for determining and assessing the ethical issues involved in mergers.
- Each model adds a needed dimension to the deliberations involved in the merger process.

The Stages of a Merger

In evaluating the decision whether or not to merge, the initiating parties are confronted with a series of complex questions that require a systematic method of deliberation. These questions emerge at every distinct stage of the merger process—from planning to implementation and beyond. We are convinced that this procedure must not only entail the basic operational considerations, but also it must include the key ethical issues that emerge in each stage. Just what are these distinct stages? Space permits us only a thumbnail sketch of each stage.[21]

Stage One is *the decision to consider the option of merging*. At this stage the primary question is whether or not a merger is a viable option. Maybe it is the only option for corporate survival. In any case, the initiating party must consider how a merger with another company will help or hinder the achievement of corporate objectives and whether or not there are alternatives to a merger. These and other operational considerations are weighed in light of the likely impact of such a decision on the corporate stakeholders. At this stage it is critical to establish criteria for measuring these likely harms and benefits, to determine whether or not the potential harms are serious enough to merit the abandonment of any merger strategy, and to develop procedures for lessening the losses to stakeholders.

Stage Two is *the search for a prospective merger partner*. At this stage it is important to develop an operational profile of the ideal merger partner and then to measure prospective partners by this profile. This includes a comparative examination of the physical resources, management styles, personnel, the economic strengths and weaknesses, and corporate cultures of all prospective mergers. In essence, which company will help us to achieve our corporate objectives? These objectives include the ethical standards and code of conduct that form the fabric of the company. If any prospective partner will strengthen the ethical climate, so much the better. If the opposite is likely, they should be dropped from further consideration.

Stage Three is *the decision to merge with a specific partner.* This phase is a refinement of Stage Two. The field is narrowed to a couple of potential partners. At this stage operational and ethical expectations are solidified into a very specific and realistic set of criteria to be applied to the prospective partners. For example, what operational measurements do we use in making the final selection—return on investment, total sales, new product development, financial ratios based upon combined balance sheets, or research-and-development capability? Similarly, what ethical criteria do we use—stated corporate commitment to stakeholders, management's "track record" in relating to the concerns of stakeholders, or the solicited opinions of selected stakeholders? Above all, we must determine how the prospective partners might react to a merger proposal.

Stage Four is *the process of making a proposal to the prospective partner.* The goal here is to develop a realistic merger proposal that will not be rejected out of hand. The pros and cons for both parties must be directly addressed in a proposal that stresses the respective advantages. And points of contention or impediments must be considered. The initiating company should determine what concessions are feasible in order to remove these potential impediments. In addition, the merger proposal must identify the key areas where certain stakeholder groups will suffer loss, e.g., management consolidation, job relocation, job displacement, plant closures, and job seniority. And a plan for addressing these probable changes should be developed with room for modification.

Stage Five, *negotiating the merger agreement,* determines whether or not the merger has a chance to succeed. It is at this point that both parties must be candid and flexible. Concessions and trade-offs in the negotiating process are critical determinants in whether or not the parties are a good fit. Each party must be certain that the operational concessions make economic sense and that any ethical concessions do not arbitrarily or unfairly undercut any critical moral commitments to any stakeholder. The ease or difficulty of this process will be an early indication of how the new company will operate and how it will treat its various stakeholders.

Stage Six, *formulating a plan for implementation,* is directed at the actual steps needed to fully implement the merger. We need to be sure that this plan includes both the letter and spirit of the merger agreement. This plan must include a realistic time frame for full implementation, procedures for resolving unforeseen impediments, a detailed description of operational and logistical responsibilities, and provisions for arbitration when disagreements occur. The need for mediation techniques is particularly important in protecting the interests of the various stakeholders. Clearly the plan must also include a description of steps that will be taken to formulate the new corporation's policy on corporate ethics.

Stage Seven, *carrying out the implementation plan,* centers on the logistics of the merger. We are concerned with any glitches that may develop. In particular, are these glitches that were simply overlooked in the merger planning, or are they the result of our eagerness to complete the merger within the designated time frame? It is important that these difficulties are also evaluated in reference to the ethical consequences they may pose for various stakeholders. For example, will the proposed remedies to these impediments treat stakeholders with respect and dignity? Should any stakeholders have a role in resolving these difficulties?

The final phase, Stage Eight, entails an *ongoing review and evaluation* of the merger. Here we are measuring the operational successes and failures and introducing modifications in the process. At both the operational and ethical levels of analysis, we are concerned with determining whether or not our objectives have been met. If not, we need to determine what has gone awry. The bottom line is that the harmful and beneficial effects for all stakeholders must be monitored long after the merger is completed.

The basic point of this paper is that any decision to merge must be carefully thought out. Each stage of the process from the initial deliberations to the review process requires a structured strategy that incorporates all of the critical issues that may arise. This requires a fine balance between operational and ethical considerations. We believe the stakeholder analysis is a good framework to use in devising this merger strategy. When companies fail to integrate the ethical dimension into the decision procedures, they increase the probability that certain stakeholders will be unnecessarily hurt by the consolidation.

The discussion we offer is not an exhaustive analysis of the various issues that must be considered, but it is a useful framework for sensitizing people to the potential difficulties that may ensue. Of course, the reader may reasonably argue that we have failed to address some obvious practices that dominate the news today, e.g., hostile takeovers, golden parachutes, and greenmail. There is no doubt that such practices immediately raise serious ethical questions, but we believe the frameworks discussed in the paper and the questions raised can easily be applied to these problem areas. Certainly stakeholder analysis provides such an application. Even if we wanted to focus on these issues, thoroughness would require a separate paper on each topic.

We have concentrated on friendly mergers because this type of consolidation is one that most stakeholders are likely to encounter. More importantly, the ethical issues that emerge in this context are often overlooked. The resulting harm may be more insidious, but it may be just as damaging as any that emerges from a hostile takeover.

NOTES

1. To better examine these types of trends, one should read the journal *Mergers & Acquisitions,* which is published by M. L. R. Publishing Company of Philadelphia.

2. This flexibility was fortuitous for ailing industries such as the steel industry.

3. Significant changes at Beatrice have reduced the number of basic companies to a handful.

4. Of course, not all acquisitions are hostile.

5. In fact, some companies have promoted themselves as white knights in order to diversify.

6. Some would dispute the claim that these individuals are reformers.

7. For example, a very traditional company may not choose to experiment in ways that will alter corporate history or culture.

8. This is a strategy that the Chicago Tribune Companies adopted in April 1989, to discourage any potential takeovers.

9. See: Sloan, Allan, "Why Is No One Safe?" *Forbes,* March 11, 1985, pp. 134–140 and Ansley, Mary Holm, "Fighting Off the Raiders: Do Repellents Serve Shareholders?" *Chicago Tribune,* March 17, 1985, Section 7, p. 1.

10. For example, a corporation may acquire a supplier to lower operational costs.

11. This activity has become prevalent in many industries as competition increases and the need for consolidation is required.

12. The double effect is a traditional problem in ethics. For example, performing an abortion to save the life of the mother has the effect of both saving and taking a life.

13. Daily, Jo Ellen, "Do Mergers Really Work?" *Business Week,* June 3, 1985, pp. 80–92.

14. For a more thorough discussion, see: Cooke, Robert Allan, "Business Ethics: A Perspective," *Arthur Andersen Cases on Business Ethics,* Arthur Andersen & Co., 1988, pp. 1–10.

15. It is important to remember that some stakeholders have more at stake than others.

16. Frankena, William, *Ethics,* Englewood Cliffs, NJ: Prentice-Hall, Inc., 1963.

17. These operational models are commonly used in business; e.g., J. C. Penney and the Golden Rule.

18. We are assuming the individual is rational and has normal moral sensibilities.

19. Most notably stockholders.

20. Weighting is crucial for utilitarians.

21. For a more thorough examination of this decision analysis see: Cooke, Robert Allan and Earl Young, "Mergers from an Ethical Perspective," *Business and Professional Ethics Journal,* Volume 5, 1986, pp. 111–128.

CHAPTER 5

THE CORPORATE SOCIAL RESPONSIBILITY DEBATE

Introduction

The constant debate over corporate social responsibility is an instructive example of the complexities of contemporary business decision making and the realities of doing business in the modern industrial arena. The concept of corporate social responsibility emerged as a direct response to the growing power and influence that American business gained directly after World War II. Business organizations grew in size and wealth, thanks to the war effort, and in the two decades following it they made even greater economic strides. In fact, the corporation attained the status of an all-pervasive institution in American life and had far-reaching effects, not only upon the economic well-being of the nation but also upon its social fabric. According to many sociologists, the corporation has become the most significant social institution, displacing government, religion, and even the family in its power to influence the lives of people.

As the corporation accrued the benefits of such status, critics began to raise questions about the responsibilities of these institutional giants. A countermovement to the power of business emerged, which challenged the corporation to become a member-in-good standing of the national and international community by using some of its massive, private resources to address the many public ills that plagued society. In the 1960s, poverty and discrimination were the main problems that the early proponents of corporate social responsibility focused on as they urged corporations to become good citizens. The critics suggested that corporations creatively use part of their accumulated wealth to help eradicate these blotches on the American social scene. Their argument in support of this idea, however, went beyond mere suggestion.

Proponents of corporate social responsibility claim that business organizations have a moral and ethical duty to contribute to social well-being. In his *Corporations and Morality* (Englewood Cliffs: Prentice Hall, 1982), Thomas Donaldson, of Georgetown University, has argued that the relationship between business entities and society is based upon an implicit compact that spells out and defines the idea of corporate social responsibility. According to Donaldson, corporations and society have entered into a "social contract" where each party has rights, as well as duties, to the other party. This social-contract theory of the corporation holds that in return for the right to conduct business and reap a profit within a given social context, corporations are obliged to protect and enhance the interest of consumers, workers, and the communities in which a firm conducts its business. In this view, then, corporations have a number of social responsibilities by the mere fact that they conduct business and use the natural and human resources of a community to further their own private economic ends. For Donaldson and other proponents of corporate social responsibility, then, there is no question that the management of business organizations must take definitive actions to use the accumulated resources of their organizations to assist society in tackling the ills that befall it. Not to take such action would be corporate irresponsibility in the sense that the social contract would be violated.

Of course, not everyone interested in this essential issue would agree that there is a moral obligation on the part of managers to expend corporate resources on social problems. Milton Friedman, the world-renowned economist, takes issue with the idea that business organizations have specific social responsibilities and that managers must take definitive actions to fulfill them. In his view, because managers are employees hired by the owners of a firm—that is, the shareholders—they have first and foremost an obligation to ensure that the owner's interests are protected and enhanced. Spending money on social problems would be unacceptable in this instance because shareholder interests would be placed second to the interest of society. According to Friedman, the resolution of social problems is the task of governments, not businesses, and managers who so spend money on them act irresponsibly. In "The Social Responsibility of Business Is to Increase Its Profits," reprinted from the *New York Times Sunday Magazine,* Friedman makes a classic statement of laissez-faire economics on the essential issue of corporate social responsibility.

While most proponents of corporate social responsibility would argue that business can do more in the creative use of their resources to help advance the status of society and address social problems, it can still be said that the concept of social responsibility is one that has been embraced in general by the corporate community. It is rare to find a firm espousing the arguments of a Milton Friedman today. Rather we see many business organizations openly avowing a commitment to social responsibility and making strategic business decisions based upon it. This social philosophy of business has been expressed as the opportunity for a firm to "do well by doing good." It is a philosophy that sees profit making as compatible with a social agenda and a social contract.

One of the early corporations to take this proactive stance was Control Data Corporation. Founded by William Norris, who espoused a "do well by doing good" philosophy as early as 1957, when the company was first offered on the open market for one dollar a share, Norris steered the firm into a profitable computer giant while at the same time making social issues central ones in Control Data's business plan. For example, the firm made plant-location decisions based upon community needs for economic revitalization rather than upon the company's own explicit business needs. They built plants in ghetto locations, hiring the inner-city poor, many of whom had long arrest records and probably would not have gained employment in any other corporation. And as Control Data flourished and grew, Norris and his social conscience became centerpieces in the arguments of the proponents of corporate social responsibility, which proved that doing well and doing good can go hand in hand. But there were also detractors from Norris's social strategy, and the second article in this chapter, "Corporate Do-gooder: Control Data's Bill Norris," allows us a firsthand look at how Norris navigated his firm in the sometimes choppy waters of corporate social responsibility.

Another way to view the turmoil concerning the concept of corporate social responsibility is provided by Rogene A. Buchholz in "The Evolution of Corporate Social Responsibility." What Buchholz outlines are the passages of the notion of corporate social responsibility over the years, from a concept tied to the social upheavals of the 1960s to its latest manifestation ·in what has been called "corporate social responsiveness." This piece does a fine job in detailing the ways in which this concept has undergone change over the years but how it nevertheless remains an essential issue in business ethics. It will be interesting to watch how corporate social responsibility evolves over the next twenty years, and what factors will continue to transform it.

The Social Responsibility of Business Is to Increase Its Profits

Milton Friedman

For the Nobel Prize–winning economist Milton Friedman, the doctrine of corporate social responsibility is a well-disguised bit of managerial irresponsibility. His argument against business spending corporate funds for social ends is relatively straightforward. According to Friedman, the managers of a corporation are hired by the owners of a firm—the shareholders—for only one solitary purpose: to increase the profits of the firm so that the owners can achieve a fair return on their investment. Since corporate expenditures

SOURCE: *The New York Times Sunday Magazine,* September 13, 1970. Copyright © 1970 by The New York Times Company. Reprinted with permission.

earmarked for alleviating society's ills will cut into profit and thereby into return on investment, managers who undertake such expenditures are not fulfilling their fiduciary responsibility to the owners and are acting contrary to their contractual obligations. Such actions are inherently irresponsible. Furthermore corporate expenditures for social causes function as a form of taxation without representation. The task of alleviating social problems is not within the purview of business; rather, it is the prerogative and obligation of government. When management spends funds for social ends, they are acting like governmental decision makers but without the legitimizing feature of having been elected. Consequently, the doctrine of corporate social responsibility is ultimately a "subversive doctrine" for the conservative-minded Friedman.

When I hear businessmen speak eloquently about the "social responsibilities of business in a free-enterprise system," I am reminded of the wonderful line about the Frenchman who discovered at the age of 70 that he had been speaking prose all his life. The businessmen believe that they are defending free enterprise when they declaim that business is not concerned "merely" with profit but also with promoting desirable "social" ends; that business has a "social conscience" and takes seriously its responsibilities for providing employment, eliminating discrimination, avoiding pollution and whatever else may be the catchwords of the contemporary crop of reformers. In fact they are—or would be if they or anyone else took them seriously—preaching pure and unadulterated socialism. Businessmen who talk this way are unwitting puppets of the intellectual forces that have been undermining the basis of a free society these past decades.

The discussions of the "social responsibilities of business" are notable for their analytical looseness and lack of rigor. What does it mean to say that "business" has responsibilities? Only people can have responsibilities. A corporation is an artificial person and in this sense may have artificial responsibilities, but "business" as a whole cannot be said to have responsibilities, even in this vague sense. The first step toward clarity in examining the doctrine of the social responsibility of business is to ask precisely what it implies for whom.

Presumably, the individuals who are to be responsible are businessmen, which means individual proprietors or corporate executives. Most of the discussion of social responsibility is directed at corporations, so in what follows I shall mostly neglect the individual proprietor and speak of corporate executives.

In a free-enterprise, private-property system, a corporate executive is an employee of the owners of the business. He has direct responsibility to his employers. That responsibility is to conduct the business in accordance with their desires, which generally will be to make as much money as possible while conforming to the basic rules of the society, both those embodied in law and those embodied in ethical custom. Of course, in some cases his employers may have a different objective. A group of persons might establish a corporation for an eleemosynary purpose—for example, a hospital or a school. The manager of such a corporation will not have money profit as his objective but the rendering of certain services.

In either case, the key point is that, in his capacity as a corporate executive, the manager is the agent of the individuals who own the corporation or establish the eleemosynary institution, and his primary responsibility is to them.

Needless to say, this does not mean that it is easy to judge how well he is performing his task. But at least the criterion of performance is straightforward, and the persons among whom a voluntary contractual arrangement exists are clearly defined.

Of course, the corporate executive is also a person in his own right. As a person, he may have many other responsibilities that he recognizes or assumes voluntarily—to his family, his conscience, his feelings of charity, his church, his clubs, his city, his country. He may feel impelled by these responsibilities to devote part of his income to causes he regards as worthy, to refuse to work for particular corporations, even to leave his job, for example, to join his country's armed forces. If we wish, we may refer to some of these responsibilities as "social responsibilities." But in these respects he is acting as a principal, not an agent; he is spending his own money or time or energy, not the money of his employers or the time or energy he has contracted to devote to their purposes. If these are "social responsibilities," they are the social responsibilities of individuals, not of business.

What does it mean to say that the corporate executive has a "social responsibility" in his capacity as businessman? If this statement is not pure rhetoric, it must mean that he is to act in some way that is not in the interest of his employers. For example, that he is to refrain from increasing the price of the product in order to contribute to the social objective of preventing inflation, even though a price increase would be in the best interests of the corporation. Or that he is to make expenditures on reducing pollution beyond the amount that is in the best interests of the corporation or that is required by law in order to contribute to the social objective of improving the environment. Or that, at the expense of corporate profits, he is to hire "hard-core" unemployed instead of better-qualified available workmen to contribute to the social objective of reducing poverty.

In each of these cases, the corporate executive would be spending someone else's money for a general social interest. Insofar as his actions in accord with his "social responsibility" reduce returns to stockholders, he is spending their money. Insofar as his actions raise the price to customers, he is spending the customers' money. Insofar as his actions lower the wages of some employees, he is spending their money.

The stockholders or the customers or the employees could separately spend their own money on the particular action if they wished to do so. The executive is exercising a distinct "social responsibility," rather than serving as an agent of the stockholders or the customers or the employees, only if he spends the money in a different way than they would have spent it.

But if he does this, he is in effect imposing taxes, on the one hand, and deciding how the tax proceeds shall be spent, on the other.

This process raises political questions on two levels: principle and consequences. On the level of political principle, the imposition of taxes and the expenditure of tax proceeds are governmental functions. We have established elaborate constitutional, parliamentary and judicial provisions to control these functions, to assure that taxes are imposed so far as possible in accordance with the preferences and desires of the public—after all, "taxation without representation" was one of the battle cries of the American Revolution. We have a system of checks and balances to separate the legislative function of imposing taxes and enacting expenditures from the executive function of collecting taxes and administering expenditure programs and from the judicial function of mediating disputes and interpreting the law.

Here the businessman—self-selected or appointed directly or indirectly by stockholders—is to be simultaneously legislator, executive and jurist. He is to decide whom to tax by how much and for what purpose, and he is to spend the proceeds—all this guided only by general exhortations from on high to restrain inflation, improve the environment, fight poverty and so on and on.

The whole justification for permitting the corporate executive to be selected by the stockholders is that the executive is an agent serving the interests of his principal. This justification disappears when the corporate executive imposes taxes and spends the proceeds for "social" purposes. He becomes in effect a public employee, a civil servant, even though he remains in name an employee of a private enterprise. On grounds of political principle, it is intolerable that such civil servants—insofar as their actions in the name of social responsibility are real and not just window-dressing—should be selected as they are now. If they are to be civil servants, then they must be selected through a political process. If they are to impose taxes and make expenditures to foster "social" objectives, then political machinery must be set up to guide the assessment of taxes and to determine through a political process the objectives to be served.

This is the basic reason why the doctrine of "social responsibility" involves the acceptance of the socialist view that political mechanisms, not market mechanisms, are the

THE CORPORATE SOCIAL RESPONSIBILITY DEBATE

appropriate way to determine the allocation of scarce resources to alternative uses.

On the grounds of consequences, can the corporate executive in fact discharge his alleged "social responsibilities"? On the one hand, suppose he could get away with spending the stockholders' or customers' or employees' money. How is he to know how to spend it? He is told that he must contribute to fighting inflation. How is he to know what action of his will contribute to that end? He is presumably an expert in running his company—in producing a product or selling it or financing it. But nothing about his selection makes him an expert on inflation. Will his holding down the price of his product reduce inflationary pressure? Or, by leaving more spending power in the hands of his customers, simply divert it elsewhere? Or, by forcing him to produce less because of the lower price, will it simply contribute to shortages? Even if he could answer these questions, how much cost is he justified in imposing on his stockholders, customers and employees for this social purpose? What is his appropriate share and what is the appropriate share of others?

And, whether he wants to or not, can he get away with spending his stockholders', customers' or employees' money? Will not the stockholders fire him? (Either the present ones or those who take over when his actions in the name of social responsibility have reduced the corporation's profits and the price of its stock.) His customers and his employees can desert him for other producers and employers less scrupulous in exercising their social responsibilities.

This facet of "social responsibility" doctrine is brought into sharp relief when the doctrine is used to justify wage restraint by trade unions. The conflict of interest is naked and clear when union officials are asked to subordinate the interest of their members to some more general social purpose. If the union officials try to enforce wage restraint, the consequence is likely to be wildcat strikes, rank-and-file revolts and the emergence of strong competitors for their jobs. We thus have the ironic phenomenon that union leaders—at least in the U.S.—have objected to government interference with the market far more consistently and courageously than have business leaders.

The difficulty of exercising "social responsibility" illustrates, of course, the great virtue of private competitive enterprise—it forces people to be responsible for their own actions and makes it difficult for them to "exploit" other people for either selfish or unselfish purposes. They can do good—but only at their own expense.

Many a reader who has followed the argument this far may be tempted to remonstrate that it is all well and good to speak of government's having the responsibility to impose taxes and determine expenditures for such "social" purposes as controlling pollution or training the hard-core unemployed, but that the problems are too urgent to wait on the slow course of political processes, that the exercise of social responsibility by businessmen is a quicker and surer way to solve pressing current problems.

Aside from the question of fact—I share Adam Smith's skepticism about the benefits that can be expected from "those who affected to trade for the public good"—this argument must be rejected on grounds of principle. What it amounts to is an assertion that those who favor the taxes and expenditures in question have failed to persuade a majority of their fellow citizens to be of like mind and that they are seeking to attain by undemocratic procedures what they cannot attain by democratic procedures. In a free society, it is hard for "good" people to do "good," but that is a small price to pay for making it hard for "evil" people to do "evil," especially since one man's good is another's evil.

I have, for simplicity, concentrated on the special case of the corporate executive, except only for the brief digression on trade unions. But precisely the same argument applies to the newer phenomenon of calling upon stockholders to require corporations to exercise social responsibility (the recent GM crusade, for example). In most of these cases, what is in effect involved is some stockholders trying to get other stockholders (or customers or employees) to contribute against their will to "social" causes favored by the activists. Insofar as they succeed, they are again imposing taxes and spending the proceeds.

THE CORPORATE SOCIAL RESPONSIBILITY DEBATE

The situation of the individual proprietor is somewhat different. If he acts to reduce the returns of his enterprise in order to exercise his "social responsibility," he is spending his own money, not someone else's. If he wishes to spend his money on such purposes, that is his right, and I cannot see that there is any objection to his doing so. In the process, he, too, may impose costs on employees and customers. However, because he is far less likely than a large corporation or union to have monopolistic power, any such side effects will tend to be minor.

Of course, in practice the doctrine of social responsibility is frequently a cloak for actions that are justified on other grounds rather than a reason for those actions.

To illustrate, it may well be in the long-run interest of a corporation that is a major employer in a small community to devote resources to providing amenities to that community or to improving its government. That may make it easier to attract desirable employees, it may reduce the wage bill or lessen losses from pilferage and sabotage or have other worthwhile effects. Or it may be that, given the laws about the deductibility of corporate charitable contributions, the stockholders can contribute more to charities they favor by having the corporation make the gift than by doing it themselves, since they can in that way contribute an amount that would otherwise have been paid as corporate taxes.

In each of these—and many similar—cases, there is a strong temptation to rationalize these actions as an exercise of "social responsibility." In the present climate of opinion, with its widespread aversion to "capitalism," "profits," the "soulless corporation" and so on, this is one way for a corporation to generate goodwill as a by-product of expenditures that are entirely justified in its own self-interest.

It would be inconsistent of me to call on corporate executives to refrain from this hypocritical window-dressing because it harms the foundations of a free society. That would be to call on them to exercise a "social responsibility"! If our institutions, and the attitudes of the public, make it in their self-interest to cloak their actions in this way, I cannot summon much indignation to denounce them. At the same time, I can express admiration for those individual proprietors or owners of closely held corporations or stockholders of more broadly held corporations who disdain such tactics as approaching fraud.

Whether blameworthy or not, the use of the cloak of social responsibility, and the nonsense spoken in its name by influential and prestigious businessmen, does clearly harm the foundations of a free society. I have been impressed time and again by the schizophrenic character of many businessmen. They are capable of being extremely far-sighted and clear-headed in matters that are internal to their businesses. They are incredibly short-sighted and muddle-headed in matters that are outside their businesses but affect the possible survival of business in general. This short-sightedness is strikingly exemplified in the calls from many businessmen for wage and price guidelines or controls or incomes policies. There is nothing that could do more in a brief period to destroy a market system and replace it by a centrally controlled system than effective governmental control of prices and wages.

The short-sightedness is also exemplified in speeches by businessmen on social responsibility. This may gain them kudos in the short run. But it helps to strengthen the already too prevalent view that the pursuit of profits is wicked and immoral and must be curbed and controlled by external forces. Once this view is adopted, the external forces that curb the market will not be the social consciences, however highly developed, of the pontificating executives; it will be the iron fist of government bureaucrats. Here, as with price and wage controls, businessmen seem to me to reveal a suicidal impulse.

The political principle that underlies the market mechanism is unanimity. In an ideal free market resting on private property, no individual can coerce any other, all cooperation is voluntary, all parties to such cooperation benefit or they need not participate. There are no "social" values, no "social" responsibilities in any sense other than the shared values and responsibilities of individuals. Society is a collection of individuals and of the various groups they voluntarily form.

The political principle that underlies the political mechanism is conformity. The individual must serve a more general social interest—whether that be determined by a church or a dictator or a majority. The individual may have a vote and a say in what is to be done, but if he is overruled, he must conform. It is appropriate for some to require others to contribute to a general social purpose whether they wish to or not.

Unfortunately, unanimity is not always feasible. There are some respects in which conformity appears unavoidable, so I do not see how one can avoid the use of the political mechanism altogether.

But the doctrine of "social responsibility" taken seriously would extend the scope of the political mechanism to every human activity. It does not differ in philosophy from the most explicitly collectivist doctrine. It differs only by professing to believe that collectivist ends can be attained without collectivist means. That is why, in my book *Capitalism and Freedom,* I have called it a "fundamentally subversive doctrine" in a free society, and have said that in such a society, "there is one and only one social responsibility of business—to use its resources and engage in activities designed to increase its profits so long as it stays within the rules of the game, which is to say, engages in open and free competition without deception or fraud."

Corporate Do-gooder: Control Data's Bill Norris

Inc. magazine

The thoughts and actions of William Norris, founder and past chairman and chief executive officer of Control Data Corporation, stands in sharp contrast to the critique of the

SOURCE: From *INC.* magazine, May 1988. Copyright © 1988 by Goldhirsh Group, Inc., 38 Commercial Wharf, Boston, MA 02110. Reprinted with permission.

doctrine of corporate social responsibility just presented by Milton Friedman. In the following *INC.* magazine interview with Norris, the thesis that corporate social responsibility is a fundamental obligation of business organizations is developed and supported. Moreover, Norris claims that in the case of Control Data—which embarked upon a number of projects driven by a social conscience—doing good for society also meant doing well for the business and the bottom line. Norris contends that corporate contributions for charitable purposes will not suffice to demonstrate that a firm is a good corporate citizen. Rather, as his leadership at Control Data suggests, social responsibility means devising corporate strategies and building a business with society's needs in mind. Social responsibility should be ingrained in business decision making; business should be in a cooperative posture with society—not in an adversarial one. For Norris, the mandate for business–society cooperation is clear, and in his concluding remark he intimates that because the Japanese have also seen this mandate and acted upon it, America is faced with the challenge to change its ways in order to compete adequately with the Japanese.

INC.: Where did the original spark come from that made you think, "I've got to do more than just make a profit"? Is there a particular event that changed your views about the social responsibilities of corporations?

NORRIS: I think there were several events. First, I graduated from the University of Nebraska with a degree in electrical engineering right at the bottom of the Great Depression. No one in our class could get a job in engineering. It was a shock. Added to that was the enormous suffering of many, many people who had it a lot worse than I did. They didn't have jobs, or any means of making a living, which is something I always had. Since I was born on a farm, I went back and helped my mother operate the farm. That experience was always a reference point.

And in 1967 there was another significant event—the fires and riots that swept through dozens of cities. Minneapolis was one of them—the north side of Minneapolis, which was predominately black. Even though some of those events had occurred in other places, it was just inconceivable that it had happened here. It was very serious. And the reason was that the people who'd rioted didn't have jobs.

INC.: After the riot did you go and look?

NORRIS: Yes. Before the riots, I had not been to the north side of Minneapolis. I had been lulled into the same feeling of benign benevolence as everyone else. I was thinking more in terms of all these slums in Detroit, New York City, and so forth. Once I saw it, I just felt that with the success that Control Data was having, I had better stop and think about this situation. So I decided to put jobs out there, good jobs. Control Data built a new plant on the north side of Minneapolis. We put one of our most important products in it, peripheral controllers, so no one would get the idea that we were just throwing something out there.

INC.: Was the plant an immediate success?

NORRIS: No. It wasn't spontaneous. We ran into some unexpected problems. One example: we were using standard employment forms. One of the questions was, "Have you ever been arrested?" Well, it turned out there wasn't enough room on the form to recount all the times these applicants had been arrested. And they had no real work experience, so that question was pretty useless, too. The form was completely ridiculous. Finally, we just tore up the regular form and devised a very simple one. You want a job, describe why you want it, and if you have anything else to say, just put it down. In other words, we made it clear that we weren't so interested in where they had been as where they wanted to go.

Another important point is that we had government funds. This was never simply a Control Data project. We were in partnership with the government, both the city as well as the federal government. I think the start-up costs for the north-side plant were around $6 million and the government paid maybe a third of them.

INC.: Could you have done it without some sort of government help?

NORRIS: Certainly, but I don't think that would have been wise. We all share in the responsibility, so we ought to share in the cost, especially in the cost of training these people. The educational system had failed them, or they'd failed the system—it didn't matter, there was failure. The point is, that wasn't just the responsibility of business, it was also the responsibility of government.

INC.: Is the plant still there?

NORRIS: Oh yes, it's very successful. And based on that success, we decided we should replicate it. At the peak, we had seven plants. We have two left, simply because the technology has changed dramatically. There's not the requirement for unskilled labor that there used to be in the computer business.

Here's something else important, though: we warned each one of those communities that that plant would probably not be there forever. And yet we also knew that the need for jobs was as pressing as ever. We didn't want to turn our backs on these people. So that led us to the concept of setting up the structure we call a job-creation network, which really should more appropriately be called a small-business innovation network. It is a community-based structure that will help start small businesses so that there are employment alternatives. We would let them have part of the plant as one element, which we call a business-and-technology center. The usual term is "incubator," which makes me want to throw up. The idea was to use part of the plant to house small businesses, a high-quality space at lower cost than a small business could get on its own. You also get a cooperation office started, which is the community working together to assist small businesses. Control Data was involved not only in leasing the plant space, but also in giving them access to our computer technology and so on. These small-business centers were put under the aegis of our Commercial Credit unit.

INC.: Could Control Data have saved money by being a lot more ruthless about closing down the plants? I am asking this especially in light of all the financial problems Control Data had at about the same time the plants were being shut down.

NORRIS: Oh, sure. For example, in one case we invested $250,000 in seed capital funds, and provided part of the building at no cost. But it really wasn't all that costly as far as the company was concerned.

Two-hundred fifty thousand dollars at Control Data is postage-stamp money, unless you want to make an issue out of it. All told, we could have saved $4 million to $5 million by just shutting things down and walking away. But when you have a loss of $150 million, and you have a chance to do something right that increases the loss by only a few million, you are a fool if you don't do it right. Now if you were a little company, and the difference between profit and loss was only $3 million, well, then you'd be in a different ball game.

INC.: I think most people would agree that handling the plant closings the way you did was extremely admirable. But it's hard to describe what you did as being business-minded, in a hard-nosed, corporate way. In effect, Control Data, at a time when it was already losing money, spent some $5 million more than it had to. Yet one of the major themes of your career is that Control Data's social efforts have always been expected to be good business efforts, too. Doesn't this example contradict your point?

NORRIS: It was good business—in the long term. And this, of course, is one of the tragedies in the modern business world. Everything is short-term-oriented now. I can't tell you the enormous amount of goodwill Control Data has been able to generate for itself with these programs. Looking at it in a broader sense, being lean and mean is not enough.

Short-term actions are going to be self-defeating in the long run. Yes, you can keep doing everything to maximize that bottom line. You can let people go just the instant that you don't need them, you don't have to go out of your way to try to condition their transition, and so on. But then you'll see the day when we'll have some more fires and riots. And probably even worse.

You look at these inner cities. Things are worse than they were back in 1967 when the riots occurred. Look out in the rural areas. My God, there's an enormous amount of misery. We're developing a two-class society. You don't think business is going to be called upon to do something about these problems? But it's useless to talk to businesspeople along these lines.

INC.: Why is it useless? Why wouldn't it have been sensible as you were doing all these things to try to sell your ideas to the business community and even to Wall Street? To say, "Look, we know this is costing us money, but we think it's worth it, not necessarily for bottom-line reasons, but for social good." Couldn't that have deflected some of the criticism you've received from Wall Street and the business community over the years?

NORRIS: First of all, we always did things for bottom-line reasons. Second, you don't know how many violent discussions I've had with securities analysts. They don't want to understand. We've never had a "social project." We've had projects addressing social needs, in cooperation with the government and other sectors, that we've also seen as profitable business opportunities.

INC.: And what would the securities analysts say when you told them that?

NORRIS: They'd say that we had social projects. So we'd get together again and finally I'd say, "Hell, you know, you're dishonest. You come in here, and I explain to you that we don't have social projects, and you agree. Then, damn it, you go out and write about 'social projects.' When are you going to quit doing it?" When you're getting that sort of thing from securities analysts, how can you get across to business in general that this is good business?

INC.: Why do you think Wall Street's been so negative? Are they mean-spirited, greedy folks?

THE CORPORATE SOCIAL RESPONSIBILITY DEBATE

NORRIS: I believe that they can't grasp that it's a new style of management. For example, I never said that these projects were something that Control Data would do by itself. Never. Never. That's impossible. That's ridiculous. But what is possible—and what is profitable in the long run—is addressing society's needs in conjunction with the government and with other sectors. That's what they don't understand.

For example, one of Control Data's most profitable growing areas now is in agriculture. I think that Control Data is the largest private supplier of knowledge to farmers. And it has grown out of one of the projects that was ridiculed by Wall Street.

INC.: This is Rural Ventures?

NORRIS: It started with Rural Ventures. Rural Ventures, which was a consortium to develop and provide computer-based assistance to farmers, was set up to find a new direction for agriculture. By the time we got it set up, the amount of government money that was available for rural revitalization had started going downhill. Today, there's virtually no money available. Without that government support, Rural Ventures itself could never hope to be profitable.

But what came out of Rural Ventures for Control Data was a whole spectrum of profitable computer-based education courses covering the operation of different types of farming—dairy farming, hog farming, beekeeping. There are fifteen or twenty of them. And they're making money.

INC.: Rural Ventures was sold not long after you stepped down as chairman of Control Data. Does the company still have a commitment to addressing social needs?

NORRIS: Yes, but Rural Ventures was a means to help point the way. It was a very small operation. I learned a lot from it. From my point of view, it was very successful, and the loss was never more than $100,000 a year. And yet you read the Wall Street analysts' reports, and they make a big deal out of Rural Ventures.

INC.: Perhaps the issue was not the amount of money that was spent but the focus of top management. In other words, these were the things that Bill Norris considered the most important. Therefore, to the extent that top managers were thinking about Rural Ventures, they weren't thinking about the peripheral business. Is that a valid criticism? It didn't divert money, it diverted attention?

NORRIS: No. Listen, Control Data is a multidivision company. There was a guy who was in charge of peripherals. He had enormous success. The thing just exploded. You couldn't tell him anything because of that success. I kept telling him the Japanese were coming in here very strong, for instance. They're going to put a lot in research. Well, you can't argue with somebody who has success. He would go around the corner and say, "Aw, you can never satisfy the old bastard."

INC.: But you're the boss.

NORRIS: What do you do? Do you kick him out? In retrospect, sure. Hindsight is great.

INC.: Another project that was on your special list was the business centers that were put under Commercial Credit. You started with two hundred of them. They really didn't take off. It became a much smaller thing, and, of course, they were unprofitable. Was the reason in part because of the lack of good marketing and research ahead of time?

NORRIS: No. It was just dumb management.

INC.: Well, that may be the same thing. Was it researched thoroughly enough in a business sense?

NORRIS: This is exactly the sort of thing I mean when I say that people don't understand our new style of management. When you're doing something new, the worst thing you can do is a lot of research and studies beforehand. All that will uncover is all the problems—all the reasons you shouldn't do something. I've learned by bitter experience that you just go do it. Now that doesn't mean you have to go out and do it a hundred times over. This was what got out of control with Commercial Credit. I was appalled to find the amount of money they sank into individual business centers. They went first class. Put a lot of money into furnishings and equipment and so forth. My perspective was to start small, and make it part of their loan offices. I never could get that point across. Instead, they fixed up the plush office space and got the overhead without the business. That's what I call stupid management.

INC.: Does this speak at some level to your own shortcomings as a manager? It's understandable not to get your point across to Wall Street or to another CEO. But weren't these people under your direct control?

NORRIS: Well, sure, I could have done a better job. On the other hand, I have always been a great believer in giving people a free hand. I started at Sperry Rand, and the reason I left was the fact that there were too many people with their spoons in my soup. I couldn't do anything.

INC.: But can you let a manager handle a project himself when the goals are not clearly understood by everyone?

NORRIS: It's a pertinent question, but it doesn't fit in this case. For an operation like Commercial Credit, the business-center idea wasn't all that far-out. It made real business sense. Small business had always been its major thrust. I just wanted them to enlarge the scope of the effort.

INC.: Still, for whatever reasons, they have never been truly successful, and certainly not profitable. It's one thing to profess a desire to make a profit with these programs and another actually to go out and do it. So one keeps coming back to the question: can these things work the way you hope they will when you first conceive of them?

NORRIS: In this case, there is no community in which it has been fully implemented . . . but I know it works because we started a cooperation office in the Twin Cities, called the Minnesota Cooperation Office. It's been very, very successful. It's started up something like twenty businesses. I was just talking to the president the other day. He estimates that with the businesses they've started up, plus those they will start in the next ten years, that ten years from now they will have created 20,000 jobs. That's a hell of a lot of jobs. And there's been little support within the community for it.

INC.: There are, of course, plenty of traditional ways that corporations give to society. In Minnesota, they have a tradition called the Five Percent Club, in which companies donate 5% of their pretax earnings to worthy groups. But you've never been much of a fan of the Five Percent Club, have you?

NORRIS: You can never meet basic needs by simply contributing 5% of pretax earnings. First of all, there's a limit on the amount. And second, once a company gives its 5%, that's it, it has done its bit. The company forgets about it until the next year.

Whereas if it's part of your business, and your future's involved in it, then you don't forget it. Let's face it: you're never in this God's world going to get the magnitude of resources that are needed to make fundamental changes. I believe that in order to have enough decent-paying jobs, you have to make that your deliberate objective. You have to make it part of your business.

INC.: You haven't been able to convince your fellow CEOs or Wall Street about the need and benefits of investments in social projects. Do you see any hope for changing their attitudes?

NORRIS: Actually, I think things have gone the other way. I think they've hardened. And there is reinforcement for their point of view. There's the guy in the White House telling everybody how good it is.

INC.: In addition to the question of jobs, what else do you think people should be worried about? What are the things that companies should be trying to do something about?

NORRIS: Any thoughtful person ought to be concerned about what's going on here with respect to the Japanese. They're just buying us out. I got into a little bit of an argument with a person in Congress. I said it's obvious that the trade deficit is not going to be solved by a lower dollar. The problem is much more fundamental than that. I was using the example of hostile takeovers as one of the detractors from competitiveness. And he got all steamed up over that. He said, "Yeah, but if you look at the trade numbers, the trade account is going up with Japan." I said, "Yeah, but look at the value that's added to the products that we're selling them. The value added in a pork belly is a lot different from the value added in a VCR that's coming this way."

The Japanese are adding enormous value, which is providing them with all this damn money to come back here and buy everything that's around. It's a very serious situation. We've got to step up the value-added part, which is innovation.

INC.: The question then becomes—and this gets to another one of your ideas—can American corporations ever learn to innovate through cooperation? Case in point, MCC [Microelectronic & Computer Technology Corp.], which you played such a large role in setting up. There are rumblings that a number of the original technology companies in the consortium have pulled out of it. And there's talk that they're never going to have the innovation they talked about.

NORRIS: Listen, MCC is a tremendous success. Again, reporters get a better story out of problems than they do out of success. There's no question that MCC is an important bellwether operation. It is successful today. That is not as evident as it will be later.

We're going into some tough days ahead for this country. It isn't until you get some fear in your guts that you'll open up your mind. This is the reason why it was possible to start MCC. These big companies were frightened of the Japanese.

There are two major creators of wealth in our society. One is agriculture, and the other is manufacturing. And both of them are in serious trouble. These problems have got to be solved.

INC.: What about the tremendous growth in the U.S. service economy?

NORRIS: It doesn't create nearly as much wealth as manufacturing and agriculture. Furthermore, most services are hooked to manufacturing. You manufacture something, you've got to service it, you've got to sell it, you've got to finance it, you've got to transport it. But if you don't manufacture it, you won't get those other services to go with it. This is another serious problem we're facing with the Japanese. They're getting the handle on all the manufacturing.

INC.: How does a small-business man fit into the things you're talking about? Suppose he is running this $5-million company. He's got a problem on the loading dock. He's been through two CFOs in the last three years. He's trying to get his son into the business. And IBM has just decided it's going to cancel its contract for his widgets, and that's 30% of his business. Now, what is it that you want him to do, if anything?

NORRIS: There are plenty of things he can do. He can join one of these job-creation networks. And, I hasten to add, this will have benefits for him, too. For instance, part of the goal of these small-business cooperatives is to make it possible for small businesses to acquire technology from overseas and government laboratories. I don't know of any small company that doesn't need a new product. That's a serious problem for small companies. They grow up on one product, and licenses are hard to come by. They need help, and where are they going to get the technology? A big company isn't going to give it to them. But they can get it out of government labs. They can get it out of universities. But they need help to do it.

INC.: Small-business men would just think of that as smart business. They wouldn't think of that as socially responsible. You're not suggesting they go out and do the kind of things that Control Data did in terms of taking socially responsible initiatives?

NORRIS: What I'm suggesting is that they get involved. Help support a job-creation network. Get on the board of directors of a cooperation office. Help review business plans. Make a little investment in seed capital. Invest in maybe two or three small companies.

INC.: Other companies?

NORRIS: Other companies, as a means of probing for new markets, new technology, new people.

THE CORPORATE SOCIAL RESPONSIBILITY DEBATE

INC.: Is small business in a sense just as much to be faulted as big business for keeping the blinders on?

NORRIS: Yes, sir.

INC.: So, whatever the guy's problems are, they're not so time-consuming that he doesn't have time to invest something in the community?

NORRIS: Yes, because the community will turn around and help him with the problems he can't solve by himself, such as getting technology out of a government lab. You know, there are something like seven hundred government laboratories. They spend $18 billion to $20 billion a year. They employ one-sixth of the engineers and scientists. Yet very little of that technology is commercialized.

INC.: Why is that? They do something and put it on a shelf?

NORRIS: They don't know how to do it. They don't understand the commercial potential of research results. By setting up a program, administered by cooperation offices, you could select small businesses that would be qualified to look at different types of technology. Get them into government laboratories to help direct research—the applied research that's necessary to take it to the stage where it could be withdrawn from the laboratory, and handled under license or joint venture or however.

INC.: As a manager, you've had a number of innovative and highly motivated people work for you. You've talked about giving your people a free hand on projects. What about the more tangible kinds of rewards, such as employee stock ownership plans?

NORRIS: I tried it. Didn't work. As soon as the stock goes up they sell it. And what have you gained?

INC.: You've got some happier employees.

NORRIS: Yeah, but they don't remember that too long after the new car they bought wears out.

INC.: So you don't want your employees to own the company. And you certainly don't want Wall Street to own the company. So who should own companies in America?

NORRIS: I guess the system that has a lot going for it is one that allows banks to own stock in companies. One of the appalling things that has happened is the lack of responsibility of banks for business. Twenty years ago, you could talk to an investment banker, you could talk to a commercial banker with absolute confidence that it was confidential. You can't do that today. Hell, they'll put you into play if they see an opportunity. No compunction about it at all.

Now if these banks had an interest in these companies, they'd be more careful about some of the things that they did. This is the reason why the Japanese system works better. I think what we've got to do is take the best part of our system, and the best part of theirs, and get a better one out of it.

INC.: What's the best part of ours?

NORRIS: The fact that a person who wants to start a company can, most of the time, get capital to start it up. Also, this is a culture that allows you to fail. Now, the other countries are adopting that good part of our system. Venture capital is slowly becoming available in Europe and Japan. Younger people in many of these countries are willing to take more risks, because they see what's done so well for the United States.

INC.: In return for this capital, though, these guys want to feel like owners, and they want to make some money.

NORRIS: To have the employees own something is not enough. It's not meaningful. I'll tell you, it doesn't work. Under the present system, you don't have owners. You just have a bunch of speculators monkeying around with the stock. A lot of it is in the hands of arbs, pension funds.

It's true, of course, businesses did this to themselves. They set up managers for their pension funds, and they wanted to have the highest performance so that they could keep down the amount they put in the fund. In effect, the whole thing backfired on business. It's the pension-fund guy who's worrying about performance, otherwise he'll lose his job. So he'll put pressure on the corporations, and it's gotten to be a vicious cycle.

I think that there's got to be some legislation that restricts pension fund managers, and these big holders of stock, so that they can't constantly turn and sell it at the drop of a hat. We've got to identify some business owners.

INC.: Yet despite your disdain for arbs and speculators and so on, the fact remains that Control Data got into a lot of trouble a few years ago and had to do some very difficult things. The company has just gone through a huge restructuring. Subsidiaries have been spun off. People have been laid off. How different would that be from that other great Minneapolis businessman Irwin Jacobs's taking the company over?

NORRIS: He would have busted it up. There wouldn't be a Control Data. He wouldn't know how to resuscitate Control Data. He's a liquidator. He's a junk merchant. Any company he's taken over, you look at it and it hasn't done well.

INC.: Would that many more jobs have been lost? Would that much more damage have been done if you took the company into its different components? You sold Commercial Credit. You sold off some of the smaller ventures. Isn't that the same thing?

NORRIS: Not really. For example, Control Data bought Commercial Credit to solve a problem, which was financing computers. It did it very well, but it was never part of the central strategy.

INC.: How do you create innovation within the corporate structure?

NORRIS: You have to give good people a free hand. Get them out of the structure, and let them run. That doesn't always work, of course, but if you want a jump in innovation, that's the way to do it. If you want innovation to evolve, then you do that within the corporate structure.

Take, for example, Plato, our computer-based education

system that we started twenty years ago. Most people in Control Data could never perceive the opportunity in it. They didn't perceive it up until a year and a half ago, when computer-based education just started to explode.

INC.: That took a lot longer than you would have thought, didn't it?

NORRIS: Yes.

INC.: It has cost a billion dollars over a decade or so. If you'd done market research twenty years ago, it would have said don't do it, right?

NORRIS: Right.

INC.: When is that going to start to pay off?

NORRIS: It just permeates the whole company. For example, I mentioned the one in agriculture is very profitable. The computer systems business is too. One of the important applications is education. A lot of times you can't see the effect it has had on the bottom line, which is what the analysts never understand. You don't see the education part of the business getting credit for what it's done for computer systems, or what it's done for agriculture, or how it has helped us get military contracts.

INC.: How did you know Plato was the right way to go? Did you ever have any second thoughts about it? Was there ever any doubt?

NORRIS: Never. Never. If you know this will happen, the uncertainty being when, the answer is to stay with it on a basis that's affordable. It was never a burden on Control Data.

It depends on what your final objective is. I'm like the Japanese. I believe a company is forever. Maintaining that company is number one. You do more for society. You promote social justice much better that way than saying, "I'll get this company going and then I'll sell it." That's the reason I always made it damn clear that anybody who tried to take over Control Data was in for a hell of a fight. I've said it in just those words.

The point is that here in our business society we're at war with each other, whereas the Japanese are cooperating. How in the world can we ever survive that sort of thing? That's serious.

The Evolution of Corporate Social Responsibility

Rogene A. Buchholz

It is fair to say that the concept of corporate social responsibility, and the concomitant debate about the obligations of corporations to their communities and to society in general, was the impetus to the current ongoing growth of business ethics as an academic discipline. Rogene A. Buchholz provides a history of this concept that underscores both the high and low points in its progress.

Buchholz begins by examining the emergence of the idea of corporate social responsibility in the turbulent 1960s. He then traces the development of it during the 1970s, when the concept of corporate social responsibility underwent a transformation into the idea of "corporate responsiveness." Buchholz shows how the emphasis gradually switched from a concern with the moral underpinnings of the term *responsibility* to the more "morally neutral" term *responsiveness*. Here the emphasis is placed on the need for corporations to make adequate responses to the various pressures it finds within its "social environment." The latest phase in this history is the evolving role of business in shaping public policy.

Tracing the development of business ethics as a field in its own right will help to understand where ethics fits into the

SOURCE: Rogene A. Buchholz, *Fundamentals Concepts and Problems in Business Ethics,* © 1989, pp. 4–13. Reprinted with the permission of Prentice-Hall, Inc., Englewood Cliffs, NJ.

business school curriculum and what factors have been responsible for the evolution of ethical concerns. While the subject of business ethics received some attention prior to the 1960s, it was with the rise of the social-responsibility debate that ethical concerns became of major importance to business organizations.[1] The years from 1960 to 1970 were years of sweeping social change that affected business organizations and the management of those organizations. The concern about civil rights for minorities, equal rights for women, protection of the physical environment, safety and health in the workplace, and a broad array of consumer issues has had far-reaching and long-lasting impacts on business organizations. The long-term effect of this social change has been a dramatic change in the "rules of the game" by which business is expected to operate.

Given this kind of social revolution, it is not surprising that the social environment of business was given increasing attention during the 1960s and 1970s by business corporations and schools of business and management. The concept of social responsibility came into its own as a response to the changing social values of society. Business executives began to talk about the social responsibilities of business and to develop specific social programs in response to problems of a social, rather than economic, nature. Schools of business and management implemented new courses in business and society or in the social responsibilities of business.

There are many definitions of social responsibility, but in general it means that a private corporation has responsibilities to society that go beyond the production of goods and services at a profit—that a corporation has a broader constituency to serve than stockholders alone. Corporations relate to society through more than just marketplace transactions and serve a wider range of values than the traditional economic ones that are prevalent in the marketplace. Corporations are more than economic institutions and have a responsibility to devote some of their resources to helping to solve some of the most pressing social problems, many of which corporations helped to cause.

The concept of social responsibility received increasing attention during the 1960s because of the need for corporations to respond to the changing social environment of business. This change was often described as a change in the terms of the contract between business and society that reflected changing expectations regarding the social performance of business.[2] The old contract between business and society was based on the view that economic growth was the source of all progress, social as well as economic. The engine providing this growth was considered to be the drive for profits by competitive private enterprise. The basic mission of business was thus to produce goods and services at a profit, and in so doing, business was making its maximum contribution to society and, in fact, being socially responsible.[3]

The new contract between business and society was based on the view that the single-minded pursuit of economic growth produced some detrimental side effects that imposed significant social costs on certain segments of society or on society as a whole. The pursuit of economic growth, it was argued, did not necessarily lead automatically to social progress. In many cases it led instead to a deteriorating physical environment, unsafe workplaces, needless exposure to toxic substances on the part of workers and consumers, discrimination against certain groups in society, urban decay, and other social problems. This new contract between business and society involved reducing these social costs of business by impressing upon business the idea that it has an obligation to work for social as well as economic betterment. This new contract did not invalidate the old contract; it simply added new terms or additional clauses to that contract.

> Today it is clear that the terms of the contract between society and business are, in fact, changing in substantial and important ways. Business is being asked to assume broader responsibilities to society than ever before and to serve a wider range of human values. Business enterprises, in effect, are being asked to contribute more to the quality of American life than just supplying quantities of goods and services.[4]

The concept of social responsibility is fundamentally an ethical concept. It involves changing notions of human welfare and emphasizes a concern with the social dimensions of business activity that have to do with improving the quality of life in society. It has provided a way for business to concern itself with these social dimensions and pay some attention to its social impacts. The word *responsibility* implies some kind of obligation to deal with social problems that business organizations were believed to have toward the society in which they functioned.

The debate about social responsibility reflected many of these ethical or moral dimensions. Proponents of the concept argued that: (1) business must accommodate itself to social change if it expected to survive; (2) business must take a long-run or enlightened view of self-interest and help solve social problems in order to create a better environment for itself; (3) business could gain a better public image by being socially responsible; (4) government regulation could be avoided if business met the changing social expectations of society before the issues became politicized; (5) business had enormous resources that would be useful in solving social problems; (6) social problems could be turned into profitable business opportunities; and (7) business had a moral obligation to help solve social problems that it had created or at least perpetuated.

The opponents of social responsibility had equally formidable arguments. These arguments included the following: (1) the social-responsibility concept provides no mechanism for accountability as to the use of corporate resources; (2) managers are legally and ethically bound to earn the highest possible rate of return on the stockholder's investment in the companies they manage; (3) social responsibility poses a threat to the pluralistic nature of our society; (4) business executives have little experience and incentive to solve social problems; and (5) social responsibility is fundamentally a subversive doctrine that would undermine the foundations of a free-enterprise system if taken seriously.

After the smoke began to clear from this debate, it was obvious to many proponents and opponents of corporate social responsibility that there were several key issues in the debate that had not, and perhaps could not, be settled. One key issue concerned the operational definition of social re-

THE CORPORATE SOCIAL RESPONSIBILITY DEBATE

sponsibility. How shall a corporation's resources be allocated to help solve social problems? With what specific problems shall a given corporation concern itself? What priorities shall be established? Does social responsibility refer to company action taken to comply with government regulations or only to those voluntary actions that go beyond legal requirements? What goals or standards of performance shall be established? What measures shall be employed to determine if a corporation is socially responsible or socially irresponsible?

The traditional marketplace provided little or no information to the manager that would be useful in making decisions about solving social problems. But the concept of social responsibility in itself did not make up for this lack and provided no clearer guidelines for managerial behavior. Given this lack of precision, corporate executives who wanted to be socially responsible were left to follow their own values and interests or some rather vague generalizations about changing social values and public expectations. What this meant in practice, however, was often difficult to determine.

Another key problem with the concept of social responsibility was that the concept did not take into account the competitive environment in which corporations functioned. Many advocates of social responsibility treated the corporation as an isolated entity that had almost unlimited ability to engage in unilateral social action. Eventually, it came to be recognized that corporations were severely limited in their ability to respond to social problems. If a firm unilaterally engages in social action that increases its costs and prices, it will place itself at a competitive disadvantage relative to other firms in the industry that may not be concerned about being socially responsible.

The debate about social responsibility never took this institutional context of corporations seriously. Concerted action to solve social problems is not feasible in a competitive system unless all competitors pursue roughly the same policy on these problems. Since collusion among competitors is illegal, however, the only way such concerted action can occur is when some other institution, such as government, makes all competitors engage in the same activity and pursue the same policy. And that is, in fact, what happened. While the debate about social responsibility was going on and corporate executives were asking for a definition of their social responsibilities, government was rewriting the rules under which all corporations operated in society by developing a vast amount of legislation and regulation pertaining to the physical environment, occupational safety and health, equal opportunity, and consumer concerns.

The last issue that remained unresolved in the debate about social responsibility concerned the moral underpinnings of the notion. The term *responsibility* is fundamentally a moral one that implies an obligation to someone or something. It is clear to most people that business has an economic responsibility to produce goods and services efficiently and to perform other economic functions for society. These economic responsibilities constitute the reason for having something like a business organization. But why does business have social responsibilities? What are the moral foundations for a concern with social impacts?

The proponents of social responsibility produced no clear and generally accepted moral principle that would impose upon business an obligation to work for social betterment.[5] Ascribing social responsibility to corporations does not necessarily imply that they are moral agents that are then responsible for their social impacts. But various moral strictures were used to try and impose this obligation on business, and various arguments were made to try to link moral behavior to business performance. Little was accomplished, however, by way of developing solid and acceptable moral support for the notion of social responsibility. Thus, the debate about social responsibility was very moralistic in many of its aspects, a debate that often generated a good deal of heat but very little light in most instances.

The intractability of these issues, according to one scholar, "posed the dreadful possibilities that the debate over corporate social responsibility would continue indefinitely with little prospect of final resolution or that it would simply exhaust itself and collapse as a viable legitimate question."[6] But beginning in the 1970s, a theoretical and conceptual reorientation began to take place regarding the corporation's response to the social environment. This new approach was labeled corporate social responsiveness, and while initially it appeared that only semantics was involved, it gradually became clear that the shift from responsibility to responsiveness was much more substantive. The shift represented an attempt to escape the unresolved dilemmas that emerged from the social-responsibility debate. This new concept of social responsiveness was defined by one author as follows:

> Corporate social responsiveness refers to the capacity of a corporation to respond to social pressures. The literal act of responding, or of achieving a generally responsive posture, to society is the focus of corporate social responsiveness. . . . One searches the organization for mechanisms, procedures, arrangements, and behavioral patterns that, taken collectively, would mark the organization as more or less capable of responding to social pressures. It then becomes evident that organizational design and managerial competence play important roles in how extensively and how well a company responds to social demands and needs.[7]

Thus, attention shifted from debate about a moral notion, social responsibility, to a more technical or at least morally neutral term, social responsiveness. Research in corporate responsiveness reflected this same shift and focused on internal corporate responsiveness to social problems and examined the ways in which corporations responded to such problems. Attempts were made to identify key variables within the organization that related to its responsiveness and discover structural changes that would enable a corporation to respond to social pressures more effectively. The important questions asked in this research were not moral, related to whether a corporation should respond to a social problem out of a sense of social responsibility, but more pragmatic and action oriented, dealing with the ability of a corporation to respond and what changes were necessary to enable it to respond more effectively.

One of the advantages of this approach is its managerial orientation. The concept ignores the philosophical debate about responsibility and obligation and focuses on the problems and prospects of making corporations more socially responsive. One of the reasons for research into response patterns is to discover those responses that have proven to be most effective in dealing with social problems. The approach also lends itself to more rigorous analytical research in examining specific techniques, such as environmental scanning and the social audit, to improve the response process. Such research can also discover how management can best institutionalize social policy throughout the organization. Such questions can be investigated as: What organizational structures are most appropriate? What role can top management play in enabling corporations to respond? What changes in the reward structure can improve the corporation's response to social problems? What role should public-affairs departments play in the response process? and How can social policy best be formulated for the organization as a whole?

Given these advantages, however, the concept of social responsiveness was still plagued with the same key problems that faced the concept of social responsibility. The concept of social responsiveness does not clarify how corporate resources shall be allocated for the solution of social problems. Companies respond to different problems in different ways and to varying degrees. But there is no clear idea as to what pattern of responsiveness will produce the greatest amount of social betterment. The philosophy of responsiveness does not help the company to decide what problems to get involved in and what priorities to establish. In the final analysis, it provides no better guidance to management than does social responsibility on the best strategies or policies to be adopted to produce social betterment. The concept seems to suggest that management itself, by determining the degree of social responsiveness and the pressures it will respond to, decides the meaning of the concept and what social goods and services will be produced.[8]

The concept of social responsiveness does not take the institutional context of business into account any more seri-

THE CORPORATE SOCIAL RESPONSIBILITY DEBATE

ously than social responsibility did. Research in social responsiveness did not deal very thoroughly with the impact that government regulation was making on the corporation and with how the corporation was responding to this change in the political environment. Individual corporate institutions were again treated as rather isolated entities that could choose a response pattern irrespective of the institutional context in which a corporation operated. There was not enough concern with business-government relations and the role government played in the social-response process.

Finally, while the question of an underlying moral principle or theory is ignored in the research dealing with corporate social responsiveness in favor of more action-oriented concerns, this turns out to be a dubious advantage. Social pressures are assumed to exist, and it is believed as an article of faith that business must respond to them in some fashion. Consequently, business is placed more or less in a passive role of simply responding to social change. The concept of social responsiveness provides no moral basis for business to get involved in social problems. It contains no explicit moral or ethical theory and advocates no specific set of values for business to follow in making social responses.[9]

In the mid-1970s academics and business managers began to realize that a fundamental change was taking place in the political environment of business—that government was engaged in shaping business behavior and making business respond to a wide array of social problems by passing an unprecedented amount of legislation and writing new regulations pertaining to these problems. The political system responded to the social revolution of the 1960s and 1970s by enacting over a hundred new laws regulating business activity. Many new regulatory agencies were created, and new responsibilities were assigned to old agencies. These agencies issued thousands of new rules and procedural requirements that affected business decisions and operations.

This regulatory role of government continued to expand until the 1980 election of the Reagan administration. The new type of social regulation, as it came to be called, affected virtually every department or functional area within the corporation and every level of management. The growth of this new type of regulation was referred to as a second managerial revolution, involving a shift of decision-making power and control over the corporation from the managers of corporations to a vast cadre of government regulators, who were influencing, and in many cases, controlling managerial decisions in the typical business corporation.[10] The types of decisions that were becoming increasingly subject to government influence and control were basic operational decisions such as what line of business to go into, where products could be made, how they could be marketed, and what products could be produced.[11]

During the late 1970s, more and more attention was paid to the changing political environment of business. Books were written that provided a comprehensive overview of the impacts government regulation was making on business.[12] Studies were completed that attempted to measure the costs of social regulation to the private sector.[13] This activity drew attention to the political environment of business and showed that this environment had become increasingly hostile, giving rise to legislation and regulation that interfered with the ability of business to perform its basic economic mission. Largely because of this activity a national debate on regulation was initiated that culminated in the election of an administration in 1980 that promised to reduce the regulatory burden on business.

Thus began a serious concern with public policy as a new dimension of management. Many business leaders recognized the importance of public policy to business and advocated that business managers become more active in the political process and work more closely with government and other groups to help shape public policy. The motivation for this concern with public policy is clear. If the rules of the game for business are being rewritten through the public-policy process and business is being forced to respond to social values through complying with laws and regulations, then business has a significant interest to learn more about the public-policy process and become involved in helping to write the rules by which it is going to have to live. These rules should not be left solely up to the public-interest groups, congressional representatives, or agency employees.

Business has since come to adopt a more sophisticated approach to public policy, an approach that has been called the proactive stance. This term means that rather than fighting change, which has often proved to be a losing battle, or simply accommodating itself to change, business attempts to influence change by becoming involved in the public-policy process. Business can attempt to influence public opinion with regard to social issues of concern to society, and it can attempt to influence the legislative and regulatory process with regard to specific laws and regulations.

The public-policy approach has some distinct advantages over the corporate social-responsibility and social-responsiveness concepts discussed earlier. For the most part, there is no question about the nature and extent of management's social responsibilities. Once regulations are approved, these responsibilities are spelled out in excruciating detail. The government gets involved in specifying technology that can be employed, publishing labeling requirements, developing safety standards for products, specifying safety equipment, and hundreds of other such management responsibilities. Where questions arise about the legality or feasibility of regulations, the court system is available to settle disputes of this nature. Management is thus told in great detail what social problems to be concerned with and to what extent it has to respond.

Obviously, the public-policy approach treats business in its institutional context and advocates that managers learn more about government and the public-policy process so that they can appropriately influence the process. Government is recognized as the appropriate body to formalize and formulate public policy for the society as a whole. Some form of response by government to most social issues is believed to be inevitable, and no amount of corporate reform along the lines of corporate social responsibility or corporate social responsiveness is going to eliminate some form of government involvement. Government has a legitimate right to formulate public policy for corporations in response to changing public expectations.

Society can choose to allocate its resources any way it wants and on the basis of any criteria it deems relevant. If society wants to enhance the quality of air and water, it can choose to allocate resources for the production of these goods and put constraints on business in the form of standards. . . . These nonmarket decisions are made by those who participate in the public policy process and represent their views of what is best for themselves and society as a whole. . . . It is up to the body politic to determine which market outcomes are and are not appropriate. If market outcomes are not to be taken as normative, a form of regulation which requires public participation is the only alternative. The social responsibility of business is not operational and certainly not to be trusted. When business acts contrary to the normal pressures of the marketplace, only public policy can replace the dictates of the market.[14]

There is also, at least on the surface, no need for a moral underpinning for a business obligation to produce social betterment. Society makes decisions about the allocations of resources through the public-policy process based on its notions about social betterment. The result is legislation and regulation that impinge on business behavior. Business, then, has a moral obligation to obey the law as a good citizen. Failure to do so subjects business and executives to all sorts of penalties. The social responsibility of business is thus to follow the directives of society at large as expressed in and through the public-policy process.

This concept of public policy, however, which at first glance seemed to eliminate many of the dilemmas and problems with social responsibility and social responsiveness, actually fares no better on closer examination. As business becomes more politically involved in writing the rules of the game or preventing new ones from being written, the question of managerial guidelines and principles again becomes relevant. What criteria, other than self-interest, are relevant to guide the corporation in the development of its political strategies? Shall these strategies be judged solely on their short-term effectiveness, say, in helping to defeat a certain bill that business didn't like? What candidates should a corporate political action committee support—only those who are judged to have the company's best interests in mind and share traditional business values? Again, the nagging question of defining social betterment, or in a public-policy context, of defining the public interest, reappears.

Regarding the institutional context, there is the question of the appropriate role for government to play in shaping business behavior. Should government continue with a command-and-control system of regulation to accomplish social objectives, or should it adopt other incentive mechanisms more consistent with market behavior? On the other side of the coin, what is the appropriate role for business to play in the political process? If business is perceived as being too influential in the political process and constituting a threat to the pluralistic nature of American society, and if its behavior is perceived as being too self-serving and not cognizant of the broader public interest, adverse public reaction can be expected. How can business avoid this kind of reaction and yet look after its own legitimate interests in the public-policy process?

And finally, the absence of a clear moral underpinning for public-policy involvement still presents a problem. Does the proactive approach simply mean that business attempts to minimize the impact of social change on itself? Does not business have more of an obligation to society than is evident in self-serving attempts to manipulate the political environment for its own advantage? Does not business have a moral obligation that goes beyond obeying the law and complying with government regulations? If business does have social and political responsibilities as well as economic responsibilities, what is the moral basis of these responsibilities?

NOTES

1. See Richard T. DeGeorge, "The Status of Business Ethics: Past and Future," Business Ethics Research Workshop, Stanford University, August 14–17, 1985.

2. See Melvin Anshen, *Managing the Socially Responsible Corporation* (New York: Macmillan Co., 1974).

3. See Milton Friedman, "The Social Responsibility of Business Is to Increase Its Profits," *New York Times Sunday Magazine*, September 13, 1970, pp. 122–26.

The Evolution of Corporate Social Responsibility

4. Committee for Economic Development, *Social Responsibilities of Business Corporations* (New York: CED, 1971), pp. 29–30.

5. William C. Frederick, "From CSR1 to CSR2: The Maturing of Business and Society Thought," Graduate School of Business, University of Pittsburgh, 1978, working paper no. 279, p. 5.

6. Ibid.

7. Ibid., p. 6.

8. Ibid., pp. 12–13.

9. Ibid., pp. 14–16.

10. Murray L. Weidenbaum, *Business, Government, and the Public* (Englewood Cliffs, N.J.: Prentice-Hall, 1977), p. 285.

11. Murray L. Weidenbaum, *The Future of Business Regulation* (New York: AMACOM, 1979), p. 34.

12. Ibid.

13. See Murray L. Weidenbaum and Robert DeFina, *The Cost of Federal Regulation of Economic Activity* (Washington, D.C.: American Enterprise Institute, 1978); and Arthur Anderson, *Cost of Government Regulation* (New York: Business Roundtable, 1979).

14. Rogene A. Buchholz, "An Alternative to Social Responsibility," *MSU Business Topics* 25, no. 3 (Summer 1977), 12, 16.

CHAPTER 6

BUSINESS AND ENVIRONMENTAL ETHICS

Introduction

One of the more pressing issues that confronts business decision makers on many fronts is that of the protection of the environment. Problems such as pollution, the disposal of toxic waste, global warming—often called the greenhouse effect, the eroding of the earth's ozone layer—acid rain, and others are serious ecological problems that have obvious implications for everyone. Since many of the causes of these and other threats to the environment have their source in industrial production, the theme of business and environmental ethics has become an essential issue in the field of business ethics.

Here the leading question is: To what extent is business responsible for the decay of the environment, and to what extent should it be held liable for its restoration? This question, however, is complicated by several factors. First, while it is true that industrial production is a direct and identifiable cause of pollution and other adverse environmental effects, it is likewise true that the demand for and consumption of the goods produced by industry is at an all-time high. Should business be held strictly liable for our environmental plight when consumer pressure for those goods that damage the environment continues and grows? In other words, who is really to blame? Industry or the consumers of industrial goods? In "Corporations and the Physical Environment" Neil Chamberlain takes a critical look at the relationship between industrial production and consumerism and concludes that corporate interests and consumer interests are so closely tied that ecological considerations become secondary ones.

Another complication is one that deals with the actual scientific facts of environmental research. Critics of the environmental movement claim that while environmentalists may have in mind what is best for the planet, they often present evidence for their case that is unsound or lacking in scientific proof and yet go on to call for radical changes in industrial production. The controversy surrounding the problem of acid rain is a good case in point. Environmentalists claim that one of the most prevalent causes contributing to the rise of lake and soil acidity in the northeastern United States and Canada—which in turn accounts for the loss of fish, wildlife, and fertile lands in these areas—is the burning of coal by electrical utilities in the Midwest. These environmental critics of business go on to recommend sweeping and very expensive changes in the way these utilities produce energy so that the high levels of sulfur, which they argue is the real culprit in coal burning, that accounts for acid rain will be eliminated or at least reduced.

On the contrary, the executives of these Midwestern utilities and owners and operators of coal mines hold that this critique is scientifically without merit and that it amounts to overreaction on the part of the environmentalists. They call for more studies of the problem of acid rain before they would be forced to change radically the way in which they produce energy at their facilities. Thus far this position has been the favored one, as the Reagan administration did not call for new governmental regulations of utilities that would address the levels of sulfur emitted in the process of coal burning. The Bush administration does not have this issue on the top of its agenda, either.

But in other areas of environmental concern, the federal government has been active in the regulation and control of businesses, primarily through the Environmental Protection Agency. And not only does the federal government regulate business on the environment, but also major environmental laws have criminal provisions that allow the government to bring charges against individuals as well as organizations. In fact, the rise in the number of individuals who have been charged with environmental crimes is on the upswing, so that what might appear initially as an accidental occurrence that could not be prevented—an inadvertent release of a toxic substance in the air, for example—might be construed as a negligent act by the government. Managers, presidents, and directors of some of the largest U.S. corporations have been indicted, found guilty, and fined or sentenced to jail terms for environmental crimes. This development is outlined in the *Wall Street Journal* item reprinted in this chapter under the title "Government Cracks Down on Environmental Crimes," and it suggests the seriousness with which the federal government takes this essential issue in business ethics.

But there is little doubt that the most controversial aspect of the issue of environmental ethics is the question of the extent to which businesses should be regulated now, and the extent to which they should be held liable for past damages to the ecological system. Environmental activists represented by groups such as the Sierra Club and the National Wildlife Federation, among many others, have mounted large national campaigns that lobby Congress to enact legislation that will regulate industry even more than it does today. They would force corporations to pay more for the cleanup of environmental damage already done, especially in the area of toxic industrial waste.

Toxic waste has been in the forefront of environmental concerns as of late, thanks in part to the tragedy of Love Canal and other sites around the country where whole communities have been negatively affected by industrial waste. Moreover, in 1987, industry released 22.5 billion pounds of toxic chemicals into the nation's air, land, and water, according to the Environmental Protection Agency. This translates into the equivalent of 92 pounds of toxic waste released per person living in the United States. And these figures are conservative ones, because only a quarter of the companies required by law to report their 1987 toxic emissions to the Environmental Protection Agency did so. This continued release of toxic waste, coupled with the amounts of such waste currently polluting the nation in dump sites dotted throughout the U.S., has greatly angered environmental activists. G. M. Keller, chairman of the board and chief executive officer of Chevron Corporation, responds to this anger in his "Industry and the Environment," in which he calls for more levelheadedness and objectivity. It might be taken as a current and representative view of corporate America on the issue of environmental ethics.

But whether environmentalists will temper their attacks on industry remains to be seen, especially in light of the recent environmental disaster in Valdez, Alaska. When the supertanker *Exxon Valdez* ran aground and emptied ten to eleven million gallons of crude oil into Prince William Sound, the country witnessed the worst oil spill ever in North American waters. In one week the glop had spread to an area spanning over nine hundred miles. Countless marine mammals, fish, and other wildlife were killed and endangered—not to mention the effects to hatcheries, beaches, and pristine parklands. As the spill eluded early efforts to contain it, Exxon came under increasing criticism, not only for alleged negligence in allowing the captain of the *Exxon Valdez* to operate the tanker with a past record of alcohol problems (which seemed to have played a role in the accident), but also for its seeming insensitivity and lack of diligence in having an adequate oil-spill disaster plan in effect at the time.

Nearly six months after the *Valdez* ran aground, in September 1989, Exxon officially ended its cleanup operations before the harsh Alaska winter set in. After having spent $1.28 billion in its efforts, Exxon proclaimed their cleanup a "success," but admitted they would need to continue to work on oil-drenched beaches in the spring. Others, however, were not so willing to call Exxon's cleanup a success and were surprised that they had ended it so abruptly. Alaskan officials threatened lawsuits if Exxon were not to come back in the spring, and environmentalists were outraged that Exxon did not stay on through the fall and winter. So, one of the greatest marine disasters in history became an ethical issue for one of America's largest corporations and a lesson to others on how not to resolve an environmental crisis. The last two selections of this chapter discuss the tragedy at Valdez and its unfortunate consequences on Alaskan ecology.

Corporations and the Physical Environment

Neil W. Chamberlain

Neil Chamberlain examines the interrelationship between consumerism and corporate values and how this interrelationship functions as a roadblock for the conservation movement in this excerpt from his classic 1973 book, *The Limits of Corporate Responsibility*. Chamberlain points out that both the consumer culture and the psychology of consumption are closely tied to corporate interests. Consequently the response of corporations, as well as of consumers, to ecological concerns that might call for drastically reduced levels of consumption will be outright resistance to change. Because corporations have engendered the value of consumption within society, society now will not take kindly to the competing value inherent in conservation, which holds that consumption needs to be tempered and life-styles changed if the physical environment is to survive. Chamberlain reviews the role of governmental regulation, the effects of the conservation movement on workers and unions, and corporate response to ecological calamity. But given his thesis that consumption will continue to be bolstered by corporate interests, the hope that the environment will become a central social value is a dim one. Until the link between corporate interests and consumer interests is broken, there is slim chance that conservation of resources will be socially accepted.

SOURCE: From *The Limits of Corporate Responsibility,* by Neil W. Chamberlain. Copyright © 1973 by Basic Books, Inc. Reprinted by permission of Basic Books, Inc., Publishers, New York.

The centrality of consumption as a social value is splendidly displayed in the matter of environmental quality. Public alarms over pollution and resource exhaustion lead to legislative controls and regulatory actions. These can be modulated, "within reason," with incremental effects on the environment. But if they begin to bite, in the sense of threatening consumption through higher prices and taxes, industry can count on a reduction in the alarm level. Not only industry's ox but society's own horsepower is being gored. Industry's responsibility to the environment is thus limited by society's conception of the good life—a conception that . . . can be traced back ultimately to values inculcated by the corporate system itself.

No single corporation—whatever its size or however socially sensitive its management—can break out of this institutionalized constraint.

The Dark Underside of Economic Growth

Concern for the conservation of natural resources has a long history. Originating in aesthetic revulsion at the commercial despoliation of natural resources such as timberlands, scenic areas, and animal life, it eventually extended also to outcries against the unrestricted and wasteful exploitation of land and fossil fuels. Concern with pollution also has a long history. It early expressed itself in abhorrence of the concentration of smoke in Europe's growing cities and the fetid atmosphere of the "Satanic mills" of the industrial revolution. This latter, however, was viewed as a matter of entrepreneurial greed, a kind of class conflict rather than a general social disaster.

Present fears concerning depletion and pollution are more widespread, embracing imminent dangers both to life as we know it and to life itself. They are expressed in picturesque concepts such as "spaceship earth," which views the planet as a vessel in space, whose stock of provisions are all there is to sustain whatever the number of passengers, and so both provisions and number of passengers must be managed

BUSINESS AND ENVIRONMENTAL ETHICS

carefully. Others have described ours as a "throughput economy," which mines the earth for the materials out of which
it fashions articles of consumption for temporary enjoy-
ment; these, once used, are thrown back on the earth as
though it were a dumpheap. The "mines" become exhausted
and the dumpheap grows.

Let us agree at the outset that the problems of depletion
and pollution are basically the same in that both involve the
using-up of natural resources. Pollution uses up air and
water, just as extraction uses up minerals. Pollution reduces
people to using air and water of inferior quality, just as
mineral extraction drives producers to lower-grade ores.
Presumably the producer bears the cost in the latter case but
not in the former, but in both cases it is the consumer who
ultimately pays, either a money cost or a real cost, and in
any event this distinction is one that could conceivably be
erased by appropriate forms of taxation on the producer. . . .
Production that takes place without pollution may nevertheless involve depletion, by dispersing scarce natural resources,
but that distinction too, if important, could presumably be
met by some form of "recovery" tax or regulation. The
antipollution movement is founded on the "discovery" that
air and water are natural resources that should not be squan-
dered as though they were unlimited in quantity. They are
now appreciated as scarce resources requiring economic use
like any other resource. Thus, whether our discussion deals
with one or the other, it relates to both.

In the face of smoke and smog, fishkills from oil spills,
and beaches unfit for bathing, pollution control has become,
in the enduring phrase of Oliver Wendell Holmes, Jr., a
"felt necessity" of the times. Our economic system, with its
expanding production and consequent increased use of resources and discard of wastes, has come to be viewed by
many as responsible for both depletion and pollution of the
environment. But this raises an intriguing question. Until
just a few years ago, economic growth was viewed as the
preeminent national objective. Countries vied with one another to attain comparatively higher rates of increase of
GNP. The United Nations proclaimed the 1960s to be the
development decade, with a general target for each country

of a doubling of its national income. If such growth-mindedness is now regarded skeptically, even negatively, we may justifiably wonder why, within the space of only a few years, economic growth has changed from being a gleam in the eye of many intelligent observers and has become instead a mote. How has it come about that industrial dynamics, until recently viewed as a multiplier of the earth's riches, can now be regarded by some as a despoiler of man's real wealth?

There is no agreed-upon answer to those questions, but three possible causes are most commonly seized on, singly or collectively. These are: (1) the increase in population, (2) the spread of affluence, and (3) the greater impact of technology. . . .

Government Response to Environmental Concerns

As concern for the environment spread from a handful of conservationists to a more general public, the federal government reacted with legislation to curb pollution. But how does a government go about such a task, when "the problem" has scarcely been defined and means of combating it are in a trial-and-error stage? The consumer-protection movement offers something of a model. Modest legislation takes a few hesitant steps forward. Thus in 1955 the Public Health Service was authorized to conduct limited research on air pollution and to offer technical assistance to state and local governments. The Clean Air Act of 1963 moved a little further by providing grants to the states to establish and maintain air-pollution control agencies and by authorizing federal authorities to initiate proceedings against interstate polluters. A 1965 amendment to this act for the first time recognized automobile exhaust as a contributor to unclean air and empowered the Secretary of Health, Education, and Welfare to set emission standards. This was followed by the Air Quality Act of 1967, which retained the provisions of the preceding legislation, but also called for collaboration of federal and state governments and major industrial corporations in setting standards for the most seriously polluted regions. Beset with seemingly insoluble problems of determining meaningful criteria to apply to a particular region and susceptible of application to individual sources of pollution (that is to say how to measure the whole effect and allocate the partial responsibility), little headway was made under the new legislation.

In response to growing public sentiment, the Clean Air Act of 1970 was designed to meet the most serious of these weaknesses. It made state pollution-control legislation mandatory and required that enforcement procedures be approved by federal authorities. If state plans are unacceptable, the federal government may intervene to impose its own procedures. The 1970 act also provides for *national* ambient air quality standards as well as emissions standards for particular (stationary) pollutants. Automobile emissions were subjected to federally determined standards, and by statutory provision were to be reduced to specified and rigorous levels by given target dates.

Federal control of water pollution was technically inaugurated by congressional actions in 1948 and 1956, but these were largely of a token nature. These acts were amended in 1961, the Water Pollution Control Act was passed in 1965 and was further upgraded by the Water and Environmental Quality Enforcement Act of 1970. The latter was triggered largely by public repugnance at a few spectacular oil spills, the widely publicized "death" of Lake Erie, and the fouling of underground water by chemical components of detergents, which had virtually displaced soap cleansers. The new law imposed stricter liability and preventive measures in the water transport of oil, gave the federal government authority to regulate discharges of waste into bodies of water, and required state certification that any new industrial facilities would not adversely affect water quality.

In 1970 the Environmental Protection Agency (EPA) was established under administrative reorganization procedure, bringing together the water-quality office lodged in the Department of the Interior, the air-pollution control group in the Department of Health, Education, and Welfare, the pesticide control function then in the Department of Agriculture, and nuclear-radiation control previously under the jurisdiction of the Atomic Energy Commission. The new agency was mandated to conduct research, and to set and enforce standards with respect to air, water, and solid-waste pollution.

In addition to this action agency, a Council on Environmental Quality had been established under the National Environmental Protection Act of 1969. Congressional intent was that this office should develop and coordinate all policy in the extensive and amorphous "environmental field," ranging, as one journalist put it, "from protection of wildlife to the preservation of historic buildings."[1] But perhaps the most significant portion of that act, Section 102, requires all government agencies to file with the newly created council a statement of the environmental impact of any major project in which they are involved. Because such projects extend to subcontracts to private business and authorizations for private initiatives (the Alaska pipeline, for example), these "impact statements" have assumed critical importance in opening to public scrutiny and possible court challenge both public and corporate actions viewed as environmentally deleterious. The consequence, at least in the early years of this new procedure, has been to delay a number of governmentally sponsored or approved projects, to elicit changes in construction plans, and occasionally to cause their abandonment.

Federal efforts at pollution control have been supplemented by state and municipal provisions. In some jurisdictions, detergents containing phosphates have been banned, automobiles have been prohibited from certain sections of cities during hours when these are most populated, and use of incinerators in apartment buildings has been controlled. Nor does this brief summary take into account numerous other related provisions of federal acts ranging from subsidies and tax credits for industrial investment in pollution-control equipment to noise-level control under a 1969 amendment to the Walsh-Healey Public Contracts Act.

If public awareness of environmental decay is recent, government response has been relatively quick and extensive. Indeed, the Nixon Administration by 1972 had moved to the position that Congress was overreacting and that such measures as the Water Pollution Control bill (enacted later

BUSINESS AND ENVIRONMENTAL ETHICS

that same year), which required total elimination of all effluent discharges into the nation's waterways by 1985, are wasteful, if not capricious. The Chairman of the Council on Environmental Quality has pointed out that the cost of pollution control, too, has an exponential aspect, so that removal of the last 1 percent of contaminant may cost as much as the removal of the first 99 percent.[2] "Zero discharge" may thus be a goal that diverts substantial resources away from other more badly needed public works to an unnecessarily finicky scrubbing of air and water. In any event, we are safe in concluding that once the public had recognized pollution as a problem, the political authorities vied with one another in doing "something," piling laws on administrative agencies and legislative amendments on regulatory orders.

Business Reaction

Could anything be more predictable than the response of business to this flurry of political activity? We have already encountered the pattern in the case of consumerism. The first reaction is defensive and bitter: business is being made a scapegoat for society's own failings; politicians are pandering to a panicky public; the cleanup demanded will bankrupt many companies and increase the public's cost of living more than it realizes. After this initial irritation, business professionalism reasserts itself: the public-relations offices take over with the soothing message that industry is busily coping with an admittedly serious problem. Millions of dollars are being spent on the research needed to take effective action, even as billions are being spent to improve old equipment and develop new equipment in line with what is already known. This is the period when resistance to remedial action shades over into acceptance of the inevitability of some action, but this is accompanied by pressures for making standards "practical" and the time period for their enforcement "reasonable."

This reaction pattern is wholly understandable. It suggests that at least in some respects the Supreme Court was not too far afield in picturing the corporation as human. When, within the space of a decade, a cause takes on the dimensions of a crusade, with industry assuming the role of the infidels, what else but a defensive reaction can be expected? With pollution controls entailing costs running into literally unknown but clearly massive sums loosely spoken of as the "ransom" that would be legislatively demanded of business to permit it freedom to operate, how else could business feel but victimized, at least in the first fresh shock of recognition that the contest was "for real"?

The instinct to fight back, with whatever arguments come to hand, is surely understandable. Thus one leading businessman informed—mistakenly—a college audience that "U.S. Department of Commerce figures show that 219 plants last year were forced to shut down because of environmental pressures."[3] As a House-Senate conference committee pondered legislation to set strict limits on automobile pollution emissions in 1975, the executive vice president of Ford Motor Company, urging a specially called meeting of principal Ford suppliers and dealers to initiate a telegram campaign to their Washington representatives, "went so far as to claim that the bill 'could prevent continued production of automobiles after January 1, 1975.' "[4] The president of a steel company, speaking before a group of university economists, emphasized the adverse effects of ill-advised pollution control legislation: "The thrust for an improved environment has caused many of us in the steel industry to close and/or drastically alter plant operations; . . . shifted vital funds away from essential revenue producing activities, including research and development; increased the competitive advantage of foreign competitors; placed an additional annual operating cost burden on our industry of about $412 million."[5]

A sanitation engineering consultant, speaking of Detroit's costly and largely "wasted" efforts to control discharges into Lake Erie, drew more lurid conclusions: "This excessive expenditure diverts funds from other environmental blights in Detroit such as crime on the streets, ghettos, malnutrition, and the needs of education. Can Detroit afford to have such a warped concept of environmental priorities? Why

BUSINESS AND ENVIRONMENTAL ETHICS

can't a child be as important as a fish?"[6] Such costly public ventures into pollution control obviously increase business taxes and provide undesirable examples of what might be expected of business itself. A suspicious business partisan might conclude and feel justified in suggesting to others that there are "efforts afoot, avowedly to control the quality of the environment but more accurately to control industrial operations and the American way of life."[7]

Business's counterattack has included undercover efforts to "defuse" the public. A "news" item describing the movement against leaded gasoline as "misleading and irrelevant" asserted that no evidence existed that lead in the atmosphere poses a health hazard. *Natural History,* a magazine published by New York's American Museum of Natural History, traced the story to *Editor's Digest,* a division of Planned Communications Services, Inc., "a company that writes and distributes stories to small-circulation newspapers on behalf of corporate and industrial clients. This story, it turns out, originated with the Lead Industries Association. . . ."[8]

Corporate leadership is, on the whole, too sophisticated to rely solely on opposition when a problem has been shown to be real and demand for its solution has generated a popular following, however misguided. One time-tested device is to join the opposition in calling for a "common" effort. "We" have erred, but "we" can make up for our folly. Again Atlantic Richfield Company, employing reproductions of contemporary art to illustrate its "cultural" concern, offers what might paradoxically be referred to as a "good" example:

> The ideal: Seas that are permanently protected from man's abuse.
> The real: Thoughtlessly, man spews waste into the world's oceans. From the air, from the stream, from ships, all of it from ourselves.
> We must find new and better ways to guard our waters from ourselves. Our solutions must be swift. They must be creative and mature. For tomorrow the waters of the world will inherit what we do today.

Throughout the world, man must learn to function without fouling the oceans—and the air and earth that adjoin them. Until then, we cannot protect the environment in which life began—and on which our lives still depend.[9]

In place of such soothing syrup, the steel industry prefers the language of hard cash: "Our industry has put its money where its mouth is. Companies producing about 98% of the nation's iron and steel spent slightly over $735 million between '66 and '71. In '71, they spent $161.5 million, equal to 10.3% of our total capital expenditures . . . the largest of any industry and twice the average for all manufacturing. Last year, environmental control spending accounted for about 20% of net profits. An additional 12% of initial construction costs, or $142,000,000 a year, must be spent annually to keep equipment working."[10]

But communicating with the public is not enough in a situation where the stakes are so high. The real objective is to help mold the legislation which cannot be avoided. Industry finds itself, willy-nilly, engaged in a bargaining process with politicians over the shape of pollution-control laws that will satisfy the public. The politicians can ignore neither the interests of large-scale industry, which after all exercises enormous, if not dominant, influence over the very structure and functioning of the American society,[11] nor the wishes and interests of their popular constituencies, whose votes must return them to office. Bargaining is something at which both politicians and industrialists have long been adept. . . .

Acceptability of Limited Progress

These limitations on the legislative and administrative protection of the environment do not mean that public interest will be slighted and the public's will thwarted. On the contrary, such incremental measures as are forthcoming to alleviate, in whatever degree, the discomforts of pollution will probably be sufficient to satisfy public pressures. This is because any more effective environmental controls would require a larger sacrifice of immediate pleasures and preferences than the public is willing to make.

When the costs of achieving more stringent standards of air and water purity drastically affect the prices of consumer goods, we can expect public resistance to the higher standards. We have already noted the contribution made by divided political objectives to less effective pollution control. In [this] kind of consumption-oriented society . . . consumer goods and clean environment become seriously competing objectives. If, as has been estimated, the standards for automobile emissions now set for 1976 will add between $390 and $425 to the price of a car, we may confidently anticipate an outcry by the automobile-buying public. I concur with René Dubos when he says: "We would like to improve our polluted and cluttered environments, but we like gadgets and economic prosperity even more. In fact, values such as political power and gross national income so dominate our collective lives that we shall undertake the social and technological reforms essential for environmental control only if we are forced into action by some disaster."[12]

This consumption-mindedness of the American public goes beyond a desire for more goods. It is linked to a way or style of life that those goods make possible. It is thus not only the price increase that irritates car buyers, but the fact that even present emission controls increase fuel consumption and reduce engine performance. One consequence has been that some car owners have had emission controls disconnected. The manager of the auto-diagnostic clinic of the Missouri Automobile Club reported that one-fourth of the late-model cars going through his clinic had their emission controls tampered with. A Detroit automobile mechanic says that thirty of the forty automobile tune-ups he does every month involve modifications of the control system.[13]

The former head of EPA had no illusions about the unpopularity of actions necessary for effective pollution control if these begin to affect people's private lives. It has been popular to talk about "changing life styles," he observed, "but when someone finds out that means bicycling or carpooling to work, or going home at a different time, he may not be for it."[14] Nor do the politicians have any illusions on this score. When the iconoclast Admiral Hyman G. Rickover testified at House hearings on the prospects of a national energy shortage, he suggested the desirability of banning "nonessential" air conditioners and putting a high tax on such "luxuries" as clothes driers. A congressman thereupon "observed with undisguised disdain that the admiral had never run for office. 'What do you think we can do and still stay in office?' " he asked. John B. Connally, then Secretary of the Treasury and a former governor of Texas, advised the House committee that he too "was too much of a pragmatist" to embrace the Rickover program. He could live without air conditioning but would "hate to give it up." People can "save a tremendous amount of energy just by going around and turning off a few lights," Mr. Connally counseled reassuringly.[15]

Ambivalence over priorities in establishing political objectives ripens into profound disagreement between the disadvantaged minorities and the more advantaged majority within the general public. Blacks and Latins, large numbers of whom have suffered from lack of social amenities in matters of housing, health, education, and employment, often believe that the billions of dollars of expenditures that they hear advocated for clean air and water should be redirected into improving their general way of life. Appeals of the conservationists to save the marshlands near urban areas or the Everglades of Florida sound like an almost callous disregard for more fundamental reforms needed in the ghettos. It is not that the ghetto residents do not suffer from bad air and bad water; if anything, they are more the victims than the suburban whites. The polluted beaches characteristic of most large cities deprive black children of desirable recreation far more than they adversely affect white children who have access to less polluted waters of remoter areas, not to mention backyard swimming pools. Nevertheless, to blacks fighting against what often appears as a hopeless existence, pollution control emerges as a political objective rather far down the list. Consumption is more important than environment.

BUSINESS AND ENVIRONMENTAL ETHICS

As one black leader put the matter: "We suffer from pollution as much as anyone, but we're not the beneficiaries of the affluence that produced the pollution."[16] For the government to institute stricter controls over industry, an action that causes the latter to pass along higher costs in the form of higher prices, thus appears to shut the blacks off from any opportunity of achieving the material advancement that they seek. It would be as though the government had capriciously increased the cost of the goods they buy by 10 or 20% at the very time it professed to be seeking to improve their standard of living.

Blacks and Latins are not the only groups who see their economic interests jeopardized by the campaign to clean up the environment. Workers whose jobs appear threatened by new pollution standards have often joined in opposition. The previously cited example of community persecution of a citizen group that secured a court order against the Blackwell, Oklahoma, zinc smelter of American Metal Climax has numerous counterparts. The 1972 National Conference on Strip Mining, meeting in Kentucky to pass a resolution urging abolition of this form of coal extraction, was harassed by some hundred strip miners from neighboring counties, wearing their work clothes and hard hats decorated with stickers proclaiming "I Dig Coal" and "Coal Puts Bread on My Table." " 'I think you can understand the feelings of the men,' said Paul Patton, the young president of the Kentucky Elkhorn Company, who is a leading spokesman for the smaller operations. 'These people [the conferees] have the emotions of idealism, but my men have the emotions of their livelihood, which is a lot stronger.' "[17]

Although a number of national unions have adopted positions favorable to environmental protection, local union leaders often find themselves placed in an ambiguous position when the employment of their members seems to be the price of a cleaner environment.

A United Steelworkers local in El Paso lobbied hard and successfully in the city council recently to help an American Smelting & Refining Co. plant to obtain more time in which to bring its air-cleanup equipment up to par; many of the plant's 1,000 employes faced possible layoffs.

Representatives of the Teamsters Union, Glass Bottle Blowers Association and Steelworkers helped in September to stymie efforts by New Jersey legislators to impose restrictions on nonreturnable containers; there were warnings that up to 30,000 jobs were threatened.

Local 1 of the United Papermakers and Paperworkers in Holyoke, Mass., has replaced its customary fall job-safety campaign with a drive "to save jobs by halting the ecology steamroller." Union officials contend a local paper company had to abolish more than 150 jobs this year because of the "excessive cost of a pollution-control system. . . ."

A Maine labor representative arguing for a new oil refinery along the state's picturesque coast maintains, "We can't trade off the welfare of human beings for the sake of scenery. . . ."

United Auto Workers President Leonard Woodcock recently told a congressional subcommittee that "their economic circumstances require them to think first of jobs, paychecks and bread on the table. . . ."

Even A. F. Grospiron, president of the Oil, Chemical and Atomic Workers, which has taken a tougher antipollution stand than most unions, warns: "We will oppose those theoretical environmentalists who would make air and water pure without regard to whether or not people have food on their tables."[18]

Nor has management failed to perceive the advantage of encouraging closer collaboration with organized labor in opposition to more stringent environmental legislation or administrative regulation. "One of the things industry and labor have to do is get together to protect ourselves from these ecology groups that have one-track minds," one manager comments.[19] Corporate officials have also played on labor's fears and self-interest by pointing out that costly pollution standards required by the U.S. government, but not matched by foreign governments, would put American industry at a competitive disadvantage and thus would cause further loss of employment. The same argument has been used in support of federal assistance to industrial research and development and to such industry projects as the supersonic transport plane, which has been condemned by numerous scientists for both known and potential adverse environmental effects. The president's special consultant on technology asserted that the United States "needed" the program to stay competitive in technology with foreign countries.[20]

The consumer culture is too closely allied with corporate interests to subordinate the latter to ecological considerations. The dominant role of the corporation in American society derives from its ability to satisfy a mass-consumption appetite, not from its contribution to an unpolluted environment. Thus, when the Bay Area Rapid Transit was proposed for the San Francisco area, it was hailed as the answer to air pollution and traffic congestion, by substituting mass transit for the rising tide of private automobiles, and as the means for opening up a wider geographical range of jobs for blacks confined to the ghettos. "But in spite of such possible advantages, it was not ecology or job access, but the potential profits from land development and the rejuvenation of downtown San Francisco that prompted a group of influential businessmen to provide the push necessary to bring a transit system to the Bay Area. . . . Nurtured more by vested interests than by a desire of Bay Area residents to find an alternative to the automobile, BART was built without a long-range commitment to shift the emphasis to public transportation in the Bay Area. Thus highway construction continues. And the region could end up with the harmful side effects of both mass transit and the automobile."[21]

Corporate profit-mindedness is of course directly related to the nation's consumption. By hallowed tradition, the former is identified as the reward for superior performance in the service of the latter, in the supply of public needs and wants. . . . Manufactured products—especially, but not only, drugs—are often put on the market before their long-run effects on people or on the environment can be established. The purpose may be profit, but the justification lies in not keeping from a waiting public products that produce immediate gratification.

Within the prevalent American culture there is thus a coalescing of interest in improving environmental quality only within bounds that do not basically threaten the more basic consumption objective. Corporation executives who have been most responsible for nurturing that focal value; workers—organized and unorganized—whose position in the consumer culture depends on the continuity of their employment and the buying power of their wages; disadvantaged minorities who aspire to catch up with the material success that they have so far been denied; and government officials who depend for their office on performing satisfactorily a brokerage function between dominant interests and a mass electorate—all these unite in insisting that the admitted problem of protecting the environment be met by incremental measures that do not rock the economic boat. The result may be modest improvement over time, or it may be simply to slow the rate of deterioration.

NOTES

1. Juan Cameron, "The Trials of Mr. Clean," *Fortune,* April 1972, p. 130.

2. *Business Week,* February 6, 1972, p. 71. President Nixon's antipathy to "sweeping" control legislation was made evident not only by his veto of the Water Pollution Control Act of 1972 (a veto overridden by Congress), but also by his subsequent order to the EPA to withhold $6 billion of the funds appropriated by Congress for administration of that act during its first two years. The restriction, like the veto, was premised on a need for fiscal economy, but the underlying rationale was transparent.

3. *The New York Times,* June 4, 1972. Subsequently a Department of Commerce employee denied that any such figure had been released and suggested that the speaker had taken his statistic from a business-news syndicate that had misinterpreted a federal study.

4. *Business Week,* December 5, 1970.

5. Reynold C. MacDonald, "Steel and the Environment: Today," an address before the Steel Industry Seminar, University of Chicago, June 14, 1972.

6. John E. Kinney, "Economic Effects of Ecological Efforts," Earhart Foundation Lecture, University of Detroit, March 30, 1971.

7. Ibid.

8. *Natural History,* December 1971, p. 6.

9. From a series of advertisements, this one appearing in *Intellectual Digest,* June 1972, p. 48.

10. MacDonald, "Steel and the Environment: Today."

11. As I have delineated in *The Place of Business in America's Future: A Study in Social Values* (New York: Basic Books, 1973).

BUSINESS AND ENVIRONMENTAL ETHICS

12. René Dubos, *Reason Awake* (New York: Columbia University Press, 1970), pp. 193–194.

13. *Wall Street Journal*, June 22, 1972. In most states there is nothing illegal about this operation; only automobile manufacturers and dealers are covered by federal law.

14. William D. Ruckelshaus, quoted in *Business Week*, August 21, 1971, p. 58.

15. *The New York Times*, April 23, 1972. Similarly, when the Secretary of the Interior was asked about the desirability of smaller cars and fewer neon signs, he replied that in the United States "the ethic has been growth. Historically, he added, national administrations 'have responded to the demands of the people.' "

16. James Spain, urban affairs director of Allied Chemical Corp. and president of the Association for the Integration of Management, quoted in "To Blacks, Ecology is Irrelevant," *Business Week*, November 14, 1970, p. 49.

17. *The New York Times*, June 19, 1972.

18. *Wall Street Journal*, November 19, 1971. Not all local union leaders have allowed fear of unemployment to blunt their demands for pollution control. As one example, Daniel Hannan, president of the U. S. Steel local at Clairton, Pennsylvania, has fought vigorously both in the Allegheny Air Pollution Board and in congressional hearings for strict enforcement of air-pollution standards, despite suggestions that this would lead to massive layoffs. Hannan has relied on independent studies to bolster his position, such as one by the National Institute of Health and University of Pittsburgh researchers, that coke workers positioned on top of the ovens had significantly higher death and lung cancer rates. *Business Week*, December 25, 1971.

19. Walter Sherman, vice president of the Flambeau Paper Co., quoted in the *Wall Street Journal*, November 19, 1971. Sherman praised the "very beneficial" support of Local 119 of the Pulp, Sulphite and Paper Mill Workers in seeking a delay in application of waste-treatment standards that, it was claimed, would require a partial shutdown of the mill and the loss of a hundred jobs.

20. William G. Magruder, quoted in *The New York Times*, May 23, 1972.

21. Robert J. Bazell, "Rapid Transit: A Real Alternative to the Auto for the Bay Area?" *Science* CLXXI (March 19, 1971), 1125, 1128.

Government Cracks Down on Environmental Crimes

The Wall Street Journal

While many would say that not enough is being done to protect the environment, there has been, nonetheless, a heightened sense of commitment to environmental problems in certain circles of the federal government. While the Reagan administration's Environmental Protection Agency came under fierce attack for a seeming insensitivity to ecological matters, the Justice Department has of late been stepping up its enforcement of violations of environmental laws designed to safeguard the nation's land, air, and water. This article from *The Wall Street Journal* reports on recent developments in the prosecution of corporate organizations and individual managers who now face fines and/or imprisonment for environmental crimes. Such criminal charges were rare until 1982, when the Justice Department instituted a special environmental-crimes section. Between 1982 and 1989, there were 486 indictments for such crimes, while there were only 25 indictments during the 1970s. And some of America's best-known corporations are among those charged with criminal behavior. Thus the Justice Department is sending a strong signal to corporate America that environmental crime does not pay.

Orval High, a plant manager at Pennwalt Corp.'s Tacoma, Wash., storage facility, was at home on vacation when he got the call. It was Jan. 2, 1985. There had been an accident at the plant; Mr. High rushed there and found that a storage tank containing sodium chlorate had collapsed, spewing hazardous chemicals into the nearby Hylebos Waterway.

In less than two hours, his lawyers say, Mr. High surveyed the damage and called the U.S. Coast Guard and the Washington State Department of Ecology to report the spill, which he estimated at the time at 20,000 gallons of sodium chlorate. But last May [1988], more than three years later, he and Pennwalt were indicted on felony charges of negligence. They also were accused of covering up the full extent of the spill, which was later found to be 75,000 gallons. Pennwalt faces a maximum fine of $1 million, while Mr. High could be fined $650,000 and sent to jail for up to nine years.

The defendants are among a growing number of corporations —and their managers—that have felt the sting of the federal government's stepped-up criminal environmental enforcement efforts. It used to be that most cases were handled

BUSINESS AND ENVIRONMENTAL ETHICS

through civil litigation and only the most flagrant violators were prosecuted. But now, according to Judson Starr, who headed the Justice Department's environmental-crimes section for six years, "There's no longer a bright line between civil and criminal cases." Companies, he adds, "are having difficulty coming to grips with the new reality."

Mr. High and Pennwalt, which is currently trying to fend off a $698 million takeover bid from Centaur Partners, have both pleaded not guilty. Their lawyers say the government is unfairly using the criminal provisions of the federal environmental laws. They say criminal charges should be filed only in instances of deliberate misconduct, not in accidental situations such as the Tacoma spill.

Ashland Oil Co. also cried foul when it was indicted on two misdemeanor counts in January 1988 following the collapse of one of its fuel tanks in Jefferson Borough, Pa. The Kentucky oil refiner was charged with violating the Refuse Act and the Clean Water Act by discharging the fuel without a permit. Although Ashland issued a statement denouncing the charges and saying that criminal sanctions should be used only against those who "knowingly violate the environmental laws," it last week entered a plea of no contest to the charges. Sentencing in the case has been scheduled for March 6, [1989].

Corporations have had to comply with civil environmental laws for years, but criminal cases were rare until the Justice Department established a special environmental-crimes section in 1982. While only 25 such cases were prosecuted by the federal government during the 1970s, there have been 468 indictments since 1982. And the Justice Department expects to bring even more cases to trial. It is asking for additional financing for litigation expenses and for the addition of eight attorneys to the twenty currently working for the environmental-crimes section.

"It's not only the midnight dumpers who are being prosecuted, it's some of the best-known names in corporate America," says Mr. Starr, who headed the environmental-crimes section from the beginning until last fall, when he joined a Washington, D.C., law firm.

Among the companies that have been indicted on environmental charges:

- Texaco Inc., which pleaded guilty in federal court in Los Angeles to charges of failing to conduct offshore oil-drilling safety tests and was fined $750,000.
- Nabisco Brands Inc., now RJR Nabisco Inc., which pleaded guilty in federal court in Tacoma to numerous Clean Water Act violations and was fined $450,000, of which $150,000 was suspended. A Nabisco plant manager also pleaded guilty in the same matter and was sentenced to one year in jail and fined $5,000.
- Orkin Exterminating Co., which was found guilty by a federal court in Roanoke, Va., in a case involving improper use of a pesticide during a home fumigation that resulted in the death of a Virginia couple. The company was fined $500,000, of which $150,000 was suspended.

The federal government has obtained 326 pleas and convictions in criminal environmental cases, of which 231 have been against individuals, says Roger Marzulla, who recently stepped down as assistant attorney general for land and natural resources. Over $13 million in fines have been assessed against individuals, and jail terms totaling 200 years have been imposed (nearly 65 years of actual jail time already have been served by those convicted of environmental crimes).

"These figures represent cases involving presidents, directors and managers," says Mr. Marzulla. Mr. Starr says it was his policy while in the government to prosecute the highest-ranking corporate officer with any responsibility for overseeing environmental compliance.

Last November, after only seven hours of deliberation, a Houston jury returned guilty verdicts against Baytank Inc. and three of its employees, including an executive vice president. Baytank, a chemical storage and transfer company, and the other defendants were convicted of dumping pollutants over a four-year period into a basin that leads into the Gulf of Mexico. Last month, the judge in the case overturned the verdicts against the employees, citing doubts about whether they had knowingly violated the law. (The government says it will appeal the decision.) But the two felony convictions against the company were upheld, and

Baytank will have to pay a $50,000 fine and come up with a community-service plan to satisfy a five-year probated sentence.

"We're talking about responsible corporate officials with spotless records being branded as criminals," protests Jay Madrid, one of the Houston lawyers defending Baytank and its executives. "They had no inkling that the conduct cited in the indictment was criminal conduct. It was a rude awakening."

Many companies aren't even aware that nearly all of the major environmental laws contain criminal enforcement provisions, Mr. Starr says. "The level of apprehension is not yet at a healthy level."

Industry and the Environment

G. M. Keller

G. M. Keller, former chairman of the board and chief executive officer of Chevron Corporation, holds that the debate about the environment has become acrimonious: that the proliferation of environmental laws has reached absurd proportions. He criticizes both elected legislative officials and environmental activists for these unacceptable conditions. For Keller, both groups need to stop sounding the alarm because industry has made much progress in the battle to save the environment, and he documents evidence to that effect. His essay, which can be taken as a representative view of corporate America, calls for more creative problem solving from industry to tackle the major environmental concerns, such as vanishing forests and spreading deserts, global warming, and the depletion of the earth's ozone layer. He urges a practical philosophy that relies on

SOURCE: *The Corporate Board,* Vol. IX, No. 52, September/October 1988. Reprinted by permission of the author and Chevron Corporation. The article is an adaptation of a speech delivered by G. M. Keller to the California Manufacturers' Association in October 1987.

the scientific method of risk analysis rather than rash emotions, a philosophy which identifies hazards that can be tolerated and those that should not. Furthermore he asks industry to not only obey current environmental laws but also to go beyond them—to work on solutions to the various ecological problems of the day and thereby demonstrate that industry, too, holds environmental values in high esteem.

The public dialogue on environmental issues is deteriorating, and that is very distressing. It is frustrating, too, because, only a couple of years ago, it looked as if we were making real progress. The interested parties in industry, in government, and among the environmental groups were finally learning how to discuss these issues rationally, and address them cooperatively.

But more recently, we have taken several giant steps *backwards*. The dialogue has become more heated, more acrimonious, and more polarized.

For a brief time, the issues were being drawn in full color, the way scientists prefer to see them. Now, they are back to black and white, the colors of politics.

What really drove this home was the success of Proposition 65 in last year's [1987] California election.

The Law Gives Legal Standing to Chemical Vigilantes

This was a state ballot initiative explicitly founded on public *distrust*—not merely of industry and the potential sources of pollution, but distrust of the regulatory authorities as well. The language of the proposition clearly states the belief that the state agencies have not provided adequate protection for drinking water.

In effect, the new law pushes the professional regulators aside, and in their place, gives legal standing to what we might call chemical vigilantes who will seek to use lawsuits as a remedy for perceived wrongs.

It is just one example. The petroleum industry could

BUSINESS AND ENVIRONMENTAL ETHICS

easily furnish you with a dozen others where the rhetoric seems to be moving backwards.

Industry is not exempt from blame in this breakdown. On the contrary, one of the strongest concerns is that industry will yield to frustration and say "We can't *work* it out, let's fight it out."

That must not happen. It would be a terrible mistake for industry to *accept* the polarization, *accept* the role of the adversary in environmental discussions, and not only because we would be taking the short end of the stick.

To follow that path would be to abdicate the role of the problem *solver,* which has always been the special genius of American industry.

It would remove us from the side of the solutions. It would fix us forever as part of the problem.

The public health of our communities, and the economic health of our nation, cannot afford that.

We need a practical environmental philosophy, an approach that will let us heal the rift in the public dialogue, and put us back on the track of real progress.

A first step might be to take an objective look at the history of environmental issues, and take stock of our situation today.

Look back twenty years, and it can be stated that our society *needed* environmental regulation. The roof will not fall in if we acknowledge that.

Increased Pollution Was the By-product of the Population Boom

Increased pollution of all types was a direct by-product of the population boom and the great surge in U.S. industrial activity that followed World War II.

Communities and ecosystems needed protection from that pollution, and it is unlikely that industry would have cleaned up without some legal imperative to do so.

That is no slur on the ethics of industry. The company that makes such expenditures unilaterally is courting financial disaster. When controls are mandatory, all players have more or less the same handicap.

The point is that industry must accept responsibility for the problems that can be legitimately laid at our doorstep, past or present, and we must acknowledge that, in a general sense, regulation to protect the environment has been necessary. By the same token, industry deserves, and seldom receives, a large share of the credit for developing the technology to reduce wastes and control pollution.

As a nation, we have made tremendous progress in cleaning up the environment, and that, too, should be acknowledged. Pollution of all types has been significantly reduced, even as industrial activity has greatly increased.

The Total Volume of Industrial Wastes Has Been Cut by 75 Percent

There is an excellent example. We read a lot about the problems of the San Francisco Bay; but the fact is that despite tremendous growth in population, as well as in the potential sources of pollution, the bay today is far cleaner than it was in the 1960s.

Industry's record is particularly impressive. The Bay Area Regional Water Quality Control Board, in testimony before Congress, compared industrial discharges of 1960 to those of 1985. They found that the total volume of industrial wastes had been cut by about 75 percent in that period, and major types of conventional pollution reduced by more than 90 percent.

This kind of information must get across to the public, not as a way of saying "We've done enough," or "Everything is solved." But just as a way of illustrating that the situation is *not* out of hand, we *are* making progress, and we will *continue* to find solutions.

We also need to make the point that our search for solutions represents a true commitment, not merely an obligation. Our personal values are not really different from those of the general public. As individuals, we, too, want a safe and wholesome environment.

BUSINESS AND ENVIRONMENTAL ETHICS

Again, the experience with Proposition 65 tells us that people need that reassurance.

Industry, too, may need to remember what we have accomplished, if only to keep from being overwhelmed by the magnitude of the job ahead of us.

We are now at a point where the world is confronting some very large and complex environmental problems, not the least of which is the sheer pressure of our own species in some regions.

Looming before us are such potential problems as the shrinkage of forests, especially tropical rain forests, the growth of deserts (related to overgrazing and other problems in the way people use the land), the depletion of the ozone layer, the magnification of the greenhouse effect, and a batch of other worries that may or may not turn out to be serious problems.

These issues cannot be addressed by passing a few more laws or drawing up some additional regulations. These things cannot be cured by communities or states or even individual nations. They are global in reach, and will require international coordination and cooperation. All industries, but especially multinational companies, will increasingly be challenged to play a key role in addressing these issues.

Meanwhile, on a more local level, regulations governing all the familiar environmental issues such as clean air and water are still proliferating, each demanding an increasing share of attention and resources. Those resources are finite. We are simply not going to be able to fix everything, all at once.

Instead, we have to set priorities. We have to find some equivalent of what the Army medics call *triage*—a system for sorting out the most urgent cases that need surgery right *now,* from those that can wait a little while.

There is such a systematic approach, of course. The *triage* technique for environmental questions is represented by the relatively new discipline of risk assessment.

Scientific Risk Assessment Is a Very Tough Sell

Administrators of the Environmental Protection Agency have been trying to sell the notion of scientific risk assessment for the last four or five years. Unfortunately, it has been a very tough sell.

The basic problem seems to be that a significant part of the general public feels all chemicals are risky, and no risks are acceptable. It is certainly true that our ability to detect infinitesimal quantities of many substances has run far ahead of our knowledge of what those measurements really *mean*.

The popular assumption, and too often one played up for political purposes, is that *any* detectable impurities have to be harmful, that if we can measure it, we ought to get rid of it.

Ironically, one of the truths about our environment, emerging from the work of scientists like Dr. Bruce Ames, is that all sorts of fearsome substances occur in nature. We human beings have been living with them throughout our evolution. In large quantities, they can hurt us, but in smaller concentrations, they are a part of nature itself, and we can tolerate many of them without apparent harm.

The point is not that we can afford to be complacent, or ignore toxics in our environment. It is simply that we should base our environmental policies on *facts*.

Is Compound X at Exposure Level Y for Duration Z harmful or not? That is a scientific question. Let science try to answer it, and let our elected officials *listen* to the answer.

In essence, that is all that risk assessment means. We in industry have to help our neighbors understand that this is the best way, maybe the only way, of finding out what problems we need to address.

As a step in that direction, Chevron is pledging $1 million over the next several years to support environmental risk assessment research at top universities around the nation. Our objective is to help stimulate programs that will draw talented people into this field, support them in developing and improving the methodologies for this emerging discipline and, ultimately, to build a base of scientific knowledge that will help *all* of us better understand the true risks involved in toxics.

The Information Base Will Be Used to Choose the Best Route to Protection

We want our contribution to have a direct and *practical* benefit for the public. We hope that the information base will be used by industry, environmental groups, and government officials alike in choosing the best route to environmental protection.

One thing that would help the educational effort would be to talk about risk assessment in nontechnical language. It is really a common sense concept, and we ought to be able to talk to people about it in a common sense way.

When he was head of the EPA, William Ruckelshaus made a speech in San Francisco in which he portrayed the foundation for risk assessment in very simple terms. Here is the way he put it: "One of the important things EPA does is to establish 'safety' as an operational concept. Safety is not, as is sometimes thought, the absolute removal of risk. Rather, it is a social contract, an agreement, a way of directing social resources and attention toward reasonable levels of protection. If we could *not* establish safety in terms of acceptable levels of exposure for the hundreds of pollutants we control, environmental protection would be utterly paralyzed."

There it is in a nutshell. We need to base more of our environmental decisions on this type of rational approach.

Another thing that would help tremendously is if we could somehow get ideology and political grandstanding out of the regulatory process.

How Many Political Figures Can Resist a Chance to Sound the Bugle?

Environmental issues raise powerful emotions, deep fears. How many political figures can resist an opportunity to sound the bugle and come riding to rescue of the voting public? Maybe we just have to live with that.

But we should not have to live with the ambitious legislators who want to write regulations instead of writing laws. We can protest that as a misuse of power, and we should protest it vigorously. The proper job of the lawmakers is to set objectives, to mandate safe drinking water or clean air, for example, and to prohibit actions which interfere with that objective. But the specific directives for achieving those objectives, the precise limits on prohibited compounds or whatever, those must be established by the experts at the regulatory agencies, using state-of-the-art technology to guide them.

Ideally, the regulators will stop there, with setting the standard, and leave it to industry to come up with the best ways of meeting that standard. This, after all, is what we know best, the equipment and processes of our individual businesses.

Again, the point is not protecting turf or defending territory. The point is that this is the most efficient path to the desired results. The way to get the job done is to let everybody do what they do *best*.

It is actually counter-productive, and perhaps hazardous, for a lawyer in Washington to think he can determine a specified technical remedy which will assure public safety in all places, under all conditions.

Hardly Anyone Was Concerned About Industrial By-products Thirty Years Ago

Thirty years ago, hardly anyone was very concerned about the by-products of industrial activity. Today, we are, in a very real sense, a society of "environmentalists." We all want clean water and pure air and wilderness and wildlife. Most people in industry, like most people in general, place a high value on a wholesome environment.

At Chevron, we are very proud of a corporate environmental policy that says we comply *fully* with the letter and the *spirit* of all laws affecting our operations. But as long as our environmental philosophy is framed by the concept of "compliance," we will not get much credit for our positive actions. Compliance means that the moral initiative lies elsewhere, outside of industry.

Perhaps the time has come for industry to move beyond compliance, to seize that initiative, and, in doing so, *demonstrate* credibility in a way that would be beyond challenge. In the broadest sense, we might want to reexamine the assumptions about the costs and benefits of environmental controls.

In the past, we have tended to let society, in the form of the regulators, tell us when some aspect of our operations has become a matter of public concern. At that point, we fix it. But, *at that point,* the corrective action is apt to be disruptive and very costly, not only in terms of the actual dollars, but in terms of lost credibility as well.

Perhaps an objective analysis might reveal many opportunities where companies could spend less, long-term, and gain *more,* in terms of credibility and community standing, by correcting operational problems *before* they become compliance problems.

A great deal of good might be done in the name of operational efficiency. The simplest and best way to control wastes, for example, is to produce *less* of them in the first place. By applying research efforts to improving our manufacturing processes now, we can head off many environmental headaches tomorrow, and sharpen our competitive edge at the same time.

Many companies have already recognized the potential of this concept. The leader in this field, and certainly the pioneer, is 3M. I believe their "3P" program, for Pollution Prevention Pays, goes back to the mid-1970s. Dow has a similar program called "WRAP"—Waste Reduction Always Pays.

And at Chevron, we have just completed the first phase of a waste reduction program we call "SMART," for Save Money And Reduce Toxics. We have already discovered that the opportunity is even greater than we thought. Going in, we thought we could reduce wastes by 25 percent over a five-year period. We have already raised our sights, to 66 percent.

We should also look for every opportunity to work cooperatively with anyone who is making a sincere, good faith effort to address environmental problems.

The Recent Upsurge in Hostile Rhetoric Poisoned the Atmosphere

There has been a very encouraging trend toward cooperative solutions, before the recent upsurge in hostile rhetoric poisoned the atmosphere. I hope we do everything possible to make sure it is just a temporary setback.

We can offer our expertise and our resources, even in some cases that might seem like lost causes.

When Proposition 65 passed by a 2-to-1 margin, there were quite a few people in industry who looked at the potential impact and said, "Let's just play it as it lays. This one will create so much turmoil, it will completely discredit the people who sponsored it."

I can understand that view, but I cannot agree with it. We need to try to lower the emotional thermostat in our discussions and negotiations on the environment. We need to encourage a non-adversarial atmosphere in the public dialogue.

Perhaps that means we should stop using the word "environmentalist" as if it were spelled with four letters.

Certainly, we need to recognize that, though we will inevitably have our differences with these groups, we will also usually have some common ground as well. Often, objections melt once it is made clear that we share a concern for environmental values, and that we will take steps to protect those values.

Activists Are Not the Legitimate Representatives of the Public Interest in All Matters

I am not willing to concede that the environmental activists are the legitimate representatives of the public interest in all matters touching on the environment. They are part of a spectrum of views, typically, more narrow and more intense than the views of the public at large. And, though they deserve a hearing, they do not deserve a monopoly of opinion.

Nor am I willing to sit down to negotiate with just anyone who happens to wave the flag of environmentalism. The real bad apples are rare, admittedly. But it is still worthwhile to try to keep them *outside* the fence when we are looking for solutions.

I would like to challenge the sincere and dedicated individuals who work for environmental causes to repudiate the more extreme and hostile voices in their movement, and try to work with us to raise the level of the dialogue.

I would like to ask them to examine some of the assumptions that seem to make it so difficult for them to find common ground with us in industry.

There are some people for whom a love of the works of nature seems to engender a corresponding hatred of the works of man. To people with that viewpoint, *mankind* is the intruder, not merely the source of pollution, but pollution itself.

I Do Not Have to Apologize for Civilization

I do not know how to find common ground with someone who expects me to appreciate this position. I do not believe I should have to apologize for civilization. Those people need to realize that human technology, and the products of our industry, are what stand between us and the hostile elements, between us and constant hunger, between us and the ravages of disease and predation.

It is only due to the tremendous progress we have achieved,

our liberation from the harshest imperatives of nature, that we finally have the luxury to look up from the business of our own survival, and attend to the needs of the other species on the planet.

Smothering the Waters

Newsweek

The massive crude-oil spill in Alaska's Prince William Sound in 1989 was the largest yet to have occurred in North American waters. With at least ten million gallons released from the supertanker *Exxon Valdez* (which ran aground due to the alleged negligence of its captain), Alaska braced itself for catastrophic damage to its fragile ecology. Then, as the nation watched in disbelief, it appeared that Exxon Corporation dragged its feet on beginning a cleanup of the crude so that within a few short days the tragedy escalated as miles of beaches were covered with oil and great numbers of wildlife were killed. Alaska's fishing industry seemed imperiled. In "Smothering the Waters," *Newsweek* correspondents relate the immediate aftermath of the big spill. Details of the rapid spread of the oil and the dangers posed by it to the Alaskan environs are sketched, as well as the reaction to the seeming unprofessional ways in which Exxon responded to the accident. In one week the spill had spread to over nine hundred square miles within Prince William Sound, and Exxon's critics were charging ineptitude and outright irresponsibility, not only for the occurrence of the accident but also for the lackadaisical cleanup effort. In addition, citizens throughout the United States expressed their anger by boycotting Exxon at the gas pumps or by returning their Exxon credit cards. Shareholders called for the resignation of Exxon Chairman and CEO Lawrence Rawl. These devel-

SOURCE: Sharon Begley et al, "Smothering the Waters," *Newsweek,* April 10, 1989. Reprinted with permission.

opments prompted Exxon to place a series of full-page advertisements in major daily newspapers. The first of these was in the form of an apology for the spill; the second asked consumers not to boycott Exxon, since this would only punish independent Exxon service-station operators, who were in no way responsible for the ecological tragedy in Alaska.

The waves hardly rippled the clear, frigid waters of Prince William Sound; the winds, tempered by the glacial mountains, barely ruffled the feathers of the bald eagle that makes a periodic circuit above the remote town of Valdez. Stockpiled near this port on Alaska's southern coast, where 800 tankers a year load up with oil for West Coast refineries, was an arsenal of equipment to fight any slick that might foul the waters: lasers to ignite oil on the surface, booms to keep spills near a leaking tanker, skimmers to suck up the petroleum corralled by the booms. All in all, perfect conditions to contain an oil spill. But when the 987-foot-long supertanker *Exxon Valdez* plowed into a rocky reef off Valdez in the predawn hours of Good Friday, it all went for naught. As the result of confusion bordering on chaos and complacency born of the belief that no spill could be this bad, almost all of the oil that gushed from the tanker spread like a black, sticky wave through the bountiful waters of Prince William Sound. Suddenly, Valdez had become the site of what Brock Evans of the Audubon Society called "America's Chernobyl"—an accident that, through mind-boggling ineptitude, went from serious to catastrophic.

The worst oil disaster in North American waters . . . dumped 240,000 barrels of oil from the *Exxon Valdez*, one fifth of its cargo. (A barrel is 42 gallons.) . . . the oil covered some 900 square miles and had spread to islands in the Chugach National Forest . . . a pristine land of such surpassing majesty that the mountains seem to be painted by the brush of an artist rather than shaped by the brute forces of geology. The slick, glinting with the delicate colors of a prism, coated thousands of marine mammals, birds and fish. William K. Reilly, administrator of the Environmental

Protection Agency, called it "a disaster of enormous potential impact on the environment." And on businesses, including tourism and Alaska's $750 million-a-year commercial fisheries. Herring roe, a delicacy exported to Japan, may now have a glaze of Exxon oil; one of the most productive salmon fisheries in the world was also endangered. Oil prices fluctuated . . . according to news from Alaska. Gasoline retailers as far away as Chicago took advantage of the scare to raise prices 14 cents at the pumps.

Angry fishermen saw their livelihoods and way of life being choked by the spreading slick. Calling Exxon's cleanup efforts "pathetic," they organized small-boat armadas and begged, borrowed and even commandeered equipment to fight the threat. The fishermen turned press conferences into town meetings, shouting down Exxon spokesmen and vilifying the company that had promised them that the oil industry would be ecologically benign. Alyeska Pipeline Service Co., formed by the seven firms that pump crude from the North Slope in Prudhoe Bay, had confidently predicted that a spill of this magnitude was "highly unlikely." A company news release cited the "absence of substantial navigation hazards" along the tanker route and the expertise of the seamen who would be commanding the ships. Yet, according to a port pilot on board at the time, there was alcohol on the breath of the *Exxon Valdez*'s skipper as the vessel left the harbor. When the crash occurred, the ship was piloted by a third mate not certified to navigate in Prince William Sound. "Now they are telling us they are going to clean it up," said Nancy Lethcoe, a charter-boat operator. "But they are not going to be able to clean up Prince William Sound. There is oil sinking in among the rocks at hundreds of beaches."

Little Comfort

To environmentalists, the disaster was proof that the oil industry has no business in Alaska's delicate ecology—in particular, the Arctic National Wildlife Refuge on the northern coast, where oil companies are eager to begin exploring.

BUSINESS AND ENVIRONMENTAL ETHICS

Activists found little comfort, though, from President Bush, who during [1988's] campaign proclaimed himself a conservationist of the "Teddy Roosevelt" stripe. The president said . . . he saw "no connection" between the shipwreck and the question of drilling in the refuge. "We are becoming increasingly dependent on foreign oil, and that is not acceptable to any president," Bush said.

In an 1,800-page contingency plan, Alyeska assured that it could control a major oil spill in just a few hours. In fact, cleanup could take months. The only real chance to contain the spill came immediately after the accident, when the oil floated in calm water. But over the entire first weekend, cleanup crews were only able to reduce the thickness of a few small patches—by igniting them with lasers aimed at the slick from helicopters—and suck up just a few thousand barrels of crude with mechanical skimmers.

Equipment supposed to be at the ready wasn't. Booms intended to physically contain or absorb oil were available, but 7,000 feet of them had been unloaded from a barge in port. (The vessel was waiting for a bad dent in its hull to be repaired, though it was still seaworthy.) Precious hours were lost reloading the barge and getting it to the accident site. As a result, the booms did not reach the stranded vessel for ten hours after the accident—not the five hours promised in Alyeska's contingency plan. George Nelson, director of Alyeska, claimed that the delay allowed only another 2,700 barrels of oil to spread into the sound. But by the third day fierce winds had overwhelmed the booms anyway, and oil corralled inside escaped.

Waiting for Permission

Exxon argues that the main line of defense against a major spill is not containment, however, but dispersants. These chemicals, similar to detergents, break up the slick into droplets that eventually sink. This eliminates some of the messiest aspects of an oil spill, although it releases hydrocarbons that may be toxic to marine life in the short term. The *Exxon Valdez* spilled its oil in an area approved for dispersant use. But before the company could actually apply the chemicals from planes and helicopters, it needed specific permission from the Coast Guard officer at the accident scene.

That approval did not come until the end of Day Three, and Exxon and state officials [blame] one another for the delay. "We were ready" to spray the day after the accident, Exxon Corp. Chairman Lawrence Rawls told Reuters news service. "We couldn't get authority to do anything until [the following evening]." In fact, Exxon did not have the equipment in place to begin spraying dispersants until the morning of the third day anyway, admitted Exxon spokesman Don Cornett. The firm's own guidelines for dispersant use, claim Alaska officials, require 500,000 gallons to fight a spill of this size; on the day of the wreck Exxon had less than 4,000 gallons on hand. Six days later, the cleanup crews had only 110,000. But in the calm seas immediately after the accident, dispersants would not have worked anyway: they need to be agitated, as in a washing machine. Exxon sprayed 11,000 gallons of dispersants on the fifth day. By then, however, the volatile fractions of the crude in most of the spill had vaporized, leaving behind a sludgy "chocolate mousse" that does not readily yield to dispersants. The company could only use cumbersome mechanical skimmers— marine vacuums—to collect oil trapped by its containment booms. It was skimming about 2,000 barrels a day.

Cornett conceded that crews could not contain the spill "with the equipment we [had] available." That failure is now being scrutinized. In its defense, the company argues that it cannot keep cleanup gear every place an accident might occur along the hundreds of miles of tanker route. But local citizens had offered to supplement company equipment. In an eerily prescient warning the night before the spill, biologist Riki Ott from nearby Cordova told a Valdez town meeting that "fishermen feel we are playing a game of Russian roulette," with a spill possible at any time. For that reason, Valdez Mayor John Devens said, his city had volunteered to stockpile cleanup equipment. The offer, he said, had been spurned by the oil companies, which assured him they had an adequate supply of their own. And when Val-

BUSINESS AND ENVIRONMENTAL ETHICS

dez imposed a property-tax surcharge on Aleyeska to create its own cleanup fund, it was barred from spending the money; state law prohibits taxing oil companies at a rate higher than other property owners.

A Rare Victory

Fishermen, disgusted with the ineffectual cleanup, "felt we had to take things into our own hands," said Jack Lamb of Cordova. "The fishermen's strike force" started leaving Cordova and Valdez on the fourth day to try to save three hatcheries that anchor the region's $75 million salmon fishery. Seiners and gill-netters deployed containment booms at all three. At Port San Juan, where 117 million pink-salmon fry were due to be released into Prince William Sound, the petrol-busters waited anxiously as the slick spread toward the hatchery—and saw the booms deflect it. The fishermen had scored a rare victory against the spill. They continued their fight a week after the accident, deploying booms at a small channel leading to Orca Inlet, home to thousands of sea otters.

Still, the efforts seemed puny against the mammoth onslaught of oil. The slick choked coastlines eighty miles away and slapped onto island beaches with such fury that "it sloshed up into the trees," said environmental consultant Randolph Bayliss. The oil patch was so thick that its volatile components were trapped beneath, dissolving into the water instead of evaporating. As a result, such toxic hydrocarbons as toluene and benzene will almost certainly enter the food chain, contaminating organisms from tiny zooplankton up to the mammals that eat them.

The effects on other parts of the marine ecosystem won't be known for years. Thousands of sea birds, such as cormorants and loons, have died—either drowned because oil destroys their buoyancy or simply poisoned. Sea otters, the most vulnerable marine mammals, die of hypothermia if their fur becomes coated with oil, says biologist Lisa Rotterman of Alaska Pacific University. Oiled otters also sink and drown, and Rotterman says the 10,000 to 12,000 in

Prince William Sound may face "total extinction." But previous spills, such as those in Torrey Canyon off England in 1967 or from the *Amoco Cadiz* off Brittany in 1978, did not leave such a bleak legacy. Research reviewed by the American Petroleum Institute shows that both fisheries rebounded in just a few years. It's too soon to tell whether Prince William Sound will be equally resilient.

Already the master of the *Exxon Valdez* has paid for the accident with his job. Blood tests showed that Captain Joseph Hazelwood—convicted of drunk driving (on shore) twice in the last five years—was legally drunk when he was tested 10½ hours after the wreck. The real question, though, is why he retired to his cabin and apparently left the bridge to an unqualified officer. Third Mate Gregory Cousins steered the *Exxon Valdez* onto submerged rocks three miles outside the designated channel. Minutes later it grounded on Bligh Reef, ripping four large holes and an uncounted number of cracks in its bottom. Investigators are still trying to find out how the tanker managed to stray so far from the shipping lane and why Coast Guard radar did not pick up its wanderings. Said Coast Guard Commandant Paul Yost, "Obviously something went very badly wrong. Your children could drive a tanker through [the 10-mile-wide shipping channel]."

Millions in Liability

Exxon vows "to pick up, one way or another, all the oil," said Cornett. "We hope to leave Prince William Sound the way we found it." He says crews will rake beaches to get congealed oil into a pile that can be carried away; high-pressure hoses will blast the sludge off rocks and skimmers will lift it from the water; workers will literally scrub splotches with rags. Any oil remaining in the sound will eventually biodegrade, although in the arctic temperatures that will take time. Even if it recovers all the oil, Exxon is still liable for the damage it has done to fisheries: the firm would have to pay the first $14 million in damages, but a fund established by North Slope producers would pay the next $86 million. If negligence can be proven, however, Exxon could be respon-

BUSINESS AND ENVIRONMENTAL ETHICS

sible for damages up to and exceeding $100 million. Therefore, the company could be liable for many more millions in claims.

Alaska officials and the FBI are investigating whether the accident was caused by criminal negligence. Whatever the verdict, oil from the North Slope, which accounts for 24 percent of U.S. production, will continue gushing through the 800-mile-long trans-Alaska pipeline from Prudhoe Bay on the North Slope to the port of Valdez. In the Exxon Shipping Co.'s 1989 wall calendar, the picture for March shows the *Exxon Valdez*. Above it is the admonition, "Take time to be careful—now." Executives there, and at other firms operating in the North Slope, would do well to pause before turning the page to April. They had more than a decade to prepare for the Big One. When it came, despite all the careful plans and earnest promises, their technology was overwhelmed by a disaster as old as civilization itself. A shipwreck.

Sharon Begley with
Lisa Drew in Valdez and
Mary Hager in Washington

In Ten Years You'll See Nothing: Exxon's Lawrence Rawl

Fortune

This is a reprint of an interview with Lawrence Rawl, chairman of the board and chief executive officer of Exxon Corporation, conducted by *Fortune* magazine shortly after the 1989 Alaskan oil spill. Rawl, a former petroleum engineer, gives his version of how the spill occurred, with special attention to how Exxon should be judged on its initial response and commitment to an all-out cleanup effort. He

SOURCE: Interview with Lawrence Rawl, *Fortune*, May 8, 1989, © 1989, Time Inc. All rights reserved. Reprinted with permission of Time Inc. and Lawrence Rawl.

appears to shift the blame for the lack of immediate action on the part of Exxon for two major reasons. First, the severe weather at the time hampered early containment possibilities; and, second, the U.S. Coast Guard and the Alaskan Department of Environmental Conservation did not give Exxon permission to use chemical dispersants until the third day of the spill, which Rawl argues could have been used to prevent 50% of the spilled oil from reaching shore. The interview is also instructive for the comments Rawl makes about the role of a CEO in times of a corporate crisis and the responsibilities of top management when unforeseen events rock the status quo. Rawl goes on to state his confidence that the accident ultimately will not be catastrophic, as has been predicted by environmental activists. He promises that Exxon will "put a hell of an effort on it" and thus prove that "Exxon is trustworthy."

How have you felt, living and operating as Exxon's CEO, since the spill?

It is something I wouldn't recommend anybody try to get themselves into. I've felt personally very responsible for doing everything that I can—and I can do a heck of a lot within this company. One is to make sure that we do all that is humanly possible to get this thing cleaned up promptly. It's our problem the ship was on the rock. It's our problem the oil was spilled.

Did you consider immediately visiting the site of the spill yourself? Would that have enhanced Exxon's image?

You're damned if you do and damned if you don't. I concluded that we were going to be up to our butts in alligators right here. I wanted to be able to deal with Congress, as well as operate the best we could around the world. I wanted to make sure that when Exxon USA said we need all the booms you have in London, we would get them.

I've fished in Alaska, and I've been to Valdez a number of times, so I know what it physically looks like. From a public relations standpoint, it probably would have been better had I gone up there. But I would have used a lot of

BUSINESS AND ENVIRONMENTAL ETHICS

people's time gathering information, talking to the governor, and that didn't make a hell of a lot of sense.

Do you think it would have helped if you had been more visible early in the crisis?

In hindsight it would have helped. Some newspapers were comparing the spill to Johnson & Johnson's Tylenol problem in 1982 or Union Carbide's Bhopal plant disaster in 1984. Now, Jim Burke [CEO of Johnson & Johnson] did an excellent job, but he had seven people dead from poisoned Tylenol tablets. I don't think he had a lot of options. Now, whether Warren Anderson [former CEO of Union Carbide] should have gone to Bhopal or not, I don't know. As I recall, he was temporarily taken into police custody.

What have you learned from all this?

Well, take the case of the captain of the ship. We can certainly minimize this type of thing from happening again. We've had a policy on alcohol abuse since 1977. The first drink the captain had after he had been rehabilitated was a basis for dismissal. Someone in management should have been notified and our policy would not have permitted this man back on the ship. [Captain Joseph Hazelwood entered an Exxon drying-out program in 1985. He is currently awaiting trial on three misdemeanor charges and has denied that he was intoxicated at the time of the accident.]

What would you do differently?

Well, I'd go back to Genesis, and that man wouldn't have been piloting the ship. There's no question that there was bad judgment involved in even putting a person with a critical skill back in that kind of work. It is pretty clear we have to tighten those things up.

After the *Exxon Valdez* ran aground, did you have plans for such a huge disaster?

Alyeska, the consortium of seven oil companies that operate the Alaska pipeline, had the material to control spills that occur in the loading and unloading of tankers. But Alyeska was not equipped to handle an unfortunate incident like this one.

What should have been done?

With a large spill like this one, you can't get booms around it. Either there are not enough booms or the slick is spreading too rapidly. Sometimes burning the oil is useful. But of course we couldn't light that whole bunch of oil because we had a ship sitting there with people on it. There were pieces of oil that moved off that we could have lighted with a laser. But you lose that opportunity if you let the oil sit on the surface of the water.

So the plan was for the shipper, Exxon in this case, to get on the scene promptly, gather the necessary equipment, and, in a large spill, apply dispersants, the chemicals that break apart the oil. On Saturday and Sunday, the first and second days after the spill, we had a wonderful window of opportunity. The spill was about four miles square, and until the wind really came up on Sunday night, it was lying right off the ship in the channel.

Why didn't you act immediately?

One of the things I feel strongly about—this catching hell for two days' delay—is that I don't think we've gotten a fair shake. The basic problem we ran into was that we had environmentalists advising the Alaskan Department of Environmental Conservation that the dispersant could be toxic. In fact, the dispersant has been approved for use in California, which is a difficult place to get these kinds of things approved, and it was approved by the U.S. Environmental Protection Agency. It was used on the huge Ixtoc well blowout off Mexico in 1979.

Our tests on Saturday and Sunday worked to our satisfaction, and we didn't understand why we were wasting any time testing it. We finally got approval to start applying the dispersant in large quantities at 6:45 P.M. on Sunday. Then gale force winds sprang up. They were blowing 70 miles per hour; the wind took the roof off the hangar at the airport. Planes carrying the dispersant got up on Sunday, but they weren't able to do much. On Monday the weather was so bad they couldn't get up until the afternoon.

Specifically, who stopped you from applying the dispersant immediately?

It was the state and the Coast Guard that really wouldn't give us the go-ahead to load those planes, fly those sorties, and get on with it. When you get 240,000 barrels of oil on the water, you cannot get it all up. But we could have kept up to 50% of the oil from ending up on the beach somewhere.

So you are saying that a Coast Guard officer and an Alaskan state environmental official prevented you for forty-eight hours from applying dispersant that would have reduced the damage by half?

If it worked perfectly.

You have also been criticized for not mobilizing the people who were already on the scene to help with the cleanup.

You know how that gets started. Somebody talks to a fisherman and says, "Why aren't they out there doing something?" But it takes a little bit of time to mobilize the expertise that you have. There is a great deal of risk involved in working in that environment. Alaskan fishermen are fine on those boats, but less experienced people would find it hazardous to even work on shore. This is not exactly like going to the beach on Long Island. There are fifteen-foot tides, a lot of wind and current, and beaches with heavy gravel and steep cliffs. You don't want to get a lot of people killed.

So what would you do differently now?

One of the things we realize is that we're going to need people sitting somewhere in a remote place in the middle of the night who are notified in the case of an accident, and we need somebody that shows up with the authority to move quickly without a lot of recriminations.

What are the cleanups and the lawsuits going to cost Exxon? Are we talking billions of dollars?

We're not talking billions, but I don't know what we're talking.

How long will the cleanup take?

I've taken a look at a lot of old spills, many of them much larger than this one, and some of them have been relatively inexpensive because the environment has just come right back. Even with the spill at Santa Barbara in 1969, a lot of expected damage didn't occur.

What makes you so hopeful?

Well, to begin with, we're going to put a hell of an effort on it.

Ten years from now, the press will be returning to Valdez the way they've returned to the site of the nuclear accident at Three Mile Island. What will they find?

Nothing. I would think they can return to Valdez a lot sooner than ten years from now. I don't think they will find much in terms of environmental damage.

No rocks covered with goo?

No. There are a lot of things that can happen. Oil evaporates and it oxidizes. We can pick a lot of it up. It is surprising, but in World War II we lost sixteen times more oil off the East Coast of the U.S. in the early months of 1942 when our tankers were torpedoed, and there was no permanent damage to the shoreline.

Will Exxon step up development of alternative fuels in response to the accident?

As you know, most of them have drawbacks. We're in the second or third generation of a program for liquefying coal, and we've put a lot of money into it. We've been spending about $85 million a year on alternative fuel programs. The cleanest energy we've got is natural gas, but it isn't profitable to produce when it's selling at around $1.50 per thousand cubic feet.

How much damage do you think this accident has done to the oil industry's ability to develop oil elsewhere in Alaska?

It is going to delay us, obviously. We feel that while we can't remove all the damage, we might turn the situation around if we do a super job cleaning up.

How do you persuade Congress to open the Arctic National Wildlife Refuge for exploration?

Well, my ticket for persuading anybody on anything now is not so good. Before March 24 [1989], it might have been. I think Congress just has to recognize the cost to the nation if we do not explore ANWR.

Once we got a go-ahead, the next step would be to develop and produce that oil in ways that are environmentally responsible. If the environmental requirements are too expensive, the oil won't get produced.

Is it possible to develop the oil and restore the area to the way it was?

You can take care of the wildlife. But everything grows very slowly in the tundra. If you want the area to look pristine when we're done, we probably can't restore it. If you accept a reasonable compromise, we'd go ahead.

How important is the oil in the ANWR?

We found ten billion barrels at Prudhoe Bay, but production will start declining soon, and the field will be played out after the turn of the century. If ANWR is only a tenth as big as Prudhoe, it might be worth developing. But even if we start today it would take ten years before the first oil came out of there.

A lot of people are asking whether you can trust Exxon and the oil industry. They kept saying this wouldn't happen.

We're going to demonstrate that Exxon is trustworthy. We're going to do everything possible to mitigate the effects on the environmental situation up there.

What advice would you give other CEOs on handling a crisis like this?

You'd better prethink which way you are going to jump from a public affairs standpoint before you have any kind of a problem. You ought to always have a public affairs plan, even though it's kind of hard to force yourself to think in terms of a chemical plant blowing up or spilling all that oil in Prince William Sound.

I just keep putting one foot in front of the other, and I'm hoping with a little bit of luck to prove to you that we're going to make this thing work out better than the greatest, most optimistic expectations.

CHAPTER 7

MULTINATIONAL ETHICS

Introduction

Consider the following hypothetical situation: An executive from a large American corporation that has production facilities and marketing interests worldwide is assigned to manage a key unit of his company that is located in Japan. He knows that if he can succeed in this management slot, he has a good chance of breaking into upper management. Upon his arrival, though, he is welcomed to his new position by the main Japanese supplier of materials to the unit with a very handsome and expensive gift. He knows that in America an expensive gift from a supplier is considered poor business practice, since it gives the appearance of shady dealings. But he also knows that in Japan, gift giving in business is culturally accepted, and to refuse a gift would be in poor taste, creating a poor relationship with the Japanese supplier. Should this manager be guided by the ethical precepts of American business or by Japanese business?

Although this scenario is hypothetical, it does picture a real and recurring problem for multinational firms and the executives who manage them, albeit not the only problem individuals in corporations with international operations face. The dilemma portrayed is, on balance, what business ethicists refer to as the problem of "cultural relativism." Simply put, the issue is whether one should do what the Romans do when one is in Rome, especially if what the Romans do is not done at home. Cultural relativism is a philosophical position which states that ethics is a function of culture. According to this view, there are no absolute principles in ethics, only principles that are relative in nature and which will hold sway within given cultures.

For multinational firms, cultural relativism is quite problematic. If a certain chemical is banned by the Environmental Protection Agency in this country, is it permissible for a multinational firm to sell it in countries that do not ban it? If a corporation sets high standards for occupational health and safety in its U.S. operations, should they maintain the same standards—at considerable cost to them—in countries where such standards are much lower? Should overseas operations of U.S. companies engage in small bribes to get contracts, when such bribery is commonplace in a given host country?

These are among the kinds of difficult ethical questions that arise for multinational businesses and which hinge on the philosophical notion of cultural relativism. In his "Business Ethics and Cultural Relativism," written especially for this volume, Norman E. Bowie takes the position of cultural relativism to task and explores its many ramifications for ethical business practices overseas. Bowie, who holds the Elmer L. Andersen Chair in Corporate Responsibility at the University of Minnesota, shows the pitfalls of relativistic thinking in this work and emphasizes the fact that there is an inherent ethic in the actual conducting of business transactions that is universal and which should dictate the actions of multinationals in host countries.

In reaction to a rash of controversial payments to foreign officials by American businesses in the 1970s, Congress passed the Foreign Corrupt Practices Act (FCPA). The FCPA has provisions for large fines for corporations who engage in illegal bribing of foreign governmental officials, as well as for individual corporate officers who knowingly bribe. The act has been amended recently, however, by striking a provision that held top management liable for acts of bribery they should have known were occurring, as well as for those in which they engaged directly. This amendment is the result of but one claim that the FCPA is a poor regulatory law in the area of multinational enterprise. Some also insist that the act is self-contradictory in nature, inasmuch as it prohibits large, questionable payments to governmental officials overseas, but it does not prohibit what are called expediting or facilitating payments—"grease payments" in the vernacular—

to foreign government employees whose work is clerical or ministerial.

Others have argued that the FCPA is a poor law since it puts American business at a distinct disadvantage in the global marketplace, because competing countries do not regulate their business organizations in the same way. In their article titled "Ethics and the Foreign Corrupt Practices Act," Mark Pastin and Michael Hooker test the act by using traditional ethical theory as their point of reference and conclude that as a regulatory law, the FCPA itself may lack a clear moral basis. In the next selection, "Business Bribes," excerpted from *The Economist,* a good overview of the extent of the problem of foreign bribery, as well as what has been done by governments recently to address the problem, is offered.

In addition to the problems of cultural relativism and bribery, another major concern that transnational enterprises create is the question of a visitor corporation's responsibility to the host country. What constitutes ethically proper corporate conduct in a foreign country? Specifically, what obligations do multinationals have to host countries and their peoples? Here the essential issue is the possible exploitation of foreign countries and their natural and human resources. The critics of multinational business have long claimed that large multinational corporations are highly exploitive, since they take advantage of very cheap labor (when compared to the cost of labor in the United States) and remove valuable raw materials from foreign lands without making much of an effort to plow anything back into the host country. For the critics, multinational business is the worst example of capitalism's disregard for the land and for people, and where the drive for profits seems to corrupt American corporations the most. "A Borderline Case: Sweatshops Cross the Rio Grande" by James W. Russell, the last selection in this chapter, paints a picture of such exploitation in Mexico. Critics claim this is a worldwide problem hardly confined to Mexico.

More and more, one also hears the argument that multinational enterprise can be identified as one source for the loss of American manufacturing jobs and which saw many plant closings and firings in the early and mid-1980s. According to this view, large multinational American firms took advantage of the very cheap labor conditions in Third World countries; consequently, they shut down American shops and opened foreign ones to exploit these conditions. For the large multinational corporation, such a decision was quite "businesslike," since the cost of labor had continued to rise in the United States. Not to take advantage of cheaper costs would be poor business strategy, according to this argument. In short, this position seems to say that American-based multinationals have no loyalty to the U.S.

Furthermore, multinationals have come under heavy attack for various physical harm their operations have perpetrated upon indigenous populations in Third World countries. In this connection, one of the most often cited examples of multinational improprieties is Nestlé's marketing of infant-food formula to Third World mothers. This attempt to convince these women that infant formula was superior to breast feeding resulted in countless infants suffering malnutrition and death when their mothers unintentionally misused the formula or mixed it with contaminated water. Also receiving a great deal of attention has been the 1984 Bhopal, India, Union Carbide leak of methyl isocyanate, which caused the deaths of nearly 3,000, and the estimated injury of another 40,000, of which 1,700 are expected to die by 1995. And, of course, the involvement of U.S. firms in the Republic of South Africa has been a recurring theme for some time.

Multinational executives, however, do not take kindly to the criticism to which they have been subjected and rejoin their critics with statistics that purport to demonstrate that their presence in Third World countries is much more positive than their detractors are willing to admit. Arguing that their operations have a major uplifting effect on local economies; provide many with good, secure jobs and better than prevailing local wages; and contribute to the betterment of the host country's standard of living through both philanthropic gifts and employment opportunity, the multinational executive is hard pressed to understand why their operations might become the brunt of criticism.

Hence, like so many essential issues in business ethics,

there is controversy and heated debate surrounding the business practices of multinational corporations. But above all the heat and discussion, one fact is undoubtedly true. Multinational companies are here to stay and, if anything, their numbers will probably grow. Given this reality, perhaps the best direction in which the debate can go is toward the essential issue to be resolved: how worldwide social responsibility can be institutionalized within the multinationals themselves. Until such a character of responsibility can be instilled in these institutions, their checkered pasts will no doubt repeat themselves into the future.

Business Ethics and Cultural Relativism

Norman E. Bowie

Norman E. Bowie presents an extended analysis of the doctrine of cultural relativism and its relationship to the ethical decision making of multinational corporations. He begins by identifying the basic flaws of this position by first showing that what appears as different moral standards among cultures may not have any standing in fact—there may not be such differences at all. Rather, it just might be the case that the belief that there are fundamental differences among cultures with respect to ethical matters is an empirical misunderstanding that can be resolved by means of further scrutiny of a culture in such a way that the apparent differences effectively evaporate. Second, Bowie turns cultural relativism on itself to show that if it is a true philosophical position, then there could be no such thing as moral agreement among cultures. But the "knockout blow" to the position of cultural relativism comes when Bowie shows the inconsistency of it when compared to other doctrines and the reality of everyday practice by multinationals in host countries. The remainder of his analysis is devoted to a

SOURCE: Previously unpublished article. Used with permission of the author.

discussion of the necessity of universal and objective ethical rules for the very possibility of international business. Bowie contends that without such an ethical framework, which is already supplied by a number of established treaties and conventions, that multinational business dealings could not be possible at all. Given this perspective, Bowie concludes that only in special circumstances is it right to do what the Romans do when one is in Rome.

Business people doing business abroad know full well that ethical practices, including ethical practices in business, differ among cultures. You can't rely on what is ethical in the U.S. when you do business abroad. How should American companies practice business in other countries? A popular way of raising this issue is to ask whether U.S. multinationals should follow the advice "When in Rome, do as the Romans do."

In discussing this issue, a distinction must be made between home and host countries. The home country is where the corporation has its charter of incorporation. Usually the multinational has major facilities in the home country and has had a long history of business practice there. The host country is any other country where the multinational does business. If European and Japanese companies build manufacturing plants in the U.S., the United States is the host country. The fact that we are a host country comes as something of a shock to most Americans. We are used to being the home country. Foreign firms face their own version of the U.S. multinational question: When in America, should you do as the Americans do?

Some companies have answered the question in the negative. Japanese companies have been reluctant to adopt American unions or American management techniques; they have brought their own ways of managing with them. Is that appropriate? If it is, should American multinationals export their management philosophy when they build plants in Japan? When two cultures have different moral traditions and a corporation does business in both, how should the company behave? There are at least four possibilities. The first is that the company follow the moral practices of its own country. Most Americans would find this option unacceptable and would not, for example, want foreign companies to treat American women the way women allegedly are treated in certain other countries.

Another alternative is for the company to follow the moral practices of the host country. Most Americans would find that option unacceptable as well. If that option were required, American corporations would have to treat women in foreign countries where they do business as women are treated in those countries. In many cases Americans would object, just as they would object if American corporate officials treated black South Africans the way South Africa does.

The principle "When in Rome do as the Romans do" might seem like a reasonable and tolerant position to adopt, and many officers and managers of multinationals often speak as if this is the position they have adopted. Who are we, they argue, to impose our moral standards on the rest of the world? For example, the Foreign Corrupt Practices Act, which prohibits the payment of unrecorded bribes to foreign governments or officials, has come under intense attack. After all, if the payment of bribes is morally acceptable in country x, why should we impose our moral views about bribery on that country? Besides, if American multinationals don't bribe, German and Japanese multinationals will—or so the argument goes. Former President Jimmy Carter's attempt to include a country's record on violating or not violating fundamental human rights when making foreign policy decisions came under the same kind of criticism.

Philosophers have given a name to the when-in-Rome-do-as-the-Romans-do position. Cultural relativism is the doctrine that what is right or wrong, good or bad, depends on one's culture. If the Irish consider abortion to be morally wrong, abortion *is* morally wrong in Ireland. If the Swedes do not consider abortion to be morally wrong, then abortion *is not* morally wrong in Sweden. There is no universal principle to which the Swedes and the Irish can appeal that determines whether abortion really is wrong or not.

This relativistic way of thinking has always been prominent in the thinking of many social scientists. After all, the discoveries by anthropologists, sociologists, and psychologists documented the diversity of moral beliefs and punctured some of the pseudo-justifications that had been given for the superiority of white Western male ways of thinking. Philosophers, by and large, welcomed the corrections to prejudicial moral thinking but nonetheless found the doctrine of cultural relativism to be seriously flawed. That people and cultures disagree as to what is right or wrong, good or bad, and behave accordingly can be accepted as a fact. But what implications does this fact have for ethical decision making? Some have argued that the diversity of "moral" behavior shows that the theory of moral relativism is true. How do relativists establish their position? Many relativists have pointed to the fact that different individuals and cultures hold different views about what constitutes moral behavior as evidence for the truth of their position. Philosophers are virtually unanimous in the opinion that this is an invalid argument.

First, many philosophers claim that the "facts" aren't really what they seem. Several writers refer to the fact that in some cultures, after a certain age parents are put to death. In our culture such behavior would be murder. We take care of our parents. Does this difference in behavior prove that the two cultures disagree about matters of ethics? No, it does not. Suppose the other culture believes that people exist in the afterlife in the same condition that they leave their present life. It would be very cruel to have one's parents exist eternally in an unhealthy state. By killing them when they are relatively active and vigorous, you insure their happiness for all eternity. The underlying ethical principle of this culture is that children have duties to their parents, including the duty to be concerned with their parents' happiness as they approach old age. This ethical principle is identical with our own. What looked like a difference in ethics between our culture and another turned out, upon close examination, to be a difference based on factual evidence alone.

Here is another example that shows how the "facts" really aren't what they seem. Cultures differ in physical setting, in economic development, in the state of their science and technology, in their literacy rate, and in many other ways. Even if there were universal moral principles, they would have to be applied in these different cultural contexts. Given the different situations in which cultures exist, it would come as no surprise to find universal principles applied in different ways. Hence the differences in so-called ethical behavior among cultures would be superficial differences only. The cultures would agree on fundamental universal moral principles. One commonly held general principle appeals to the public good; it says that social institutions and individual behavior should be ordered so that they lead to the greatest good for the greatest number. Many different forms of social organization and individual behavior are consistent with this principle. The point of these two arguments is that superficial differences among cultures on so-called ethical behavior may not reflect genuine disagreement about ethics. Unless the relativist can establish basic differences about matters of ethics, the case for relativism cannot be made.

This discussion is important because it shows that ethical judgments are bound up in some complicated way with the facts. The existence of simple, safe birth-control methods has implications for sexual morality. The existence of sophisticated mechanical techniques for prolonging human life has implications for medical ethics. Since our ethical judgments depend in part upon what the facts are, the first step in resolving disputes about ethics should be to determine whether or not the disputants are disagreeing over the facts. If the disagreement is factual, it will need to be resolved before tackling any ethical disagreement. If the factual disagreement is resolved, the ethical disagreement often dissolves.

Some philosophers have made the strong claim that ultimately all the disagreement between cultures is either about the facts or about nothing more than the attempt to apply universal moral principles to specific situations. These philosophers claim that the apparent diversity in behavior among cultures is only apparent, and that ultimately cultures do agree on certain fundamental ethical standards. A discussion of this claim would take us beyond philosophy to anthropology, history, theology, and a host of other disciplines. The analysis thus far, though, should have established the early contention that you can't claim that cultural relativism is true just because cultures have different moral standards.

Another common strategy for criticizing relativism is to show that the consequences of taking the perspective of ethical relativism lead to some rather bizarre results. One of the bizarre results is that if relativism is true, then agreement on morals is, in principle, impossible. Of course, in this context *agreement* means agreement on the basis of reasons. There can be agreement by force. That's equivalent to "Worship my God or I'll cut off your head." Why there can be no rational agreement is obvious when an examination is made of the definition of relativism. Cultural relativism is the view that what is right or wrong is determined by culture. So if one culture says that abortion is right and another says it is wrong, that has to be the end of the matter. Abortion *is* morally permissible in some cultures and morally wrong in others.

But suppose a person from one culture moves to another and tries to persuade the other culture to change its view. Suppose someone moves from a culture where slavery is immoral to one where slavery is morally permitted. Normally, if a person were to try to convince the culture where slavery was permitted that slavery was morally wrong, we would refer to such a person as a moral reformer. But if cultural relativism were true, there would be no place for the concept of a moral reformer. Slavery is right in those cultures that say it is right and wrong in those cultures that say it is wrong. If the reformer fails to persuade a slaveholding country to change its mind, the reformer's antislavery position was never right. If the reformer is successful in persuading a country to change its mind, the reformer's antislavery views would be wrong—until the country did, in fact, change its view. Then the reformer's antislavery view was right. Now that's a bizarre result.

Underlying these two objections is the broader objection that relativism is inconsistent with our use of moral language. When Russia and the United States argue about the

MULTINATIONAL ETHICS

moral rights of human beings, they seem to be genuinely disagreeing about a matter of ethics. How unfortunate it would be if that dispute had to be resolved by nonrational means, since rational agreement is in principle impossible. People do marshal arguments in behalf of ethical views. If relativism is true, such arguments are doomed to failure or are a mere subterfuge to creating agreement. Similarly, we do have a place in our language for the concept of a moral reformer. Is this use of language really deviant, as it would have to be if relativism were true?

By virtue of the arguments developed so far, we see that you can't move from the facts of diversity in so-called ethical behavior and disagreement in ethics to moral relativism. The facts really don't establish ethical relativism, and the facts about our use of moral language are inconsistent with a relativist theory.

Although these arguments are powerful ones, they do not deliver a knockout blow to cultural relativism. A cultural relativist might admit that cultural relativism doesn't follow from the fact of cultural diversity. However, in the absence of universal moral principles, cultural relativists could argue that cultural relativism is the only theory available to help make sense of moral phenomena. Some cultural practices might be shown to be based on common moral principles, but the relativists doubt that all can.

Similarly, the cultural relativist might argue that our language does reflect a commitment to universal moral principles but that since we are mistaken about the existence of such principles, our language should be reformed. We should talk differently. At one time people used to talk and act as if the world were flat. Now they don't. Surely we can change our ethical language in the same way. Future historians could note that people used to talk as if there were universal moral principles, but of course we don't talk that way anymore. The cultural relativist insists that the only knockout blow against cultural relativism is to establish the truth or correctness of at least one universal moral principle that applies to all cultures.

Such confidence by the cultural relativist might not be warranted. Consider this argument against cultural relativism:[1] A spectrum of moral positions is laid out in Figure 1.

Figure 1

| Individual Relativism | Cultural Relativism | Universalism |

Individual relativism is the view that what is right or wrong, good or bad, depends on the feelings or attitudes of the individual. If an individual believes abortion is wrong, then abortion is wrong for that individual. If another individual believes abortion is not wrong, then abortion is not wrong for *that* individual. There is no valid cultural norm that will tell us which individual is objectively right.

The strategy is to show that any argument the cultural relativist uses against universalism can also be used by the individual relativist against cultural relativism. Similarly, any argument the cultural relativist uses against the individual relativist can be used by the universalist against the cultural relativist. The cultural relativist is constantly fighting a war on two fronts.

For example, against an individual relativist, a cultural relativist would often argue that if individual relativism were the prevailing view, a stable society would be impossible. Arguments from Thomas Hobbes or decision theory would prove the point. If individual relativism were the prevailing norm, life would be "nasty, brutish, and short" in the words of Hobbes' *Leviathan* (1650).

But in the world of 1989, any arguments that appeal to social stability will have to be applied universally. In the atomic age and in an age where terrorism is in some societies an acceptable form of political activity, the stability problems that afflict individual relativism equally afflict cultural relativism. If the necessity for social stability is a good argument for a cultural relativist to use against an individual relativist, it is an equally good argument for a universalist to use against a cultural relativist.

Multinational CEOs are likely to accept the argument thus far, however, because multinationals need a stable international environment if they are to make a profit in the long run. As any adviser for any multinational will tell you, one of the chief factors affecting an investment decision in a foreign country is the political stability of both that individual country and of the region surrounding it. An unstable country or region is highly inimical to the conduct of international business.

On the other hand, if the cultural relativist argues that there is no objective basis for asserting a universal moral principle, an individual relativist could make the same charge against the cultural relativist. What justification can a culture give for saying that the moral principles of some people are right but that the moral values of others, e.g., the reformer or prophet, are wrong? My hypothesis is that the types of argument available for the cultural relativist against the individual relativist are also available to the universalist against the cultural relativist. The real battle in ethics is not between the cultural relativist and the universalist but between the individual relativist and the universalist.

Even if this argument succeeds, the international business person has not been helped very much. She still doesn't know what her company should do when behaving abroad, and executives with other companies don't know what to do when they practice business in the United States. Despite appearances to the contrary, a great deal of morality has already been internationalized, either explicitly, by treaty or by belonging to the U.N.; or implicitly, through language and conduct.

For example, American business leaders engaged in business abroad often complain that the Foreign Corrupt Practices Act puts American business at a competitive disadvantage in doing business abroad. They argue that bribery is standard business practice abroad and that our laws against bribery put American firms at a disadvantage. You get the impression from reading the press that the U.S. is fairly unique in making bribery illegal and that bribery is a common practice in many parts of the world.

Such an impression is seriously mistaken, however. As Michael Bogdan, Professor of International Law at the University of Lund, Sweden, has pointed out, bribery—at least of public officials—is prohibited by the laws of practically every nation.[2] Member countries of the OECD have adopted guidelines, albeit voluntary ones, against bribery.

Both the International Chamber of Commerce and the Permanent Council of the Organization of American States have called on states to pass antibribery legislation outlawing the bribery of officials in host countries. Sweden has enacted such a law. Finally the General Assembly of the United Nations adopted Resolution 3514, condemning bribery among other practices. Research has also shown that U.S. multinationals were involved in Middle East scandals nearly twice as often as multinational corporations of other nationalities.[3] Moreover, for those scandals involving non-U.S. multinationals, the host countries in the Mideast generally originated the investigation. The notion that bribery is generally permitted and practiced abroad does not stand up to empirical scrutiny.

Whereas the explicit acceptance of a universal morality has often been commented upon, the implicit acceptance of universal standards has not. Note the following: The words *democracy* and *democratic* have become honorific terms. Nearly all national states claim they are democracies—people's democracies, worker democracies, but democracies nonetheless. The August 4, 1986 issue of *Newsweek* carried a story about repression and the denial of civil rights in Chile. The president of Chile responded to his critics by calling his dictatorship "a democratic government with authority." I have yet to come across a state that brags that it is not a democracy and has no intention of being one. (Some nations do indicate they don't want to be a democracy like the U.S.)

A notion of shared values can be of assistance here as well. There is a whole range of behavior—e.g., torture, murder of the innocent, racism—that nearly all agree is wrong. A government accused of torture does not respond by saying that a condemnation of torture is just a matter of subjective morality. It doesn't respond by saying, "We think torture is right but you don't." Rather, the standard response is to deny that any torture took place. If the evidence of torture is too strong, a finger will be pointed either at the victim or at the morally outraged country: "They do it too." In this case the guilt is spread to all. Even the Nazis denied that genocide took place. What is important to note

MULTINATIONAL ETHICS

is that *no* state replies that there is nothing wrong with genocide or torture.

This conceptual argument is buttressed by another. Suppose an anthropologist discovers a large populated South Pacific island. How many tribes are on the island? Part of the answer to that question will be determined by seeing if such things as killing and murder are permitted, and if so, against whom? If they are not permitted, that counts as evidence that there is only one tribe. If people on the northern half of the island permit stealing directed against southerners but do not permit northerners to steal from one another, that provides evidence that there are at least two tribes. What often distinguishes one society from another is the fact that society *A* does not permit murder, lying, and stealing against members of *A*—society *A* couldn't permit that and still be a society, but society *A* does permit that kind of behavior against society *B*. What this strategy shows is that one of the criteria for having a society is that there be a shared morality among the individuals that comprise it.

What follows from this is that there are certain basic rules that must be followed in each society; e.g., don't lie, don't commit murder. There is a moral minimum in the sense that if these specific moral rules aren't generally followed, then there won't be a society at all. These moral rules are universal, but they are not practiced universally. That is, members of society *A* agree that they should not lie to each other, but they think it is permissible to lie to the members of other societies. Such moral rules are not relative; they simply are not practiced universally.

However, multinational corporations are obligated to follow these moral rules. Since the multinational is practicing business in the society, and since these moral norms are necessary for the existence of the society, the multinational has an obligation to support those norms. Otherwise multinationals would be in the position of benefiting from doing business with the society while at the same time engaging in activity that would undermine the society. Such conduct would be unjust.

Since the norms constituting a moral minimum are likely to be few in number, it can be said that the argument thus far has achieved something—i.e., multinationals are obligated to follow the moral norms required for there to be a society at all—but it hasn't achieved very much, and most issues surrounding multinationals do not involve alleged violations of these norms. Perhaps a stronger argument can be found by making explicit the morality of the marketplace. That there is an implicit morality in the market is a point that is often ignored by most economists and many business people.

Although economists and business people assume that individuals are basically self-interested, they must also assume that people involved in business transactions will honor their contracts. In most economic exchanges the transfer of product for money is not simultaneous. You deliver and I pay, or vice versa. As the economist Kenneth Boulding put it:

> . . . without an integrative framework, exchange itself cannot develop, because exchange, even in its most primitive forms, involves trust and credibility.[4]

Boulding's point can be illustrated by considering whether a business person should keep her contract when it is to her advantage not to. The contract device is extremely useful in business. The hiring of employees, the use of credit, the ordering and supplying of goods, and the notion of warranty, to name but a few, all make use of the contract device. Indeed, the contract is such an important part of business operation that it is often overlooked. This is a serious blunder. I maintain that if contract breaking were universalized, then business practice would be impossible. If a participant in business were to universally advocate violating contracts, such advocacy would be self-defeating, just as the universal advocacy of lying and cheating are self-defeating in a given society.

In fact, one can push this analysis to the generalization that business practice requires the adoption of a minimum standard of justice. In the U.S., a business person who engages in the practice of giving bribes or kickbacks is behaving unjustly. Why? Because the person is receiving the

benefits of the rules against such activities without supporting the rules personally. This is an example of freeloading.
A freeloader is one who accepts the benefits without paying
any of the costs. A similar argument could be used against
activities such as theft, fraud, and the use of kickbacks. All
these activities take a free ride at the expense of honesty. If
all people were dishonest, no one could gain an advantage
from theft and fraud.

This argument does not show that if bribery really is an
accepted moral practice in country X, that moral practice is
wrong. What it does show is that practices in country X that
permit freeloading are wrong, and if bribery can be construed as freeloading, then it is wrong.

To establish this point, consider what would happen if
everyone bribed. A bribe undermines the competitive process so that a purchaser pays more than the competitive
price; it is designed to enable a firm to get a contract
without making the lowest bid possible. But the successful
briber freeloads off those who offered competitive bids.
Consider an example: Suppose in a two-firm universe that
the two firms are sufficiently alike to be able to build an
airport in a foreign country for $50 million. Neither could
afford to build for less than that. Suppose firm A bids $50
million and firm B bribes official X to give it the contract for
$60 million, in return for a $5-million bribe. The foreign
country would pay $10 million more than it needed to pay.
In practice, the briber has to free-ride off those who make
competitive bids. Otherwise, if everyone bribed, they would
bid the cost of the project up to where the country cannot
afford it. If the contract is lost by all parties, nobody wins
the contract and the bribery has become self-defeating.

The implications of this analysis for multinationals are
broad and important. If activities that are permitted in other
countries violate the morality of the marketplace, e.g., undermine contracts or involve free-loading on the rules of the
market, they are nonetheless morally prohibited to multinationals that operate there. Such multinationals are obligated
to follow the moral norms of the market. Contrary behavior
is inconsistent and ultimately self-defeating.

Our analysis here has rather startling implications. If the

moral norms of a host country are in violation of the moral norms of the marketplace, then the multinational is obligated to follow the norms of the marketplace. Systematic violation of marketplace norms would be self-defeating. Moreover, whenever a multinational establishes businesses in a number of different countries, the multinational provides something approaching a universal morality—the morality of the marketplace itself. If Romans are to do business with the Japanese, then whether in Rome or Tokyo, there is a morality to which members of the business community in both Rome and Tokyo must subscribe—even if the Japanese and Romans differ on other issues of morality. As we have seen from our analysis of lying, contract breaking, theft, fraud, kickbacks, and bribery, these activities, prohibited by norms of the market, are quite extensive.

However, many would point out that the norms of the market are not extensive enough. They have nothing to say about how companies should behave in countries where human rights are violated, e.g., should companies behave in South Africa as the law requires them to? Violating the rights of a minority class allegedly is not a violation of market morality. Does that mean that when in South Africa a company should do as the South African government does?

It seems that the answer to this last question should be no, but some arguments for a negative answer are needed. First, an argument can be made that the morality of the market does require that the rights of economic agents in the country be recognized and respected. Business activity on the market model assumes that contracts are made voluntarily. An involuntary contract is usually not considered to be a valid contract. Market morality explicitly requires that market transactions be voluntary and hence implicitly recognizes the right to liberty of participants in business. What justifies the voluntariness requirement? The right to liberty.

But what about the right to liberty in the political realm? What arguments can be given for civil and political liberty? A common argument is to appeal to a general right to liberty. Think of the argument in the Declaration of Independence. If economic, political, and civil liberties are *all* justified by the human right to liberty, then a recognition of the right to liberty brings with it a recognition of the other rights that are justified by it as well. You have to take the whole package. Thus it would be wrong for business to behave in South Africa as the South African government does.

Does that mean that American companies shouldn't do business in South Africa? That depends on whether or not international business can serve as a catalyst for democratic reform and the promotion of human rights. If business actively promotes democracy and human rights, despite laws against such activity on the part of business, then a moral argument can be made to justify business activity there. The multinational is serving the moral end of making the government less repressive. By the way, this is precisely the argument that many have used to justify business practice in South Africa. Indeed the South African situation can serve as an interesting case study. The point of the Sullivan principles, a set of ten criteria for ethical corporate behavior offered by Rev. Leon Sullivan, is to provide moral guidelines so that a company may be morally justified in having plants in South Africa without becoming part of the system of exploitation. The Sullivan principles also prevent profit-seeking corporations from morally justifying immoral behavior. No company can passively do as the South Africans do and then claim that their presence will bring about a more democratic, less racist regime. After all, if it is plausible to argue that capitalism can help create a democracy, it seems equally plausible to argue that a totalitarian regime may corrupt capitalism. The Sullivan principles help keep multinationals with South African facilities morally honest.

Moreover, the morality of the Sullivan principles depends on an empirical claim that profit-seeking corporations behaving in accordance with marketplace morality and acknowledging universally recognized human rights will in fact help transform totalitarian or repressive regimes into more democratic, more human regimes. If that transformation does not take place within a reasonable amount of time, the moral justification for having facilities in that country disappears. Leon Sullivan recognized that point when he set May 31, 1987, as the deadline for reform of the South African government. When the deadline passed, he insisted that American companies suspend operations in South Africa.

At this point some special remarks must be made about our relationship with the Soviet Union, since some hold that because there is little evidence that doing business with the Soviets will end their oppressive regime, the U.S. should not do business with them. An obvious response to that charge is to point out how much less oppressive the Soviet Union is under Gorbachev and *glasnost*. But suppose Gorbachev disappears from the scene?

Another argument remains. The ability to destroy one another perversely binds us in a special relationship. Even if increased business transactions between the two countries do not transform the Soviet system of government, moral justification for doing business with the Soviets remains. If such business transactions lessen the chance of war between us and the Soviets, then such business activity is justified on those grounds alone. Hence, there need be no inconsistency in saying that a multinational has an obligation not to do business in South Africa but does not have a similar obligation with respect to the Soviet Union. What is needed is a similar code or set of codes for doing business in the Soviet Union or in any other nondemocratic country. The existence of such a code would go far toward promoting the required consistency.

This brings up the human-rights issue again. Part of what it means to be a democracy is that respect be shown for fundamental human rights. The only justification for a multinational doing business with a regime that violates human rights is the claim that in so doing, the country's human-rights record will improve. Again, business activity under that justification will have to be judged on results.

Hence, only in special circumstances is it right to do in Rome as the Romans do. Similarly it is only right in certain circumstances for the Japanese to do in New York as the Japanese do in Tokyo. What settles this question are moral principles that either have been accepted by all parties—as in U.N. treaties and other multinational agreements—or the principles of morality required by the practice of business itself. Since the practice of business requires an underlying business ethic, the international practice of business brings with it an international ethic that must be practiced everywhere. And the ethic is a demanding one!

NOTES

1. This is an adaptation of an argument against prudentialism by Derek Parfit, *Reasons and Persons* (New York: Oxford University Press, 1986), pp. 126–27.
2. Michael Bogdan, "International Trade and the New Swedish Provisions on Corruption," *American Journal of Comparative Law,* Vol. 29, #4 (Fall 1979), p. 665.
3. Kate Gillespie, "Middle East Response to the U. S. Foreign Corrupt Practices Act," *California Management Review,* Vol. XXIX, Number 4 (Summer 1987), pp. 21–22.
4. Kenneth Boulding, "The Basis of Value Judgments in Economics," in *Human Values and Economic Policy,* ed., Sidney Hook (New York: New York University Press, 1967), p. 68.

Ethics and the Foreign Corrupt Practices Act

Mark Pastin and Michael Hooker

In the wake of a number of overseas bribery scandals, Congress passed, and President Jimmy Carter signed into law, the Foreign Corrupt Practices Act (FCPA) of 1977 as a stopgap measure to prevent American corporations from making questionable payments to officials of foreign governments. The law has come under attack by many as being naïve and antibusiness in the sense that it does not permit activities that competitors of U.S. business interests are permitted to engage in, thereby placing American firms at a distinct disadvantage in the global marketplace. The authors take this criticism a step further by asking if the act itself is

SOURCE: Reprinted from *Business Horizons* (December 1980). Copyright © 1980 by the Foundation for the School of Business at Indiana University. Used with permission.

an ethical law. After reviewing the history of the FCPA, the authors test its ethicality by appealing to two kinds of approaches that ethicists traditionally have used to assess social institutions. They apply "end-point assessment," a utilitarian approach that emphasizes consequences; and "rule assessment," a deontological approach that emphasizes the importance of a moral standard or code. Both approaches independently establish that the FCPA does not possess a "sound moral basis." They conclude that this kind of regulatory legislation fails to recognize the complexity of contemporary business and is more akin to a "righteous condemnation of business," which has no place in law.

Not long ago it was feared that as a fallout of Watergate, government officials would be hamstrung by artificially inflated moral standards. Recent events, however, suggest that the scapegoat of post-Watergate morality may have become American business rather than government officials.

One aspect of the recent attention paid to corporate morality is the controversy surrounding payments made by American corporations to foreign officials for the purpose of securing business abroad. Like any law or system of laws, the Foreign Corrupt Practices Act (FCPA), designed to control or eliminate such payments, should be grounded in morality, and should therefore be judged from an ethical perspective. Unfortunately, neither the law nor the question of its repeal has been adequately addressed from that perspective.

History of the FCPA

On December 20, 1977 President Carter signed into law S.305, the Foreign Corrupt Practices Act (FCPA), which makes it a crime for American corporations to offer or provide payments to officials of foreign governments for the purpose of obtaining or retaining business. The FCPA also establishes record keeping requirements for publicly held corporations to make it difficult to conceal political payments proscribed by the Act. Violators of the FCPA, both corporations and managers, face severe penalties. A company may be fined up to $1 million, while its officers who directly participated in violations of the Act or had reason to know of such violations, face up to five years in prison and/or $10,000 in fines. The Act also prohibits corporations from indemnifying fines imposed on their directors, officers, employees, or agents. The Act does not prohibit "grease" payments to foreign government employees whose duties are primarily ministerial or clerical, since such payments are sometimes required to persuade the recipients to perform their normal duties.

At the time of this writing, the precise consequences of the FCPA for American business are unclear, mainly because of confusion surrounding the government's enforcement intentions. Vigorous objections have been raised against the Act by corporate attorneys and recently by a few government officials. Among the latter is Frank A. Weil, former Assistant Secretary of Commerce, who has stated, "The questionable payments problem may turn out to be one of the most serious impediments to doing business in the rest of the world."[1]

The potentially severe economic impact of the FCPA was highlighted by the fall 1978 report of the Export Disincentives Task Force, which was created by the White House to recommend ways of improving our balance of trade. The Task Force identified the FCPA as contributing significantly to economic and political losses in the United States. Economic losses come from constricting the ability of American corporations to do business abroad, and political losses come from the creation of a holier-than-thou image.

The Task Force made three recommendations in regard to the FCPA:

- The Justice Department should issue guidelines on its enforcement policies and establish procedures by which corporations could get advance government reaction to anticipated payments to foreign officials.
- The FCPA should be amended to remove enforcement from the SEC, which now shares enforcement responsibility with the Department of Justice.

• The administration should periodically report to Congress and the public on export losses caused by the FCPA.

In response to the Task Force's report, the Justice Department, over SEC objections, drew up guidelines to enable corporations to check any proposed action possibly in violation of the FCPA. In response to such an inquiry, the Justice Department would inform the corporation of its enforcement intentions. The purpose of such an arrangement is in part to circumvent the intent of the law. As of this writing, the SEC appears to have been successful in blocking publication of the guidelines, although Justice recently reaffirmed its intention to publish guidelines. Being more responsive to political winds, Justice may be less inclined than the SEC to rigidly enforce the Act.

Particular concern has been expressed about the way in which bookkeeping requirements of the Act will be enforced by the SEC. The Act requires that company records will "accurately and fairly reflect the transactions and dispositions of the assets of the issuer." What is at question is the interpretation the SEC will give to the requirement and the degree of accuracy and detail it will demand. The SEC's post-Watergate behavior suggests that it will be rigid in requiring the disclosure of all information that bears on financial relationships between the company and any foreign or domestic public official. This level of accountability in record keeping, to which auditors and corporate attorneys have strongly objected, goes far beyond previous SEC requirements that records display only facts material to the financial position of the company.

Since the potential consequences of the FCPA for American businesses and business managers are very serious, it is important that the Act have a rationale capable of bearing close scrutiny. In looking at the foundation of the FCPA, it should be noted that its passage followed in the wake of intense newspaper coverage of the financial dealings of corporations. Such media attention was engendered by the dramatic disclosure of corporate slush funds during the Watergate hearings and by a voluntary disclosure program established shortly thereafter by the SEC. As a result of the SEC program, more than 400 corporations, including 117 of the Fortune 500, admitted to making more than $300 million in foreign political payments in less than ten years.

Throughout the period of media coverage leading up to passage of the FCPA, and especially during the hearings on the Act, there was in all public discussions of the issue a tone of righteous moral indignation at the idea of American companies making foreign political payments. Such payments were ubiquitiously termed "bribes," although many of these could more accurately be called extortions, while others were more akin to brokers' fees or sales commissions.

American business can be faulted for its reluctance during this period to bring to public attention the fact that in a very large number of countries, payments to foreign officials are virtually required for doing business. Part of that reluctance, no doubt, comes from the awkwardly difficult position of attempting to excuse bribery or something closely resembling it. There is a popular abhorrence in this country of bribery directed at domestic government officials, and that abhorrence transfers itself to payments directed toward foreign officials as well.

Since its passage, the FCPA has been subjected to considerable critical analysis, and many practical arguments have been advanced in favor of its repeal.[2] However, there is always lurking in back of such analyses the uneasy feeling that no matter how strongly considerations of practicality and economics may count against this law, the fact remains that the law protects morality in forbidding bribery. For example, Gerald McLaughlin, professor of law at Fordham, has shown persuasively that where the legal system of a foreign country affords inadequate protection against the arbitrary exercise of power to the disadvantage of American corporations, payments to foreign officials may be required to provide a compensating mechanism against the use of such arbitrary power. McLaughlin observes, however, that "this does not mean that taking advantage of the compensating mechanism would necessarily make the payment moral."[3]

The FCPA, and questions regarding its enforcement or

repeal, will not be addressed adequately until an effort has been made to come to terms with the Act's foundation in morality. While it may be very difficult, or even impossible, to legislate morality (that is, to change the moral character and sentiments of people by passing laws that regulate their behavior), the existing laws undoubtedly still reflect the moral beliefs we hold. Passage of the FCPA in Congress was eased by the simple connection most Congressmen made between bribery, seen as morally repugnant, and the Act, which is designed to prevent bribery.

Given the importance of the FCPA to American business and labor, it is imperative that attention be given to the question of whether there is adequate moral justification for the law.

Ethical Analysis of the FCPA

The question we will address is not whether each payment prohibited by the FCPA is moral or immoral, but rather whether the FCPA, given all its consequences and ramifications, is itself moral. It is well known that morally sound laws and institutions may tolerate some immoral acts. The First Amendment's guarantee of freedom of speech allows individuals to utter racial slurs. And immoral laws and institutions may have some beneficial consequences, for example, segregationist legislation bringing deep-seated racism into the national limelight. But our concern is with the overall morality of the FCPA.

The ethical tradition has two distinct ways of assessing social institutions, including laws: *End-Point Assessment* and *Rule Assessment*. Since there is no consensus as to which approach is correct, we will apply both types of assessment to the FCPA.

The End-Point approach assesses a law in terms of its contribution to general social well-being. The ethical theory underlying End-Point Assessment is utilitarianism. According to utilitarianism, a law is morally sound if and only if the law promotes the well-being of those affected by the law to the greatest extent practically achievable. To satisfy the utilitarian principle, a law must promote the well-being of those affected by it at least as well as any alternative law that we might propose, and better than no law at all. A conclusive End-Point Assessment of a law requires specification of what constitutes the welfare of those affected by the law, which the liberal tradition generally sidesteps by identifying an individual's welfare with what he takes to be in his interests.

Considerations raised earlier in the paper suggest that the FCPA does not pass the End-Point test. The argument is not the too facile one that we could propose a better law. (Amendments to the FCPA are now being considered.[4]) The argument is that it may be better to have *no* such law than to have the FCPA. The main domestic consequences of the FCPA seem to include an adverse effect on the balance of payments, a loss of business and jobs, and another opportunity for the SEC and the Justice Department to compete. These negative effects must be weighed against possible gains in the conduct of American business within the United States. From the perspective of foreign countries in which American firms do business, the main consequence of the FCPA seems to be that certain officials now accept bribes and influence from non-American businesses. It is hard to see that who pays the bribes makes much difference to these nations.

Rule Assessment of the morality of laws is often favored by those who find that End-Point Assessment is too lax in supporting their moral codes. According to the Rule Assessment approach: A law is morally sound if and only if the law accords with a code embodying correct ethical rules. This approach has no content until the rules are stated, and different rules will lead to different ethical assessments. Fortunately, what we have to say about Rule Assessment of the FCPA does not depend on the details of a particular ethical code.

Those who regard the FCPA as a worthwhile expression of morality, despite the adverse effects on American business and labor, clearly subscribe to a rule stating that it is unethical to bribe. Even if it is conceded that the payments proscribed by the FCPA warrant classifications as bribes, citing a rule prohibiting bribery does not suffice to justify the FCPA.

Most of the rules in an ethical code are not *categorical* rules; they are *prima facie* rules. A categorical rule does not allow exceptions, whereas a prima facie rule does. The ethical rule that a person ought to keep promises is an example of a prima facie rule. If I promise to loan you a book on nuclear energy and later find out that you are a terrorist building a private atomic bomb, I am ethically obligated not to keep my promise. The rule that one ought to keep promises is "overriden" by the rule that one ought to prevent harm to others.

A rule prohibiting bribery is a prima facie rule. There are cases in which morality requires that a bribe be paid. If the only way to get essential medical care for a dying child is to bribe a doctor, morality requires one to bribe the doctor. So adopting an ethical code which includes a rule prohibiting the payment of bribes does not guarantee that a Rule Assessment of the FCPA will be favorable to it.

The fact that the FCPA imposes a cost on American business and labor weighs against the prima facie obligation not to bribe. If we suppose that American corporations have obligations, tantamount to promises, to promote the job security of their employees and the investments of shareholders, these obligations will also weigh against the obligation not to bribe. Again, if government legislative and enforcement bodies have an obligation to secure the welfare of American business and workers, the FCPA may force them to violate their public obligations.

The FCPA's moral status appears even more dubious if we note that many of the payments prohibited by the Act are neither bribes nor share features that make bribes morally reprehensible. Bribes are generally held to be malefic if they persuade one to act against his good judgment, and consequently purchase an inferior product. But the payments at issue in the FCPA are usually extorted *from the seller*. Further it is arguable that not paying the bribe is more likely to lead to purchase of an inferior product than paying the bribe. Finally, bribes paid to foreign officials may not involve deception when they accord with recognized local practices.

In conclusion, neither End-Point nor Rule Assessment uncovers a sound moral basis for the FCPA. It is shocking to find that a law prohibiting bribery has no clear moral basis, and may even be an immoral law. However, this is precisely what examination of the FCPA from a moral perspective reveals. This is symptomatic of the fact that moral conceptions which were appropriate to a simpler world are not adequate to the complex world in which contemporary business functions. Failure to appreciate this point often leads to righteous condemnation of business, when it should lead to careful reflection on one's own moral preconceptions.

NOTES

1. *National Journal*, June 3, 1978: 880.
2. David C. Gustman, "The Foreign Corrupt Practices Act of 1977," *The Journal of International Law and Economics*, Vol. 13, 1979: 367–401, and Walter S. Surrey, "The Foreign Corrupt Practices Act: Let the Punishment Fit the Crime," *Harvard International Law Journal*, Spring 1979: 203–303.
3. Gerald T. McLaughlin, "The Criminalization of Questionable Foreign Payments by Corporations," *Fordham Law Review*, Vol. 46: 1095.
4. "Foreign Bribery Law Amendments, Drafted," *American Bar Association Journal*, February 1980: 135.

Business Bribes

The Economist

Continuing our analysis of corruption and multinational firms, this article from *The Economist* offers a review of the extent of bribery overseas and the effects of the Foreign Corrupt Practices Act (FCPA) upon the ability of American corporations to compete with foreign companies. The article suggests that although there has been a good deal of criticism about how the FCPA has hampered America's busi-

---

ness interests and competitive standing in the world, empirical studies tend to show that such criticism is unfounded. The percentage of the U.S. share of imports to countries where bribery is standard has actually grown at a faster rate in the eight years since the passage of the FCPA than from countries where bribery is not practiced as a culturally accepted form of business. In short, the expected consequences of the FCPA as a set of unwelcome handcuffs on American multinationals has not become a reality. The widespread belief about the acceptability of bribery in overseas markets may be a fiction. Most business people tend to think that they will automatically be required to engage in corrupt practices in a foreign country. In actuality, most foreign countries do not condone bribery as a business condition and have laws against it themselves. Hence these expectations may lead to corrupt acts so that a country's standards are brought down by the multinationals rather than vice versa. Yet while the acceptability of bribery by foreign governments may be low, the practice of it in many countries is still prevalent.

There are parallels between bribery and nuclear weapons. A bribe can win a contract, just as a nuclear bomb can win a war. But to offer bribes and to make nuclear weapons invites rivals to do the same. When all companies bribe, none is sure of winning the contract, but each must pay so as not to be outdone. As bribers bid against each other, the cost rises; bribery's effectiveness does not. All companies— and the countries whose officials are corrupted—would gain from an agreement to scrap bribes.

In 1975 the United Nations began work on an international ban on bribery. Progress is even slower than on arms control. Frustration has bred an urge for unilateralism; but here the nuclear comparison stops. Unilateral nuclear disarmament would hardly serve the interests of a country like the United States. But America is bribery's unilateralist, and its experience indicates that renouncing bribery need not damage the fortunes of a country's businessmen.

In 1977 America passed the Foreign Corrupt Practices Act, which forbids American companies from making pay-

MULTINATIONAL ETHICS

ments to foreign officials. Companies are liable to a fine of $1 [million] for each violation; individuals to a fine of $10,000 and five years in jail. Prison terms are the more powerful half of the deterrent, since the potential revenues from some bribes make a $1 [million] fine look like loose change. The PEMEX scandal in the 1970s, in which Mexico's national oil company received bribes from a Texan businessman, involved contracts worth $293 [million].

After the anti-bribery legislation was passed, American businessmen complained that they were losing orders to Japanese and European competitors for whom bribery was sometimes not merely legal but tax free, since it could be counted as a business expense. Business lobbyists have repeatedly demanded that the act be repealed or diluted, citing the country's $150 billion trade deficit as a reason for urgent action.

America's law suffers from being vague. It does not, for instance, forbid "facilitating payments" to government employees "whose duties are essentially ministerial or clerical." Only a handful of companies have been prosecuted under the Foreign Corrupt Practices Act. But though the act has its faults, damage to American exports is apparently not one of them.

Studies by Mr. John Graham of the University of Southern California and Mr. Mark McKean of the University of California at Irvine suggest that the businessmen's cries of pain are exaggerated. Using information from American embassies in 51 countries that together account for four-fifths of America's exports, Mr. Graham divides the countries into two groups: one where bribery is endemic, the other where it is not. He then checks the embassies' impressions against American press reports of bribery, which broadly confirm the corrupt/noncorrupt classification. He has found that in the eight years after the Foreign Corrupt Practices Act was passed, America's share of the imports of corrupt countries actually grew as fast as its share of the imports of non-corrupt ones. . . . His findings are convincing even though, over the period studied, a few of the baddies may have become goodies (and vice versa).

Shady Folk in Sunny Places

The need to pay bribes to win business is, it seems, over-estimated. Bribes are awkward to distribute: it is not always clear in a foreign country whom should be bribed, or with how much. "Commissions" are sometimes not passed on. Sometimes they are, but the enriched official then awards the contract on the basis of merit. Costs are incurred and risks are run for uncertain benefits. As well as being expensive, bribes can be embarrassing if exposed. Many man-hours are therefore spent fudging accounts and keeping things quiet. Low prices and high quality are often an easier way to win contracts.

The success of the Foreign Corrupt Practices Act ought to have encouraged other governments to copy America's virtuous example. None has: nearly all countries have laws against the bribing of their own officials, but only America forbids the bribing of other people's. Despite the evidence from America, bribery is still thought of as a necessary part of doing business in the third world. Anthropologists' studies of gift-giving are wheeled in to show that bribery is part of the culture of many poor countries: non-bribers are presented as cultural imperialists as well as naive businessmen. The way share-ownership is becoming more international is cited as another reason for business managers to bribe freely: whatever their personal moral scruples, they should not impose them on shareholders to whom such morals might be alien.

Such attitudes once prevailed in America, too. Lockheed, an American aircraft manufacturer, admitted in 1975 that it had paid out $22 [million] in bribes since 1970; but it protested that: "Such payments . . . are in keeping with business practices in many foreign countries." Yet the Lockheed scandal—along with the humiliating revelations of corrupt political practices that came with the Chilean-ITT and Watergate hearings—helped to bring about a change of mood among America's politicians, even if not among its businessmen.

In 1977 the Senate was told that the Securities and Exchange Commission had discovered that more than 300 American companies had paid bribes abroad. The image both of American government and of American business was suffering, and so were America's relations with friendly foreign governments. Lockheed's bribes to Mr. Kakuei Tanaka when he was Japan's prime minister in 1972–74 led to his arrest in 1976 and a protracted trial that has still not been completed. The Senate report also made a point that has grown with the fashion for *laisser-faire* [sic] economics. A free-market economy is based on competition—which corruption subverts.

The report's result was the Foreign Corrupt Practices Act. Far from being patronising, the act's proponents argued, it enforced American compliance with other countries' anti-corruption laws. Even Saudi Arabia, renowned for the lush bribing that goes on there, has anti-corruption legislation on its books. Indeed, it may often be developing countries' standards that are brought down by multinational firms, rather than the other way round.

Innocents Abroad

Two researchers from the University of Western Ontario, Mr. Henry Lane and Mr. Donald Simpson, argue that foreign businessmen on brief visits to Africa presume corruption too easily, and so make it worse. If they fail to win a contract, they prefer to believe that the rivals won with larger bribes than that their own products were not up to scratch. Once sown, rumours of corruption spread quickly among the expatriates of an African capital. This leaves westerners with the impression that they have little choice but to bribe: the rumours are self-fulfilling.

The style of western business also encourages bribery. Executives from head office spend fleeting days in a poor country's capital. Few know their way about, or understand the workings of the cumbersome local bureaucracy. The foreignness of foreign cities makes it hard to resist the speakers of excellent English who hang around the hotel bars: a westerner gets conned, and quickly spreads the news that the city is corrupt. Alternatively, his lack of time makes him impatient with local bureaucratic rules. The simplest solution, so it seems, is to cut through the rules with bribes.

Mr. Lane and Mr. Simpson base their views on private talks with officials and businessmen. None, for obvious reasons, wants to be named, so the theories cannot be checked. But they fit with Mr. Graham's conclusions. First, the moral justification for bribery abroad—that it is part of local custom—is sometimes spurious. Second, the business justification does not stand up either: since bribery is not expected of foreign firms, contracts can be won without it. Yet European governments show no signs of heeding such research and legislating against bribery abroad.

Their mistakes need not be repeated by European companies, which could also learn from their counterparts in the United States. More and more American companies are telling their employees to act ethically as well as profitably. Managers have three standard weapons in their armoury. Company codes of practice lay down general ethical guidelines. These are fleshed out with training courses, based mainly on case studies. Then there are ways of catching offenders by encouraging colleagues to report them. One is to create an ethics ombudsman to whom employees may report anonymously. Another is IBM's "skip level" management reporting, whereby everybody spends periods working directly for his boss's boss, and so has a choice of two familiar superiors to report to.

According to the Ethics Resource Center, a Washington-based research group, 73% of America's largest 500 companies had codes of ethics in 1979; by 1988 the figure had risen to 85% of the 2,000 biggest. In 1980 only 3% of the companies surveyed had ethics training for their managers; now 35% do. In 1985 the centre knew of no company that had an ethics ombudsman; by 1987 more than one in ten had created the post.

Most American business courses now include a training course in ethics. At Harvard nearly a quarter of the business-school students opt for the ethics course. More European business schools are also starting to teach business ethics. Last year an umbrella body, the European Business Ethics Network, was set up in Brussels.

Down to Self-defence

Yet the fight against corruption remains a peculiarly American concern. The Europeans and Japanese (whose own country is pretty corrupt) hurt themselves by their complacency, but they hurt developing nations more. In the end it is up to poor countries to defend themselves from foreigners' corruption—as well as from their own.

Sheer poverty makes this hard to do. By 1900 Britain had beaten the worst of its corruption. But in 1900 the average Briton had a yearly income (GDP per person in today's prices) of $4,000—more than ten times that of the average person in the developing world today. Britain had acquired a middle class, whose belief in reward for hard work was the antithesis of corruption. Few of today's poor countries have a sizable middle class; the rest are sat upon by elites accustomed to acquiring money through inheritance and other gifts.

Poverty goes with a weak state, which makes corruption worse. If the state cannot enforce laws, nobody will respect it. Disrespect quickly breeds disloyalty among civil servants: corruption seems eminently sensible, since it involves robbing from the state in order to give to relatives and friends who provide the security that the state is too feeble to deliver. Thus impoverished, the state's strength diminishes further; the rival authority of the clan is consolidated.

Though hampered by their poverty, developing countries can dent the worst of their corruption. The first step is to **admit corruption exists.** It hides behind respectable masks. Mexican policemen ask for "tips." Middlemen in business deals demand "consultancy fees" and "commissions." A favourite trick in Pakistan is for the post-office teller to be out of stamps. Terribly sorry, but there happens to be a street vendor just outside the post office who sells them—at a premium. Not everybody guesses that half the premium goes to the teller.

It is also necessary to admit it is damaging. The Mexican policeman gets the national minimum wage (a bit over $3 a day), so it may seem natural that he should supplement his pay. The bribes accepted by an official before he awards a government contract do not necessarily distort competition among rival tenderers: sometimes, all are accompanied by a similar bribe, which serves as an entry fee. Equally, a judge may offer the plaintiff with justice on his side the first chance to make a "contribution." For businessmen, a modest bribe may seem an efficient way to secure a licence quickly.

Even these apparently mild examples of corruption are harmful. Mexican policemen refuse to investigate crimes reported by those who cannot afford to pay the tip: access to public services, which should be equal, is thus restricted to the better off. While refusing to investigate crimes that do not pay, the Mexican police assiduously tackle non-crimes that do: innocent motorists are stopped to extract a bribe.

The poor and innocent suffer, but there is wider damage too. The tip for a quickly issued licence encourages officials to invent new licences. The tangle of lucrative red-tape strangles would-be entrepreneurs—and the economy suffers. The state's venality diminishes its standing in the eyes of its citizens. No sane Mexican respects the police. South Africa's supposedly independent homelands are made all the more despicable because their rulers are thieves.

By weakening the state, corruption can even prompt—or at least provide the excuse for—political violence, as when Nigeria's President Shehu Shagari was deposed in 1984. Honest regimes, by contrast, are generally strong enough to get even their unpopular policies accepted. Ghana's Flight Lieutenant Jerry Rawlings, who overthrew his civilian predecessors because of their corruption, has imposed an awesome dose of economic austerity on his people, but still survives in power.

Once corruption's harmfulness is acknowledged, **train civil servants to spot and stop it.** The polite silence that surrounds corruption often blocks the passing on of useful tips on how to tackle it. The story is told of an engineer responsible for an irrigation system in India. The rich farmers in the area bribed a local politician, who in turn ordered the irrigation engineer to divert water from poor farms to rich ones. The engineer agreed to do as he was told, so long as the politician would speak his order into the engineer's tape recorder: whereupon the politician backed down. If this was made a case study for trainee water engineers, India's water might be better managed.

As well as instructing the virtuous on how to beat corruption, training should explain to the not-so-virtuous why corruption is so damaging. It may not be a bad idea to explain the benefits to a country of an honest civil service, much as student lawyers learn some jurisprudence. The same goes for businessmen. Some Latin countries—Mexico, Chile—are making ethics training part of their business-school curriculums, which should make businessmen aware of the harm that corruption does to the economy, and to the standards of their firms.

Next, let **journalists and other snoops** help in exposing corruption. It is not enough for governments to break their silence on the subject; general openness is essential for having corruption discussed. In the Soviet Union, parts of which are pretty poor, Mr. Mikhail Gorbachev is allowing more press freedom than before partly in order to expose the corruption that festered under the secretive rule of Leonid Brezhnev.

Greater openness is the first step towards increased accountability. Mr. Gorbachev also wants some party officials to be exposed to elections, so that they can be judged on the records that *glasnost* has made known. Elections are one good way of holding people to account. Another is the separation of powers. Independent executives, judiciaries and legislatures can keep tabs on each other.

Even strong and open states have difficulty retaining civil servants' loyalty, so the wise ones **reduce bureaucrats' discretion:** fewer licenses will mean fewer bribes. In famously corrupt Indonesia, the government's economic-reform programme includes the burning of red tape. To build a hotel only one licence is now required; once, an entrepreneur needed thirty-three.

In particular, do away with economic controls that create black markets. If the state fixes the exchange rate artificially high, foreign currency will be scarce, and distributing it will be the task of bureaucrats. Bribes will flow, because businessmen who need to import spare parts will pay generously for dollars or import quotas. The same happens when state food-marketing boards force farmers to sell their crops at artificially low prices: farmers are encouraged to bribe the board's officials to overlook their grain, and then to bribe customs officials to allow it across the border into a country where it will fetch more. Five years ago Ugandan coffee could be sold in Kenya for ten times its domestic price.

Slimming down the state will make possible the next corruption-beating move that is sometimes needed: **pay public employees more**, so that they no longer depend on "tips." The Indonesian government is likely to find its anti-corruption policies damaged by the freeze it has put on civil servants' pay. It may do wonders for Indonesia's budget, but it will probably encourage civil servants to find pay of their own. Along with better training, better pay will improve morale. The more pride that officials take in working for their governments, the less likely they are to subvert them by accepting bribes.

Another way to raise the professional morale of bureaucrats is to make the civil service **meritocratic.** Competitive entry examinations and promotion on merit helped diminish corruption in nineteenth-century England. In Mexico today, the relatively high professional standards of the Finance Ministry, Bank of Mexico and Foreign Ministry go with their relatively clean reputations. The Indian civil service has competitive examinations but, in some states at least, civil-service jobs are known by the size of bribe needed to obtain them. So long as that persists, those who do the jobs will see them as an instrument of plunder, not as a chance to serve the state.

Tolerated, corruption spreads easily. The civil servant who buys his job will reimburse himself corruptly. In the Philippines corruption has even infected the body investigating corruption under the country's deposed ruler, Mr. Ferdinand Marcos. Because it is so hard to beat, and because all societies and institutions develop taboos against snitching on colleagues, corruption is too often met with defeatism or indulgence. That is an unkindness to bureaucracies and businessmen, whether poor or rich.

A Borderline Case: Sweatshops Cross the Rio Grande

James W. Russell

Multinational enterprises are often criticized for exploiting their host country's labor force because such labor is usually quite cheap when compared to the cost of labor in their home country. James Russell offers a snapshot of such exploitation in his exposé of the effects that the presence of foreign-owned business has had on the people of Ciudad Juárez, Mexico—just across the border from El Paso, Texas. Russell examines the life of those who work in the *maquiladoras*, the 125 or so assembly plants owned by multinationals mostly from the United States. The picture Russell develops in "A Borderline Case" is not a very flattering one for the multinationals. He reports on the decline of the wage rate in the *maquiladoras* from 1981 to 1983, where a $9.19 per day take-home pay had slipped to $6.80, thanks to the economic troubles Mexico has had, and the devaluation of its peso. He tells of very young workers working in not so desirable conditions. And he details some highly questionable employment practices by management that have the effect of keeping the Mexican workers in line so that labor costs remain low. According to Russell, these practices earn multinationals "superprofits" because they are based upon "superexploitation" of the *maquiladoras* worker.

The Third World and the First World meet on Juárez Avenue, a strip of bars, restaurants, and curio shops catering to tourists who spill over the border from El Paso. For Americans who want to photograph, purchase, or eat a bit of Mexicana, Ciudad Juárez is a convenient sally. They drive

---

SOURCE: Reprinted with permission from *The Progressive,* 409 East Main Street Madison, WI 53703. Copyright © 1984, The Progressive, Inc.

in, soak up the ambience around the "mariachi plaza," and go home.

But there is a permanent American presence in Ciudad Juárez, invisible to the sightseers though manifest to the city's inhabitants. To see it, one must take a frustrating drive through streets choked by traffic, bus fumes, and food vendors. On the outskirts of the city, in the barren Chihuahua desert, it rises like a gleaming mirage: row upon row of modern buildings and well-manicured lawns.

The buildings are *maquiladoras,* assembly plants run by foreign-based multinational corporations, most of which are headquartered in the United States. Juárez is home to about 125 foreign-owned factories that employ 45,000 people—a manufacturing nexus larger than Youngstown, Ohio, in its steel-producing heyday. Most of the *maquiladoras* operate within spanking new industrial parks, where security is tight and rent is cheap.

U.S. companies import American parts into Mexico, assemble the parts in *maquiladoras,* and export the products back to the United States. The finished goods are usually stamped, ASSEMBLED IN MEXICO OF U.S. MATERIALS. A host of U.S. corporate giants—including General Electric, Zenith, RCA, and General Motors—as well as many smaller subcontractors have set up shop along the 2,000-mile Mexican frontier, dominating the economies of such cities as Juárez, Tijuana, and Mexicali.

The companies have turned the border zone into a terminal on their global production line. More than 70 per cent of *maquiladora* work involves electronics or apparel, both product lines that require intensive labor for final assembly. U.S. companies farm out, or "outsource," the fabrication work to Mexico to save on labor costs.

If the day trippers from the United States bring dollars and leave with knickknacks, the multinational employers bring capital and leave with ready profits—superprofits, in fact, derived from superexploitation.

Maquiladora managers prefer to hire teen-aged women, believing them to be more dexterous and tractable than men. Since electronics assembly must be done in a clean, temperature-controlled environment, the new factories are air-conditioned, to protect the parts, not the workers, from sweltering desert heat that can send the mercury to 114 degrees. Garment manufacturers do not have that concern, so many of their factories are scattered about Juárez in old, uncooled buildings.

The *maquiladoras* are a tremendous boon to the corporations. Labor costs generally run 20 to 25 per cent of what they would be in the United States; the work week is 25 per cent longer; the pace of work is faster, and Mexico's high unemployment rate disciplines the labor force. Richard Michel, who manages General Electric's seven *maquiladoras* in Mexico, boasts of a 2 per cent absentee rate in his factories, compared with 5 to 9 per cent in the United States. Productivity, he adds, is 10 to 15 per cent higher south of the Rio Grande.

Though *maquiladora* wages lag far behind those in the United States and represent a fraction of the workers' productive output, the pay is good by Mexican standards. However, border-zone wages are declining in real terms because of unfavorable exchange rates with the dollar. U.S. prices affect Mexican prices; moreover, the workers spend between a third and half of their earnings on the U.S. side.

Gustavo de la Rosa, a lawyer who specializes in *maquiladora* workers' cases, found that the government's peso devaluations have markedly reduced real pay in Juárez: In February 1981, 80 per cent of the *maquiladora* employees were taking home the equivalent of $9.19 a day; one year later, take-home pay had slipped to $8.00; by late 1983, it had shrunk to $6.80.

Maria Munoz, who began sewing for Acapulco Fashions in Juárez at age sixteen, was earning $48 for a fifty-hour week in 1981—and she had accumulated eleven years of seniority. That year, she and her co-workers planned to strike for an 18 per cent raise and a reduction in hours from fifty to forty-five. Preempting the strike, the company abruptly shut down operations. The managers of Acapulco Fashions returned to the United States carrying the workers' last paychecks and some $6,000 in credit union funds. The company never paid indemnities to the employees for closing down, as required by Mexican law.

In response, the workers seized the factory to prevent management from retrieving machinery and finished goods. Funds were raised from passing motorists and, after more than a year of occupying the plant, the workers sold the goods and machinery and divided the revenues. They recovered about half their losses. A small group continues to occupy the abandoned offices.

The story of Acapulco Fashions is unusual, not in its description of management but in its portrayal of border-zone labor relations. More revealing is the annual May Day in Juárez, when there are two parades—the government's and the Left's. Both take place on the city's main street, separated by ninety minutes.

In the first parade, most of the approximately 30,000 participants march behind banners of government-controlled unions. The signs proclaim loyalty to the ruling Partido Institucional Revolucionario (PRI). Other workers, including many from the *maquiladoras,* fall in behind company standards: Young women predominate the formations, which could be mistaken for girls' high school contingents. RCA goes so far as to dress up its workers in red-and-white cheerleader skirts, and male managers bark out marching orders through megaphones.

The second parade shatters the image of labor pliancy projected by the first. Dressed in red and black, members of the Comite de Defensa Popular (CDP) march behind portraits of Marx, Engels, Lenin, Pancho Villa, guerrilla leader Arturo Gamiz, the Haymarket martyrs, and effigies of Uncle Sam and a *charro syndicalista,* or sell-out labor leader.

Participation in the CDP-sponsored parade has steadily increased—from 2,000 three years ago to 15,000 last May—as the nation's economic crisis has intensified. The CDP, the largest left-wing organization in Juárez, is a leading political force in two dozen of the city's poor and squatter neighborhoods.

But the militance of the CDP has not moved *maquiladora*

workers. A tenuous labor peace reigns within the assembly plants, though there have been isolated and sometimes violent confrontations.

The *maquiladoras* run smoothly, but not because the interests of the workers are protected. Between 1971 and 1978, the government's Board of Arbitration issued 482 judgments involving *maquiladora* employees. Only fourteen were favorable to the workers.

Mexican law requires that senior workers be assured job security, but there are many ways for multinational corporations to get around the requirement. Employers can slash hours or shut the plant down for a period, thereby forcing the employees to seek work elsewhere. Companies have also been known to swap workers, eliminating accrued seniority in the process. High turnover is seen as a key to high productivity, and workers are pressured to leave when they reach their late twenties.

The border cities were opened to *maquiladora* exploitation in 1965 with the inauguration of the Border Industrialization Program. A year earlier, the Bracero Program, which provided U.S. growers with seasonal armies of unorganized Mexicans, had been canceled. President Gustavo Diaz Ordaz was facing skyrocketing unemployment in the border region—and rising unrest.

In fact, guerrilla warfare had erupted in Chihuahua. Arturo Gamiz, a rural school teacher, had organized a base of guerrillas to combat fraudulent land reform, fight the sale of forest and mineral concessions to corporations, and defend the Tarahumara Indians. The Mexican Army engaged Gamiz and his followers in battle on September 23, 1965. Most of the guerrillas were killed, and their bodies were thrown into a common grave.

The Mexican government sensed that tensions in the border area would exacerbate as growing numbers of impoverished peasants left the land and filled the already swollen ranks of the urban unemployed. So Diaz Ordaz designated the frontier region a free-trade zone, waived import duties, and granted tax breaks to the U.S.-based multinational companies.

This bonanza came at an opportune time for U.S. corporations. After a long period of unbridled expansion, they were facing heightened competition from Japan, West Germany, and other nations. As foreign garment and electronics manufacturers began making inroads into the U.S. market, labor costs became a vital factor in maintaining a competitive edge. U.S. multinational companies started shifting production to such cheap labor suppliers as South Korea, Taiwan, Singapore, and the Mexican border zone.

In choosing a Third World outpost, business executives consider three variables: labor costs, freedom of operations, and stability. Even before the Bracero Program ended, Mexico's border cities suffered unemployment rates of 30 to 40 per cent; wages, following the law of supply and demand, were accordingly low. The unemployment rate in the region remains at least 40 per cent [in 1984].

The Border Industrialization Program ensured multinational corporations absolute freedom. The Mexican government absolved them of tax obligations, and the U.S. Government molded the U.S. tariff code to the companies' advantage. Two provisions pegged customs duties on *maquiladora* products to the low wages paid in Mexico, not to the value added to the materials in the production process.

The PRI, which exercises firm control over Mexican affairs, has coopted most of the popular movements, including the unions, and brutally suppressed the rest. It simply rigged the 1983 state elections: "Privately, PRI officials admit that votes were manipulated," *U.S. News & World Report* recently noted, "because 'it was too dangerous to lose elections during a major economic crisis.' "

Cheap labor, freedom from regulation, and political stability have conspired to bring U.S. multinational corporations across the border. The total number of *maquiladoras* grew from twelve in 1965 to more than 600 by 1980.

The border zone is hardly unique: It competes with similar corporate havens in Asia and in other parts of Latin America. But the Mexican frontier has a special selling point—the "twin plant" concept. A firm can maintain its capital-intensive operations in the United States and meet its labor-intensive needs a short distance away. For example, U.S. workers can cut cloth—a task that is relatively skilled and requires major capital investment—and *maquiladora* employees can then sew it.

Runaway plants deprive U.S. workers of jobs, and the *maquiladora* competition drives down wages in the United States, particularly along the border, where there is a palpable threat that more shops will flee to Mexico.

The damage north of the border has not been offset by benefits to the south. Unemployment in Mexico's frontier area has not been reduced, and living conditions have remained, at best, unchanged. The assembly plants have become magnets for displaced peasants; local newspapers warn that 100 families a day are moving into Juárez. A marginalized, "surplus" population lives in cardboard shacks and feeds its young by begging or selling items scavenged from American parks, alleys, and dumps. Some of the poor become servants on the U.S. side; a full-time, resident maid in El Paso earns $30 to $40 a week.

The movement of women into the *maquiladoras* has strained traditional sex roles. Family strife has increased, and the idle men often turn to alcohol or crime. Many abandon their families to take jobs as undocumented workers in the United States. Spanish-language radio and television stations in El Paso and Juárez regularly broadcast appeals from wives searching for runaway husbands.

Desperation is what keeps the workers mute. Challenges to the system are few. The official unions enroll only a quarter of the work force, and seem to do little more than maintain discipline for the employers. The independent unions, which are more militant than the major labor groups, have yet to make significant inroads into the *maquiladoras*.

Opposition to the system is most visible among the squatter organizations, such as the CDP, and among the leftist electoral parties. A new and important component of the opposition is the Catholic lay communities.

As in the rest of Latin America, the currents of liberation theology flow through Juárez. When the 1979 Puebla Conference of the Latin American Church called for a Christian-based community movement to raise the social and political consciousness of the poor, a number of churches in Juárez responded.

One of them was Father Oscar Enriquez's parish in the working-class *colonia* of Alta Vista. From his church, Enriquez can see across the Rio Grande into the United States. He can also see the smoke of ASARCO's copper smelter as it poisons both sides of the border with lead and other toxic chemicals. Enriquez has become a leader of the Christian community movement, which now encompasses about seventy groups, with ten to fifteen members in each, that meet weekly to discuss social and political issues. The study groups have been growing, fostering a healthy skepticism toward capital among Juárez's citizens.

But even as the skepticism builds, new *maquiladoras* rise against the desert sky—concrete reminders that for the people of the Third World, growth is not necessarily development and industrialization is not necessarily salvation. If a tag could be placed on the profits of the corporate giants who have plants along the border strip, it might read, ASSEMBLED IN THE U.S. OF MEXICAN LABOR.